TEACH YOURSELF BOOKS

BUSINESS
JAPANESE

A COMPLETE COURSE FOR BEGINNERS

NTC *NTC Publishing Group*

Peta

TEACH YOURSELF BOOKS

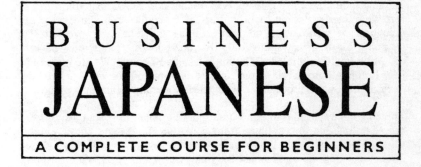

BUSINESS
JAPANESE

A COMPLETE COURSE FOR BEGINNERS

Michael Jenkins
and
Lynne Strugnell

Japan Business Consultancy

NTC *NTC Publishing Group*

Acknowledgements

We would like to thank the many people who have contributed towards the writing of this book. In particular we are grateful to Michiko Sugino and Miki Ishikawa Clibbon for their invaluable help in contributing ideas, suggestions and advice, and for their untiring help in checking the various drafts of the text. Our thanks also go to Yoko Luetchford for her contributions to the dialogues and proofreading; to Tomoko Boyd and Julie De Looze for their help with proofreading; and to Julie De Looze, Joyce Jenkins, Alex Stewart and Mike Luetchford for contributing Business Briefings. We are grateful to John Pearson, Rosemary Sansome and Rachel Sparrow for working faithfully through the lessons providing us with valuable comments and suggestions.

The authors would like to thank the following companies who allowed the use of their logos in this book: Autodoor, Ena, ILI Design, Japan Airlines, Kictec, Meito and Teraoka. The authors feel particularly indebted to Keisuke Okuma and Graeme Paterson of ILI Design for contributing their business card designs. Last but not least they wish to thank their colleagues at Bath College of Higher Education for their support in this project.

This edition was first published in 1993 by NTC Publishing Group, 4255 West Touhy Avenue, Lincolnwood (Chicago), Illinois 60646 – 1975 U.S.A. Originally published by Hodder and Stoughton Ltd.

Library of Congress Catalog Card Number: 93-83165

Printed in England by Cox & Wyman Ltd, Reading, Berks

LIST OF
CONTENTS

suggestions; telephone phrases; how to explain when
something hasn't been done yet
Business Briefing: Advertising in Japan

── INTRODUCTION ──

───── Who is this book for? ─────

More and more people these days are getting the opportunity to go to Japan on short-term business or long-term work assignments, or have dealings with Japanese people outside of Japan. You may be going to Japan on a business trip for the first time or the tenth time; you may be someone who often receives Japanese visitors to the company; you may have Japanese families in your neighbourhood who have come to work at the new Japanese factory down the road; you may even be studying for business examinations, and are looking towards the Japanese market of the future. Whatever your reason for being interested in Japanese, *Teach Yourself Business Japanese* aims to give you a good grounding in the Japanese language, and an introduction to various aspects of the business culture of Japan.

───── Why study Japanese? ─────

There is no doubt that understanding some of the language of your Japanese business partners will bring a wealth of advantages. At the very least it is a courtesy, and shows that you are willing to make that extra effort to meet them halfway. It also gives a tremendous confidence boost to know that if you are in Japan you can communicate, and enjoy some independence in being able to get around without having to rely on others all the time. Most importantly, all sorts of opportunities open up when you can talk to a wider range of people from more varied backgrounds than is possible if you only speak English. If you tried Japanese once before and gave it up as impossible – try again. It's not!

What will I learn from *Business* Japanese?

By the end of this book, you should feel comfortable using Japanese in social situations with Japanese business colleagues, have an idea of what is going on in business meetings conducted in Japanese, be able to survive in Japan on your own, and have an appreciation of the similarities and differences between doing business in Japan and doing business in the West. In short, it should help you to achieve better results in your business and social dealings with the Japanese. Be under no illusions – you will not be able to conduct high level negotiations in Japanese simply with the aid of this book. However, it aims to set you on the right road.

Composition of the lessons

There are 20 lessons altogether, and apart from Lesson 1, which concentrates on pronunciation, all have the same format. Each begins with a short description of the contents of the lesson, and what you should know and be able to do by the end of it. After this come the following sections:

The story so far

This short description sets the scene for the dialogue to come. It appears in English for the first 11 lessons, but from Lesson 12 it is given in Japanese, first in Japanese script, and then in romanised Japanese.

Dialogue

The dialogue continues the story line, and introduces new vocabulary, structures and ideas which are the themes of the lesson. Like **The Story So Far**, the dialogue appears first in Japanese script, and then in romanised Japanese. Following each dialogue is a list of the new vocabulary, and a short comprehension exercise to help you see if you have understood the dialogue correctly.

Notes

This section gives a brief explanation, with examples, of any new structure patterns, colloquial phrases or unusual vocabulary that are introduced in the dialogue. Lengthy grammatical explanations have been avoided as far as possible. Instead, it is hoped that you will get a feel for the meaning and usage of new material through the examples given in this section, and through practice in the **Expansion Activities** that follow. You may want to read this section before starting on the main dialogue in order to help you understand the new material introduced there. With very few exceptions, all the new vocabulary that you will need for the **Expansion Activities** that follow will have been introduced either in the dialogue or in the examples given in the **Notes,** so that you can see how the vocabulary is used and what its English equivalent is.

Expansion activities

This is perhaps the most important section of the lesson, as it gives you a chance to practise the new structures, vocabulary and situations that have been introduced so far. In each lesson there are six or seven activities of various kinds, finishing with Now It's Your Turn, an exercise designed to test what you can remember from the lesson.

Reading corner

This section is written entirely in Japanese script as a challenge to those who want to practise their reading skills, and contains material such as memos, pages from a diary, faxes, etc. No new vocabulary that is essential for the following lessons is introduced in this section, so if you decide to work with romanised Japanese only and omit this section, you will not miss out on any important aspects of the language or the story. However, giving it a try will provide you with more opportunities to practise and expand on material from the lesson.

Business briefing

To be successful in business in Japan, a knowledge of the language must go hand-in-hand with a knowledge of business practices and etiquette. This section, in English, gives you background information about doing business with the Japanese which is essential for getting off to a good start with Japanese colleagues and business partners.

In the answer key at the back of the book you will find translations of **The Story So Far**, the **Dialogue** and the **Reading Corner**, with answers to the exercises in the **Expansion Activities**. As far as possible, we have tried to give translations in natural-sounding English. In some cases, however, we felt that a more literal translation would give a better idea of how to form equivalent Japanese sentences. This is particularly true of the example sentences given in the **Notes**, which are presented specifically to illustrate the new structure points. Therefore, you may find some cases where the English sounds somewhat awkward, but this should not detract from the meaning.

The story

The story revolves around Wajima Trading Company, a medium-sized, well-established trading company with its head office in Tokyo.

The British company Dando Sports, which manufactures sports equipment and clothing, wants to market its sporting goods in Japan through Wajima, so there are several visits to and from the UK and Japan to draw up the contract.

Yamamoto san is the buchō, or general manager, of the Overseas Planning Department at Wajima Trading Company in Tokyo. He is in his early 50s, solidly-built, and content with life.

Okamoto san is the kachō, or manager, of the Overseas Planning Section. In his late 30s, he is rather small and thin, and somewhat fussy. He works long hours, and though no doubt he has a family somewhere in the background, they do not have a place in his business life.

Maeda san is the kakarichō, or deputy manager, in his mid-30s. He is an honest, hard-working person who tends to look overworked and worried about life, but he tries to keep cheerful, and is well-respected by his staff.

Noguchi san is just 27, and likes to think of himself as internationalised as he spent a year studying in the US while at Waseda University. He is smooth, trendy, and fancies himself with the ladies.

Hotta san is 22, and has just joined Wajima on graduation from Tohoku University in Sendai. He is something of a contrast to Noguchi san, being rather short, plump and unsophisticated, so he admires Noguchi san for being everything that he is not.

Koyama san, Ikeda san and Watanabe san are OLs (or 'office ladies') at Wajima, and they perform general duties around the office such as typing, copying and greeting visitors. They are all originally from outside Tokyo, and they now live in Wajima's all-female company dormitory.

Mr Lloyd is the marketing manager for Dando Sports, and has to make several business trips to Japan in order to discuss contract matters with the people at Wajima.

Barbara Thomas is in charge of advertising at Dando Sports, and visits Japan with Mr Lloyd to learn more about the Japanese way of doing business.

Written Japanese

It is outside the scope of this book to provide learning materials for all aspects of written Japanese, but following is a brief description of the writing system. For those interested in pursuing this subject further, there are now several excellent texts and workbooks available from most large bookshops.

Japanese uses three different ways of writing used in combination: **kanji, hiragana** and **katakana. Kanji** characters first found their way into Japan via Korea around the fourth century, and gradually came to be used to write Japanese, which until then had had no written form. Today there are about 3,000 **kanji** in everyday use, although there are many more used for specialist subjects. As **kanji** are not phonetic, and represent meanings rather than sounds, it is not possible to tell the pronunciation simply from looking at them. (This is rather similar to our arabic numbers, which when written down also have meaning independent of their pronunciation. For example, think about how the symbol '2' is pronounced in the numbers 2, 12, 20.) Hence, all **kanji** and the different ways of reading them have to be learned by heart, which even for the Japanese is a formidable task. Although there is not space in this book to teach **kanji**, several are introduced in each lesson for your interest and for recognition purposes. You will find a list of all these in the appendices at the end of the book.

Hiragana are phonetic characters, and in theory can be used to write any Japanese word. In practice, they are generally used to write words which have no **kanji** representation, words where the **kanji** are so rare that the average person cannot be expected to know them, and in reading materials for young children who have not yet learned **kanji**. In cases where **kanji** are complex or unusual, tiny **hiragana** characters, known as **furigana**, are sometimes written above them to help the reader with pronunciation.

Hiragana are also used in combination with **kanji** to show the grammatical role played by the word. For example, a **kanji** may be used to represent the meaning 'play,' and then **hiragana** added to the end to show the equivalents of '-ed, -ing,' etc. **Hiragana** used in this way are known as **okurigana**. There are 46 **hiragana** characters.

Katakana are also phonetic characters, and are another way of representing the same sounds as **hiragana**. All sounds can therefore be written either in **hiragana** or **katakana**, but in practice **katakana** is used almost exclusively for writing foreign words which have been imported into Japanese, or words which are given stress in a text. In these ways it is somewhat similar to the use of italics in English text. So if you want to write 'London' or 'The Times' or your name in Japanese, you would use **katakana** characters. Many words for food and drink have been imported from English and other European languages, so if you learn **katakana** you will be able to read much of the menu in coffee shops and restaurants. **Katakana** is also used where the characters need to be very clear, such as in telegrams, and in comic books for effect to represent words like 'wham! whoosh! zoom!' Like **hiragana**, the **katakana** syllabary contains 46 characters. Both **hiragana** and **katakana** syllabaries are shown at the beginning of Lesson 1.

You may wonder if it is worth the trouble of learning the Japanese writing system. Perhaps one reason for trying is that the only place you will ever find Japanese written in roman letters is in a textbook for foreigners, so if that is all you know, then the world of the Japanese language will be very narrow for you. However, you will see that the dialogues in this book are written in both Japanese script and roman script, and the expansion activities appear only in roman script. Therefore, if you are not convinced of the usefulness of learning written Japanese, you can ignore it and work with the romanised version only. Nevertheless, if you do decide to have a go at learning to read, you will have the advantage of eventually learning Japanese more quickly, having better pronunciation, and being able to make more sense of the world around you if you go to Japan.

There are several systems in existence for writing Japanese in roman letters, but the most common, and that used in this book, is known as the modified Hepburn system. We have made exceptions to this system in some of the English sentences, where the accepted English spellings of familiar Japanese words and placenames are used. For example, the Japanese capital city appears as Tōkyō in romanised Japanese sentences, but as Tokyo in the English translation.

Hints on how to study

There are many ways of studying, and what suits one person may not be appropriate for someone else. Studying alone requires discipline and hard work, and it is all too easy to fall behind when you are busy, or tired, or feeling that you are not making progress. Below are some ideas which may help you to maintain a steady and successful study pattern.

- Keep a special notebook for new vocabulary and useful phrases, and refer to it frequently.
- Try to study with another person so that you can set targets together, encourage each other, and test each other.
- Read the dialogue and example sentences aloud, paying attention not only to pronunciation but also to intonation. Try reading them in different voices, or at different speeds.
- Record yourself on cassette tape as you speak aloud, and then listen carefully to your pronunciation.
- Try not to look at the translation of the dialogue until you have worked through the lesson, however tempting it may be. If you already know what the English meaning is, you will tend not to try so hard to understand the Japanese.
- When you read a sentence, don't worry if you cannot think of an exact English translation as long as you understand the general meaning of the Japanese.
- Don't do the exercises with one finger permanently in the answer key at the back, flipping back and forth. If you are not sure of the answer to a question, have a go anyway before you refer to the answers.
- Try writing out the answers to the exercises without referring to the answer key.

- After finishing a lesson, go back and read the main dialogue again as a review.
- Occasionally, go back three or four lessons and review the new vocabulary and structures there.
- Use your spoken Japanese whenever you can, and try not worry about making mistakes. By all means aim for flawless Japanese, but remember that in the real world it is much better to communicate successfully but with a few grammatical mistakes than not to communicate at all.

Symbols

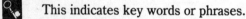

This indicates that the cassette is needed for the following section.

This indicates dialogue.

This indicates exercises – places where you can practise using the language.

This indicates key words or phrases.

This indicates grammar or explanations – the nuts and bolts of the language.

This indicates a section which gives some advice on what to expect when on a business trip to Japan or dealing with Japanese business people in this country. It also provides some background information about their industry and culture.

This indicates a section where you can practise your reading skills of Japanese script, and where you can revise vocabulary already met in the same lesson.

DAI 1 KA

—— HAJIMEMASHŌ ——

In this first lesson, you will learn how to pronounce Japanese correctly and you may also discover a number of Japanese words which you already know. Japanese pronunciation is relatively simple for the English-speaker for the following reasons:

- Most of the sounds are already familiar, as they exist in English.
- The rhythm of Japanese speech is very regular – each syllable takes about the same amount of time to pronounce.
- There is only one way to pronounce each written **kana** character (unlike English letters, which change their pronunciation depending on which letters they are placed next to).
- There are no strong stress patterns. For example, each syllable of the placename **Yokohama** has equal stress – quite different from the English pronunciation of *YokoHAAAma*!

Overleaf are two charts showing the **hiragana** and **katakana** syllabaries along with their equivalent sounds written in roman letters. (For a short description of the uses of **hiragana** and **katakana**, please see the **Introduction**.)

Note that, apart from the individual vowels (**a**, **i**, **u**, **e**, and **o**) at the beginning and the single **n** at the end, all the sounds are whole syllables, made up of a consonant and a vowel.

Hiragana syllabary

	A	I	U	E	O
	あ a	い i	う u	え e	お o
K	か ka	き ki	く ku	け ke	こ ko
S	さ sa	し shi	す su	せ se	そ so
T	た ta	ち chi	つ tsu	て te	と to
N	な na	に ni	ぬ nu	ね ne	の no
H	は ha	ひ hi	ふ fu	へ he	ほ ho
M	ま ma	み mi	む mu	め me	も mo
Y	や ya		ゆ yu		よ yo
R	ら ra	り ri	る ru	れ re	ろ ro
W	わ wa				を wo
	ん n				

Some of these hiragana characters can be modified using the marks ゛ and ゜ to represent the remaining sounds of Japanese, as shown below:

	A	I	U	E	O
G	が ga	ぎ gi	ぐ gu	げ ge	ご go
Z	ざ za	じ ji	ず zu	ぜ ze	ぞ zo
D	だ da	ぢ ji	づ zu	で de	ど do
B	ば ba	び bi	ぶ bu	べ be	ぼ bo
P	ぱ pa	ぴ pi	ぷ pu	ぺ pe	ぽ po

Note that ぢ (ji) and づ (zu) are only rarely used.

Katakana syllabary

	A	I	U	E	O
	ア a	イ i	ウ u	エ e	オ o
K	カ ka	キ ki	ク ku	ケ ke	コ ko
S	サ sa	シ shi	ス su	セ se	ソ so
T	タ ta	チ chi	ツ tsu	テ te	ト to
N	ナ na	ニ ni	ヌ nu	ネ ne	ノ no
H	ハ ha	ヒ hi	フ fu	ヘ he	ホ ho
M	マ ma	ミ mi	ム mu	メ me	モ mo
Y	ヤ ya		ユ yu		ヨ yo
R	ラ ra	リ ri	ル ru	レ re	ロ ro
W	ワ wa				ヲ wo
	ン n				

As with hiragana, some of the katakana characters can be modified with the symbols ˚ and ° to give these sounds:

	A	I	U	E	O
G	ガ ga	ギ gi	グ gu	ゲ ge	ゴ go
Z	ザ za	ジ ji	ズ zu	ゼ ze	ゾ zo
D	ダ da	チ ji	ヅ zu	デ de	ド do
B	バ ba	ビ bi	ブ bu	ベ be	ボ bo
P	バ pa	ビ pi	ブ pu	ベ pe	ボ po

Note: The symbol — after a character serves to lengthen the previous vowel sound for example データ (dēta) *data*, and ステーキ (sutēki) *steak*.

チ (ji) and ジ (zu) are only rarely used.

📷 —— **Notes and expansion activities** ——

For those of you who are learning to read and write **hiragana** and **katakana** (good luck – you'll find it well worth the effort) the pronunciation exercises below have been written out in **kana** too. When working through the exercises, try not to look at the romanised version until you've had a go at the **kana**.

Vowels

There are only five main vowel sounds.

a is pronounced as in the English *father* or *ha ha* or *after*, but quite short (**not** *faaaather*). Say the following words aloud, pronouncing **a** the same way whenever there is a blank space and keeping the pitch level – don't stress any particular syllable.

1	Y__m__h__ K__w__s__ki Hond__ Yokoh__m__ m__m__ - s__n	やまは かわさき ほんだ よこはま ママさん

i is pronounced as in the English *machine* or *ease* or *key*, but short and clipped (**not** *keeeey*). Say the words below, remembering this **i** sound wherever there is a blank.

2	or__gam__ harak__r__ n__nja Nagasak__ Ok__nawa	おりがみ はらきり にんじゃ ながさき おきなわ

In some cases the **i** is hardly sounded. **Deshita** (*was*), for example, is pronounced **desh'ta**.

u is pronounced as in *noodles* or *hula* or *book*, but without pursing your lips. This is the correct **u** sound for the words in the following box. Don't forget that the stress is equal on all the syllables.

Like **i**, in some cases, the **u** is hardly sounded. **Futon** for example, is pronounced **f'ton**, and **sukiyaki** as **s'kiyaki**.

—— **12** ——

3	F___ji	ふじ
	s___shi	すし
	ts___nami	つなみ
	sam___rai	さむらい
	S___z___ki	すずき

e is pronounced as in *end* or *get* or *bet*. Say the following words aloud taking care with this **e** sound. (Most of these words are mispronounced when used in English!)

4	sak___	さけ
	kamikaz___	かみかぜ
	ik___bana	いけばな
	karat___	からて
	Z___n	ぜん

The vowel sound **o** is similar to that in *old* or *go* but shorter and more clipped, as in *Honda*.

5	kim___n___	きもの
	___rigami	おりがみ
	kara___ke	からおけ
	Hir___shima	ひろしま
	T___y___ta	とよた

When two vowels appear together, remember that each one should be given the same value and keep its own pronunciation. Don't slide them together. **Samurai**, for example, has four syllables of equal length: **sa.mu.ra.i**. Say the following words aloud, giving each syllable equal time. (For ease of pronunciation, the syllables have been separated by dots.)

6	ko.i *(carp)*	こい
	sa.mu.ra.i	さむらい
	ge.i.sha	げいしゃ
	ha.i *(yes)*	はい

Long and short vowels

Japanese also has some long vowel sounds, which are simply the same sound as the short vowels, but held for twice as long. The vowel sounds in **Tōkyō**, for example, are not said the same as the **o** in **Honda** – they are double the length, as they are made up of the two sounds **o** and **u** together. If said slowly and carefully, the placenames **Tōkyō** and **Ōsaka** have four beats, as does the word **jūdō**, which has a long vowel in the middle and at the end. Practise saying these words.

7	To.u.kyo.u	とうきょう
	O.o.sa.ka	おおさか
	ju.u.do.u	じゅうどう
	sho.u.gu.n	しょうぐん
	su.mo.u	すもう

In the remaining lessons of this book, short and long vowels are written as follows: **a** and **ā**, **i** and **ii**, **u** and **ū**, **e** and **ei**, **o** and **ō**. With words borrowed from English or other Western languages, **ē** is used instead of **ei** (for example **kēki**, *cake*).

Syllables

As you can see from the **hiragana** and **katakana** charts at the beginning of this lesson, each **kana** character represents either a vowel or a syllable, and there are no single consonants except for **n**, which also has the length of a syllable. (So the name **Honda**, for example, is written with three **kana** and pronounced with three beats: **Ho.n.da.**) This is most clearly noticeable with words which have been borrowed from English into Japanese, where each consonant in the English word becomes a whole syllable in Japanese. Read the following words, giving equal stress to each syllable, and see if you can guess which English words they come from. (Answers are in the answer key at the back of the book.) The accompanying **katakana** will show you how the words have been formed.

8	ta.ku.shi.i	タクシー
	pa.su.po.o.to	パスポート
	ko.n.pyu.u.ta.a	コンピューター
	ne.ku.ta.i	ネクタイ
	de.e.ta	データ

Consonants

Most of the consonant sounds are already familiar to English speakers, but there are a few which will be new to you and need to be practised. The sound which is written in roman letters as **fu** is in fact halfway between the English **fu** and **hu**. (Notice from the **hiragana** chart that the other characters in this group are written with **h**.) The main difference between the pronunciation of these two is that the top teeth touch the bottom lip with the English **fu** but not with **hu**. To get the correct Japanese **fu** sound, try saying the word **futon**, but without letting your top teeth touch your bottom lip (rather like the initial sound of *phew*!). Now try saying these other words. What do they mean?

9		
	furūtsu	フルーツ
	furaido-chikin	フライドチキン
	pirafu	ピラフ
	biifusutēki	ビーフステーキ
	naifu	ナイフ

Another sound that does not exist in English is the Japanese **r**. To our ears, it sometimes sounds like an English *l* or *d*. Try saying *look*, *rook* and notice how the tip of your tongue flicks against the roof of your mouth when you say *look* but not with *rook*. Now try saying *rook* but with the top of your tongue briefly touching as it does with *l*. It will probably feel like a *d*. That's the sound you're aiming for. This is not an easy sound, but it is an important one to practise if you want to have good Japanese pronunciation, so listen out for it when you have a chance to hear Japanese spoken. When reading the words below, all originally from English, remember that the Japanese do not differentiate between the English *l* and *r* sounds, so they are both written in roman letters with **r**. What are the English equivalents?

10		
	Rondon	ロンドン
	esukarētā	エスカレーター
	purintā	プリンター
	Amerika	アメリカ
	ereganto	エレガント
	gorufu	ゴルフ

The sound **tsu** may look odd to you when it occurs at the beginning of a word, but it is simply a variation of the Japanese **t** when it occurs before **u**. In English, this sound comes only in the middle or at the end of a word, for example in *cats, bits, Patsy*. Try reading the following words.

11		
Mitsubishi	みつびし	
tsuna	ツナ	
sūtsu	スーツ	
tsū-piisu	ツーピース	
tsuiido	ツイード	

Doubled consonants

You will come across some words with double consonants, and these sounds should be held for twice as long as a single consonant. **Kata**, for example, has two beats (**ka.ta**) whereas **katta** has three beats (**ka.t.ta**). If this sounds confusing, think of the *tt* sound in the middle of *hot toast*. Try saying it aloud, and note the way the *t* sound is held for longer than a single letter. Now say the words below, remembering to hold on to the doubled sounds. (Apart from the first two, these are all words which were originally English, but which have now been accepted into Japanese. See if you can recognise them.)

12			
Ni.s.sa.n	にっさん	(as in *less salt*)
Ni.p.po.n	にっぽん	(as in *top person*)
po.ke.t.to	ポケット	(as in *hot toast*)
ka.se.t.to	カセット	(as in *hot toast*)
pa.ni.k.ku	パニック	(as in *take care*)
sa.k.ka.a	サッカー	(as in *take care*)
ra.s.shu (*hour*)	ラッシュ	(as in *fresh shrimps*)
ma.t.chi	マッチ	(as in *hot chocolate*)

Combined syllables

The **kana** for the sounds **ya**, **yu** and **yo** are sometimes written very small after another **kana**, which means the two sounds combine together to make one syllable. For example, if the **kana** for **ni** and **ya** are written the same size (にや), the sound would be pronounced **ni.ya** with two beats, but if the **kana** for **ya** is written small (にゃ), the sound would be **nya**, with only one beat. Look at the following pairs of words and practise saying them aloud.

13

ki.ya.ku (*agreement*) きやく	→ kya.ku (*visitor*) きゃく
bi.yo.u.i.n (*beauty salon*) びようLん	→ byo.u.i.n (*hospital*) びょうLん
hi.yo.u (*expense*) ひよう	→ hyo.u (*chart, diagram*) ひょう
ri.yu.u (*reason*) りゆう	→ ryu.u (*dragon*) りゅう

Some English sounds don't exist in Japanese. This means that when English words are imported into Japanese, not only do all individual sounds have to be turned into syllables, but pronunciation has to be adapted to sounds which exist in Japanese. As we have seen above, there is no English *l* sound, so this becomes the Japanese **r**. Other English sounds which do not exist are *v* (which becomes **b**), *u* as in *sun* (which becomes **a**), *wi* (which becomes a combination of the two Japanese sounds **u** and **i**) and *th* (which becomes **s** or **z**). Some examples of words with these sounds are given below.

14

violin	becomes	**ba.i.o.ri.n**	バイオリン
whisky	becomes	**u.i.su.ki.i**	ウイスキー
bus	becomes	**ba.su**	バス
lunch	becomes	**ra.n.chi**	ランチ
milk	becomes	**mi.ru.ku**	ミルク
leather	becomes	**re.za.a**	レザー

Can you guess how you might say the following?

15

waitress	_____
salad	_____
video	_____
elevator	_____
pub	_____

How many Japanese words do you already know? Quite a lot, though you may not realise it. Read through the following story, and see how many of the Japanese words (printed in bold type) you can understand or guess at. You may find it helpful to read the words aloud.

16

Monday **Burūsu**

It had been a bad day for Mr Tanaka right from the start. The trains were on **sutoraiki** again, so he had to get to work by **basu** and **takushii**. He had a very tight **sukejūru**, so it didn't help to begin the day by arriving late. As head **sērusuman**, he was supposed to be giving a **repōto** at today's **sērusu** meeting, but when he got to his desk, he found a **messēji** to say that the **purintā** on the **konpyūtā** had broken down, so he couldn't get the **dēta** he needed for his **repōto**. He sent a **memo** to the **taipisuto** to see if she could **taipu-appu** the details for him, but she was too busy at the **kopii** machine with other work.

He didn't have much time for **ranchi**, so he just bought a **hamu sandoitchi** and a **kōhii** at the **kōhii shoppu** next door. However, taking them to his **tēburu**, he tripped on the **kāpetto** and spilled the **kōhii** all over his **sūtsu** and **nekutai** ...

When he got back to the office, he found everyone in a **panikku**. It seemed that the **erebētā** had got stuck between floors with the **manējā** of the **sērusu** department inside, so they had to **kyanseru** the **sērusu** meeting and wait for the building **enjinia** to arrive to free the **manējā**. This was the only good thing that happened to Mr Tanaka that day.

The final straw was when he called his **gārufurendo** to see if she'd like to go to a **resutoran** that evening, but it seemed she had another **dēto** with someone else. So he got a take-out **piza** on the way home, opened a can of **biiru**, put the **sutereo** on very loud, and prepared to spend a miserable evening alone. And it was still only Monday.

DAI 2 KA

—— O-NAMAE WA? ——

In this lesson you will learn how to:

- greet someone
- say thank you
- count up to 99
- say telephone and room numbers

Begin by reading the opening dialogue together with the vocabulary list following it, but don't worry if you don't understand it too well at first. Come back to it again after you have read the **Notes** and finished all the **Expansion Activities** and you should be pleasantly surprised at how much easier it has become.

—— The story ——

Wajima Trading Company is an old-established, medium-sized trading company with its head office in Tokyo. Maeda Tadahisa, an assistant manager at Wajima, is just checking out of a hotel after a short business trip. He is returning to Tokyo today to take part in an interview panel for new recruits.

—— Dialogue ——

Try to read this without referring to the **romaji** (roman script) version of the dialogue which comes after it.

フロントのひと　おはよう　ございます。
まえだ　　　　　おはよう　ございます。
フロントのひと　チェックアウト　ですか。
まえだ　　　　　はい、おねがい　します。
フロントのひと　おなまえ　は?
まえだ　　　　　まえだ　です。
フロントのひと　おへや　ばんごう　は?
まえだ　　　　　3812 (さん　はち　いち　に)です。
フロントのひと　3812　です　か。
まえだ　　　　　はい,そう　です。
フロントのひと　(handing over the bill) はい　どうぞ。
まえだ　　　　　どうも。あぁ!かぎ!
フロントのひと　ありがとう　ございました。

Furonto no hito	Ohayō gozaimasu.
Maeda	Ohayō gozaimasu.
Furonto no hito	Chekku-auto desu ka.
Maeda	Hai, onegai shimasu.
Furonto no hito	O-namae wa?
Maeda	Maeda desu.
Furonto no hito	O-heya bangō wa?
Maeda	3812 (san hachi ichi ni) desu.
Furonto no hito	3812 desu ka.
Maeda	Hai, sō desu.
Furonto no hito	(handing over the bill) Hai dōzo.
Maeda	Dōmo. Ā! Kagi!
Furonto no hito	Arigatō gozaimashita.

dai 2 (ni) ka *lesson 2*
furonto no hito *reception clerk (in a hotel)*
ohayō gozaimasu *good morning*
chekku-auto *to check out (of a hotel)*
desu *am, is, are*
ka [indicates a question]
hai *yes*
onegai shimasu *please (do that)*
o- [prefix to indicate politeness]
namae *name*
wa [indicates topic of sentence]

heya *room*
bangō *number*
san *three*
hachi *eight*
ichi *one*
ni *two*
sō desu *that's right*
dōzo *please (take it), here you are*
dōmo *thanks*
kagi *key*
arigatō gozaimashita *thank you very much*

Comprehension

Choose the correct answers to the questions below.

1 What time of day is it?
  (*a*) Morning.
  (*b*) Afternoon.
  (*c*) Evening.

2 What does Maeda san want to do?
  (*a*) Get his room key.
  (*b*) Give his name.
  (*c*) Get the bill.

Notes

These notes explain and expand on new sentence structures, vocabulary and cultural points which appear in the opening dialogue.

1 Ohayō gozaimasu (Good morning)

Other greetings are **Konnichiwa** in the daytime and **Konbanwa** in the evening, although you would not use them in formal situations to someone in a higher position, or in very informal situations such as within the family. These phrases might be used, for example, to greet a person of similar rank to yourself or the receptionist when you are visiting an office.

2 Chekku-auto (To check out of a hotel)

This word is an adaptation of the English *check out*. The number of words imported from other countries into the Japanese language is growing all the time, the majority of them coming from American English. There will be more practice with **gairaigo**, or *words from abroad*, later in the lesson.

3 Desu (Is, am, are)

Desu can mean *is*, *am* or *are*, since Japanese verb forms do not make the distinction between singular or plural. In addition, it is not generally considered necessary to use personal pronouns where the meaning is implicit. Therefore **desu** can be used for *I am, you are, he is, she is, we are, they are*. The verb always comes at the end of the sentence.

For example:

| Taipisuto **desu**. | *I'm a typist.* |
| Tanaka san **desu**. | *He/She's Tanaka san.* |

Note that although **desu** is two syllables, the final **-u** is hardly sounded, and it is perhaps closer in pronunciation to *dess*.

4 Ka

Simply adding **ka** after the verb at the end of a sentence turns it into a question.

Maeda san desu **ka**.	*Is he Maeda san?/ Are you*
	Maeda san?
Nan desu **ka**.	*What is it?*

As a final **ka** always indicates a question in Japanese, it does not need to be followed by a question mark.

Note that there are no equivalents to *a* and *the* in Japanese, so where they appear in English they can simply be ignored in Japanese.

5 Hai, onegai shimasu (Yes, please)

This is a handy way of saying, *Yes, that (what you just offered me) is what I would like*.

| A | Kōhii? | *Coffee?* |
| B | Hai, **onegai shimasu**. | *Yes please.* |

6 O-namae (Name)

With certain words, **o-** added at the beginning makes the whole tone of the sentence more polite and formal. Hence you will often hear this used in shops, hotels and restaurants by the staff to the customers, as well as in other situations which require a degree of formality. It is used rather more by women than by men.

7 O-namae wa? (Your name?)

Japanese uses a number of small words called particles, whose function is to show what job a word or phrase does in a sentence.

Particles are sometimes called 'post-positions' because they come after the word they are related to. One of the most common particles is **wa**, which indicates what the topic of a sentence is by following immediately after it. The pattern **A wa B desu** means *A is B* or *A equals B.*

Maeda san **wa** kakarichō desu.	*Maeda san is assistant manager.*
Namae **wa** Tanaka desu.	*The name's Tanaka.*
Wajima **wa** shōsha desu.	*Wajima is a trading company.*
Denwa bangō **wa** nan-ban desu ka.	*What (number) is your telephone number?*

8 *Maeda desu* (I'm Maeda)

The word **san** is used after a person's name as a term of respect, whether the person is male or female, married or unmarried, so it is the equivalent of *Mr, Mrs, Ms* and *Miss*. (It can also be used with first names, so do not be surprised if your Japanese colleagues call you **John san** or **Sue san**.) However, as **san** is used to show respect to others, it is never used when speaking of yourself.

9 *O-heya bangō wa?* (Your room number?)

As in English, it is not always necessary to use a complete sentence or question for the meaning to be understood. In particular, when two questions have the same grammatical pattern, you don't need to repeat the whole question a second time.

A	Maeda san wa kakarichō desu ka?	*Is Maeda san an assistant manager?*
B	Hai, sō desu.	*Yes, that's right.*
A	**Okamoto san wa?**	*How about Okamoto san?*
B	Okamoto san wa kachō desu.	*Okamoto san is a manager.*

Note, however, that you still need to include the particle **wa** to show that you are using **Okamoto** in the same way as **Maeda**.

10 *San hachi ichi ni* (Three, eight, one, two)

Giving your hotel number, as Maeda san does, is a straightforward case of saying each digit individually. Learn the following numbers:

1	ichi	6	roku
2	ni	7	nana, shichi
3	san	8	hachi
4	yon, shi	9	kyū, ku
5	go	10	jū

There are two ways of saying the numbers 4 and 7: which you use generally depends on what you are counting. For example, when you are talking about room numbers or telephone numbers, use **yon** (4) and **nana** (7). Other uses will be explained as they arise.

Counting beyond 10 is very straightforward in Japanese. For the numbers 11 to 19, think of them as 10 and 1, 10 and 2, etc.

11	jū-ichi	16	jū-roku
12	jū-ni	17	jū-nana, jū-shichi
13	jū-san	18	jū-hachi
14	jū-yon, jū-shi	19	jū-kyū
15	jū-go		

If **ni** means 2, and **jū** means 10, can you guess before looking at the list below how to say 20? What about 30? And 40?

10	jū	60	roku-jū
20	ni-jū	70	nana-jū
30	san-jū	80	hachi-jū
40	yon-jū	90	kyū-jū
50	go-jū		

For numbers in between, such as 23 or 26, simply add on the appropriate single digit: **ni-jū-ichi** is 21, **ni-jū-ni** is 22, **ni-jū-san** is 23, etc.

11 *Hai, sō desu* (Yes, that's right)

Sō is a very useful little word and is roughly the equivalent of the English *so* in the sense of *Yes, that's so.*

A	Orenji jūsu desu ka?	*Is this orange juice?*
B	Hai, **sō** desu.	*Yes, it is* (Lit. *Yes, that's so*).

12 *Hai, dōmo* (Thanks)

As with the English *thank you, thank you very much, thanks* and *thanks very much*, so in Japanese there are several ways of expressing thanks using the same words in different combinations. As a very general rule, the longer the phrase, the more polite it is.

Dōmo.	*Thanks.*
Dōmo arigatō.	*Thank you.*
Arigatō gozaimasu.	*Thank you very much.*
Dōmo arigatō gozaimasu.	*Thank you very much indeed.*

If **gozaimashita**, the past tense, is used with this last phrase, it indicates thanks for something which has happened previously, even if only a moment ago, rather than for something which will happen in the future.

If someone uses one of these phrases to thank you for doing something for them, you can respond with **Dō itashimashite**, or *You're welcome*.

A	Dōmo arigatō.	*Thank you.*
B	**Dō itashimashite.**	*You're welcome.*

—— Expansion activities ——

These activities provide practice with the new structure patterns and vocabulary introduced in the dialogue and explained in the Notes. If you have difficulty with any of the activities, read through the relevant Notes once more before having another try.

1 How would you greet someone in the street at the following times of day?

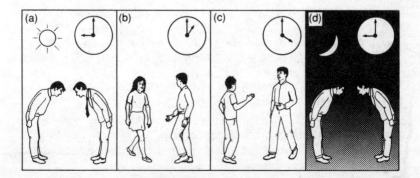

2 Watanabe san, an OL (or 'office lady') in the personnel department at Wajima Trading Company, is checking the telephone extension numbers of some of the staff members for the new company handbook. Read aloud her dialogue with Koyama san, another OL, using the information from the floor plan to complete it.

Takeshita **774**	**Yamamoto** **598**	**Okamoto** **312**
Tani Ono **569 839**	**Noguchi** **698**	**Maeda** **211**
Yamada **238**	**Koyama** **146**	**Ikeda** **435**

Watanabe	Noguchi san wa roku-kyū-hachi desu ka.
Koyama	Hai, sō desu.
Watanabe	Ikeda san wa nan-ban desu ka.
Koyama	(*a*) _____
Watanabe	Maeda san wa?
Koyama	(*b*) _____
Watanabe	Okamoto san wa?
Koyama	(*c*) _____
Watanabe	Tani san wa?
Koyama	(*d*) _____
Watanabe	Ono san wa?
Koyama	(*e*) _____
Watanabe	Dōmo arigatō.
Koyama	Dō itashimashite.

3 You need only two more small pieces of information to be able to tell people your telephone number. The number 0 is **zero** (careful of pronunciation!) and where in English we might say *dash* to separate groups of numbers, the Japanese equivalent is **no**. Now say the following numbers aloud. Example: (03–3416–7709) zero-san no san-yon-ichi-roku no nana-nana-zero-kyū.

(*a*) 0565–264–264   (*d*) 0427–97–2661
(*b*) 03–4665–3107   (*e*) 078–861–3343
(*c*) 03–3920–1776   (*f*)   your telephone number

If you are studying with someone else, ask him or her to read aloud the telephone numbers above while you write them down without looking at the book.

4 Rearrange the words below to make complete sentences.

(a) kachō desu san Okamoto ka wa
(b) ni-san-go wa bangō desu o-heya ka
(c) bangō nan-ban wa denwa ka desu
(d) desu wa Wajima shōsha
(e) bangō desu denwa wa 03–4836–0865

5 Can you work out what the following **gairaigo** words mean? Say them aloud and concentrate on the sound, rather than the spelling, to give you a clue.

Food and drink	At the office	Jobs
hanbāgā	fairu	uētoresu
uisukii	taipuraitā	enjinia
sarada	konpyūtā	konsarutanto
biiru	dētabēsu	anaunsā

6 Now it's your turn. Imagine that you have just come back to the hotel where you are staying and you go up to the front desk clerk to pick up your key. Using the cues given in English, complete the following dialogue.

Clerk Kagi desu ka.
You (a) *Yes, please.* _____
Clerk O-namae wa?
You (b) *It's* _____
Clerk O-heya bangō wa?
You (c) *It's 204.* _____
Clerk Hai, dōzo.
You (d) *Thank you.* _____

—————— Reading corner ——————

Watanabe san has finished her check of everyone's office extension number and home telephone number. To complete the company handbook, she only has to confirm everyone's rank. Read aloud her conversation with Koyama san below.

わたなべ　まえだ　さん　は　かかりちょう　です　か。
こやま　　はい、そう　です。
わたなべ　おかもと　さん　は?
こやま　　おかもと　さん　は　かちょう　です。

📖 ───────── **Business briefing** ─────────

Japan: the country

Although Japan is one of the world's great powers both economically and industrially, it is comparatively small and cramped in land area. It is a long, thin, crescent-shaped country stretching almost 3,000 km north to south, and it is made up of four main islands – Honshu, Hokkaido, Kyushu and Shikoku – along with hundreds of smaller ones. Japan covers an area of 337,435 square km, which makes it just a little smaller than California and about 1½ times the size of the UK. The capital city of Tokyo is on roughly the same latitude as Gibraltar, Cyprus and Las Vegas.

Around 70% of the country is taken up with heavily forested mountains which are virtually uninhabitable, so all housing, industry, farming and transportation networks are concentrated in the remaining 30% of land area. The most densely populated part of the country is the narrow strip of coastal plain between Tokyo and the northern part of Kyushu, where approximately 70% of Japanese people live.

Japan is situated on one of the most seismologically active areas in the world, and there are thousands of earthquakes every year, although most are too small to worry about or even feel. The last really serious one was the Great Kanto earthquake in 1923, which killed about 140,000 people. Japan is also a volcanic country and eruptions are not uncommon, though they are generally harmless. The most famous volcano, Mt Fuji, is now dormant and has not erupted since 1707.

The volcanic ranges which run through the country give it a great deal of scenic variety. There are short, fast-flowing rivers, deep gorges, beautiful mountain lakes, and dramatic, rocky coastlines. In addition, there is great variety in the climate. There are four distinct seasons, although the length of the country and the effect of the mountain ranges mean weather patterns vary greatly in different parts of the country at any one time. With this kind of variety in the weather and the landscape, with the mountains and the lakes, the volcanoes and the forests, the sea and the plains, wherever the traveller goes outside the cities, he or she cannot help but be impressed by the scenic beauty of Japan.

BENTŌ WA IKURA DESU KA

In this lesson you will learn how to:

- ask for something
- express numbers up to 9,999
- ask the price of something
- talk about your interests, likes and dislikes

The story so far

Maeda san, assistant manager at Wajima Trading Company, is on his way back to Tokyo to interview job candidates. One of these candidates is Hotta Yūichirō, a final-year economics student at university in Sendai, who at this moment is waiting on the train platform for the **Shinkansen** (*Bullet train*) to Tokyo. While waiting, he goes to the kiosk to buy some food for the journey.

Dialogue

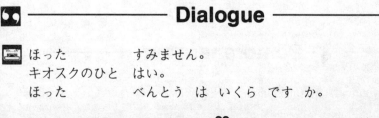

ほった	すみません。
キオスクのひと	はい。
ほった	べんとう は いくら です か。

キオスクのひと　￥800（はっぴゃく　えん）です。
ほった　　　　サンドイッチ は?
キオスクのひと　チーズ サンド は ￥700（ななひゃく　えん）
　　　　　　　　です。ツナ サンド は ￥750（ななひゃく　ご
　　　　　　　　じゅう　えん）です。
ほった　　　　じゃ、ツナ サンド を ください。ツナ は
　　　　　　　　だいすき です。
キオスクのひと　はい どうぞ。
ほった　　　　あぁ! にっけい しんぶん も ください。
キオスクのひと　はい，ありがとう ございます。

Hotta	Sumimasen.
Kiosuku no hito	Hai.
Hotta	Bentō wa ikura desu ka.
Kiosuku no hito	￥800 (hap-pyaku en) desu.
Hotta	Sandoitchi wa?
Kiosuku no hito	Chiizu sando wa ￥700 (nana-hyaku en) desu. Tsuna sando wa ￥750 (nana-hyaku-go-jū en) desu.
Hotta	Ja, tsuna sando o kudasai. Tsuna wa dai-suki desu.
Kiosuku no hito	Hai dōzo.
Hotta	Ā! Nikkei Shinbun mo kudasai.
Kiosuku no hito	Hai, arigatō gozaimasu.

sumimasen *excuse me*
kiosuku *kiosk*
bentō *packed lunch*
ikura *how much (money)?*
en *yen*
sando(itchi) *sandwich*
chiizu sando *cheese sandwich*
tsuna *(canned) tuna*
ja *well, in that case* [contraction of dewa]
o [indicates object of verb]
kudasai *please (give me)*
dai-suki *like very much*
suki *like*
Nikkei *Japan's leading economic newspaper*
shinbun *newspaper*
mo *also, too*

Comprehension

1 Why does Hotta san choose a tuna sandwich?

(*a*) Because it's cheaper than the cheese sandwich.
(*b*) Because he likes tuna.
(*c*) Because the **bentō** is too expensive.

2 How many items does Hotta san buy at the kiosk?
  (*a*) One.
  (*b*) Two.
  (*c*) Three.

Notes

1 *Sumimasen* (Excuse me)

This is similar to the English *Excuse me* both in the sense of an apology (when stepping on someone's foot, for example) and also when attracting someone's attention, as in this case.

2 *Bentō* (Boxed lunch)

A **bentō** is a kind of picnic meal, packaged in a box, which can be bought at places like train stations and bus stations to eat on long journeys, in the same way we might buy sandwiches. **Bentōs** are also often bought (or made by loving wives or mothers) to eat as packed lunches at work or school. They will typically contain rice, some pickled vegetables, some fish or meat, a small container of soy sauce and a pair of chopsticks.

3 *¥800 desu* (It's ¥800)

Remember the numbers 1–10? If the word for 100 is **hyaku**, how do you think you say 200? What about 400? and 700?

100	hyaku	600	rop-pyaku
200	ni-hyaku	700	nana-hyaku
300	san-byaku	800	hap-pyaku
400	yon-hyaku	900	kyū-hyaku
500	go-hyaku		

Note that there are some phonetic changes with the numbers 300, 600 and 800.

A Pen wa ikura desu ka.   *How much are the pens?*
B ¥300 (**san-byaku** en)   *They're ¥300. Here you are.*
    desu. Dōzo.

As one yen has almost no value, even relatively cheap articles can run into the thousands of yen. This is why it is important to know how to say and recognise large numbers in Japanese. Practise counting in thousands:

1,000	sen	6,000	roku-sen
2,000	ni-sen	7,000	nana-sen
3,000	san-zen	8,000	has-sen
4,000	yon-sen	9,000	kyū-sen
5,000	go-sen		

For complex numbers simply say the thousands, hundreds, tens and units one after the other. For example 5,325 is **go-sen, san-byaku ni-jū-go**.

4 *Sando* (Sandwich)

Many words borrowed from other languages are shortened for convenience, sometimes to the extent that you may not recognise them at first sight. Below are some of the most common ones.

depāto	(*depart*ment store)	sūpā	(*super*market)
terebi	(*televi*sion)	wāpuro	(*word pro*cessor)
apāto	(*apart*ment)	eakon	(*air con*ditioner)

5 *Tsuna sando o kudasai* (A tuna sandwich, please)

The pattern **A o kudasai** is the commonest and most straightforward way of politely asking for something. The particle **o** indicates that the noun preceding it is the grammatical object of the verb. **Kudasai** is the polite form of a verb meaning *give to me*.

Kōhii o **kudasai**.	*Could I have some coffee, please?*
Kasa o **kudasai**.	*I'd like an umbrella, please.*
Fairu o **kudasai**.	*The file, please.*

6 *Tsuna wa dai-suki desu* (I really like tuna)

The construction of this sentence is very different from the English, as **suki**, the word for *like*, is not a verb. In Japanese, the thing or person liked is the topic of the sentence. If you visit Japan, you will hear questions like the following very often, as your hosts will be eager to find out if you like things Japanese.

Nihon wa **suki** desu ka.	*Do you like Japan?* (Lit. *Is Japan liked [by you]?*)
Nihonshu wa **suki** desu ka.	*Do you like sake?*

The opposite of **suki** is **kirai**, a rather strong statement of dislike. Even stronger is **dai-kirai**.

Gorufu wa **kirai** desu.	*I can't stand golf.*
Shigoto wa **dai-kirai** desu.	*I hate work.*

A less direct way of indicating that you don't particularly like something is to respond using **mā-mā**, meaning *so-so*.

A	Tenisu wa suki desu ka.	*Do you like tennis?*
B	**Mā-mā** suki desu.	*So-so. It's okay.*

Here is a summary of the words you can use to show varying levels of like or dislike.

dai-suki	*love, like very much*
suki	*like*
mā-mā suki	*Ok, so-so*
kirai	*dislike*
dai-kirai	*hate*

7 *Nikkei Shinbun* (Nikkei Newspaper)

The **Nikkei** is Japan's leading daily economic newspaper, with the name coming from the first syllables of **Nihon** (*Japan*) and **Keizai** (*economy*). There is a weekly English-language version of this paper known as *The Nikkei Weekly*. Other leading dailies are the **Asahi Shinbun**, the **Yomiuri Shinbun** and the **Mainichi Shinbun**.

8 *Mo* (Too)

Note that where **mo** (*too, also*) is used, it is not necessary also to include the particles **wa** or **o**.

Biiru **mo** suki desu ka.	*Do you like beer too?*
Kōhii **mo** ¥500 desu.	*Coffee is also ¥500.*

✓ ——— Expansion activities ———

1   Maeda san has to be careful with the rather meagre allowance he
has been given by Wajima for this business trip and so always has
to ask the price of things in shops. Following his example below,
ask how much the items in the pictures are, and give the answers
too. The words you need are given below the pictures, but try not
to refer to them.

Example:

          Maeda   Shinbun wa ikura desu ka.
Kiosuku no hito   ¥170 (hyaku-nana-ju en) desu.

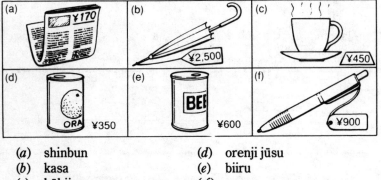

(a)   shinbun   (d)   orenji jūsu
(b)   kasa   (e)   biiru
(c)   kōhii   (f)   pen

2   Not only is it raining in Tokyo, but Hotta san has left his briefcase
on the Shinkansen platform in Sendai. He philosophically decides
that it is time he had a new one anyway, so goes to buy one in
Tokyo. What does he say when he asks for the things on the
shopping list?

Example: (briefcase) Kaban o kudasai.

> briefcase
> file
> pen
> Yomiuri newspaper
> umbrella

3   Hotta san is appalled at Tokyo prices and, being only a student, goes for the cheaper option if given a choice. Practise reading the following conversation he has in a coffee shop. (Before saying each line, try looking at it first, and then looking away from the text as you say it aloud.)

Hotta   *Tsuna sando* wa ikura desu ka.
Uētoresu   *¥850* desu.
Hotta   *Chiizu sando* wa?
Uētoresu   *¥750* desu.
Hotta   Ja, *chiizu sando* o kudasai.

Now substitute the italicised words with those given below for other shopping situations. Try to do so without looking at the dialogue.

(*a*)   Asahi Shinbun (¥130), Mainichi Shinbun (¥150)
(*b*)   orenji jūsu (¥550), kōhii (¥500)
(*c*)   biiru (¥650), nihonshu (¥600)

4   Imagine someone is asking whether you like the things pictured below. What would their questions be, and how would you answer? Look at the example.

Example:

A   Kōhii wa suki desu ka.
B   Hai, dai-suki desu. / Hai, suki desu./ Mā-mā suki desu. /Kirai desu.

Here are the words you need, though not necessarily in the same order as the pictures: **biiru, terebi, tenisu, shigoto, Nihon, gorufu.**

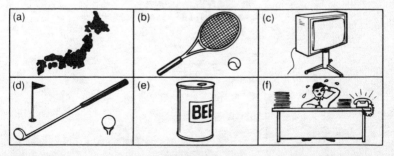

5 Each of the questions below has two answers, only one of which is appropriate. See if you can work out which one it is.

(a)	Gorufu wa suki desu ka.	(i)	Hai, suki desu.
		(ii)	Hai, kirai desu.
(b)	Denwa bangō wa nan-ban desu ka.	(i)	Sō desu.
		(ii)	403-ban desu.
(c)	Okamoto san wa kachō desu ka.	(i)	Kachō desu ka.
		(ii)	Sō desu.
(d)	Kōhii?	(i)	Hai, onegai shimasu.
		(ii)	Kōhii o kudasai.
(e)	Shinbun wa ¥180 desu ka.	(i)	Hai, sō desu.
		(ii)	Hai, shōsha desu.

6 Now it's your turn. Imagine that you are staying at a business hotel, and that you go to the bookshop in the lobby to buy some reading matter. Complete the following dialogue.

You (a) *Excuse me.* _____

Clerk Hai!

You (b) *How much is 'Newsweek'?* _____
_____

Clerk ¥850 desu.

You (c) *And 'Time'?* _____

Clerk Taimu mo ¥850 desu.

You (d) *I'll have 'Time', please.* _____

Clerk Hai, dōzo.

You (e) *Oh, a pen, too, please.* _____

Clerk Hai, arigatō gozaimasu. ¥1,150 desu.

Reading corner

What are the items on this shopping list?

ショッピングリスト
かさ
べんとう
かばん
あさひしんぶん
にほんしゅ
かぎ

Business briefing

Recruitment in Japanese companies

The lifetime employment system is one aspect of the Japanese business world already familiar to most foreigners. The larger corporations and government agencies which follow this system have the pick of the best recruits when hiring, and there is a great deal of competition among young people to get into them. To be hired by one of these prestigious companies or organisations usually means an end to any worries about future job security.

As permanent employees are, in effect, being hired for life, great care must be taken in the selection process. At this point the company is not really looking for specialists – with a lifetime of employment ahead there is plenty of time to learn specific skills on the job – but rather young people with a well-rounded personality and good education, and who look as if they will fit in with the company's particular style and philosophy. New recruits get only a low salary and do not expect more, but they know that this is the beginning of a steady investment in a long and secure future.

Hiring generally takes place once a year directly from schools or universities. Candidates must sit company entrance examinations and survive a series of interviews. The Japanese educational year ends in March, so companies wanting to hire from any one year's graduating class will approach the university the previous autumn to begin the recruitment process. The fruits of this process can be seen each April 1st during morning rush hour: on station platforms throughout the country, crowds of smartly dressed young men and women, easily identifiable by their sober new clothes, new briefcases and new haircuts, wait nervously for the train to take them to their first day at the company. Their working lives are just beginning.

DAI 4 KA

SENDAI NO HOTTA DESU

In Lesson 4, you will find out how to

- introduce yourself
- ask how someone is
- express the names of positions and departments within a company
- ask where something is

——————— The story so far ———————

Hotta san has just finished his job interview at Wajima Trading. He is relieved it is over, as it involved paper tests as well as several interviews. He won't know the results of the interview until December. Now he has to make a courtesy telephone call to Tanaka san, a retired industrialist who is a friend of his father and who lives in Tokyo.

——————— Dialogue ———————

ほった　もしもし。
たなか　もしもし。
ほった　たなか　さん　ですか。

たなか　はい、たなか　です。

ほった　あの、ほった　です　が。

たなか　(*unable to hear because of background noise*)
　　　　えっ？　おおた　さん　です　か。

ほった　いいえ、ほった　です。せんだい　の　ほった　です。

たなか　ああ、ほった　さん！　こんにちは！　おとうさん　は
　　　　おげんき　です　か。

ほった　はい、げんき　です。

たなか　いま　どこ　です　か。

ほった　いま　しんじゅく　の　えき　です。

たなか　かんこう　です　か。それ　は　いい　です　ね。

ほった　いいえ、ちがいます。かいしゃ　の　めんせつ　です。

Hotta	Moshi moshi.
Tanaka	Moshi moshi.
Hotta	Tanaka san desu ka.
Tanaka	Hai, Tanaka desu.
Hotta	Anō, Hotta desu ga.
Tanaka	(*unable to hear because of background noise*) Ē? Ōta san desu ka.
Hotta	Iie, Hotta desu. Sendai no Hotta desu.
Tanaka	Ā, Hotta san! Konnichiwa! O-tōsan wa o-genki desu ka.
Hotta	Hai, genki desu.
Tanaka	Ima doko desu ka.
Hotta	Ima Shinjuku no eki desu.
Tanaka	Kankō desu ka. Sore wa ii desu ne.
Hotta	Iie, chigaimasu. Kaisha no mensetsu desu.

moshi moshi　*Hello? (on the telephone)*

anō　*er...*

ga　[sentence ending to soften the tone of the sentence]

iie　*no*

Sendai no Hotta desu　*Hotta from Sendai*

o-tōsan　*your father*

genki　*well, fine, healthy*

ima　*now, at the moment*

doko　*where?*

Shinjuku　*a business and entertainment area of Tokyo*

eki　*station*

kankō　*sight-seeing*

sore　*that*

ii　*nice, good*

ne　*isn't it*

chigaimasu　*that's not correct*

kaisha　*company*

no　[indicates possession]

mensetsu　*interview*

✔ ———————— **Comprehension** ————————

Choose the correct answers to the questions below.

1 Whom does Tanaka san ask about?
   (a) About Hotta.
   (b) About Hotta's family.
   (c) About Hotta's father.

2 Where is Hotta during the conversation?
   (a) With his father.
   (b) In Shinjuku station.
   (c) In Sendai.

🎙 ———————————— **Notes** ————————————

1 Moshi moshi (Hello?)

This phrase is used almost exclusively to begin conversations on the telephone, rather like the English *Hello?*, although without the question intonation. You may also hear it in the middle of a telephone conversation if you have been quiet at your end for some time – in this case it means something like, *Hello? Are you still there?*

2 Hotta desu ga (This is Hotta...)

Ga is added to the end of the sentence in order to soften it a little, by sounding as if it is unfinished. Without this, the statement would sound too terse and direct.

A	Ano, sumimasen **ga**...	*Er, excuse me, but...*
B	Hai.	*Yes?*
A	O-tearai wa doko desu ka.	*Where are the toilets?*

3 Sendai no Hotta desu (Hotta from Sendai)

Hotta explains who he is by saying where he comes from. It is very common when introducing yourself in Japanese to use this pattern (group) **no** (name) **desu**, to identify yourself as a member of a particular group. For business people this will most commonly mean mentioning the company name, but in some circumstances it may be appropriate to mention the name of a university, club or other group.

Hajimemashite. Wajima **no**   *How do you do? My name is*

Maeda **desu**.

Maeda, from Wajima (company).

Hajimemashite. Jinji-bu **no** Watanabe Keiko **desu**.

How do you do? I'm Keiko Watanabe, of the personnel department.

This **no** can be thought of as similar to *belonging to* or *of*. It is very commonly used to indicate possession or belonging.

Buchō **no** tsukue wa doko desu ka.

Where's the general manager's desk?

Wajima **no** honsha wa Tōkyō desu.

Wajima's head office is in Tokyo.

Hotta san **no** shumi wa nan desu ka.

What are your interests (hobbies), Hotta san?

Igirisu **no** kaisha desu.

It's a British company.

4 *O-tōsan* (Your father)

There are many different words in Japanese for family members and relatives depending on whether they are 'inside' your group, i.e. part of your own family, or 'outside' your group, part of another person's family. **O-tōsan**, with the prefix **o-** to indicate respect to another person, is used when talking about someone else's father or when talking to one's own father. Using the more familiar word **chichi** indicates to other people that you are talking about your own father. Here is a summary of situations and usage.

Talking about someone else's father	**o-tōsan**
Talking about someone else's mother	**o-kāsan**
Talking to one's own father	**o-tōsan**
Talking to one's own mother	**o-kāsan**
Talking about one's own father	**chichi**
Talking about one's own mother	**haha**

The following dialogue shows examples of usage when talking to someone outside the family:

A **O-tōsan** wa sarariiman desu ka.

Does your father work in an office? (Lit. Is your father a 'salary man'?)

B Iie, **chichi** wa gakkō no sensei desu.

No, he's a school teacher.

A	**O-kāsan** wa?	*How about your mother?*
B	**Haha** mo gakkō no sensei desu.	*She's a school teacher too.*

The next short dialogue shows examples of usage within the family.

A	**O-kāsan**, denwa!	*Mum, telephone!*
B	Dare?	*Who is it?*
A	**O-tōsan**.	*Dad.*

5 *O-tōsan wa o-genki desu ka* (How is your father?)

O-genki desu ka is a common greeting, being similar in usage to *How are you?* although the literal meaning is closer to *Are you well?* Note that the polite prefix **o-** is not used in Hotta's reply, because he is referring to someone within his own circle.

6 *Ima doko desu ka* (Where are you calling from?)

You will have noticed by now that it is not necessary in Japanese to specify every word in a sentence if the meaning is implicit from the context. In this sentence, it is so obvious that it is Hotta's location that is being enquired after that this does not need to be stated overtly. Although personal pronouns exist in Japanese, they are rarely used except for clarification or emphasis.

A	Sumimasen ga, Takahashi san desu ka.	*Excuse me, are you Takahashi san?*
B	**Watashi** desu ka. Iie, chigaimasu. Watanabe desu.	*Who, me? No, I'm not. My name's Watanabe.*

Generally, a person's name will be used instead of *you, he or she*, even when talking to that person directly.

Sumisu san wa enjinia desu ka.	*Are you an engineer (Mr Smith)?*

The personal pronouns are given below for your reference, but it should be remembered that they cannot all be used in the same way as English pronouns. The word **anata**, for example, is limited almost entirely to wives addressing their husbands. If in any doubt, avoid using them and use names instead, as the inappropriate use of pronouns can sound very impolite.

watashi	*I, me*
anata	*you*
kare, ano hito	*he, that person*
kanojo, ano hito	*she, that person*
watashitachi	*we, us*
anatatachi, minna	*you* (plural), *all of you*
karera, sono hitotachi	*they, those people*

7 *Sore* (That)

The English language has only two demonstrative pronouns, *this* to indicate things which are near you and *that* to indicate things which aren't. However, Japanese has three: **kore** (*this one here, near me*), **sore** (*that one just there, near you*) and **are** (*that one, over there*).

Kore o kudasai.	*I'll take this one please.*
Sore wa Furansu no sukāfu desu ka.	*Is that a French scarf?*
Are wa Fuji-san desu ne.	*That's Mt Fuji over there, right?*

The corresponding question word is **dore**?, or *which one?*

A	Watanabe san no tsukue wa **dore** desu ka.	*Which is your desk, Watanabe san?*
B	Kore desu.	*This one.*

There are several other words which fall into groups beginning with **ko-, so-, a-** and **do-** like those above. Demonstrative adjectives (*this, that*, etc.) are as follows:

kono (shigoto)	*this (work)*
sono (shisha)	*that (branch office)*
ano (kōjō)	*that (factory) over there*
dono (kaisha)?	*which (company)?*

A	**Ano** hito wa dare desu ka.	*Who is that (person) over there?*
B	**Ano** hito wa shachō desu.	*That's the president.*

8 *Ne* (Isn't it?, Aren't they?)

Ne is often used at the end of a sentence to invite agreement from the listener or to ask for confirmation of something about which the speaker is almost, but not completely, sure. It is therefore rather similar to the English *isn't it? aren't they?* or *didn't you?*

A   Hotta san no namae wa
       Yūichirō desu **ne**.

Your first name is Yūichirō, right, (Hotta san)?

B   Hai, sō desu.

Yes, that's right.

9 *Chigaimasu* (No, that's not right)

Chigaimasu is a verb which actually means *to be different from (what you said)*, but it is often used instead of a negative when you need to point out that what someone said is incorrect in its information.

A   Wajima wa depāto desu ka.
B   Iie, **chigaimasu**. Shōsha
       desu.

Is Wajima a department store?
No, it isn't. It's a trading company.

────── Expansion activities ──────

1   Read the following words and see if you can work out which is the odd man out in each group of four. If you are working with someone else, make up some more examples and try them out on him or her.

(*a*)	shachō	kaisha	shisha	honsha
(*b*)	sensei	enjinia	konsarutanto	konpyūtā
(*c*)	hachi	ano	go	ichi
(*d*)	otōsan	haha	chichi	mā-mā
(*e*)	kankō	shachō	buchō	kachō
(*f*)	Furansu	Igirisu	Tōkyō	Nihon

2   Look at the following **meishi**, or name cards. How would these people introduce themselves to a stranger?

Example: Hajimemashite.
                                  Teraoka no Terada Tetsuo* desu.

(*a*) AUTO DOOR
Managing Director
Ralph James
Auto Door Corp

(*c*) KICTEC
Purchasing Department
Assistant Manager
Susan Ellis
株式会社 キクテック

(*b*) MEITO
株式会社 メイトー
Masato Iwata
Meito Corporation

(*d*) ENE
Training Adviser
Richard Moor

Look at the name cards again, and ask and answer questions about the locations of the head offices and branch offices using the cues below.

Example: (Teraoka, honsha)

A **Teraoka** no **honsha** wa doko desu ka.
B Tōkyō desu.

(*e*)   Autodoor, shisha   (*g*)   Kictec, honsha
(*f*)   Meito, honsha   (*h*)   ENA, shisha

* Note that when Japanese people speak or write in English, they put their
family name last. However, when they speak or write in Japanese, the
family name comes first.

3   Below is part of Wajima Trading's organisation chart, taken from its company handbook. If Hotta is hired by Wajima, he will have to learn who everyone is, so he has just asked a friend back in Sendai to test him on who's who. Following the example, ask and answer questions using the cues below and the chart.

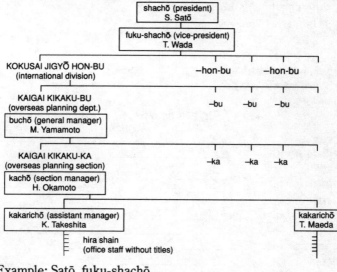

Example: Satō, fuku-shachō

Friend   **Satō** san wa **fuku-shachō** desu ka.
Hotta   Iie (chigaimasu), shachō desu.

(*a*)   Okamoto, kachō   (*d*)   Wada, shachō
(*b*)   Yamamoto, kachō   (*e*)   Takeshita, kakarichō
(*c*)   Maeda, kakarichō

4 Select the correct ending from the right-hand column to complete each sentence begun on the left.

(a) Chichi no shumi wa

(b) Hotta san no o-tōsan wa

(c) Ano hito wa

(d) Shachō no heya wa

(e) Kore wa

(f) Sono kaisha wa

(i) kokusai-bu no buchō desu ka.

(ii) Watanabe san no kaban desu.

(iii) Nihon no kaisha desu ne.

(iv) gorufu desu.

(v) doko desu ka.

(vii) o-genki desu ka.

5 Before Hotta returns to Sendai, he has to buy some souvenirs for his family. He is now in a department store, looking for a scarf for his mother. Re-arrange the sentences from his conversation with the shop assistant into the correct order. (Two of the lines have already been put in for you.)

(a) Hai!

(b) Sono Igirisu no sukāfu desu.

(c) ¥8,000? Ja, ano Furansu no sukāfu wa?

(d) Hai, arigatō gozaimasu.

(e) Sumimasen.

(f) Sono sukāfu wa ikura desu ka.

(g) Ā, kore desu ka. Kore wa ¥8,000 desu.

(h) Are wa ¥5,500 desu.

(i) Dore desu ka.

(j) Ā, sō desu ka. Ja, Furansu no sukāfu o kudasai.

Hotta	
Depāto no hito	
Hotta	
Depāto no hito	Dore desu ka.
Hotta	
Depāto no hito	Aa, kore desu ka. Kore wa ¥8,000 desu.
Hotta	
Depāto no hito	
Hotta	
Depāto no hito	

6 Now it's your turn. You are in Japan on a business trip, and the company you are visiting has asked if they can do a profile of you for their in-house newsletter. Takahashi san, who edits the newsletter, is now sitting with pencil poised about to ask you the first question.

Takahashi	Sumimasen ga, o-namae wa?
You	(a) *It's* (*your name*) _____
Takahashi	Kaisha no o-namae wa?
You	(b) *It's...* _____
Takahashi	Amerika no kaisha desu ka.
You	(c) *Yes, it is. /No, it isn't.* (as appropriate) _____
Takahashi	Honsha wa doko desu ka.
You	(d) *It's in...* _____
Takahashi	Sō desu ka. Ja, Nihon wa o-suki desu ka.
You	(e) *Yes, I do.* _____
Takahashi	Sō desu ka. Anō, shumi wa nan desu ka.
You	(f) *My interests are...* _____
	_____
Takahashi	Dōmo arigatō gozaimashita.
You	(g) *You're welcome.* _____

📖 ——— Reading corner ———

Hotta has now been back in Sendai for some time, finishing off his studies at university and anxiously awaiting news of the job at Wajima. One day when he is at home, the phone rings, and his mother answers it.

おかあさん　もしもし、ほった です が…はい…はい…
　　　　　　ゆういちろう、でんわ！
ほった　　　だれ？
おかあさん　わじま の じんじぶ の いしい さん。
ほった　　　ええ！わじま の いしい さん?!

💼 ——— Business briefing ———

Meishi o dōzo (Here's my card)

One thing that you can be sure of when you go to Japan is that you will soon end up with a wallet full of **meishi**, or name cards. Almost all adults have one and no first meeting, especially in business, would be complete without the ritual of exchanging cards at the very beginning of the meeting.

A **meishi** is more than just an indication of who a person is or what company he or she represents. Relative rank between Japanese people is very important in defining levels of behaviour and language, so cards are presented at the very beginning of introductions in order that the parties will know how to address one another.

When a Japanese business colleague receives and looks at your card, he or she will be scanning it to ascertain your rank and to make educated guesses about the size of your company. For this reason, it is extremely important to make sure that your position in the company has been translated as accurately as possible on the Japanese side of your name card.

When you receive a card, remember to study it with the same respect accorded to yours, even if you are not sure what the information given there implies. Keep the card on the table in front of you if you are at a meeting or, if this is not possible, take the time to look closely at the information on the card before carefully putting it away in a card case or wallet. On no account pop it straight into a pocket without looking at it, as this would imply that you consider the person to be of no importance.

If you deal with the Japanese a lot, you might also consider buying a special **meishi** card file, as it is a most useful source of reference in the future to have all **meishi** on file, especially if you make a note at the same time to remind you of who the people were, when you met them and under what circumstances.

Be sure to have a good supply of **meishi** on you at all times, whether you are dealing with Japanese people in Japan or in your own country. It would be considered most unbusinesslike not to have one to give in return when a **meishi** is offered to you. Most Japanese people in business now have one side of their card printed in English, and it is only courteous, as well as good business sense, for you to have one side of yours printed in Japanese. **Meishi** are usually exchanged with the print facing towards the person receiving the card, so that it is ready for him or her to read it. They are generally handed over with a slight bow. You may feel uncomfortable bowing, but a slight inclination of the head will show that, although you may not know how to bow properly, you are at least willing to try to conform to local custom. The correct exchange of **meishi** can be an important indication of your attitudes towards Japan and doing business with the Japanese, so it is as well to get it right.

ASHITA NO YOTEI WA?

In this lesson, there is an introduction to Japanese verbs, so the range of things you can say will expand greatly. As this is an important area needing detailed explanation, the **Notes** section is rather longer than usual. In addition, there are seven **Expansion Activities** to give you practice with the new material, rather than six as previously. In this lesson you will also learn how to:

- talk about future plans
- ask where people are
- note some differences between formal and informal speech
- use two new particles: **ni** and **ga**

The story so far

Hotta san and all his family heaved a sigh of relief when they heard the news that he had been hired by Wajima Trading.

Today is his first day of work. He and the other new employees were formally introduced to the people in the Overseas Planning Department as a group, but now Noguchi san, who also works in the department, is taking him around to meet everyone individually. First he introduces Hotta to the **kachō** (*section manager*), Okamoto san.

Dialogue

Starting with this lesson, several new **kanji** (Chinese characters) will be introduced in each opening dialogue. As you will not know how to read these at first, you will need to look at the small **hiragana** characters, called **furigana**, above each **kanji**. However, when the same **kanji** reappears in different situations, you should try to get into the habit of recognising it without relying on the **furigana**.

のぐち　　　(*to Okamoto*) 課長、ほった　さんです。きょう　から

うち　の部　に　はいります。

ほった　　　ほった　です。どうぞ　よろしく　おねがい　します。

おかもと　あぁ！ほった　くん！がんばって　ください　ね。

ほった　　　はい、がんばります。しつれい　します。

(*Noguchi takes Hotta over to Yamamoto san's desk, but the buchō is not there.*)

のぐち　　　(*to Ikeda*) 部長　は　どこ　ですか。

いけだ　　　きょう　は　いません。なごや　ししゃ　に　います。

あした　かえります。

のぐち　　　あぁ　そう、ありがとう。

ほった　　　(*aside to Noguchi*) あの　ひと　は　だれ　です　か。

のぐち　　　あれ　は　いけだ　さん。

ほった　　　あぁ　そう　です　か。かわいい　です　ね！

のぐち　　　(*introducing Hotta to Ikeda*) いけださん，ほった　さん

です。

ほった　　　ほった　です。どうぞ　よろしく。

いけだ　　　よろしく。あぁ、のぐち　さん、なごや　ししゃ　から

メッセージ　が　あります。いしはら　さん　は、

らいしゅう　の　かいぎ　に　きません。

のぐち　　　えっ？どう　して？つごう　が　わるい？

いけだ　　　わかりません。なごや　ししゃ　に　電話　を　します

か。

のぐち　　　おねがい　します。

Noguchi	(*to Okamoto*) Kachō, Hotta san desu. Kyō kara uchi no bu ni hairimasu.
Hotta	Hotta desu. Dōzo yoroshiku onegai shimasu.
Okamoto	Ā! Hotta kun! Ganbatte kudasai ne.
Hotta	Hai, ganbarimasu. Shitsurei shimasu.

(*Noguchi takes Hotta over to Yamamoto san's desk, but the buchō is not there.*)

Noguchi	(*to Ikeda*) Buchō wa doko desu ka?
Ikeda	Kyō wa imasen. Nagoya shisha ni imasu. Ashita kaerimasu.
Noguchi	Ā sō, arigatō.
Hotta	(*aside to Noguchi*) Ano hito wa dare desu ka.
Noguchi	Are wa Ikeda san.
Hotta	Ā sō desu ka. Kawaii desu ne!
Noguchi	(*introducing Hotta to Ikeda*) Ikeda san, Hotta san desu.
Hotta	Hotta desu. Dōzo yoroshiku.
Ikeda	Yoroshiku. Ā, Noguchi san, Nagoya shisha kara messēji ga arimasu. Ishihara san wa, raishū no kaigi ni kimasen.
Noguchi	Ē? Dō shite? Tsugō ga warui?
Ikeda	Wakarimasen. Nagoya shisha ni denwa o shimasu ka.
Noguchi	Onegai shimasu.

---

kyō *today*
kara *from*
uchi no *our*
ni *to* [indicates location, or place towards which something moves]
hairimasu *join* [from **hairu**, to join, enter]
dōzo yoroshiku onegai shimasu *pleased to meet you*
kun *Mr* [informal]
ganbatte kudasai *do your best, try hard* [from **ganbaru**, to do one's best, try hard]
ganbarimasu *I'll do my best* [from **ganbaru**]
shitsurei shimasu *excuse me, sorry to disturb you*
imasen *isn't in* [from **iru**, to be, to exist]
ashita *tomorrow*
kaerimasu *return* [from **kaeru**, to return, come back]
kawaii *cute, pretty*
messēji *message*
ga [indicates subject of verb]
arimasu *have* [from **aru**, to have, possess, exist]
raishū *next week*
kaigi *meeting*
kimasen *won't come* [from **kuru**, to come]
dō shite *why (not)?*
tsugō ga warui *is inconvenient*
tsugō *convenience, circumstances*
warui *bad, wrong*
wakarimasen *don't know* [from **wakaru**, to know, understand]
denwa o shimasu *make a telephone call* [from **denwa o suru**]

———————— **Comprehension** ————————

1 Where is Yamamoto san, the
  buchō?
  (*a*) In Nagoya.
  (*b*) On his way home.
  (*c*) In Tokyo.

2 Who will telephone the
  Nagoya office?
  (*a*) Noguchi san.
  (*b*) Ikeda san.
  (*c*) The buchō.

———————————— **Notes** ————————————

1 *Kachō* (Manager)

It is very common, in Japanese, to address professional people by
their title rather than by name, even when talking to them directly. In
cases where there are several people of the same rank, the name
may be used as well as the title.

Kachō, o-denwa desu.

*Kachō (section manager),
telephone!*

Kore wa **Yamamoto buchō** no
  tsukue desu ne.

*This is Yamamoto buchō's
(general manager's) desk, right?*

2 *Ni* (To, into, in)

Like all particles, **ni** comes directly after the word or phrase to which
it relates. It can have several different meanings and grammatical
uses, three examples of which appear in the opening dialogue of this
lesson. In the first case, **ni** indicates a place towards which something
or someone moves.

Kyō kara uchi no bu **ni**
  hairimasu.
Shachō wa asatte Rondon **ni**
  ikimasu.

*He's joining (entering into) our
department as of today.*
*The president is going to London
the day after tomorrow.*

In the second case, **ni** indicates the location where something or
someone exists.

Nagoya shisha **ni** imasu.
Repōto wa doko **ni** arimasu ka.

He's at the Nagoya branch office.
Where's the report?

In the third situation, **ni** points out the indirect object of the sentence.

Nagoya shisha **ni** denwa o
   shimasu ka.

Shall I call the Nagoya branch?

Katō sensei wa Igirisu-jin **ni**
   Nihongo o oshiemasu.

*Katō sensei teaches Japanese to
   British people.*

3 *Hairimasu* (To enter)

You will be pleased to hear that the formation of verbs in Japanese is
rather easy. For one thing, there are only two irregular verbs, **suru**
(*to do*) and **kuru** (*to come*), both of which we meet in this lesson, and
the rest are highly regular in formation. For another, Japanese verbs
do not change to indicate number of people, so the first verb in this
dialogue, **hairimasu**, can mean *I enter, you enter, she/he enters, we
enter*, etc. However, when verbs appear in vocabulary lists in this
book, the English definition is given as the infinitive (e.g. *to enter*).

Verbs are often used without any pronouns, and although this sounds
as if it could lead to ambiguity, in fact the meaning is generally obvious from context. The verb always comes at the end of the sentence,
and in some cases a verb can form a sentence by itself.

A   **Kaerimasu?**   *Are you going home now?*
                           [informal]
B   Hai, kaerimasu.   *Yes, I am.*

Each verb has two sets of forms, usually referred to as the *plain form*
and the *polite form*. The plain form of the present tense is also known
as the 'dictionary form' when in the positive, as it is the one used to
list verbs in dictionaries, and it is the one from which the basic stem
of the verb is most easily isolated to make other forms. The polite
form (sometimes called the '**-masu** form', as all verbs end in **-masu**)
is used in much everyday conversation, as the plain form can often
sound too abrupt, except perhaps between close friends or family
members. The polite form is used when talking to colleagues and
acquaintances, as well as more obvious cases demanding special
courtesy such as talking to the boss, to one's elders or to strangers.

There will be more information on the appropriate uses of these two
forms throughout the book, but until you get a deeper understanding
of the Japanese language and the implications of its verb forms, it is
best to use the polite form, as inappropriate use of the plain form can
sound impertinent.

Almost all Japanese verbs can be divided into two groups, which differ only in the way they form the verb stems. In one group are most of the verbs which end in **-eru** or **-iru** in the dictionary form. The verbs in this group form the basic stem by dropping the final **-ru**.

Dictionary form	Basic stem	Present polite form	Meaning
hajimeru	hajime-	hajimemasu	*to start, to begin*
iru	i-	imasu	*to be, to exist*
miru	mi-	mimasu	*to see, to look at*
oshieru	oshie-	oshiemasu	*to tell, to teach*
taberu	tabe-	tabemasu	*to eat*

The other, larger group consists of all verbs which do not end in **-eru** or **-iru** in the dictionary form. (It also includes a few verbs which do have these endings, two from our dialogue appearing in the list below: **hairu** and **kaeru**.) The basic stem is formed by dropping the final **-u**.

Dictionary form	Basic stem	Present polite form	Meaning
aru	ar-	arimasu	*to have, to exist*
ganbaru	ganbar-	ganbarimasu	*to try hard, to persist*
hairu	hair-	hairimasu	*to join, to enter*
hanasu	hanas-	hanashimasu*	*to speak, to talk*
iku	ik-	ikimasu	*to go*
kaeru	kaer-	kaerimasu	*to return, to go home*
kaku	kak-	kakimasu	*to write*
kiku	kik-	kikimasu	*to ask, to hear*
nomu	nom-	nomimasu	*to drink*
okuru	okur-	okurimasu	*to send, dispatch*
wakaru	wakar-	wakarimasu	*to know, to understand*
yomu	yom-	yomimasu	*to read*

* Note the phonetic change from **-s-** to **-sh-** in the stem; the sound **si** does not exist in Japanese, so it becomes **shi**.

The two irregular verbs are only irregular in the way they form the basic stems.

kuru	ki-	kimasu	*to come*
suru	shi-	shimasu	*to do*

Although this may seem a lot to take in at the moment, Japanese verbs are so regular in the way they make their various forms that you will be surprised at how quickly you understand them.

4 *Dōzo yoroshiku onegai shimasu* (Pleased to meet you)

This is a set phrase which literally means something like *Please treat me well*. It is often said when introducing yourself, to correspond roughly to *Glad to meet you*, but in other circumstances it can also mean *Best wishes* or *Regards*. A slightly less formal version is **dōzo yoroshiku**, or simply **yoroshiku**.

5 *Kun* (informal form of Mr)

Kun is an informal, friendly form of address used to small boys, or to young men by male colleagues who are older and in more senior positions. (Women do not usually address people using **kun**, except perhaps when talking to small boys.) Therefore the **kachō**, or manager, can use **kun** with Hotta and Noguchi, but they refer to everyone by title or by using **san** because of their relatively low status.

6 *Ganbatte kudasai ne!* (Work hard!)

This is a set phrase, often said to wish people luck or to exhort them to grit their teeth and do their best. Thus it might be said to people as they go to sit an exam, take part in a sports event or start a new job. The equivalent in English might be *Good luck, go for it, keep going*, etc., depending on the situation.

A   Ne, Watanabe san, ashita no yotei wa? — *Hey, Watanabe san, what are your plans for tomorrow?*

B   Ashita wa Tōkyō marason desu! — *Tomorrow's the Tokyo marathon!*

A   Ā sō, sō! Ja, **ganbatte kudasai!** — *Oh, right! Well, good luck!*

7 *Shitsurei shimasu* (Excuse me)

This is a set phrase which is extremely useful, so practise it carefully. (To pronounce it correctly, remember that it is written with the four **hiragana** characters for **shi-tsu-re-i.**) It can mean *Excuse me, I'm sorry for interrupting* or *I beg your pardon*, and so is used in a wide variety of situations. It is also commonly used as a polite way of saying goodbye.

8   Kyō wa imasen (He's not here today)

The negative of the polite form of verbs in the present tense is very simple and regular. Simply replace the final -**masu** with -**masen**. For example: **kimasu/kimasen, arimasu/arimasen, nomimasu/nomimasen.**

A	Ashita no asa, kaisha ni **kimasu** ka.	*Are you coming to the office tomorrow morning?*
B	Iie, **kimasen**. Ashita wa kenkyū sentā ni ikimasu.	*No, I'm not (coming). I'm going to the research centre tomorrow.*

9   Imasu (To be, to exist)

The verb **iru** (**imasu**) is only used to show the existence of living things, such as people, birds, fish or animals. For inanimate objects, the verb **aru** (**arimasu**) is used. Compare the following pairs of sentences.

Kachō wa kaigi-shitsu ni **imasu**.	*The section manager's in the meeting room.*
Kachō no kaban wa kaigi-shitsu ni **arimasu**.	*The section manager's briefcase is in the meeting room.*
Kenichi kun no inu wa doko ni **imasu** ka.	*Where's Kenichi's dog?*
Kenichi kun no gakkō wa doko ni **arimasu** ka.	*Where's Kenichi's school?*

10   Ashita kaerimasu (He'll be returning tomorrow)

The Japanese verb has only two real tenses: present and past. What is termed the 'present' actually covers definite happenings in the future too. Here again, the meaning is generally clear from context or from the use of time words such as **ashita** (*tomorrow*), **asatte** (*the day after tomorrow*), **raishū** (*next week*), **konban** (*this evening*), etc.

A Itsu Eigo no benkyō o   *When will you begin your English*
   hajimemasu ka.   *(language) study?*
B Raishū hajimemasu.   *I'll be starting next week.*

11 Ā sō, arigatō (Oh really, thanks)

In informal situations between close friends or colleagues, speech patterns can be noticeably different from those used in formal situations. In this dialogue, Noguchi speaks very casually both to Hotta and to Ikeda. Hotta speaks more formally, as he is still new at Wajima Trading and thus on his best behaviour. Ikeda uses polite forms of speech as this is more natural for a woman, and because Noguchi is her superior in the company. Compare below what Noguchi says and what Hotta or Ikeda would have said in the same circumstances.

Noguchi	Hotta/Ikeda
Ā sō, arigatō.	Ā sō desu ka. Arigatō gozaimasu.
Are wa Ikeda san.	Are wa Ikeda san desu.
Dō shite?	Dō shite desu ka.

12 Messēji ga arimasu (There's a message)

As it seems possible to use both the particles **wa** and **ga** to indicate the subject of a verb, the difference between them is sometimes puzzling for the foreigner learning Japanese. However, there are some general guidelines which should help you to understand their usage. (It is as well to note that incorrect usage will not seriously hamper communication; it is somewhat similar to problems non-English speakers have with the use of *a* and *the*.)

The particle **ga** emphasises the subject of a verb and in such cases always follows the grammatical subject of that verb.

A Dare **ga** konpyūtā no   *Who's joining the computer class?*
   kurasu ni hairimasu ka.
B Ikeda san **ga** hairimasu.   *Ikeda san is.*

When **wa** is used, the emphasis is on something other than the subject.

| Ikeda san **wa** dono kurasu ni hairimasu ka? | *Which class is Ikeda san going to take?* |

In this case, it is the kind of class that the speaker is interested in hearing about and not who is taking the class. The topic indicated by **wa** may or may not be the grammatical subject of the verb and can usually be roughly translated as *as for*.

| Watashi **wa** ashita kaigi ga arimasu. | *Tomorrow I have a meeting* (Lit. *As for me, there is a meeting tomorrow*). |
| Buchō no fakkusu **wa**, watashi ga okurimasu. | *I'll send the buchō's fax* (Lit. *As for the buchō's fax, I'll send it*). |

Question words like **nani** (*what?*), **dare** (*who?*) and **doko** (*where?*) are always followed by **ga**, never **wa**, when they are the subject of the verb, and the subject of the answers take **ga** too.

| A | Kyō, dare **ga** kimasu ka. | *Who's coming today?* |
| B | Watanabe san **ga** kimasu. | *Watanabe san is.* |

| A | Shinbun wa nani **ga** arimasu ka. | *What newspapers do you have?* (Lit. *As for newspapers, what is there?*) |
| B | Mainichi to Nikkei **ga** arimasu. | *We have the Mainichi and the Nikkei.* |

13 *Denwa o shimasu* (To make a telephone call)

There are many verbs in Japanese which are formed from a noun plus **shimasu** (from **suru**) or **o shimasu**. Some other examples are:

shigoto (o) shimasu	*to (do) work*
benkyō (o) shimasu	*to study*
gorufu (o) shimasu	*to play golf*
renshū (o) shimasu	*to practise*
kenkyū (o) shimasu	*to (do) research*

The difference between a noun plus **shimasu** and a noun plus **o shimasu** is something like that between '*to telephone*' (**denwa shimasu**) and '*to make a telephone call*' (**denwa o shimasu**).

✔ ———— Expansion activities ————

Try to familiarise yourself with the dictionary form and the **-masu** form of all the new verbs given in **Note 3** before you begin these activities.

1 Look at the list of Japanese verbs below, and write in the English equivalent in the spaces next to them. (One has already been done for you.) After you have done so, you should find another Japanese verb in the box outlined vertically.

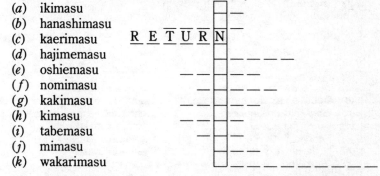

(a) ikimasu

(b) hanashimasu

(c) kaerimasu   R E T U R N

(d) hajimemasu

(e) oshiemasu

(f) nomimasu

(g) kakimasu

(h) kimasu

(i) tabemasu

(j) mimasu

(k) wakarimasu

2 Pictured below are some things that Hotta san will do during his first week in Tokyo, and a few things he won't be doing (indicated by a cross through the picture). Using the pictures and cues, choose suitable verbs and make up some sentences about his activities, using the positive or negative of the verb as appropriate. Example:

repōto o   Repōto o yomimasu.

(a) repōto o   (b) repōto o   (c) shachō ni

(d) wāpuro no renshū o   (e) denwa o   (f) Nagoya shisha ni

 (i)

(*g*) Sendai ni   (*h*) terebi o   (*i*) kōhii o

3 Complete the following sentences with **arimasu** or **imasu**, whichever is appropriate:

(a)	Buchō wa kyō Nagoya ni	arimasu/imasu.
(b)	Ikeda san no tsukue wa doko ni	arimasu/imasu ka.
(c)	Kaigi-shitsu ni dare ga	arimasu/imasu ka.
(d)	Buchō ni messeji ga	arimasu/imasu.
(e)	Konban, yotei wa	arimasu/imasu ka.
(f)	Hotta san no o-tōsan wa Sendai ni	arimasu/imasu.
(g)	Jinji-bu no Watanabe san wa doko ni	arimasu/imasu ka.
(h)	Sumimasen ga, denwa ga	arimasu/imasu ka.

4 At the morning meeting, Maeda san checks up on everyone's movements for the next couple of days. In the dialogue below, put in the appropriate polite form of the verb shown in brackets. The signs + and – indicate whether the verb should be positive or negative.

Maeda   Noguchi kun, ashita no yotei wa?
Noguchi Ashita Nagoya shisha ni (iku +). Asatte (kaeru +).
Maeda   Sō desu ka. Hotta kun wa?
Hotta   Ashita kenkyū sentā ni (iku +).
Maeda   Asa kara desu ka.
Hotta   (Wakaru -). Kore kara jinji-bu ni (kiku +).
Maeda   Ja, Ikeda san to Koyama san no yotei wa?
Koyama   Watashitachi wa ashita kara wāpuro no kurasu ni (hairu +).
Maeda   Ja, ii desu ne. Minna, yoroshiku.

5 Below is part of the schedule board on the wall of Wajima's Overseas Planning Department, showing everyone's schedule for the next day. Make sentences about what people are doing tomorrow.

Examples:
Yamamoto san wa ashita Nagoya kara kaerimasu.
Okamoto san wa ashita kaisha ni imasu.

Ashita no yotei	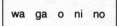
Yamamoto	Nagoya ♦ Tokyo
Okamoto	
Takeshita	Osaka ♦ Tokyo
Maeda	
Tani	
Noguchi	Tokyo ♦ Nagoya shisha
Hotta	kenkyu senta
Koyama	wapuro no kurasu
Ikeda	wapuro no kurasu

6 Particles are very important for showing what job a word or phrase does in a sentence. To practise their usage, put the appropriate particle in the spaces below to make complete sentences.

> wa   ga   o   ni   no

(*a*) Ikeda san ＿＿ itsu wāpuro ＿＿ renshū ＿＿ hajimemasu ka.

(*b*) Kaigai kikaku-bu ＿＿ buchō ＿＿ Yamamoto san desu.

(*c*) Ashita ＿＿ asa, Noguchi san ＿＿ Nagoya kara Tōkyō ＿＿ kaerimasu.

(*d*) Katō sensei ＿＿ Ikeda san ＿＿ wāpuro ＿＿ oshiemasu.

(*e*) Kono resutoran ＿＿ nani ＿＿ oishii desu ka.

(*f*) Hotta san ＿＿ raishū kara Eigo ＿＿ benkyō ＿＿ shimasu.

(*g*) Asatte ＿＿ kaigi ＿＿ dare ＿＿ kimasu ka.

(*h*) Sumimasen, chiizu sando ＿＿ kudasai.

7 Now it's your turn. You have just arrived in Japan on a business trip, and there are several important meetings planned while you are there. At one of next week's meetings, you hope to be able to meet up again with Miura san and Takagi san, two old friends from the Osaka branch office. You call Miura now to say hello and to see if he's coming to the meeting.

Miura Moshi moshi.

You (*a*) *Is that Miura san?* ＿＿＿＿＿＿＿＿＿＿＿

Miura Hai, Miura desu.

You (*b*) *This is (your name).* ＿＿＿＿＿＿＿＿＿＿＿

Miura Ā, (*your name*) san, o-genki desu ka.

You (*c*) *Yes, I'm fine. Uh* (ēto), *are you coming to next week's meeting?* ＿＿＿＿＿＿＿＿＿＿＿

Miura	Hai, ikimasu, ikimasu.
You	(d) *How about Takagi san?* _____
Miura	Takagi san wa ikimasen.
You	(e) *Why not? Is he busy?* _____
Miura	Sō desu ne. Takagi san wa raishū Amerika ni ikimasu.
You	(f) *Is it business?* _____
Miura	Iie, hanemūn (*honeymoon*) desu!

Note: As your knowledge of structure and vocabulary expands, so you will be able to find several different ways of saying the same thing, and may come up with responses for this activity other than those given in the answer key. Please note that the responses given there are only samples, reflecting sentences practised in the lesson, and that other equally valid ones may exist.

Reading corner

Tomorrow there will be a welcome party for Hotta at a local bar and Ikeda san is in charge of the arrangements. She calls Keiko Watanabe in the personnel department to invite her too, but Watanabe san is away from her desk, so Ikeda san leaves a message. Below is a copy of the message, and Watanabe san's reply. See if you can read them.

4月4日
わたなべさん
　いけださんから 電話。
　あしたは ほったさんの パーティです。
　かいがいきかく部の みんな いきます。
　わたなべさんも いきますか。
　いけださんに 電話 おねがいします。
　　　　　　　　　　みちこ

4月4日
いけださん
　電話 ありがとう。
　わたしも いきます。
　こんばん 電話 しますね。
　　　　　　　　　　けいこ

* pāatii

Business briefing

The senpai-kōhai *relationship*

Japanese children grow up in a society broadly divided into **senpai** (*seniors*), **dōkyūsei** (*contemporaries*) and **kōhai** (*juniors*). The existence of **senpai-kōhai** relationships is strongly developed by the time a person enters university. Here the strict formality of club and society life, particularly where martial arts are concerned, emphasises the vertical nature of the system. **Kōhai** are often required to stand up and greet a **senpai** who enters the room and may be required to run errands for the **senpai**.

Although the term **senpai** generally refers to older graduates of one's school or university, it carries over naturally to the company situation, where the new employee regards everyone else as his **senpai** by virtue of the fact that they joined the company before him. When a person enters a company, it is usual for him to be assigned a **senpai** who will show him the basics of the job and help him to find his way around. While the **kachō**, or section manager, is responsible for overall workload and job allocation, he will expect the **senpai** to monitor the day-to-day progress of the newcomer and inform him of any difficulties.

A **senpai** may be more than just a year or two older; a department head can also be thought of as a **senpai** if he is a graduate of the same university. This means that it is not uncommon for cliques made up of **senpai** and **kōhai** from the same university to form in the departments of large companies.

Senpai-kōhai relationships can last throughout life, with responsibilities felt on both sides. The **senpai** considers it his duty to take care of the **kōhai** and can be relied upon to help influence the **kōhai**'s progress in the company. The **kōhai** for his part feels a strong sense of loyalty and respect for the **senpai**. The influence of **senpai-kōhai** relationships can even extend outside the company into personal life: it is not unusual for a **senpai** to arrange introductions to potential marriage partners for the **kōhai**, as he considers it his responsibility to see that the **kōhai** makes a good match.

NAN-JI NI
TSUKIMASU KA

In Lesson 6 you will learn how to:

- say what the time is
- describe things, with adjectives ending in **-i**
- say by what means you do something, using the particle **de**

——————— The story so far ———————

This morning Okamoto kachō, the manager, is chairing a meeting of the Overseas Planning Department. The first topic on the agenda is the visit to Japan of Mr Richard Lloyd, marketing manager of the British company Dando Sports. Although Mr Lloyd has been in contact with Wajima for some time, this will be his first meeting with them in Japan. Also present at the meeting are the kakarichō, Maeda san, and Noguchi san.

——————— Dialogue ———————

In standard Japanese script there are no spaces between words, although until this lesson the words have been separated to help you with your reading practice. However, from here on we will follow standard practice and have no gaps between words.

課長	みなさん、おはよう。
みんな	おはようございます。
課長	ほったくんは?
まえだ	すぐ来ます。まちますか?
課長	もう10じだよ。
まえだ	では、はじめます。あしたイギリスのダンドー・スポーツからボイドさんが来ます。
のぐち	(*whispering*) まえださん、すみません。ボイドさんじゃありません。ロイドさんです。
まえだ	あぁ、はい、ロイドさんですね。すみません。ええと、たんとうしゃは、のぐちくんですね。のぐちくん、ロイドさんは何じにつきますか。
のぐち	あさの8じに、なりたくうこうにつきます。
	わたしが、むかえに行きます。
課長	はやいですね! 何で行きますか。リムジンバスで行きますか。
のぐち	まだ、わかりません。これから、電しゃとリムジンバスのじかんをしらべます。
課長	まえださんも行きますね。
まえだ	ちょっと...。
課長	むずかしい?いそがしい?
まえだ	いいえ、むずかしくありません。だいじょうぶです。
課長	じゃ、いいですね。
のぐち	まえださん、よろしくおねがいします。

Kachō	Mina san, ohayō.
Minna	Ohayō gozaimasu.

Kachō	Hotta kun wa?
Maeda	Sugu kimasu. Machimasu ka.
Kachō	Mō 10 (jū)-ji da yo.
Maeda	Dewa, hajimemasu. Ashita Igirisu no Dandō Supōtsu kara Boido san ga kimasu.
Noguchi	(*whispering*) Maeda san, sumimasen. Boido san ja arimasen. Roido san desu.
Maeda	Ā, hai, Roido san desu ne. Sumimasen. Ēto, tantō-sha wa, Noguchi kun desu ne. Noguchi kun, Roido san wa nan-ji ni tsukimasu ka.
Noguchi	Asa no 8 (hachi)-ji ni, Narita kūkō ni tsukimasu. Watashi ga, mukae ni ikimasu.
Kachō	Hayai desu ne! Nani de ikimasu ka. Rimujin basu de ikimasu ka.
Noguchi	Mada, wakarimasen. Kore kara, densha to rimujin basu no jikan o shirabemasu.
Kachō	Maeda san mo ikimasu ne.
Maeda	Chotto…
Kachō	Muzukashii? Isogashii?
Maeda	Iie, muzukashiku arimasen. Daijōbu desu.
Kachō	Ja, ii desu ne.
Noguchi	Maeda san, yoroshiku onegai shimasu.

mina san *everyone* [variation of **minna** when followed by **san**]
sugu *soon*
machimasu *wait* [from **matsu**, to wait]
mō *already*
-ji *o'clock*
da *is* [plain form of **desu**]
yo [sentence ending to show emphasis]
dewa *well then, in that case*
tantō-sha *person in charge*
ja arimasen *isn't* [negative of **desu**]
nan-ji *what time?*
tsukimasu *arrive* [from **tsuku**, to arrive]
Narita kūkō *Narita airport* (Tokyo's international airport)
mukae ni ikimasu *go to meet* [from **mukae ni iku**]

hayai *early*
nani de *how? by what means?*
rimujin basu *airport limousine bus*
kore kara *after this*
basu *bus*
de *by*
mada *(not) yet* [with negative verb]
densha *train*
jikan *time, hour*
shirabemasu *check up* [from **shiraberu**, to investigate, check up]
chotto… *it's rather…*
muzukashii *difficult*
isogashii *busy*
muzukashiku arimasen *not difficult*
daijōbu *all right, ok*
Yoroshiku onegai shimasu *Thank you for your offer of help*

Comprehension

Choose the correct answers to the questions below.

1 Does Okamoto kachō want to wait for Hotta before beginning the meeting?
   (*a*)   Yes, because it's only 10:00.
   (*b*)   No, because it's already 10:00.
   (*c*)   No, because Hotta can't come to the meeting.

2 Who will go to meet Mr Lloyd at the airport?
   (*a*)   Noguchi san.
   (*b*)   Noguchi san and Okamoto kachō.
   (*c*)   Noguchi san and Maeda san.

Notes

1   *Mō 10-ji da yo* (It's already 10:00)

Telling the time in Japanese is very straightforward. Once you know that the equivalent of *o'clock* is **-ji**, you can probably work out the hours for yourself.

1:00	ichi-ji	5:00	go-ji	9:00	ku-ji
2:00	ni-ji	6:00	roku-ji	10:00	jū-ji
3:00	san-ji	7:00	shichi-ji*	11:00	jū-ichi-ji
4:00	yo-ji*	8:00	hachi-ji	12:00	jū-ni-ji

* Note that **yo** is used instead of **yon** and **ku** instead of **kyū** when talking about the hour. The **shichi** alternative is used for 7.

Now for the minutes. The word for *minute* is **fun**. However, this changes to **pun** when preceded by certain sounds.

00:01	ip-pun	00:06	rop-pun
00:02	ni-fun	00:07	nana-fun
00:03	san-pun	00:08	hap-pun/hachi-fun
00:04	yon-pun	00:09	kyu-fun
00:05	go-fun	00:10	jip-pun/jup-pun

If these look daunting, remember that in most everyday speech we only ever talk of minutes in units of five and ten.

1:05	ichi-ji go-fun	1:10	ichi-ji jip-pun
1:15	ichi-ji jū-go-fun	1:20	ichi-ji ni-jip-pun
1:25	ichi-ji ni-jū-go-fun	1:30	ichi-ji san-jip-pun*
1:35	ichi-ji san-jū-go-fun	1:40	ichi-ji yon-jip-pun
1:45	ichi-ji yon-jū-go-fun	1:50	ichi-ji go-jip-pun
1:55	ichi-ji go-jū-go-fun		

* This is more commonly said **ichi-ji han**, or *'half past one.'*

A Kaigai kikaku-bu no kaigi wa nan-ji desu ka.

What time is the Overseas Planning Department meeting?

B **Ni-ji han** desu.

Two-thirty.

2 Yo [sentence ending to show emphasis]

Yo is added to the end of sentences in informal situations to show emphasis, especially if the speaker is giving some information the other person doesn't know. It can sometimes be thought of as similar to an exclamation mark in English.

Hotta kun, kaigi no jikan desu **yo**.

Hey, Hotta kun, it's time for the meeting!

Kachō, denwa desu **yo**.

Kachō, telephone!

Yo is commonly used when asserting something in contradiction to what has just been said.

A Roido san wa sērusu no manējā desu ka.

Is Mr Lloyd the sales manager?

B Chigaimasu **yo**! Māketingu no manējā desu **yo**.

No, he's not! He's the marketing manager.

3 Ja arimasen (Isn't, aren't)

This is the negative of **desu**. The full form is **dewa arimasen**, but **dewa** is commonly contracted to **ja** in spoken Japanese.

Tsugi no Shinkansen wa 6-ji 10-pun **ja arimasen** yo. 6-ji desu.

The next Shinkansen isn't at 6:10. It's at 6:00.

Ikeda san wa ima no shigoto wa suki **ja arimasen**.

Ikeda san doesn't enjoy her present job.

4 Asa no 8-ji ni (At 8:00 in the morning)

The particle **ni** is used when talking about a particular point in time when something happens, but not when simply saying what the time is.

A	Nan-ji **ni** kaerimasu ka.	*What time are you going home?*
B	6-ji goro **ni** kaerimasu.	*I'm going at about 6:00.*
A	Ima nan-ji desu ka.	*What time is it now?*
B	Mō 5-ji han desu.	*It's already 5:30.*

Ni is also used with days of the week and dates, which are covered in Lesson 9. There are some time expressions which do not take **ni**, including ones like **ashita** (*tomorrow*), **kyō** (*today*), **asatte** (*the day after tomorrow*) and **raishū** (*next week*).

5 Hayai (Early)

We have already come across several adjectives which, like **hayai**, end in **-i** (**ii**, *good*; **kawaii**, *pretty*; **warui**, *bad*). More examples are:

isogashii	*busy*		hiroi	*big (spacious)*
muzukashii	*difficult*		ōkii	*big (large)*
omoshiroi	*interesting*		takai	*expensive, high*
atarashii	*new*		tanoshii	*enjoyable, fun*
osoi	*late, slow*			

Nihongo wa **muzukashii** desu ka.	*Do you find Japanese difficult?* (Lit. *Is Japanese difficult?*)
Kokusai denwa wa totemo **takai** desu ne.	*International telephone calls are really expensive, aren't they!*
Densha wa **osoi** desu ne.	*The train's late, isn't it.*

In fact, these words act like verbs in many ways, with different tenses and moods. (There is also another group of adjectives, more closely related to nouns, which act in a different way – these are introduced in the next lesson.) As these adjectives are so closely related to verbs, they can be used without the verb **desu** and still make a complete sentence, although the tone becomes somewhat informal.

Kono hoteru no heya wa **hiroi** ne.	*The rooms in this hotel are big (spacious), aren't they.*
Roido san no kaisha wa **ōkii**.	*Mr Lloyd's company is big.*

These adjectives can also be used before a noun to modify it.

Ano **kawaii** hito wa Ikeda san desu ne.	*That pretty woman is Ikeda san, right?*
Kyō wa **ii** tenki desu ne.	*It's nice (weather) today, isn't it.*

6 Nani de ikimasu ka (How [Lit. by what] are you going?)

The particle **de** indicates that the word preceding it shows the means of or instrument for doing something. It can often be translated as '*by*' or '*with*'.

Shinkansen **de** ikimasu.	*I'm going by Shinkansen [Bullet train].*
Kikaku-bu no repōto o Eigo **de** kakimasu ka.	*Are you going to write the planning department report in English?*
Sono shorui o fakkusu **de** okurimasu.	*I'll send those documents by fax.*
'Product' wa Nihongo **de** nan desu ka.	*What's 'product' in Japanese?*

7 Chotto... (Well, it's rather...)

Chotto means *just a little, slightly, a bit,* but used by itself and followed by a pause, it is a device for avoiding an explicit statement. In the dialogue, for example, Maeda san obviously does not relish the thought of the long trip out to Narita airport to meet Mr Lloyd, although he decides not to say so in the end.

A Ima no shigoto wa suki desu ka.	*Do you like your present job?*
B Chotto...	*Well... (not really).*

8 Muzukashiku arimasen (It isn't difficult)

Adjectives which end in **-i** also have a negative form. In the present tense, this is made by dropping the final **-i** and then adding **-ku arimasen** to the stem. Note that **ii** *'good'* has an alternative form **yoi**, from which the negative is formed.

Positive	Stem	Negative	Meaning
hayai	haya-	hayaku arimasen	isn't early
omoshiroi	omoshiro-	omoshiroku arimasen	isn't interesting
atarashii	atarashi-	atarashiku arimasen	isn't new
warui	waru-	waruku arimasen	isn't bad
ii/yoi	yo-	yoku arimasen	isn't good

Kare no hanashi wa
omoshiroku arimasen ne.

He's boring, isn't he? (His conversation is uninteresting, isn't it?)

Jinji-bu no atarashii kikaku wa
yoku arimasen yo.

The personnel department's new plan is no good.

9 *Yoroshiku onegai shimasu*

This phrase appeared in the previous lesson as an equivalent to '*Glad to meet you*,' but it can also mean something more like '*Please be kind enough to take care of this*.' It can therefore be used instead of a direct request when the meaning is implicit. For example, a boss giving some papers to a typist may say **Yoroshiku onegai shimasu** instead of the specific words for '*Please type this*.' It can also be said to someone who has offered to do something, as in this case where Maeda, however unwillingly, has agreed to go with Noguchi to the airport to meet Mr Lloyd. In this kind of situation it means *Thank you in advance for taking care of the matter we just discussed.*

☑ ——— Expansion activities ———

1 How would you say the following times in Japanese?

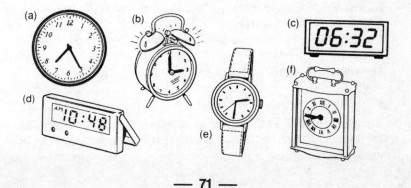

2 In the entrance lobby of Wajima Trading is a large wall map showing the time in various parts of the world. Unfortunately, a tem-
   porary electrical fault this morning has meant that all the clocks
   have stopped. The *caretaker* (**kanrinin**) is putting them right,
   with the help of the *reception* (**uketsuke**) clerk. Look at the dialogue below, and mark the correct times on the map.

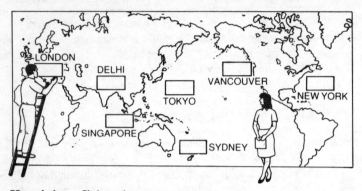

Kanrinin	Ii desu ka.
Uketsuke	Hai dōzo.
Kanrinin	Ja, Rondon. Rondon wa ima nan-ji desu ka.
Uketsuke	Rondon desu ka. Ima yo-ji han desu.
Kanrinin	Arigatō. Derii wa?
Uketsuke	Ēto...Derii wa ku-ji go-fun desu.
Kanrinin	Ku-ji go-fun, hai. Sore kara, Shingapōru.
Uketsuke	Shingapōru wa jū-ichi-ji yon-jip-pun.
Kanrinin	Dōmo. Tsugi wa, Tōkyō. Tōkyō wa ima jū-ni-ji yon-jū-go-fun desu ne.
Uketsuke	Hai, sō desu.
Kanrinin	Ja, Shidonii wa nan-ji desu ka.
Uketsuke	Shidonii desu ka. Shidonii wa jū-ni-ji go-jip-pun desu.
Kanrinin	Dōmo. Sore kara, Bankūbā to Nyū Yōku desu ne. Bankūbā wa?
Uketsuke	Bankūbā wa jū-ku-ji go-jū-go-fun desu. Ii desu ka?
Kanrinin	Hai, dōzo.
Uketsuke	Nyū Yōku wa ima ni-jū-san-ji desu.
Kanrinin	Hai, dōmo arigatō.
Uketsuke	Iie, dō itashimashite.

3 Complete the following sentences by using one of the words from
   the box. You may find some cases where several words can be
   used.

| fakkusu | densha | Eigo |
| terebi | denwa | Shinkansen |

(a) _____		Tōkyō ni kaerimasu.
(b) _____		Roido san ni hanashimasu.
(c) _____	de	nani o mimasu ka.
(d) _____		shorui o okurimasu.
(e) _____		kikimasu.
(f) _____		kaisha ni ikimasu.

4 How would you answer the questions below? Look at the following example to see some typical responses.

Example:

Q Anata no kaisha wa ōkii desu ka.
A Hai, ōkii desu.
or Mā-mā ōkii desu.
or Iie, ōkiku arimasen.

(a) Nihongo no benkyō wa tanoshii desu ka.
(b) Igirisu no uisukii wa takai desu ka.
(c) Shigoto* wa omoshiroi desu ka.
(d) Igirisu no densha wa osoi desu ka.
(e) Kyō wa isogashii desu ka.
(f) Kyō no tenki wa warui desu ka.

* Or **benkyō** if you are a student.

5 Below are some sentences about Mr Lloyd. Unscramble the words to find out more about him.
(a) wa desu manējā no san māketingu Roido
(b) ni no asa kūkō tsukimasu ashita Narita
(c) gorufu no shumi wa desu Roido san
(d) ja Rondon arimasen suki wa
(e) kaisha kaisha no no desu wa kare Igirisu
(f) isogashii Roido wa hito san desu totemo
(g) Wajima kenkyū ikimasu raishū ni no sentā

6 Now it's your turn. Imagine you are in a taxi on your way to Tokyo Station, where you will take the last Shinkansen of the evening to Kobe. After you have told the taxi driver where you want to go, he begins chatting to you.

Taxi	Kankō desu ka. Shigoto desu ka.
You	(*a*) *It's business. I'm going to Kobe on the Shinkansen.* ____

Taxi	Nan-ji no Shinkansen desu ka.
You	(*b*) *8:00. It gets to Kobe at about 11:20.* _____

Taxi	Sore wa osoi desu ne.
You	(*c*) *Yes, it is.* _____
Taxi	Anō, shitsurei desu ga, Nihongo wa muzukashiku arimasen ka.
You	(*d*) *It's a bit difficult.* _____
Taxi	Omoshiroi desu ka.
You	(*e*) *Yes, it's very interesting. Studying Japanese is fun.* ____

Taxi	(*as the taxi draws up outside Tokyo Station*) Hai, Tōkyō eki desu yo.
You	(*f*) *Thank you. How much is it?* _____
Taxi	¥2500 desu.
You	(*g*) *¥2500?! That's expensive!* _____
Taxi	Sumimasen ne! Ja, Nihongo, ganbatte kudasai.
You	(*h*) *Yes, I will. Thanks.* _____

📖 —————— **Reading corner** ——————

FRIDAY, APRIL 16

8:15　えいごの class
9:30　あたらしい part-timer
　　　のめんせつ
11:00　かいがい きかく部のかいぎ
12:00　Lloyd さん lunch
2:00　Singapore に こくさい電話
4:00　とうきょう えきに しゃ長を
　　　むかえに 行きます
6:00　Marathon の れんしゅう
MEMO
・なごやししゅの いしはらさんに 電話
・Dando Sports の しりょうを
　よこはまに Fax
・あしたの golf は 何じから？

— **74** —

This is a page from Okamoto kachō's diary, showing what he will be doing on the day Mr Lloyd first visits Wajima. If you are studying with someone else, practise asking and answering questions such as **Okamoto kachō wa 8-ji 15-fun ni nani o shimasu ka.**

Business briefing

Transportation

Japan is accessible by air through cities such as Osaka, Nagoya and Fukuoka, but still the majority of foreign business people arrive in Japan via Tokyo's international airport at Narita. From Narita, about 60 kilometres from central Tokyo, the most convenient connections are made using the Narita Express. This train makes the journey to the capital in under 60 minutes, but it is very popular so be prepared for a wait before being able to board a train.

In Tokyo itself, there is a clean, efficient and comprehensive train system which criss-crosses the city both above and below ground and which connects it with Yokohama and other satellite cities such as Chiba. Most train stations have signs in English, and the system is not difficult to use. Although everything you have heard about Tokyo's rush hour trains is probably true, with trains full to bursting point, the trains are nevertheless frequent, punctual, clean, and probably the most efficient way of getting around the city.

Taxis are numerous and can be flagged down on the street by holding out your hand as if you are waving to the driver. If the taxi is unoccupied, you will often see a sign in red **kanji** characters inside the front windscreen. Taxis are fairly expensive, but they all have meters, and there is no tipping, so you can keep track of how much you will have to pay as you go along.

For travel around the country, there are extensive air networks served by Japan Airlines and others, reaching up to Sapporo in the north and down to Okinawa in the south. As an alternative, you may prefer to use the Shinkansen, or *Bullet Train*, which provides easy access along the main trunk routes west, south and north from Tokyo.

The Shinkansen is not cheap, but it is fast and reliable and well worth the expense. At most times you will be able to get a comfortable seat with a **jiyūseki,** or unreserved ticket, but at rush hour or holiday times it is advisable to get a **shiteiseki,** or reserved seat ticket. There is also a first class section, known as the Green Car.

If you are on a business trip to Japan, you may want to consider buying a Japan Rail Pass before travelling to the country. For a fixed cost this allows you virtually unlimited travel on JR (Japan Railways) trains and ferries, and if your travel plans include frequent use of the Shinkansen, it is bound to save you a lot of money.

Whichever way you travel in Japan, it is likely to be crowded, but you can also be assured of a fast, reliable, safe and punctual service.

DAI 7 KA

IMA SHITE
IMASU

In Lesson 7 you will learn how to:

- talk about things happening at the moment (using the **-te iru** form of the verb)
- make polite requests (using **-te kudasai**)
- describe things or people with another kind of adjective (called **-na** adjectives)
- talk about two contrasting ideas, joined together by **ga** (*but*) in one sentence

——— The story so far ———

Maeda san and Noguchi san got up very early this morning to go to Narita airport to meet Mr Lloyd, but the flight is late and they have to wait another hour before he arrives. To kill some time, Maeda san decides to call the office to check on the preparations for the meeting. He's now talking to Koyama san, one of the OLs 'office ladies'.

——— Dialogue ———

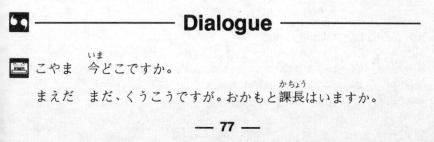

こやま　今^{いま}どこですか。

まえだ　まだ、くうこうですが。おかもと課長^{かちょう}はいますか。

こやま　ちょっと... (*looking around*) 今、電話をしていますが。

まえだ　じゃ、いけださんにかわって下さい。

こやま　いけださんは今、ファックスをおくっていますが、ちょっとまって下さい。(*calling to Ikeda*)　いけださん、まえださんです。

いけだ　はい、すぐ行きます。(*comes over and takes the receiver*)
　　　　もしもし、いけだですが。

まえだ　おはようございます。まえだですが、どうも。ええと、ところで、あしたのかいぎのじゅんびはどうですか。

いけだ　今、しています...すぐおわりますよ。

まえだ　あ、そうですか。じゃ、ほったくんは? 何をしていますか。

いけだ　ほったさんですか。あさからいろいろなことをしています。今はワープロのれんしゅうをしていますが、まだ、じょうずじゃありませんね。

まえだ　(*laughing*) おそいですか。

いけだ　えぇ、ほんとうにおそいですよ! でも、とてもがんばっていますよ。ところで、まえださんたちは、何じのバスでかえりますか。

まえだ　まだ、わかりません。のぐちくんが、今バスのじかんをしらべています。

いけだ　あぁ、そうですか。わかりました。

Koyama　Ima doko desu ka.
Maeda　Mada, kūkō desu ga. Okamoto kachō wa imasu ka.
Koyama　Chotto... (*looking around*) ima, denwa o shite imasu ga.
Maeda　Ja, Ikeda san ni kawatte kudasai.

Koyama Ikeda san wa ima, fakkusu o okutte imasu ga, chotto matte kudasai. (*calling to Ikeda*) Ikeda san, Maeda san desu.

Ikeda Hai, sugu ikimasu. (*comes over and takes the receiver*) Moshi moshi, Ikeda desu ga.

Maeda Ohayō gozaimasu. Maeda desu ga, dōmo. Ēto, tokoro de, ashita no kaigi no junbi wa dō desu ka?

Ikeda Ima, shite imasu... Sugu owarimasu yo.

Maeda Ā, sō desu ka. Ja, Hotta kun wa? Nani o shite imasu ka.

Ikeda Hotta san desu ka. Asa kara iroiro-na koto o shite imasu. Ima wa wāpuro no renshū o shite imasu ga, mada, jōzu ja arimasen ne.

Maeda (*laughing*) Osoi desu ka.

Ikeda Ē, hontō ni osoi desu yo! Demo, totemo ganbatte imasu yo. Tokorode, Maeda san-tachi wa nan-ji no basu de kaerimasu ka.

Maeda Mada, wakarimasen. Noguchi kun ga, ima basu no jikan o shirabete imasu.

Ikeda Ā, sō desu ka. Wakarimashita.

---

mada *still*	**owarimasu** *finish* [from
denwa o shite imasu *is making a*	**owaru**, to finish, end]
telephone call [from **suru**]	**iroiro-na** *various, all kinds of*
...ni kawatte kudasai *please get*	**koto** *things, matters*
me...instead [from **kawaru**, *to*	**ga** *but*
replace, take the place of]	**jōzu** *skilful, good at*
okutte imasu *is sending* [from	**hontō ni** *really, truly*
okuru]	**demo** *but, however*
tokorode *well, by the way*	**Maeda san-tachi** *Maeda san and*
junbi *preparations*	*others with him*
dō *how?*	**wakarimashita** *I see*

Comprehension

1 What is Ikeda san doing at the moment?
   (*a*) Sending a fax.
   (*b*) Writing a fax.
   (*c*) Reading a fax.

2 What is Hotta san doing?
   (*a*) Writing various things.
   (*b*) Learning how to use the word processor.
   (*c*) Typing a report slowly.

Notes

1 Mada kūkō desu ga (We're still at the airport)

When used with a positive verb in the present tense, **mada** has the meaning of *still*.

Nihonshu wa **mada** arimasu ka.   *Is there still some sake left?*
Buchō wa **mada** Kōbe ni imasu.   *The buchō is still in Kobe.*

However, as we saw in the previous lesson, **mada** has the meaning of *not yet* when followed by a negative verb.

A   Ashita nani o shimasu ka.   *What are you doing tomorrow?*
B   Sā, **mada** wakarimasen.   *Well, I don't really know yet.*

2 Shite imasu (Is doing)

This form of the verb is often called the **-te** form as it always ends in **-te** (or in some cases the variation **-de**). It is an important form to learn, as it has a wide variety of uses. For example, it is used in the opening dialogue to form the progressive tense which indicates action happening at the moment. The **-te** form is also used to make polite requests and commands, to join certain kinds of sentences together and when asking permission to do something.

You will remember from Lesson 5 that most verbs can be divided into two groups, those that drop **-ru** and those that drop **-u** from the dictionary form to make other verb forms. To make the **-te** form with verbs in the first group, simply drop the final **-ru** and add **-te** to the basic stem.

plain form	-masu form	-te form
ireru (*to put in, to insert*)	iremasu	irete
hajimeru (*to begin*)	hajimemasu	hajimete
miru (*to see*)	mimasu	mite
deru (*to come out, to appear*)	demasu	dete
shiraberu (*to investigate*)	shirabemasu	shirabete

It is not quite so simple with the group of verbs that drop **-u** from the dictionary form, as the ending of the word differs depending on the last letter of the stem. These endings are shown below in five groups, but you might find it easier simply to learn them by heart.

	plain form	-masu form	-te form
(a)	**-tsu, -ru, -u** verbs end in **-tte:**		
	matsu (*to wait*)	machimasu	matte
	kawaru (*to change, to replace*)	kawarimasu	kawatte
	ganbaru (*to persist*)	ganbarimasu	ganbatte
	narau (*to learn*)	naraimasu	naratte
(b)	**-su** verbs end in **-shite:**		
	hanasu (*to talk*)	hanashimasu	hanashite
	osu (*to push, to press*)	oshimasu	oshite
(c)	**-ku** verbs end in **-ite:**		
	kiku (*to ask, to hear*)	kikimasu	kiite
	kaku (*to write*)	kakimasu	kaite
	(An exception is iku, *to go*, which becomes **itte**)		
(d)	**-gu** verbs end in **-ide:**		
	isogu (*to hurry*)	isogimasu	isoide
(e)	**-mu, -bu, -nu** verbs end in **-nde:**		
	nomu (*to drink*)	nomimasu	nonde
	yomu (*to read*)	yomimasu	yonde
	asobu (*to play*)	asobimasu	asonde
	shinu (*to die*)	shinimasu	shinde
	The two irregular verbs are:		
	kuru (*to come*)	kimasu	kite
	suru (*to do*)	shimasu	shite

The progressive tense of the verb, which indicates action over a period of time, is formed from the **-te** form with **iru**, *to be*. In this way, the **-te** form corresponds very closely to the *-ing* form of English verbs.

Nani o **shite** imasu ka.	*What are you doing?*
Kanojo wa Nihongo o **naratte** imasu.	*She's learning Japanese.*
Ima buchō to hanashi o **shite** imasu.	*She's talking with the general manager at the moment.*

3 Ikeda san ni kawatte kudasai (Could you get Ikeda san, please? [Lit. Please change to Ikeda san])

You will already have used **kudasai** in previous lessons to ask for something (e.g. **Kōhii o kudasai**, *Could I have some coffee please?*). When it is used after the **-te** form of a verb, it becomes a polite way of asking someone to do something.

Chotto **matte kudasai**.   *Just a moment, please* (Lit. *Please*

	wait a little.)
Māketingu no buchō ni **kiite kudasai.**	*Please ask the marketing buchō.*
Ikeda san, kono shorui o kopii **shite kudasai.**	*Ikeda san, could you make a copy of these papers?*

4 Sugu ikimasu (Just coming)

Although the meaning of **iku** is generally given as *to go*, and **kuru** as *to come*, their use is sometimes a little different from the English equivalents. **Iku** means *to go to any other place*, whereas in English *to go* means *to go to any place except where the person you are speaking to is*. Hence in the example given above from the dialogue, Ikeda san uses **iku** where in English we would use *come*.

A	(*phoning from Tokyo*) Itsu Tōkyō ni **kimasu** ka.	*When are you coming to Tokyo?*
B	(*in Kobe*) Raishū **ikimasu.**	*I'll be coming next week.*

5 Iroiro-na koto (Various things)

In addition to the adjectives ending in **-i** which we came across in the previous lesson (**hiroi, omoshiroi**, etc.) there is another group of adjectives like **iroiro** which act in a different way. They are much more like nouns, so they need a verb like **desu** to make a complete grammatical sentence. Some more examples of these are:

suki	*like, likeable*	kirai	*dislike, hateful*
kirei	*pretty, clean*	jōzu	*clever, skilful*
genki	*healthy, energetic*	yūmei	*famous*
taihen	*tough, terrible*	shinsetsu	*kind*
hen	*strange, odd*		

Kaigi no junbi wa **taihen** desu yo.	*The preparation for the meeting is really hard work.*
Sore wa **hen** desu ne!	*That's strange!*

When this kind of adjective is used with a noun, **-na** needs to be added. (Therefore they are usually referred to as **-na** adjectives.)

Satō sensei wa hontō ni **shinsetsu-na** hito desu yo.	*Professor Satō is a really kind man.*

Suki-na supōtsu wa tenisu to gorufu desu.	*The sports I like are tennis and golf.*
Shinjuku ni **yūmei-na** kaisha ga takusan arimasu.	*There are a lot of famous companies in Shinjuku* [an area of Tokyo].

The words **ōkii** (*large*) and **chiisai** (*small*) can belong either to the **-i** group or to the **-na** group of adjectives when in the positive. Hence you can say **ōkii kaisha** or **ōki-na kaisha** (*a large company*) and **chiisai inu** or **chiisa-na inu** (*a small dog*).

6 Ima wāpuro no renshū o shite imasu ga, mada jōzu ja arimasen ne (He's practising on the word processor, but he's not very good yet)

When the conjunction **ga** joins two sentences, it acts rather like the English *but*, especially if the two sentences are contrasting. Note that, while *but* comes in the second part of an English sentence after the comma, in Japanese **ga** comes before the comma.

Maeda san wa kaigi ni demasu **ga**, Noguchi san wa demasen.	*Maeda san will attend the meeting, but Noguchi san won't.*
Kanojo wa totemo shinsetsu desu **ga**, chotto hen-na hito desu.	*She's very kind, but a bit odd.*

However, **ga** is much weaker than *but* and is often used simply to join sentences together even if there is no element of contrast.

Iroiro-na hanashi ga arimasu **ga**, jikan wa arimasu ka.	*There are lots of things to talk about – do you have some time?*
Kore kara Nagoya shisha ni denwa shimasu **ga**, messēji wa arimasu ka.	*I'm going to call the Nagoya office – do you have any messages?*

7 Jōzu (Skilful, good at)

When using the word **jōzu**, the thing one is skilled at is the subject of the verb. Therefore, it is marked by **wa** or **ga**, and not **o** as might be expected.

Roido san wa Nihongo **ga** jōzu desu yo.   *Mr Lloyd is good at Japanese.*

Other similar adjectives which take **ga** are **heta** (*unskilful, poor at*), **suki** and **kirai**.

Nihon no sarariiman wa gorufu **ga** dai-suki desu ne!   *Japanese businessmen really like golf, don't they!*

8 *Hontō ni osoi* (Really slow)

Although the correct pronunciation is **hontō**, in everyday conversation **honto** (with a shorter final **o** sound) is very common.

A Wajima wa Derii ni mo shisha ga arimasu yo.   *Wajima has a branch in Delhi too, you know.*

B Ē?! **Honto?**   *What? Really?*

9 *Maeda san-tachi* (Maeda san and his group)

-tachi can be added to the end of personal pronouns or other words indicating people, to show that they are plural.

watashi**tachi**   *we*
sensei**tachi**   *the teachers*
anata**tachi**   *you* [plural]
OL**tachi**   *the OLs*

-tachi can also be added to people's names to indicate that the person's group is also included. **Maeda san-tachi**, for example, could mean *Maeda san and the person/people with him, the Maeda family* or *Maeda's crowd*, depending on the circumstances.

10 *Wakarimashita* (I understand, I see)

The verb **wakaru** means *to understand, to comprehend* and, used in the present tense, it generally refers to an ongoing situation.

Nihongo ga **wakarimasu** ka.   *Do you understand Japanese?* (Lit. *Is Japanese understandable?*)

However, when talking about something which has just now been learned or discovered, the past tense is used, meaning *Now I have understood*. More colloquially, it is the equivalent of *Oh, I see* or *Got it!*

A Roido san wa sērusu no
   manējā ja arimasen.
   Māketingu no manējā
   desu yo.

*Mr Lloyd isn't the sales manager,
he's the marketing manager.*

B Ā sō desu ka.
   Wakarimashita.

Oh really, I see.

Note that the verb **wakaru** usually takes the particle **ga**.

Expansion activities

1 This first exercise practises **-na** adjectives. Repeat the exchange
   below and then substitute the words in bold type with the cues
   which follow. Practise this with a partner if possible.

   A **Ano hito** wa **genki** desu ne.
   B Ē, hontō-ni **genki-na hito** desu ne.

   (*a*) kono heya, kirei
   (*b.*) kono shigoto, taihen
   (*c*) ano kōjō, ōkii

   (*d*) ano sensei, shinsetsu
   (*e*) ano kaisha, yūmei
   (*f*) kono messēji, hen

2 Below is a picture of Wajima's Overseas Planning Department.
   Look at the sentences following the picture, and circle T or F,
   depending on whether you think they are true or false. (If you are
   working with a partner, get him or her to read the sentences
   aloud to you while you look only at the picture.)

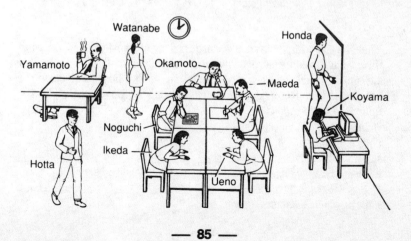

(a) Ima jū-ji han goro desu.   T   F
(b) Maeda san wa denwa o shite imasu.   T   F
(c) Ikeda san wa Ueno san to hanashite imasu.   T   F
(d) Yamamoto buchō wa isogashiku arimasen.   T   F
(e) Noguchi san wa kyō kaisha ni imasen.   T   F
(f) Honda san wa hanashi o shite imasu.   T   F
(g) Hotta san wa kōhii o nonde imasu.   T   F
(h) Watanabe san wa Hotta san o mite imasen.   T   F

3   Look at the picture again and complete the sentences below.
   (a) Yamamoto buchō wa ima kōhii o _____
   (b) Noguchi san wa ima repōto o _____
   (c) _____ wa Ikeda san no hanashi o _____
   (d) Maeda _____ shorui _____
   (e) _____ denwa de _____
   (f) _____ wāpuro no renshū o _____
   (g) Ikeda _____ to _____

4   **Part A**

The Overseas Planning Department has just received some new
word processors. See if you can work out the meaning of the
Japanese instructions below, which are not in the correct order,
by matching them to the appropriate English sentences.

   (a) *Press the 'ON' switch.*   (i) Furoppi o ireru.
   (b) *Wait ten seconds.*   (ii) Menyū ga deru.
   (c) *Insert the floppy disk.*   (iii) Jū-byō matsu.
   (d) *Enter the time.*   (iv) 'ON' suitchi o osu.
   (e) *Press the 'RETURN' key.*   (v) Jikan o entā suru.
   (f) *The menu will appear.*   (vi) 'RETURN' kii o osu.

Part B

The Nagoya office have also ordered new word processors, but
theirs have been delivered without manuals, so Ikeda san is now
explaining over the phone to one of the clerks how to start up the
new machine. Referring to the instructions above, complete the
following dialogue.

Ikeda   Ja, 'ON' suitchi o oshite kudasai.
Clerk   Hai.
Ikeda   10-byō _____
Clerk   Hai.
Ikeda   Ēto, _____ kudasai, ne.
Clerk   Hai, iremasu.

Ikeda	Tsugi wa _____
Clerk	Jikan desu ka. Ima 5-ji desu ne.
Ikeda	Sō desu ne. Sore kara _____
Clerk	Ā, menyū desu!
Ikeda	Ii desu ne.
Clerk	Hai. Arigatō gozaimasu.

5 Things are especially busy in the Overseas Planning Department, so the section manager, Okamoto kachō, asks the two OLs Ikeda san and Koyama san to do some jobs for him. Complete the dialogue below by replacing the dictionary form of the verb in brackets with the **-te kudasai** or **-te imasu** form of the verb, as appropriate.

Kachō	Ikeda san, Nagoya shisha ni kono fakkusu o (okuru) yo.
Ikeda	Hai, kore kara okurimasu.
Kachō	Sore kara, raishū no kaigi no junbi mo (hajimeru) yo!
Ikeda	Hai, ima (suru) ga.
Kachō	Ā sō, arigatō. Koyama san, kono shorui o kopii (suru).
Koyama	Hai.
Kachō	Sore kara, sono kopii o Dandō Supōtsu no fairu ni (ireru).
Koyama	Wakarimashita.

6 Look at the following example, which joins two sentences together with **ga**. Then make similar sentences using the cues which follow.

Example:

A Tanaka san wa genki desu ka. (totemo isogashii)
B Hai, genki desu **ga**, totemo isogashii desu.

(a) Wāpuro no renshū wa muzukashii desu ka. (omoshiroi)
(b) Ano hoteru wa dō desu ka. Takai desu ka. (yoku arimasen)
(c) Ano kaisha wa chiisai desu ka. (yūmei)
(d) Atarashii shigoto wa dō desu ka. Omoshiroi desu ka. (taihen)
(e) Gorufu wa suki desu ka. (jōzu ja arimasen)
(f) Kopii wa takusan arimasu ka. (sugu owarimasu)

7 Now it's your turn. Your company is conducting some market research for Wada san's organisation and Wada san has just called from Japan to see how the report is coming along. Unfortunately, you have given it very low priority, so there is still a long way to go before it will be finished.

Wada	Repōto no koto desu ga…
You	(a) *The report? Uh, we're writing it at the moment…*

Wada	Ā sō desu ka. Itsu Nihon ni okurimasu ka.
You	(b) *Well, we're still checking up on various things…*

Wada	Ē? Mada? Ja, itsu owarimasu ka.
You	(c) *Just a moment, I'll ask the person in charge.* (pause) *I'm sorry, the person in charge isn't here.*

Wada	Ē?!
You	(d) *He's having a meeting at the moment, but…*

Wada	Wakarimashita. Ja, ashita.
You	(e) *Yes, we'll call you tomorrow.*

Wada	Un, sō shite kudasai.

Reading corner

Ikeda san is stopped outside the main entrance to Wajima one morning and asked to fill in a questionnaire prepared by the Health and Welfare section of the Personnel Department. See if you can read and answer these questions from the first part of the questionnaire.

Ⓜ Questionnaire

今のじかんをかいて下さい。　　　　　_____
部、課のなまえをかいて下さい。　　　_____

1.　あさ、何をたべますか。　　　　　　_____
2.　あさ、何をのみますか。　　　　　　_____
3.　あさ、テレビをみますか。　　　　　_____
4.　しんぶんは何をよみますか。　　　　_____
5.　何じに、かいしゃに行きますか。　　_____
6.　電しゃで行きますか。　　　　　　　_____
7.　何じにかいしゃにつきますか。　　　_____
8.　しごとは何ですか。　　　　　　　　_____
9.　何じにかえりますか。　　　　　　　_____

▯ ──────── Business briefing ────────

Women in business

The world of Japanese business is still very much a male-dominated society. Although women make up over 40% of the workforce in Japan and roughly half of all married women work, only a tiny majority are in supervisory or managerial positions. Most of the others who work in offices belong to a group of workers known simply as OLs, or 'office ladies', whose duties consist of such simple tasks as making tea for guests, answering the telephone, making photocopies and filing.

The traditional pattern is for women to stay at work only until they get married or at the latest until they have their first child, so companies are often reluctant to spend a lot of time and money on training women who are likely to leave within a few years of being hired. This in turn leads to frustration on the part of many women employees who, even though they may have high academic qualifications, are given boring and menial jobs to do, with no opportunity of competing equally with men. Faced with such bleak job prospects, it is perhaps not surprising that they decide to quit when they get married, and so the cycle is perpetuated.

However, there are signs that things are beginning to change. In 1986 the Equal Opportunity Law was passed, forbidding discrimination against women in hiring, training, assignment of job responsibilities or promotion. This has led to an increase in the number of companies considering women for positions of responsibility and a greater awareness among women of the opportunities open to them. In particular, many have been attracted to non-Japanese companies, which take advantage of the pool of highly-educated female workers to recruit women for high status jobs and which pay salaries comparable to men's – unlike many Japanese companies.

Nevertheless, it is still an uphill struggle for the woman who wants to combine a job with a family. As yet, childcare facilities are few and far between, there is no tradition of leaving children with babyminders, and husbands do not expect to share equally in household duties. Things are beginning to change and the last few years have seen more and more women appointed to posts of responsibility, but it is likely to be a long time before women catch up with men at work.

DAI 8 KA

O-TSUKARE SAMA DESHITA

Lesson 8 concentrates on practice with talking about things which happened in the past. You will also find out a new form of the verb for making suggestions and offering help, and there are a number of new phrases for greetings and thanks.

The story so far

Maeda san and Noguchi san have just arrived back at the Wajima office after meeting Mr Lloyd at Narita airport and then taking him to his hotel in downtown Tokyo. Koyama san, one of the OLs, greets them as they come in, tired out after a very long day.

Dialogue

まえだ　ただいま。
こやま　あぁ、おかえりなさい。
まえだ　あぁ...つかれた!!

こやま　けっきょくロイドさんのひこうきは何時につきました
　　　　か。

まえだ　11時はんにつきました。

こやま　それはずいぶんおくれましたね!

まえだ　かえりはもっとたいへんでした。くうこうからホテル
　　　　まで3時かんはんもかかりましたよ。

こやま　ほんとうにおつかれさまでした。おちゃでもいれましょ
　　　　うか。

まえだ　はい、おねがいします。えぇと、いけださんは?

こやま　もう、うちへかえりましたが...

まえだ　えぇ?! 会議のじゅんびは?

こやま　もうおわりましたよ。しょるいはそこにありますが、
　　　　みせましょうか。

まえだ　えぇ、でも、さきにおちゃをいれて下さい。

Maeda	Tadaima.
Koyama	Ā, o-kaeri nasai.
Maeda	Aaaaa, tsukareta!!
Koyama	Kekkyoku Roido san no hikōki wa nan-ji ni tsukimashita ka.
Maeda	11-ji han ni tsukimashita.
Koyama	Sore wa zuibun okuremashita ne!
Maeda	Kaeri wa motto taihen deshita. Kūkō kara hoteru made san-jikan han mo kakarimashita yo.
Koyama	Hontō ni o-tsukare sama deshita. O-cha demo iremashō ka.
Maeda	Hai, onegai shimasu. Ēto, Ikeda san wa?
Koyama	Mō... uchi e kaerimashita ga....
Maeda	Ē?! Kaigi no junbi wa?
Koyama	Mō owarimashita yo. Shorui wa soko ni arimasu ga, misemashō ka.
Maeda	Ē, demo, saki ni o-cha o irete kudasai.

tadaima　*I'm back*		**kekkyoku**　*finally, in the end*	
o-kaeri nasai　*welcome back*		**hikōki**　*plane*	
tsukareta　*I'm exhausted* [from		**tsukimashita**　*arrived* [from **tsuku**]	
tsukareru, *to get tired*]		**deshita**　*was* [from **desu**]	

kakarimashita took [from **kakaru**, to take, need, require]	**o-cha demo** some tea or something
o-tsukare sama deshita You must be very tired!	**iremashō ka** shall I make (some tea)? [from **ireru**, to put in]
zuibun extremely	**uchi** home, house
okuremashita was late [from **okureru**, to be late]	**e** to, towards
kaeri return trip	**kaerimashita** went home [from **kaeru**]
motto more	**owarimashita** finished [from **owaru**]
made to, until, as far as	**soko** there
san-jikan han three and a half hours	**misemashō ka** shall I show you? [from **miseru**, to show]
mo as much as	**saki ni** first of all, ahead

Comprehension

1   Was Mr Lloyd's plane:
   (a)   more or less on time?
   (b)   a bit late?
   (c)   very late?

2   Why is Maeda san concerned?
   (a)   Because he thinks he will be late home.
   (b)   Because he thinks the preparations for the meeting haven't been done.
   (c)   Because Ikeda san has gone home.

Notes

1   Tadaima (I'm back)

This is a greeting which is said when returning home, and is a contraction of **Tadaima kaerimashita**, or *I have just come back*. It can also be said when returning to one's office or other place which is regarded as a base. The response used to welcome someone home is **O-kaeri nasai**, or *Welcome back*.

2   Tsukareta! (I'm exhausted!)

This exclamation is actually the plain past tense of the verb **tsukareru**, *to become tired*. As it is treated like a comment said to oneself (even if there are actually other people around) it is perfectly acceptable to use the plain form. When talking about other people, the polite form **tsukaremashita** should be used. There is more information on the plain form in later lessons.

3 Tsukimashita (Arrived)

To talk about something which happened in the past, simply replace the **-masu** of the present tense of the verb with **-mashita**. Note that the pronunciation is **-mash' ta** with the **-i-** hardly sounded. (There is) also a plain form which we will learn in a later lesson.)

dictionary form	-masu form	past tense	meaning
tsuku (*to arrive*)	tsuki-masu	tsuki-mashita	arrived
kaeru (*to return*)	kaeri-masu	kaeri-mashita	returned
katazukeru (*to tidy up*)	katazuke-masu	katazuke-mashita	tidied up
au (*to meet*)	ai-masu	ai-mashita	met
kuru (*to come*)	ki-masu	ki-mashita	came
suru (*to do*)	shi-masu	shi-mashita	did

The simple past tense in Japanese is roughly equivalent not only to the English past tense (e.g. *he returned*) but also to the present perfect form (e.g. *he has returned*).

Kekkyoku kuruma de **ikimashita**.	*In the end we went by car.*
Sore kara dō **shimashita** ka.	*So what happened after that?* or *What did you do after that?*
Ikeda san wa mō kaigi-shitsu o **katazukemashita**.	*Ikeda san has already cleared up the meeting room.*

If you want to talk about things which were continuing to happen in the past over a period of time, simply treat the **-te iru** form of the verb in the same way, replacing the final **imasu** with **imashita**.

A	Kinō no 8-ji goro nani o **shite imashita** ka.	*What were you doing at around 8:00 yesterday?*
B	Terebi o **mite imashita**.	*I was watching television.*

The negative of the polite past tense is also very regular: it is necessary only to add **deshita** (the past form of **desu**; see below) to the negative of the polite present tense.

| Ni-jikan mo **kakarimasen deshita.** | *It didn't take as much as two hours.* |
| Kachō wa ikimashita ga, buchō wa **ikimasen deshita.** | *The section manager went, but the general manager didn't.* |

4 *Deshita* (Was)

The polite past form of **desu** is **deshita.**

| Kinō no kaigi wa taihen **deshita** ne. | *Yesterday's meeting was tough, wasn't it!* |
| Shūmatsu wa dō **deshita** ka. | *How was the weekend?* |

The negative follows the same pattern as described above for regular verbs: simply add **deshita** to the negative of the present tense, which in the case of **desu** is **de wa** (or **ja**) **arimasen.**

| Yamada san wa shachō **ja arimasen deshita.** Fuku-shachō deshita. | *Yamada san wasn't the president, he was the vice-president.* |

5 *Kūkō kara hoteru made* (From the airport to the hotel)

Note that the words **kara** (*from*) and **made** (*to*) come after the place, time, etc., to which they refer.

| Kaigi wa nan-ji **kara** nan-ji **made** desu ka. | *How long will the meeting be?* (Lit. …*from what time to what time…*) |
| Tōkyō **kara** Ōsaka **made,** Shinkansen de nan-jikan gurai kakarimasu ka. | *About how many hours does it take by Shinkansen from Tokyo to Osaka?* |

6 *O-tsukare sama deshita* (You must be very tired)

This is a set phrase said in praise or gratitude to someone who has put a great deal of effort and energy into something, and so may be translated as *Thank you, you must be tired after that* or *Thank you for all your hard work*. It is also often said in response to the parting phrase **O-saki ni** or **O-saki ni shitsurei shimasu** said by someone who leaves the office before you at the end of the day's work.

A O-saki ni (shitsurei shimasu).	I'm off (Lit: *Excuse me for leaving ahead of you*).
B O-tsukare sama (deshita).	Bye. (Lit: *Thank you for your hard work*).

7 *O-cha demo* (Some green tea or something)

Demo (*or something*) is sometimes added to imply that there are other choices possible than the one suggested, otherwise it might seem that one is presuming to impose one's own preferences on someone else. When **demo** is used, particles such as **wa, ga** and **o** can be omitted.

Sushi **demo** tabemasu ka.	*Would you like some sushi or something?*
Konban Akasaka no pabu **demo** ikimasu ka.	*Would you like to go to a pub in Akasaka or somewhere this evening?*

8 *O-cha demo iremashō ka* (Shall I make some tea?)

This form of the verb ending in **-mashō** is used very often in Japanese to suggest doing something, and corresponds roughly to the English *Let's....* It is formed simply by replacing the final **-masu** of the verb with **-mashō**.

Ganbarimashō.	*Let's have a go.*
Mina san, okuremasu yo! **Isogimashō!**	*We're late, everyone. Let's hurry!*

If this form of the verb is followed by the question particle **ka**, it corresponds to the English *shall we...?* or *shall I...?*

Doko de **aimashō ka**.	*Where shall we meet?*
Watashi wa saki ni kuruma de **ikimashō ka**.	*Shall I go on ahead by car?*
Chotto **nomimashō ka**.	*Shall we have a quick drink?*

9 *Uchi e* (To home)

The particle **e**, like **ni**, indicates the direction towards which something moves. Although there are some very slight grammatical differences in usage between **e** and **ni** (**e** concentrates on the direction, whereas **ni** concentrates on the point of contact), in practice native speakers use them more or less interchangeably.

Shutchō wa doko **e/ni** ikimasu ka.	*Where are you going on your business trip?*
Kanojo wa Shinkansen de Hiroshima **e/ni** kaerimashita.	*She went home to Hiroshima by Shinkansen.*

10 *Soko* (There)

The set of words indicating location is another of the **ko-, so-, a-, do-** group we met in Lesson 4. The others in this set are **koko** (*here*), **asoko** (*over there*) and **doko** (*where?*).

Asoko ni arimasu yo.	*It's over there.*
Koko kara Shinjuku made ikura desu ka.	*How much does it cost from here to Shinjuku?*

Expansion activities

1 We have come across a number of set phrases and sayings in the lessons so far. Which ones would you say in the following situations?

  (*a*) You have just arrived back home.
  (*b*) You greet someone who has just arrived home.
  (*c*) You've just understood something that has been explained to you.
  (*d*) You are meeting someone for the first time.
  (*e*) You want to say hello on the telephone.
  (*f*) You want to encourage someone to keep trying.
  (*g*) You excuse yourself for disturbing someone.
  (*h*) You fall exhausted into a chair.
  (*i*) You thank someone for having worked so hard on a project.
  (*j*) You are leaving the office at the end of the working day.
  (*k*) Someone has just thanked you for doing something for them.

2 Mr Lloyd is going to do a lot of travelling during the next few weeks in Japan, so he goes to the travel centre in his hotel to

check on travelling times before making business appointments in the various cities.

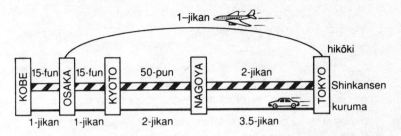

Ask questions like those in the example, using the cues provided.

Example:

Shinkansen, Tōkyō, Nagoya

A Shinkansen de, Tōkyō kara Nagoya made, nan-jikan kakarimasu ka.

B Ni-jikan gurai kakarimasu.

(a) Shinkansen, Tōkyō, Ōsaka
(b) kuruma, Ōsaka, Kōbe
(c) kuruma, Tōkyō, Nagoya
(d) hikōki, Ōsaka, Tōkyō
(e) Shinkansen, Kyōto, Nagoya

3 Below is Ikeda san's list of things she was supposed to do today, but she didn't manage to do all of them. She has put a tick [✓] against the jobs she finished. Read through the list to make sure you understand it.

- Ōsaka no Ishii san ni denwa o suru ✓
- Shingapōru ni fakkusu o okuru
- kaigi-shitsu o katazukeru ✓
- mensetsu no junbi o suru ✓
- Shinkansen no jikan o shiraberu
- kikaku-bu no repōto o kopii suru ✓
- Dandō Supōtsu no dēta o konpyūtā ni ireru

Maeda san goes over to Ikeda san's desk to check on what she did and didn't do today. Make questions and answers like the ones below using the information from Ikeda san's list. (Practise this together with another person if possible.)

Examples:

Maeda Ōsaka no Ishii san ni denwa o shimashita ka.
Ikeda Hai, denwa shimashita.
Maeda Shingapōru ni fakkusu o okurimashita ka.
Ikeda Iie, okurimasen deshita.

4 A few minutes later, Hotta san comes over to see if he can lend Ikeda san a hand. Using her checklist above again, make offers and responses like the ones in the examples following.

Hotta Ōsaka no Ishii san ni denwa o shimashō ka.
Ikeda Mō denwa shimashita.
Hotta Shingapōru ni fakkusu o okurimashō ka.
Ikeda Hai, onegai shimasu. (*or*) Hai, okutte kudasai.

5 Okamoto kachō knows that Maeda san has had a long day, and so goes over to see if he'd like to have a drink on the way home. In order to complete their dialogue, fill in the blanks with the **-mashō** form of the verb which follows in brackets.

Kachō Maeda kun, o-tsukare sama. Pabu demo _____ (iku) ka.

Maeda Mada 6-ji desu ga...

Kachō Ii yo, ii yo! _____ (owaru)!

Maeda Ii desu ne. Sō _____ (suru). Doko ni ikimasu ka.

Kachō Shinjuku no 'Tampopo' ('*Dandelion*' [name of bar]) de _____ (nomu) yo.
(*Calls to Noguchi*) Noguchi kun mo _____ (iku) yo!

Noguchi Hai. Demo Shingapōru kara no denwa o matte imasu. Mō chotto kakarimasu ga.

Maeda Kachō, _____ (matsu) ka.

Kachō Iie, saki ni _____ (iku). Noguchi kun, 'Tampopo' de _____ (au)!

6 Now it's your turn. It's Monday morning in the office, and one of your Japanese colleagues, Saitō san, is asking you about your trip to Yokohama last weekend. You will need a few new words, which are given in brackets.

Saitō Ohayō gozaimasu.
You (a) *Good morning.* _____

Saitō Shūmatsu wa dō deshita ka. Yokohama e ikimashita ka.
You (b) *Yes, I did, but the return trip was terrible.* _____

Saitō Dō shite?
You (c) *There was a big accident (**jiko**) at Yokohama station.*

Saitō Ā sō, sō, watashi mo terebi de mimashita yo. Taihen deshita ne.
You (d) *Yes, I waited for an hour but no trains came.* _____

Saitō Sore de, dō shimashita ka.
You (e) *I went to the taxi stand (**takushii noriba**) but a lot of people were waiting for taxis. I waited again there for forty minutes. I finally got home at 10:00.* _____

Saitō Sore wa o-tsukare sama deshita. Demo, takushii wa takai deshō.
You (f) *Yes, they're really expensive! But what came next (**sore kara ga**) was worse.* _____

Saitō Ē? Dō shimashita ka!
You (g) *I didn't have my house key!* _____

Reading corner

Look at the **kanji** for the numbers 1 to 10, 100 and 1,000 given below, and learn to recognise them.

一 (1)   六 (6)   百 (100)
二 (2)   七 (7)   千 (1,000)
三 (3)   八 (8)
四 (4)   九 (9)
五 (5)   十 (10)

Can you read the following sentences? Note that when Japanese is written vertically, it begins from the right and works towards the left.

一　かいがいきかく部の会議は二時から四時までです。

二　課長の電話ばんごうは（〇五二）三八二ー三五四九です。

三　かえりのタクシーは三千五百六十えんでした。たかいですね。

四　あの六千えんのスカーフを下さい。

五　十時のしんかんせんでなごやに行きます。

Business briefing

Nemawashi

Nemawashi literally means *preparing the roots*, and it describes a process which has been used in Japan for hundreds of years when moving a tree to a new site. First the soil is carefully excavated from around the roots, so as to gradually expose them without damage, and then the root ball is bound firmly with strips of hessian which can be kept moist. In this way, the tree is prepared for the impending change in its circumstances slowly and with great care.

In Japanese business, the word **nemawashi** is used to mean the practice of talking about a particular course of action with all the parties involved, individually and usually informally, prior to a meeting where a final decision will be made. In this way, all parties to the decision can work out their differences and reach a consensus before the meeting even takes place. The meeting itself is very often convened only to put an official seal of approval on a course of action which has already been decided upon by all the participants during the process of **nemawashi**.

Typically, pre-meeting **nemawashi** is done with great care as regards timing, and deciding on the best time to approach a certain section leader to get his agreement to something is often an intuitive decision. The discussions which form part of the **nemawashi** process are usually informal and down-to-earth, and people feel more able to verbalise their real feelings about an impending change in the company, something which they do not often do in the more formal atmosphere of a meeting.

Before big corporate decisions are taken, a great deal of **nemawashi** will take place over an extended period, often in bars after work or in odd moments during the working day. The conversation will start casually with, 'By the way, what do you think about...' and the participants will talk person-to-person about a particular course of action, again something which is rarely done in the meeting situation itself.

Nemawashi is a vital part of the Japanese approach to business. Meetings in the West tend to be forums for thrashing out a course of action, often between strongly opposing parties, and then deciding action points. A Japanese business meeting tends to be a place where the official seal can be put to the consensus of the group – a consensus reached by careful and often prolonged **nemawashi**. After all, if a tree is to be moved, it is vital to ensure that the tree will survive the move. To ensure the success of a proposed plan of action, in the world of Japanese business it makes sense to spend as much time as possible preparing the parties to that decision – because those people form the roots of the company itself.

TSUITACHI WA AITE IMASU KA

In Lesson 9 you will learn dates and days of the week, and using these you will then be able to practise making appointments. You will also learn another use of the **-te iru** form for talking about ongoing or routine situations, and a new particle **de** to indicate the place where something happens.

The story so far

Mr Lloyd has arrived safely in Japan. He has already had a preliminary meeting with Wajima and lunch with Yamamoto buchō, but business meetings do not start in earnest until after the weekend. This evening, Saturday, he has met up with Shimada san, an old friend whom he knew when Shimada san was working in London some years ago.

Dialogue

島田　ロイドさんは今もかいがいきかく部にいますか。

ロイド　ええ、そうですが、今はべつの課ではたらいています。

二月からマーケティングをたんとうしています。

島田　たいへんですね。いそがしいでしょう。

ロイド　ええ、ざんぎょうもたくさんありますよ。

島田　どよう日とにちよう日はやすみでしょう。

ロイド　そうですが、ときどきどよう日も会しゃに行きます。
しゅっちょうもあります。

島田　ところで、このしゅっちょうは五月三日までですよね。

ロイド　はい、そうです。

島田　一日はいそがしいですか。

ロイド　(*looking at his diary*) 一日はどよう日ですね。ええ、
あいていますよ。何か…?

島田　じつは、その日はけっこんしきです。

ロイド　だれのけっこんしきですか。

島田　ぼくのです!!

ロイド　あぁ!それはおめでとうございます!

Shimada	Roido san wa ima mo kaigai kikaku-bu ni imasu ka.
Lloyd	Ē, sō desu ga, ima wa betsu no ka de hataraite imasu. Ni-gatsu kara māketingu o tantō shite imasu.
Shimada	Taihen desu ne. Isogashii deshō.
Lloyd	Ē, zangyō mo takusan arimasu yo.
Shimada	Doyōbi to nichiyōbi wa yasumi deshō.
Lloyd	Sō desu ga, tokidoki doyōbi mo kaisha ni ikimasu. Shutchō mo arimasu.
Shimada	Tokorode, kono shutchō wa go-gatsu mikka made desu yo ne.
Lloyd	Hai, sō desu.
Shimada	Tsuitachi wa isogashii desu ka.
Lloyd	(*looking at his diary*) Tsuitachi wa doyōbi desu ne. Ē, aite imasu yo. Nanika…?

Shimada   Jitsu wa, sono hi wa kekkon-shiki desu.
Lloyd   Dare no kekkon-shiki desu ka.
Shimada   Boku no desu!!
Lloyd   Ā! Sore wa omedetō gozaimasu!

ni-gatsu *February*	**tokorode** *by the way*
betsu no *another, separate*	**go-gatsu** *May*
de *at, in*	**mikka** *the 3rd (of the month)*
hataraite imasu *I am working* [*from*	**tsuitachi** *the 1st (of the month)*
hataraku]	**aite imasu** *is open, unoccupied*
tantō shite imasu *I'm in charge of*	[*from* **aku,** *to be open, free*]
[*from* **tantō suru**]	**Nanika...** *Is there something...?*
isogashii deshō *You must be busy*	**jitsu wa** *in fact, to tell the truth*
zangyō *overtime work*	**hi** *day*
doyōbi *Saturday*	**kekkon-shiki** *wedding ceremony*
nichiyōbi *Sunday*	**boku** *I, me* [*male, informal*]
yasumi *holiday, day off*	**omedetō gozaimasu**
tokidoki *sometimes*	*congratulations*

Comprehension

1 Does Mr Lloyd work at the weekend?
  (*a*) No, he doesn't.
  (*b*) He works on Saturdays.
  (*c*) Sometimes he works on Saturdays.

2 When is Mr Lloyd leaving Japan?
  (*a*) On the 1st.
  (*b*) On the 3rd.
  (*c*) On Saturday.

Notes

1 *Ni-gatsu* (February)

The words for the months are very straightforward in Japanese, as they do not have special names, but are simply called after the number of the month.

ichi-gatsu	*January*	shichi-gatsu	*July*
ni-gatsu	*February*	hachi-gatsu	*August*
san-gatsu	*March*	ku-gatsu	*September*
shi-gatsu	*April*	jū-gatsu	*October*
go-gatsu	*May*	jū-ichi-gatsu	*November*
roku-gatsu	*June*	jū-ni-gatsu	*December*

The particle **ni** is used when referring to a specific point in time when something happens.

Ikeda san wa **shi-gatsu ni** kono kaisha ni hairimashita.
Ikeda san joined this company in April.

Kaisha no ryokō wa **hachi-gatsu ni** arimasu.
The company trip is in August.

2 *Betsu no ka de* (In a different section)

The particle **de** indicates the place where something happens. (Therefore it is not used with verbs like **imasu** or **arimasu** which only show existence.) It comes directly after the word or phrase showing the location, and can often be translated as *at* or *in*.

Doko **de** kaimono o shimasu ka.
Where do you go shopping?

Yamamoto buchō wa kaigi-shitsu **de** Roido san to hanashite imasu.
Yamamoto buchō is talking to Mr Lloyd in the meeting room.

Ano Shinjuku no sushi-ya **de** aimashō.
Let's meet in that sushi bar in Shinjuku.

3 *Hataraite imasu* (I work)

Some actions which are formed with **-te iru** in Japanese describe situations which are ongoing or routine, and would not be translated as *-ing* forms in English as they are not necessarily happening right at the moment. Some of these verbs are given below.

dictionary form	-masu form	-te form
hataraku (*to work*)	hatarakimasu	hataraite
suku (*to become empty*)	sukimasu	suite
oshieru (*to teach, to tell*)	oshiemasu	oshiete
aku (*to be open, be unoccupied*)	akimasu	aite
tsutomeru (*to be employed*)	tsutomemasu	tsutomete
shiru (*to know, be acquainted*)	shirimasu	shitte

Satō san wa mō kono kaisha ni **tsutomete imasen.**	*Satō san isn't employed at this company any more.*
Kanojo wa, Wajima no shain ni Eigo o **oshiete imasu.**	*She teaches English to the staff at Wajima.*
O-naka ga **suite imasu** ka.	*Are you hungry? (Lit. Is your stomach empty?)*
Watanabe san no denwa bangō o **shitte imasu** ka.	*Do you know Watanabe san's telephone number?*

(Note that a negative reply to this last question is **shirimasen,** *I don't know.*)

4 Ni-gatsu kara māketingu o tantō shite imasu (I've been in charge of marketing since February)

If an action or situation is still continuing even though it began some time ago (*have been -ing* in English), Japanese simply uses the present tense.

| Senshū no getsuyōbi kara totemo isogashii desu. | *I've been really busy since last Monday.* |
| San-gatsu kara Ikeda san to konpyūtā o naratte imasu. | *He's been learning about computers with Ikeda san since March.* |

5 Isogashii deshō (You must be pretty busy)

Deshō comes from **desu** and can have several different shades of meaning depending on how it is used.

(*a*) When it is said with falling intonation, the sentence is a comment on something the speaker is already fairly sure of.

| Nihongo wa muzukashii **deshō.** | *Japanese must be difficult.* |
| Jūgatsu no Kyōto wa kirei **deshō.** | *Kyoto must be beautiful in October.* |

(*b*) When used with rising intonation, it is asking for confirmation.

| Dandō Supōtsu wa Igirisu no kaisha **deshō?** | *Dando Sports is a British company, right?* |
| Ano hito wa kaigai kikaku-bu | *That's the general manager of the* |

no buchō **deshō?**   *Overseas Planning Department,*
                        yes?

(c)   When **deshō** is used with a question word (**dare?**, **doko?**, **nani?** etc.) or with the question marker **ka** at the end of the sentence, it means *I wonder....* It is said with falling intonation.

Koko wa Shinjuku **deshō** ka.	*I wonder if this is Shinjuku.*
Dō shite **deshō.**	*I wonder why.*
Dare **deshō.**	*I wonder who that is.*
Kore wa nan **deshō.**	*Whatever is this, I wonder.*

(d)   When **deshō** replaces **desu** in an ordinary question, it has the result of making the tone of the question very polite.

Shitsurei desu ga, Tanaka san **deshō** ka.	*Excuse me, but would you be Ms Tanaka?*
Sumimasen ga, tsugi wa Ōsaka **deshō** ka.	*Sorry to bother you, but is the next stop Osaka?*

6   *Doyōbi to nichiyōbi* (Saturday and Sunday)

The days of the week are as follows:

getsuyōbi	*Monday*		kinyōbi	*Friday*
kayōbi	*Tuesday*		doyōbi	*Saturday*
suiyōbi	*Wednesday*		nichiyōbi	*Sunday*
mokuyōbi	*Thursday*			

Karate no renshū wa **kinyōbi** desu.	*Karate practice is on Fridays.*
Nagoya shutchō wa raishū no **kayōbi** kara desu.	*My business trip to Nagoya begins next Tuesday.*
Doyōbi ni eiga o mimashō ka.	*Shall we see a movie on Saturday?*

7   *Go-gatsu mikka* (May 3rd)

The names of the days of the month are irregular up to the 10th, so try to learn them by heart.

tsuitachi	1st		muika	6th
futsuka	2nd		nanoka	7th
mikka	3rd		yōka	8th
yokka	4th		kokonoka	9th
itsuka	5th		tōka	10th

After the 10th, they are much more regular, except for the 14th, 20th and 24th.

jū-ichi-nichi	11th	ni-jū-ichi-nichi	21st
jū-ni-nichi	12th	ni-jū-ni-nichi	22nd
jū-san-nichi	13th	ni-jū-san-nichi	23rd
jū-yokka	14th	ni-jū-yokka	24th
jū-go-nichi	15th	ni-jū-go-nichi	25th
jū-roku-nichi	16th	ni-jū-roku-nichi	26th
jū-shichi-nichi	17th	ni-jū-shichi-nichi	27th
jū-hachi-nichi	18th	ni-jū-hachi-nichi	28th
jū-ku-nichi	19th	ni-jū-ku-nichi	29th
hatsuka	20th	san-jū-nichi	30th
		san-jū-ichi-nichi	31st

Hotta san no tanjōbi wa hachigatsu **tōka** desu ne.
Tsuitachi kara **yokka** made Pari ni imashita.

Your birthday is on August 10, isn't it, Hotta san?
We were in Paris from the lst to the 4th.

8 *Nanika* (Something)

When **ka** is added to the end of the question word **nani**, it changes the meaning from *what?* to *something*. **Ka** can also be added to other question words to produce similar changes as follows:

doko	where?	doko**ka**	somewhere, anywhere
nani	what?	nani**ka**	something, anything
dare	who?	dare**ka**	someone, anyone
itsu	when?	itsu**ka**	sometime, anytime

Kaigi-shitsu ni **dareka** imasu ka.
Nanika nomimasu ka.

Is there anyone in the meeting room?
Would you like something to drink?

9 *Boku* (I, me [male, informal])

There are many different ways of saying *I* in Japanese depending on the situation and who you are speaking to, although as we have seen, in many cases it is not necessary to use the equivalent of *I* at all where the meaning is implicit. **Boku**, meaning *I* or *me*, is generally used by small boys, or between men in casual and informal situations.

This is perhaps an appropriate point for a word of warning. It is very tempting for the learner of Japanese to try to use such words as **boku, kun**, etc., in what appear to be suitably informal situations. You may tire of hearing that you are learning 'polite' Japanese and long to use the 'informal' patterns on the mistaken assumption that they will sound more natural and colloquial. Remember that it is all too easy to misjudge the situation, and that informal Japanese sounds anything but natural if used in the wrong place. There are very few situations where it is correct for the foreign visitor to Japan to use it, although it is useful to be able to recognise it.

10 *Boku no desu* (It's mine)

As in English, it is not always necessary to state exactly what it is you are talking about in situations where it is apparent from the context. In the sentence given above, for example, it is obvious in both English and Japanese that it is the wedding that is being talked about.

A Shitsurei desu ga, sono kaban wa **dare no** (kaban) desu ka.

Excuse me, but that briefcase – whose (briefcase) is it?

B **Maeda san no** (kaban) desu.

It's Maeda san's (briefcase).

11 *Omedetō gozaimasu* (Congratulations)

This is a set phrase which can be said on any occasion needing congratulations, such as birthdays, the start of the new year, passing exams, or promotion in the company.

Tanaka san, tanjōbi, **omedetō gozaimasu**!

Tanaka san, happy birthday!

Expansion activities

1 Hotta is still feeling a bit lost and lonely in the big city, and so is asking Noguchi what he does in his free time and where. Look at the train map of Tokyo below, then make up questions and answers like the following example.

Example: kaimono, suru

Hotta Doko de kaimono o shimasu ka.
Noguchi Harajuku de (kaimono o) shimasu.

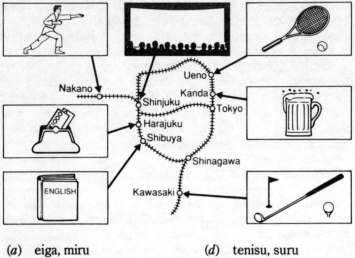

(a) eiga, miru
(b) biiru, nomu
(c) Eigo no benkyō, suru

(d) tenisu, suru
(e) gorufu no renshū, suru
(f) karate no renshū, suru

2 Shimada san is getting busier and busier as his wedding day approaches, so he checks his diary to make sure he hasn't forgotten any important dates such as birthdays. Look at the calendar below and make sentences about the dates he has circled.

Example: o-tōsan, tanjōbi

Shimada san no o-tōsan no tanjōbi wa san-gatsu futsuka desu.

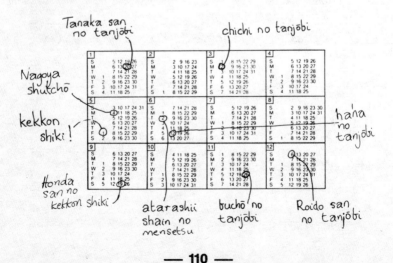

(*a*)	o-kāsan, tanjōbi	(*e*)	Honda san, kekkon-shiki
(*b*)	kekkon-shiki	(*f*)	Nagoya shutchō
(*c*)	Roido san, tanjōbi	(*g*)	atarashii shain, mensetsu
(*d*)	buchō, tanjōbi	(*h*)	Tanaka san, tanjōbi

3   Shimada san is eager to show off his fiancée to Mr Lloyd, and calls him again on Monday morning to see when Mr Lloyd might be free for lunch. Look at their conversation below as Mr Lloyd consults his diary, and then fill in the rest of the engagements in the diary. (Today is the 19th.)

Shimada	Ja, kyō no yotei wa?
Lloyd	Sumimasen, 1-ji kara Wajima de kaigi ga arimasu.
Shimada	Sō desu ka. Ēto, mokuyōbi wa dō desu ka?
Lloyd	Mokuyōbi mo tsugō ga warui desu. 10-ji 15-fun no Shinkansen de Nagoya e ikimasu. Sore ni kinyōbi mo isogashii desu ne. Kyōto ni ikimasu... Ni-jū-shichi-nichi ni Tōkyō e kaerimasu.
Shimada	Ni-jū-shichi-nichi desu ka. Sore wa kayōbi desu ne.
Lloyd	Sō desu ne. Sono hi wa aite imasu yo. Sore kara, suiyōbi mo aite imasu.
Shimada	Sumimasen, kayōbi mo suiyōbi mo isogashii desu. Muzukashii desu ne!
Lloyd	Ā, asatte wa dō desu ka? Watashi wa 2-ji han made aite imasu ga.
Shimada	Ah! Watashi mo aite imasu! Ja, doko de aimashō ka.

APRIL	APRIL
MON 19 (*a*) _____ Dinner with Okamoto san	MON 26 10.30 meeting at Wajima in Nagoya
TUE 20	TUE 27 (*e*) _____
WED 21 (*b*) _____ p.m. meet Tanako san at Honda	WED 28
THUR 22 (*c*) _____	THUR 29 National holiday Greenery day
FRI 23 a.m. ~call London office (*d*) _____	FRI 30 confirm return flight
SAT 24 Sight-seeing in Kyoto	SAT MAY 1 Shimada's wedding!!
SUN 25 Mother's birthday	SUN MAY 2

4 Join the halves of the sentences together with a line to make whole sentences.

(*a*)	Kono densha wa	(*i*)	tantō shite imasu ka.
(*b*)	Raishū no nichiyōbi wa	(*ii*)	shitte imasu ka.
(*c*)	Ano hito no namae o	(*iii*)	suite imasu ne.
(*d*)	Tanaka sensei wa doko no gakkō de	(*iv*)	aite imasu ka.
(*e*)	Maeda san wa ima mo Wajima de	(*v*)	oshiete imasu ka.
(*f*)	Roido san wa nani o	(*vi*)	hataraite imasu ka.

5 Mr Lloyd has just finished another round of talks with the people at Wajima, and though it is still rather early, Yamamoto buchō suggests heading over to Shinjuku for something to eat. Look at the sentences below and put them in the correct order to make a conversation. (The third line of the dialogue has been indicated to help you.)

(*a*) ____	**Lloyd**	Getsuyōbi desu yo.
(*b*) ____	**Lloyd**	Hai, dai-suki desu. Watashi mo tokidoki Rondon de sushi o tabemasu yo.
(*c*) ____	**Lloyd**	Ē, suite imasu.
(*d*) _3_	**Yamamoto**	Anō, Shinjuku ni yuumei-na sushi-ya ga arimasu ga, sushi wa daijōbu desu ka.
(*e*) ____	**Yamamoto**	Aa, getsuyōbi wa yasumi desu. Sono sushi-ya wa aite imasen!
(*f*) ____	**Yamamoto**	O-naka wa suite imasu ka.
(*g*) ____	**Yamamoto**	Ē?! Rondon de?! Sore wa ii desu ne. (*suddenly thinking of something*) Ā! chotto matte kudasai – kyō wa nanyōbi desu ka.

6 Now it's your turn. You have arranged to meet an old friend, Tanaka san, who is on a business trip from Japan. You haven't seen him for quite a while, so there is a lot of news to catch up on. Right now you're talking about work.

You	(*a*) *You must be busy!* _____
Tanaka	Mā, isogashii desu ne.
You	(*b*) *Are you still working in the personnel department?*
	_____
Tanaka	Iie, kaigai kikaku-bu de hataraite imasu. (*your name*) wa? Ima mo māketingu o tantō shite imasu ka.
You	(*c*) *No, I'm employed at a different company now.* _____

Tanaka	Ā, sō desu ka. Doko no kaisha desu ka. Igirisu no kaisha desu ka.
You	*(d)* *No, it's a Japanese company.* _____
	_____
Tanaka	Ōki-na kaisha desu ka.
You	*(e)* *It's still small.* _____
Tanaka	Zangyō wa arimasu ka?
You	*(f)* *There's really a lot! Sometimes I go in to the office on Saturdays, too.* _____
Tanaka	Sore wa taihen desu ne.

Reading corner

Below is a page from the file kept by Ikeda san to record the birthdays of everyone in the office. Practise reading the dates by seeing if you can make sentences about the birthdays. For example, the first one would be:

Hotta san no tanjōbi wa san gatsu-mikka desu.

な まえ 名 前	がっ び 月 日
ほっ た 堀 田	三月　三日
おか もと 岡 本	四月　十日
の ぐち 野 口	六月　十六日
まえ だ 前 田	七月　五日
いけ だ 池 田	九月二十一日
こ やま 小 山	十月　一日
やま だ 山 田	十一月　四日
たけ した 竹 下	十二月二十六日

Business briefing

Working hours

Japan Standard Time is nine hours ahead of GMT, which means that it is difficult for Japanese and British companies to communicate during the course of a normal working day. Nevertheless, when the British business man or woman arrives at work in the morning, it is usually still possible to call a company in Japan and find many of the staff still at their desks, even though it is already early evening there.

Japan has been criticised abroad as a workaholic nation, and despite the efforts of the government to encourage a shorter working week, the Japanese still work longer hours than any other advanced nation. The strong sense of loyalty and belonging that the Japanese feel for the company and their sense of personal involvement in the success of the company mean that they do not simply stop work when the clock says it is time to do so. It is quite usual to work several hours beyond the official end of the working day in order to finish tasks and especially if the boss is also working late. The company man does not want to let his group down and as long as he feels his boss may need him he will stay at the office until late into the evening, even though he may wish to go home and spend more time with his family.

The company provides the essential framework on which the salary-man builds his life, providing him with a network of relationships, support and social life as well as job security. There is not such a clear division between working life and private life as there is in the west. The company man spends a lot of time with his colleagues even outside working hours. He may go drinking with them after work, play mah-jong until late into the night and go on weekend company trips without the family. The pressures to conform to the group consensus are great, and he will rarely risk destroying the consensus by acting independently.

There is some evidence to suggest that things may be changing a little. The young graduates of today are not so eager to commit themselves totally to one company and they are more willing to take risks, and even change jobs. There is a trend towards developing interests and a social life away from the company and being more independent and individual.

However, such changes in attitude will only come about very gradually and it is unlikely that the effect on society at large will be anything other than marginal. There are not likely to be any fundamental changes to the Japanese attitude to work in the near future.

ICHIBAN ŌKI-NA
—— SHIJŌ WA DOITSU ——
DESU

In Lesson 10 you will learn how to make more complex sentences than previously. There is practice with giving reasons, using sentences joined with **kara** (*because*), and qualifying statements with **kedo** (*although, however*). You will also learn how to:

- talk about the frequency with which you do something
- use superlatives (e.g. *biggest, best, highest,* etc.)
- describe your company

—————— The story so far ——————

This afternoon Mr Lloyd is going to make a major presentation to the people at Wajima, but right now he is chatting to Okamoto buchō about his company, Dando Sports, before they go to lunch.

————————— Dialogue —————————

岡本　　イギリスはストライキが多いでしょう。

ロイド　　まあ、時々ストライキがありますけど、ダンドー・スポー

　　　　　ツはストライキをぜんぜんしません。

おかもと
岡本　どうしてですか。

ロイド　たいぐうがいいですから、じゅうぎょういんはストライ

キをしません。きゅうりょうもいいです。

おかもと
岡本　ダンドー・スポーツさんはヨーロッパにゆしゅつしてい

ますね。

ロイド　はい、しています。ドイツがうちの一ばん大きな

しじょうです。

おかもと
岡本　ひがしヨーロツパは?

ロイド　あまり、ゆしゅつしていません。これから、もっととうし

をしますが。

おかもと
岡本　あぁ、そうですか。ダンドー・スポーツさんはほんとう

かいしゃ
にエネルギッシュな会社ですね。

ロイド　ありがとうございます。

Okamoto	Igirisu wa sutoraiki ga ōi deshō.
Lloyd	Mā, tokidoki sutoraiki ga arimasu kedo, Dandō Supōtsu wa sutoraiki o zenzen shimasen.
Okamoto	Dō shite desu ka.
Lloyd	Taigū ga ii desu kara, jūgyōin wa sutoraiki o shimasen. Kyūryō mo ii desu.
Okamoto	Dandō Supōtsu san wa Yōroppa ni yushutsu shite imasu ne.
Lloyd	Hai, shite imasu. Doitsu ga uchi no ichiban ōki-na shijō desu.
Okamoto	Higashi Yōroppa wa?
Lloyd	Amari, yushutsu shite imasen. Kore kara, motto tōshi o shimasu ga.
Okamoto	Ā, sō desu ka. Dandō Supōtsu san wa hontō ni enerugisshu-na kaisha desu ne.
Lloyd	Arigatō gozaimasu.

sutoraiki *strike*	**yushutsu suru** *to export*
ōi *lots of, many*	**Doitsu** *Germany*
mā *well, I think, let me see*	**ichiban ōki-na** *the biggest*
kedo *however, but, although*	**shijō** *market*
zenzen *not at all*	**higashi** *east*
taigū *treatment*	**amari** *not very much, not usually*
kyūryō *salary*	**tōshi** *investment*
kara *since, because*	**enerugisshu-na** *energetic,*
jūgyōin *employees, workers*	*go-ahead*
Yōroppa *Europe*	

Comprehension

1 What does Mr Lloyd say about strikes at Dando Sports?
   (*a*)   There are no strikes, so the employees are treated well.
   (*b*)   The employees are treated well, so there are no strikes.
   (*c*)   There are some strikes, but the employees are treated well.

2 What does Dando Sports plan to do in the future?
   (*a*)   Invest more in Eastern Europe.
   (*b*)   Export more to Germany.
   (*c*)   Make Germany the biggest market.

Notes

1 *Igirisu wa sutoraiki ga ōi deshō* (There are a lot of strikes in Britain, aren't there?)

This construction clearly shows the difference between the job of **wa** (to point out the general topic of a sentence) and that of **ga** (to focus in on the specific subject). In the sentence above, *Britain* is the general topic, about which a specific comment is then made. A literal translation would be *As for Britain, there are a lot of strikes, aren't there?* Some other sentences using this same pattern are shown below.

Watashi **wa** o-naka **ga** sukimashita.	*I'm hungry* (Lit. *As for me, my stomach has become empty*).
Uchi no kaisha **wa**, kinmu jikan **ga** 8-ji han kara desu.	*At our company, working hours are from 8:30.*

There are also certain verbs and adjectives which usually use this **A wa B ga C** pattern, including **wakaru** (*understand, be understandable*), **suki desu** (*like, be liked*), **kirai desu** (*dislike, be disliked*) and **jōzu desu** (*be skilful at*).

Maeda san **wa** Eigo **ga** wakarimasu ka.	*Does Maeda san understand English?* (Lit. *As for Maeda san, is English understandable?*)
Watashi **wa** shutchō **ga** kirai desu.	*I hate business trips* (Lit. *As for me, business trips are detestable*).
Roido san **wa** Nihongo **ga** jōzu desu ne!	*Your Japanese is very good, Mr Lloyd!*

2 Tokidoki sutoraiki ga arimasu kedo,... (Although sometimes there are strikes,...)

Kedo (or its more formal equivalents **keredo** and **keredomo**) can often be translated as *but* or *although* and as such can be used to join two sentences together. It is somewhat similar in usage to **ga** (*but*) described in Lesson 7. Note that **kedo** comes at the end of the first part of the sentence, before the comma, whereas the English equivalent *but* comes after the comma.

Kinō ano hito ni aimashita **kedo**, namae o kikimasen deshita.	*I met him yesterday, but I didn't ask his name.* (Lit. *Although I met him yesterday,...*)
Kyōto wa ii machi desu **kedo**, chotto hito ga ōi desu.	*Kyoto is a nice town, but there are rather a lot of people.*
Ii kaisha desu **kedo**, kyūryō wa yasui desu.	*It's a good company, but the saleries are low.* [Lit. *cheap*]

In general, it is the form of the final verb at the end of a sentence which denotes the level of politeness. It is therefore perfectly acceptable in everyday speech to use the plain form of the verb in the middle of a sentence – for example, in the first part of a sentence when it is followed by **kedo** – as long as the final verb is in the **-masu** form. (In very formal speech, you can continue to use the **-masu** form throughout the sentence.)

Shigoto de tokidoki kaigai
shutchō **suru kedo**,
Yōroppa no kuni wa amari
suki ja arimasen.

*I sometimes go abroad on
business, but I don't like
European countries very much.*

Kinmu jikan wa 9-ji kara 5-ji
made **da kedo**, zangyō ga ōi
desu.

*Although our working hours are
from 9am to 5pm, there's a lot
of overtime.*

In a similar way, **-i** adjectives do not need to be followed by **desu**
when they occur in the middle of a sentence.

Rondon no dairiten wa **chiisai
kedo**, shigoto wa takusan
arimasu.

*Our representative office in
London is only small, but they
have a lot of work.*

Na adjectives need only be followed by **da** (the plain form of **desu**),
although **desu** can be used in more formal situations.

Kono sukejūru wa taihen **da
kedo**, ganbarimashō.

*This schedule is tough, but let's
give it a go.*

The plain form of the negative will be discussed in the next lesson.

3 *Zenzen* (Never, not at all)

Some of the most commonly used adverbs of frequency are shown
below.

itsumo	*always*
yoku	*usually, often*
tokidoki	*sometimes, occasionally*
amari (+ negative)	*not very often, not usually*
zenzen (+ negative)	*never, not at all*

These may come either at the beginning of the phrase or just before
the verb.

Uchi no kaisha wa Amerika
kara **zenzen** yunyū
shimasen.

*We don't import from America at
all.*

Shūmatsu ni **yoku** yama e
ikimasu ka.

*Do you often go to the mountains
at the weekend?*

4 *Taigū ga ii desu kara, jūgyōin wa sutoraiki shimasen* (The workers don't strike because they're treated well)

The word **kara** is used to join two sentences together when one shows the reason for something happening and the other shows the result. In other words, it has a similar function to the English *because* or *so*. Note that **kara** comes at the end of the first part of the sentence showing the reason, before the comma. Remember that you can use the plain form of verbs and adjectives in the middle of a sentence without it sounding rude, as long as the sentence ends with a polite form.

Kyō wa totemo isogashii **kara**, ashita shimashō.	*I'm really busy today, so let's see to it tomorrow.* (Lit. *Because I'm really busy today, let's do it tomorrow.*)
Kare wa ichi-gatsu ni Amerika e iku **kara**, ima Eigo o naratte imasu.	*He's learning English now because he's going to America in January.* (Lit. *Because he's going to America in January...*)

As in English, it is possible to reverse the order of the two sentences, depending on where you want the stress.

Mina san, shigoto o shimashō yo! Shachō ga kimashita **kara**.	*Ok everybody, get on with your work! Because the president has just arrived.*

5 *Ichiban ōki-na shijō* (The biggest market)

To talk about the biggest or best of something is a relatively easy construction in Japanese: simply put **ichiban** before the adjective, which is rather like adding *-est* in English.

Kore ga **ichiban** ii desu yo.	*This one is best.*
Yōroppa de, **ichiban** chiisai kuni wa doko desu ka.	*Which is the smallest country in Europe?*
Fuji-san wa Nihon de **ichiban** takai yama desu ka.	*Is Mt Fuji Japan's highest mountain?*

6 Higashi Yōroppa (Eastern Europe)

The four points of the compass are **kita** (*north*), **minami** (*south*), **higashi** (*east*) and **nishi** (*west*).

Shinjuku eki no **minami**-guchi de aimashō.	*Let's meet at the south exit of Shinjuku station.*
Yōroppa de ichiban **kita** no kuni wa doko desu ka.	*What is Europe's northernmost country?* (Lit. *Where is...?*)

7 Dandō Supōtsu san (The people at Dando Sports)

The courtesy title **san** is often added to a company name when referring to it in the sense of a collection of people, rather than simply the organisation or the building. It may be heard in business meetings or on the telephone when someone is discussing a topic as one company to another, rather than as one individual to another.

Dandō Supōtsu san no kōjō wa doko ni arimasu ka.	*Where are your (Dando Sports') factories?*
Wajima san wa doko kara yunyū shite imasu ka.	*Where do you (Wajima company) import from?*

8 Enerugisshu-na kaisha (An energetic company)

To make an adjective from a **gairaigo** (*non-Japanese*) word, just add **-na. Enerugisshu**, for example, is simply the Japanese pronunciation of the German word *energisch*.

romanchikku-na otoko no hito	*a romantic man*
sekushii-na onna no hito	*a sexy woman*

(As an emergency measure when you are stuck for the right Japanese adjective, use the equivalent English word, said with Japanese pronunciation, and followed by **-na** – it sometimes works!)

Expansion activities

1 The latest craze in Hotta san's company dormitory is to play general knowledge games late into the night. See how many of the questions you can answer.

(a)

Q Nihon de, ichiban takai yama wa dono yama desu ka.
A _____

(b)

Q Igirisu de, haha no hi wa nan-gatsu desu ka.
A _____

(c)

Q Nihon de, ichiban ōkii machi wa doko desu ka.
A _____

(d)

Q Yōroppa no ichiban chiisai kuni wa doko desu ka.
A _____

(e)

Q Nihon de, ichiban hayai densha wa nan desu ka.
A _____

(f)

Q Tōkyō no kokusai kūkō wa doko desu ka.
A _____

---

2 Match the halves of the following sentences, using **kedo** to join them together.

(*a*) Uchi no kaisha wa chiisai

(*b*) Ano hoteru wa takai

(*c*) Nihon no shinbun wa omoshiroi

(*d*) Ano kaisha wa Furansu ni tōshi suru

(*e*) Ano machi wa yūmei da

(*f*) Uchi no kaisha wa zangyō ga ōi

(*g*) Dairiten ga ōi

K E D O

(*i*) omoshiroku arimasen.

(*ii*) amari yomimasen.

(*iii*) totemo enerugisshu desu.

(*iv*) shisha wa amari arimasen.

(*v*) Igirisu ni wa shimasen.

(*vi*) amari yoku arimasen.

(*vii*) yasumi mo ōi desu.

3 Below is Yamamoto buchō's schedule for the past couple of weeks. Make up sentences like the following about his activities.

Example:

Itsuka wa yasumi deshita.
Muika ni Yokohama ni ikimashita.

M 5	T 6	W 7	T 8	F 9	S 10	S 11
yasumi	Yokohama ni iku		Kaigai kikaku-bu no kaigi	Kenkyū sentā		

M 12	T 13	W 14	T 15	F 16	S 17	S 18
	kōjō no jūgyōin no mensetsu o suru	kaigai kikaku-bu no kaigi	Nagoya ni shutchō	Roido san ni au	Satō san no kekkon-shiki ni deru	gorufu o suru

This schedule is very different from his original one, however – he had to re-arrange his appointments several times as new things came up. A colleague is now asking yamamoto buchō about the things he has been doing recently, not knowing about the schedule changes. Using the information from his schedule again, give answers like the one in the example below, using **kara**.

A Getsuyōbi ni Yokohama ni ikimashita ka.
B Iie, getsuyōbi wa yasumi deshita kara, kayōbi ni (Yokohama ni) ikimashita.

(*a*) Mokuyōbi ni kenkyū sentā ni ikimashita ka.
(*b*) Kayōbi ni kaigai kikaku-bu no kaigi o shimashita ka.
(*c*) Kinyōbi ni Nagoya ni shutchō shimashita ka.
(*d*) Doyōbi ni gorufu o shimashita ka.

4 Below is part of an extensive survey made by Wajima comparing Dando Sports to their nearest UK rival, Dell Sporting Goods. Make some more sentences about the two companies like the example given below.

Example:

Dandō Supōtsu no honsha wa Rondon ni arimasu ga, Deru no honsha wa Ribapūru ni arimasu.

	Dando Sports	Dell Sporting Goods
Head office	London	Liverpool
Representative offices	New York, Seoul	Houston, Manila
Factories	Glasgow, Bristol	Derby, Cardiff
Working hours	9:00–6:00	9:00–5:00
Biggest market	Germany	France
Export to USA?	Yes	No

Now make up similar sentences about your own company.

5 Answer the following questions truthfully! Use one of the words in the box in your answers.

itsumo	yoku	tokidoki	amari	zenzen

Example:

Q Tenisu o yoku shimasu ka.
A Iie, zenzen shimasen. /Iie, amari shimasen. /Hai, tokidoki shimasu. / Hai, yoku shimasu. /

(*a*) Biiru o yoku nomimasu ka.
(*b*) Kaisha de tokidoki zangyō shimasu ka.
(*c*) Shisha ni yoku shutchō shimasu ka.
(*d*) Doyōbi to nichiyōbi ni yoku terebi o mimasu ka.
(*e*) Shinbun o yoku yomimasu ka.
(*f*) Tokidoki Nihon ni ikimasu ka.

(g) Nihongo de yoku hanashimasu ka.

(h) Kaisha no jūgyōin wa yoku sutoraiki o shimasu ka.

6 Look at the questions below, and then choose which of the two possible answers is most appropriate.

(a) Dō shite Kyōto ni ikimashita ka.
   (i) Tōkyō ga suki desu kara.
   (ii) Kaigi ga arimashita kara.

(b) Dō shite shain ryokō ni ikimasen deshita ka.
   (i) Enerugisshu-na kaisha deshita kara.
   (ii) Sono hi ni tomodachi no kekkon-shiki ga arimashita kara.

(c) Dō shite doyōbi mo kaisha ni ikimasu ka.
   (i) Totemo isogashii kara.
   (ii) Amari isogashiku arimasen kara.

(d) Dō shite okuremashita ka.
   (i) Kaigi ga arimasen deshita kara.
   (ii) Jiko ga arimashita kara.

(e) Dō shite Nihongo o naratte imasu ka.
   (i) Kore kara Nihon e ryokō ni ikimasu kara.
   (ii) Nihonshu ga suki desu kara.

7 Now it's your turn. You are at a Chamber of Commerce reception in Tokyo and are having a conversation with a Japanese businessman about your respective companies.

Him Shitsurei desu ga, [*your name*] no kaisha no ichiban ōki-na shijō wa doko desu ka.

You (a) *Right now it's France.* _____

_____

Him Nihon wa?

You (b) *Not at all at the moment, but we hope to invest here soon. That's because Japan is a really go-ahead country.* _____

_____

Him Sore wa arigatō gozaimasu! Tokorode, [*your name*] san no kaisha no honsha wa Rondon desu ka.

You (c) *No, it isn't. We have a representative office in London, but the head office is in Liverpool.* _____

_____

Him Ribapūru wa totemo yūmei-na machi desu ne.

You (d) *What? Do you know Liverpool?* _____

_____

Him Hai, Biitoruzu (the Beatles) no machi deshō? Nihon-jin wa ima mo yoku Biitoruzu o kikimasu yo.

You (e) *Really. In Britain we don't listen to them much any
more.* _____

📖 ——————— Reading corner ———————

Hotta san realises that there are still a few questions remaining
which he should be able to answer before he goes into the Dando
Sports presentation, so he notes down the questions and goes off to
ask Noguchi.

💼 ——————— Business briefing ———————

Trade unions in Japan

While strikes in Japan are not unknown, industrial relations between
Japanese employers and employees are generally less contentious
than those of their European counterparts. Japanese unions tend
to be established on a company-by-company basis, and the union
negotiates pay settlements with management at prescribed times of
the year, the principal period being that of **shunto**, the *spring wages
offensive*, in April. This is where union representatives sit down with
company bosses and members of the personnel department to dis-

cuss working conditions, salary levels and the size of the annual bonuses. Bargaining can last several weeks. In sectors where redundancies are likely, the company and union will work together on diversification programmes in order to avoid the mass laying-off of workers. When strikes do occur, they are generally of very short duration and are organised to cause as little disruption as possible. Train strikes, for example, tend to be between midnight and 5:00 a.m. so as not to inconvenience commuters. In other words, strike action tends to be symbolic rather than a way of getting results in itself.

In all, it is estimated that there are over 35,000 unions in Japan. This reflects the single-union policy common to many Japanese industrial sectors, and is one of the tenets of Japanese industry which is often so difficult to export to other countries, particularly to Western Europe. Japanese unions are less powerful in general than their counterparts overseas. One of the main reasons for this is historical. At the time of the Korean War, unions became dominated by communist and socialist activities and, as a result, union activities were viewed with deep suspicion by the Washington administration of the time. General Douglas MacArthur organised an anti-communist purge which effectively removed the left from union activities, stunting union growth. The legacy of these moves is a Japan where the union has a relatively close association with the management structure of the company and where labour relations are perhaps less divisive than the traditional 'us' and 'them' relationship which exists between unions and management in the west.

DAI 11 KA

BIIRU WA DŌ DESU KA

This lesson concentrates on some more uses of the plain form of verbs in everyday speech. You will also learn how to:

- introduce yourself
- make adverbs from adjectives
- count cylindrical objects, using the counter **-hon**

—————— The story so far ——————

Yamamoto buchō, of Wajima Trading, has introduced Mr Lloyd to one of their distributors, Ishikawa san. After a long and fruitful meeting, Ishikawa san invited everyone at the meeting for drinks and something to eat at a bar in Shinjuku. They have just arrived at the bar.

—————— Dialogue ——————

石川　ロイドさん、こちらへどうぞ。
ロイド　あぁ、どうも。

石川　ビールにしましょうか。(*to waiter*) ビールを五本下さい。

(*The waiter brings the beer.*) ロイドさん、ビールはどうですか。

ロイド　(*holding his glass to be filled*) はい、いただきます。

石川　じゃ、みなさん、今日は、本当におつかれさまでした。かんぱい！

みんな　かんぱい！

石川　ロイドさん、日本へようこそ。何か一ことおねがいします。

ロイド　じこしょうかいのことですか。でも、まだ、わたしの日本ごはじょうずじゃないんですけど...。

石川　だいじょうぶですよ。かんたんに、どうぞ。

ロイド　イギリスのダンドー・スポーツのリチャード・ロイドです。かいがいマーケティングをたんとうしています。これから、いろいろおせわになります。どうぞ、よろしくおねがいします。

石川　どうも、ありがとうございます。ロイドさんは、いつまで日本にいますか。

ロイド　五月三日までです。ちょっと、みじかいですけど...

石川　かんこうの時間はありますか。

ロイド　あまり、ないんですけど、にっこうへ行くつもりです。

石川　それはいいですね。

Ishikawa　Roido san, kochira e dōzo.
Lloyd　Ā, dōmo.
Ishikawa　Biiru ni shimashō ka. (*to waiter*) Biiru o go-hon kudasai.
　　　　　(*The waiter brings the beer*)
　　　　　Roido san, biiru wa dō desu ka.

Lloyd	(*holding his glass to be filled*) Hai, itadakimasu.
Ishikawa	Ja, mina san, kyō wa, hontō ni o-tsukare sama deshita. Kanpai!
Minna	Kanpai!
Ishikawa	Roido san, Nihon e yōkoso. Nanika hitokoto onegai shimasu.
Lloyd	Jiko shōkai no koto desu ka. Demo, mada, watashi no Nihongo wa jōzu ja nai n' desu kedo...
Ishikawa	Daijōbu desu yo. Kantan ni, dōzo.
Lloyd	Igirisu no Dandō Supōtsu no Richādo Roido desu. Kaigai māketingu o tantō shite imasu. Kore kara, iroiro o-sewa ni narimasu. Dōzo yoroshiku onegai shimasu.
Ishikawa	Dōmo arigatō gozaimashita. Roido san wa, itsu made Nihon ni imasu ka.
Lloyd	Go-gatsu mikka made desu. Chotto, mijikai desu kedo...
Ishikawa	Kankō no jikan wa arimasu ka.
Lloyd	Amari, nai n' desu kedo, Nikkō e iku tsumori desu.
Ishikawa	Sore wa ii desu ne.

---

kochira *this way*
...ni shimashō ka *shall we have...?*
go-hon *five (bottles)*
itadakimasu *thank you* [when receiving something]
kanpai *Cheers!*
Nihon e yōkoso *Welcome to Japan*
hitokoto *a word (or two)*
jiko shōkai *self-introduction*

ja nai n' desu *isn't* [from **desu**]
kantan ni *simply, briefly*
iroiro o-sewa ni narimasu *We look forward to your support*
mijikai *short*
aru n' desu ka *do you have?*
nai n' desu *don't have* [from **aru**]
Nikkō *a city north of Tokyo*
tsumori desu *intend to*

Comprehension

1 Why is Mr Lloyd hesitant to do a self-introduction?
   (*a*) Because he doesn't know what to say.
   (*b*) Because he's so tired.
   (*c*) Because he thinks his Japanese is not very good.

2 Will Mr Lloyd have any time for sightseeing while he is in Japan?
   (*a*) No.
   (*b*) Only a little.
   (*c*) Only on the 3rd.

Notes

1 Kochira (This way)

This is another in the **ko-, so-, a-, do-** series. The others are **sochira** *that way*, **achira** *that way over there*, and **dochira** *which way?*

Shitsurei desu ga, kaigai kikaku-shitsu wa **dochira** desu ka.	*Excuse me, which way is the Overseas Planning Office?*
Shachō no heya wa **kochira** desu.	*The president's office is this way.*

These words can also be used as polite substitutes for **koko, soko, asoko** and **doko**, and when referring to people.

Kochira wa Yamada san desu.	*This is Ms Yamada.*

2 Biiru ni shimashō ka (Shall we have beer?)

The phrase **(noun) ni suru** means *to have, to decide on* and so is often used when making decisions, such as what to order in a restaurant or when to do something.

Nani ni **shimashō** ka.	*What shall we have?*
Dandō Supōtsu san to no kaigi wa getsuyōbi ni **shimasu.**	*We've decided to hold the meeting with Dando Sports on Monday.*
Tsugi no jinji-bu no ryokō wa Kyōto ni **shimashita.**	*We decided on Kyoto for the next Personnel Department trip.*

3 Biiru o go-hon (Five bottles of beer)

There are many special words used in Japanese for counting different kinds of things. Although this also happens in English (*a bar of chocolate, a piece of pie, a sheet of paper, a slice of cake*, etc.) there are far more counters in Japanese, and we shall be coming across several of them in the next few lessons. The counter used for long, cylindrical objects such as pencils, bottles of beer, cigarettes and cans of juice is **-hon**. (Beer is generally sold in bottles in Japanese bars, so this is a useful counter to know if you plan on going out for a drink.) Note that there are some phonetic changes to the **-hon** ending which are best learned by heart.

ip-pon	*one*	rop-pon	*six*
ni-hon	*two*	nana-hon	*seven*
san-bon	*three*	hap-pon	*eight*
yon-hon	*four*	kyu-hon	*nine*
go-hon	*five*	jip-pon	*ten*

Biiru o mō **ip-pon** kudasai.   *Another (bottle of) beer, please.*
Noguchi kun no pātii de,   *We drank two bottles of whisky at*
  uisukii o **ni-hon**   *Noguchi's party!*
  nomimashita yo!

Note that in Japanese the counter comes after the noun.

4 *Hai, itadakimasu* (Yes, thank you, I'd like some)

Itadakimasu is a verb meaning *to receive*, but the subject of the verb must always be the speaker or someone from the speaker's group, so in fact it can be thought of as meaning *I receive* or *we receive*. It is a very polite way of saying *Thank you very much, I accept*, especially when your host or hostess offers you something to eat or drink.

The other common usage of **itadakimasu** as a set phrase is before beginning a meal. In this case it is similar in usage to *Bon appétit*, except that it is said much more frequently. At the end of a meal, the set phrase is **gochisō sama deshita**, the equivalent of *Thank you for the meal*.

5 *Kantan ni* (Simply, briefly)

We have already come across several adverbs in Japanese, and some which, although not true adverbs, translate into English as such (**mada**, *yet*, **motto**, *more*, **takusan**, *a lot*, **tokidoki**, *sometimes*, etc.). It is also possible to turn adjectives into adverbs, as in English. With **-i** adjectives, this is done by replacing the final **-i** with **-ku**.

Adjective		Adverb	
hayai	*fast*	hayaku	*quickly*
ii, yoi	*good*	yoku	*well, often*
isogashii	*busy*	isogashiku	*busily*
kuwashii	*detailed*	kuwashiku	*minutely, in detail*
mijikai	*short*	mijikaku	*briefly*

Watanabe san wa **yoku** benkyō shimasu ne.	*Watanabe san studies hard, doesn't she?*		

Watanabe san wa **yoku** benkyō shimasu ne.
Watanabe san studies hard, doesn't she?

Kyō wa **hayaku** kaerimasu kara, yoroshiku o-negai shimasu.
I'm going home early today, so please just carry on the good work.

Mō chotto **kuwashiku** kaite kudasai.
Write it out in a little more detail, please.

With **-na** adjectives, simply replace the **-na** with **ni**.

kantan-na	*simple, brief*	kantan ni	*simply, briefly*
kirei-na	*pretty, clean*	kirei ni	*prettily, cleanly*
shinsetsu-na	*kind*	shinsetsu ni	*kindly*
shizuka-na	*quiet*	shizuka ni	*quietly*
jōzu-na	*skilful*	jōzu ni	*skilfully*

Jikan ga arimasen kara, shijō no repōto o **kantan ni** setsumei shite kudasai.
We don't have much time, so could you explain the market report briefly, please?

Sono heya de ima kaigi o shite imasu kara, **shizuka ni** hanashite kudasai.
They're having a meeting in that room, so could you speak quietly, please?

6 *Jiko shōkai* (Self-introduction)

It is very common at gatherings in Japan where not everyone knows each other for every person to give a brief self-introduction. Most Japanese business people define themselves in terms of the company they work for, rather than the job they do. Hence they will say *I work for Bloggs Plumbing*, rather than *I am a plumber*. The information given in a self-introduction is in the opposite order from its English equivalent; that is, the largest, most general group is given first (the name of the company, for example), with the most specific information – your name – given last. Therefore Yoko Tanaka, of the Overseas Planning Department at the Nagoya branch of Wajima, might introduce herself as **Nagoya shisha no kaigai kikaku-bu no Tanaka Yoko desu** (*Nagoya-branch's Overseas-Planning-Department's Yoko Tanaka*).

7 *Ja nai* (Isn't)

As has been mentioned previously, the plain, or dictionary, form of the verb is generally considered to be too abrupt to use at the end of a sentence in everyday polite conversation, except between very close friends or family members. However, the plain form is commonly used in the middle of sentences and in various set phrases which we practise in the next few lessons.

You have already come across the positive forms (e.g. **iku, taberu, miru**) which have been given each time a new verb has been introduced. Each of these has a separate negative form.

In the boxes below, the first column shows the dictionary form, the second column shows the plain negative and the third contains the meaning.

For the verbs which drop **-ru** from the dictionary form, simply add **-nai** to the basic stem.

oshie-ru	oshie-**nai**	*doesn't teach*
shirabe-ru	shirabe-**nai**	*doesn't investigate*
tabe-ru	tabe-**nai**	*doesn't eat*
i-ru	i-**nai**	*isn't in*
mi-ru	mi-**nai**	*doesn't see*

For the verbs which drop **-u** from the basic stem, add **-anai**. If the basic stem ends in a vowel, add **-wanai**.

ik-u	ik-**anai**	*doesn't go*
yom-u	yom-**anai**	*doesn't read*
hanas-u	hanas-**anai**	*doesn't speak*
nara-u	nara-**wanai**	*doesn't learn*
a-u	a-**wanai**	*doesn't meet*

The irregular verbs are:

kuru	konai	*doesn't come*
suru	shinai	*doesn't do*
aru	nai	*there isn't*

Watashi wa Eigo ga **wakaranai** kara, Nihongo de setsumei shite kudasai.	*I don't understand English, so could you explain in Japanese?*
Biiru wa amari **nomanai** kedo, uisukii wa dai-suki desu.	*I don't drink much beer, but I really like whisky.*

Uchi no kaisha wa minami Amerika ni wa yushutsu shite **inai** kedo, Afurika ni wa shite imasu.	*We aren't exporting to South America, but we are to Africa.*

The negative of **-i** adjectives is formed in the same way, with the final **-ku arimasen** changing to **-ku nai**.

Ano kaisha no taigū wa **yoku nai** kara, jūgyōin wa yoku sutoraiki o shimasu.	*The workers at that company often go on strike because the working conditions aren't good.*

The plain form of **desu** is **da**, and the negative is **ja nai** or **dewa nai**.

Watashi wa tantō-sha **ja nai** kara, buchō ni kiite kudasai.	*I'm not in charge of that, so please ask the buchō.*

8 *Jōzu ja nai n' desu* (I'm not very good so...)

Although the basic meaning of a sentence does not change by the addition of **no desu** (often abbreviated to **n' desu**) nevertheless it does give a slightly different nuance from the simple addition of **desu**.

N' desu is most commonly seen in sentences which indicate an explanation for something which was said or done, or when asking for an explanation. For example, someone may ask **Omoshiroi desu ka**, simply to get factual information about the book you are reading. However, if they ask **Omoshiroi n' desu ka**, they are probably asking to see if that is the explanation for your being deeply engrossed in the book or having spent a lot of money on the book or having gone to a lot of trouble to borrow it. The addition of **n' desu** can also imply slightly more emphasis than just **desu**. **N' desu** can follow the plain form of a verb, an **-i** adjective or a **-na** adjective, and is pronounced almost as if it is joined on to the previous word (e.g. **Omoshiroi-n desu ka**).

A	Konai **n' desu** ka. Dō shite?	*You're not coming? Why not?*
B	Chotto tsugō ga warui **n' desu**.	*It's a bit inconvenient.*
A	Zannen desu ne.	*That's a pity.*

9 *Iroiro o-sewa ni narimasu* (We look forward to your support)

The word **sewa** by itself means *help, assistance*, but when it is used in the set phrase **iroiro o-sewa ni narimasu,** the speaker is anticipating a situation where help will be requested and will be forthcoming, so it is a kind of thanks in advance. If someone has been very good to you and has helped you in many ways, **Iroiro o-sewa ni narimashita** is a courteous way of thanking them for their assistance. It is very often used in speeches, introductions and formal greetings between potential business partners.

10 *Nikkō*

The town of Nikkō is a very popular tourist destination. It is about 140 kilometres north of Tokyo, and can be reached in under two hours by train. It is famous not only for its many beautiful old buildings, including the stunning Toshogu shrine, but also for the beauty of the surrounding countryside, with mountains, forests, a lake and Kegon Waterfall.

11 *Iku tsumori desu* (Intend to go)

When **tsumori desu** follows the plain form of a verb, it means *have the intention of doing, intend to do.*

Ashita nani o suru **tsumori desu** ka.	*What do you plan on doing tomorrow?*
Kyō wa, zangyō wa shinai **tsumori desu.**	*I don't intend to do any overtime today.*
Senshū Kyōto ni iku **tsumori deshita** ga, kekkyoku ikimasen deshita.	*I intended to go to Kyoto last week, but in the end I didn't go.*

✅ ——————— Expansion activities ———————

1 The crossword on page 137 gives practice with the plain form of some of the verbs you have come across so far. Notice that some of the clues are in the positive, and some in the negative.

ACROSS

4 *get tired*
5 *be employed*
7 *don't understand*
11 *doesn't finish*
12 *isn't here*
14 *don't drink*
15 *doesn't come*
16 *doesn't wait*
17 *there isn't*
18 *doesn't do*
19 *teach*

DOWN

1 *go home*
2 *send*
3 *don't eat*
4 *doesn't arrive*
6 *doesn't listen*
8 *don't meet*
9 *don't read*
10 *don't learn*
13 *don't go*

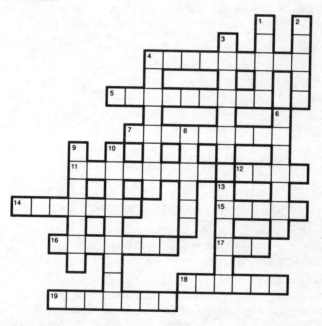

2 Read through the following mini dialogue, with a partner if possible. After two or three readings, see if you can say it without looking at the book.

A **Ashita no pātii ni iku** n' desu ka.
B Iie, **ikanai** n' desu.
A **Ikanai** n' desu ka.
B Ee, **kaigi ga aru** kara.
A Zannen desu ne.

Now make similar dialogues by replacing the words in bold, where necessary, with the following cues.

(*a*)   Nikkō e iku; jikan ga nai

(*b*)   Tanaka san wa kuru; yotei ga aru

(*c*)   buchō wa ashita no kaigi ni deru; shutchō ga aru

(*d*)   kyō wa hayaku kaeru; zangyō ga takusan aru

3   Nagai san, of the Tōyō Matsumoto Bank, has invited you and several other people out for something to eat this evening. As most of you don't know each other, he decides that self-introductions would be a good idea, and begins by introducing himself.

Mina san, konbanwa. Tōyō Matsumoto Ginkō no jinji-bu no Nagai Jirō desu. Dōzo yoroshiku o-negai shimasu.

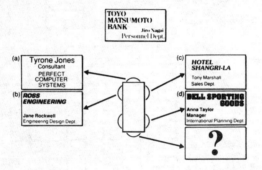

How would the others at the table introduce themselves? How would you introduce yourself?

4   Look at the pictures below, and make up sentences like the one in the example, using the words which accompany each picture.

Example:

Shizuka ni hanashimashita.

If you need help, use the cues following the pictures, but note that they are not in the same order as the pictures.

jiko shōkai o suru	kaigi-shitsu o katazukeru
Nihongo o hanasu	repōto o kaku
kaisha ni tsuku	uchi ni kaeru

5 Below are two separate dialogues which have been mixed together. One is between a waiter and a customer, and the other is between two people having a drink. See if you can separate the two. You may find it helps to write the dialogues out again below.

A	Kochira e dōzo.	*or*	Menyū o kudasai.
B	Hai, dōzo.	*or*	Ā, dōmo.
A	Biiru o kudasai.	*or*	Biiru wa dō desu ka.
B	Hai, itadakimasu.	*or*	Nan-bon desu ka.
A	Ip-pon onegai shimasu. Sore kara, supagetti (*spaghetti*) o kudasai.	*or*	Ja, kanpai shimashō.
B	Hai, wakarimashita.	*or*	Kanpai!

Dialogue 1

A Kochira e dōzo.
B _____
A _____
B _____
A _____
B Kanpai!

Dialogue 2

A Menyū o kudasai.
B _____
A _____
B _____
A _____
B _____

6 Now it's your turn. You are in a Japanese restaurant where you are entertaining a group of visiting Japanese businessmen, led by Tanaka san.

You   (*a*) *Tanaka san, please come this way.* _____

_____

Tanaka	Ā, dōmo.
You	(b) *Shall we have some beer?* _____
Tanaka	Ē, sore wa ii desu ne.
You	(c) (*to the waiter*) *Six beers, please.* _____
	(d) (*to Tanaka san*) *How long will be you be in Britain?*
	_____
Tanaka	Shichi-gatsu tōka made desu. Chotto mijikai desu kedo.
You	(e) *Will you have any time for sightseeing?* _____
Tanaka	Amari nai n' desu kedo, Okkusufōdo (*Oxford*) e iku tsumori desu.
You	(f) *That's nice. (The beer arrives) Would you like some beer?* _____
Tanaka	Ā, itadakimasu.
You	(g) *Well, everyone, welcome to Britain. Cheers!* _____
	_____
Everyone	Kanpai!
You	(h) (*looking at the menu*) *Well, what shall we have?* _
	_____

📖 ──────── Reading corner ────────

Below is part of a typical coffee shop menu. As most of the drinks and snacks served in coffee shops in Japan are called by their original western names, they are written in **katakana** characters. See if you can work out what the items on the menu are. (Even those of you who have not been learning **katakana** should be able to work these out if you refer to the **katakana** chart at the beginning of Lesson 1!)

```
◆◇◆◇◆◇◆◇◆◇◆◇◆◇◆◇◆◇◆◇◆◇◆◇◆◇◆◇◆
                  コーヒーショップ　リン

  ── ★ソフト・ドリンク★ ──      ── ★ジュース★ ──
  ブレンドコーヒー ……… 600    オレンジジュース ……… 700
  カフェオレ …………… 750    グレープフルーツジュース …… 700
  レモンティー ………… 680    トマトジュース ………… 650
  ミルクティー ………… 680    コーラ ………………… 580
  ミルク ……………… 600    クリームソーダ ……… 650
  ココア ……………… 750

◆◇◆◇◆◇◆◇◆◇◆◇◆◇◆◇◆◇◆◇◆◇◆◇◆◇◆◇◆
```

🧳 ─────────── **Business briefing** ───────

Drinking

Alcohol plays a very important part in lubricating the wheels of business in Japan and in offsetting the stresses and strains of business life and long working hours. The stereotypical Japanese office worker is a man who has a long and crowded commute each day, who stays late at the office each evening, who takes few holidays and who is totally dedicated to his company. Although this picture may be exaggerated, there is more than a grain of truth in it. Such a man, however, is also human and needs some release from this constant pressure. He very often finds it in going out with his colleagues after work for a few drinks.

It is very common after work for the men, and sometimes the women, of an office to stop off at one of the many drinking places that cluster around the main commuter stations, and more often than not several of them will go on to a second or third place before returning home slightly the worse for wear. Going out for a drink after work with colleagues is not only about drinking, however. Its purpose is also to strengthen group cohesion and consciousness. It allows for an atmosphere of relaxation and lowered barriers in which anything can be discussed, most commonly work, and for seniors and juniors to mix together in an unstressful environment. In fact, even non-drinkers will go along if the boss suggests a quick drink after work precisely because of this opportunity to relax together and to strengthen the bonds between the group members.

Japanese drinking etiquette also encourages the sense of cohesiveness within the group. Generally everyone drinks the same drink – at the beginning of the evening it will be beer, later on many people will change to sake and by the end of the evening some will be finishing things off with whisky. Beer, sake and whisky are all served by the bottle rather than by the glass, so they are all drinks to be shared by the group, rather than to be ordered individually. Etiquette also demands than you never pour your own drink, but that you always watch out for your fellow drinkers and make sure that their glasses are full. In other words, you are always at the service of your colleagues.

This continual filling up of glasses, however, can also mean drinking somewhat more than was originally intended. The Japanese are traditionally rather permissive of drunkenness, which tends to manifest itself in silly jokes, loud voices and an urge to sing traditional songs, rather than violent or aggressive behaviour. Nevertheless, if you find yourself thinking that you really shouldn't have any more to drink, the trick is not to drain the glass (which protocol would demand needs to be filled again by colleagues immediately), but to leave it full, and just take tiny sips occasionally. In this way, there is just a chance you may be able to remain sober.

DAI 12 KA

DŌ SHITA N'
DESU KA

In Lesson 12 you will find more practice with the plain form of verbs, but this time when talking about things that happened in the past. There is practice with the past form of adjectives too. In this lesson you will also learn how to:

● count people
● talk about two things happening at once, using **toki**
● talk about the weather

From this lesson on, **The Story So Far** is in Japanese rather than English. It is given first in Japanese script, and then in romanised Japanese. You will find a translation in the Answer Key at the back of the book, but try reading **The Story So Far** together with the dialogue once or twice to see if you can get an idea of the meaning before looking at the translation.

——— The story so far ———

きのう、ロイドさんは、ともだちの島田さんと二人でにっこうへ
行きました。今日は山本部長と会議があるから輪島に来ました。
部長は、今ロイドさんに、にっこうでのことをきいています。

Kinō, Roido san wa, tomodachi no Shimada san to futari de Nikkō e ikimashita. Kyō wa, Yamamoto buchō to kaigi ga aru kara, Wajima ni kimashita. Buchō wa, ima Roido san ni Nikkō de no koto o kiite imasu.

Dialogue

山本 けっきょく、にっこうへ行ったんですか。

ロイド えぇ、ともだちの島田さんと二人で行きました。
たいへんたのしかったです。

山本 てんきはどうでしたか。ちょっとさむかったでしょう。

ロイド いいえ、そんなにさむくなかったです。にっこうに
ついた時、あめがふっていましたが、そのあといいてんき
でした。

山本 どこが一ばんよかったですか。

ロイド とうしょうぐうがとてもよかったです。それから、
けごんのたきがたいへんきれいでした。

山本 しゃしんをたくさんとりましたか。

ロイド えぇ、三本もとったんですが、ぜんぶだめにしました。

山本 どうしたんですか。

ロイド けごんのたきのしゃしんをとっていた時、ころびまし
た。そして、フィルムを川におとしました‥‥‥

山本 (laughing) それはざんねんでした。

ロイド 本当にばかなことをしました!!

Yamamoto	Kekkyoku Nikkō e itta n' desu ka.
Lloyd	Ē, tomodachi no Shimada san to futari de ikimashita. Taihen tanoshikatta desu.
Yamamoto	Tenki wa dō deshita ka. Chotto samukatta deshō.
Lloyd	Iie, sonna ni samuku nakatta desu. Nikkō ni tsuita toki, ame ga futte imashita ga, sono ato ii tenki deshita.
Yamamoto	Doko ga ichiban yokatta desu ka.
Lloyd	Tōshōgū ga totemo yokatta desu. Sore kara, Kegon no taki ga taihen kirei deshita.
Yamamoto	Shashin o takusan torimashita ka.
Lloyd	Ē, san-bon mo totta n' desu ga zenbu dame ni shimashita.
Yamamoto	Dō shita n' desu ka.
Lloyd	Kegon no taki no shashin o totte ita toki, korobimashita. Soshite, fuirumu o kawa ni otoshimashita…
Yamamoto	(*laughing*) Sore wa zannen deshita.
Lloyd	Hontō ni baka-na koto o shimashita!

---

tomodachi *friend*
to *with*
futari de *the two of us, two people*
itta *went [from **iku**]*
taihen tanoshikatta *was very enjoyable [from **tanoshii**]*
samukatta *was cold [from **samui**, cold]*
sonna ni *that much, to that extent*
samuku nakatta *wasn't cold [from **samui**]*
tsuita *arrived [from **tsuku**]*
toki *a time, the time when…*
ame *rain*
futte ita *was falling [from **furu**, to fall, come down]*
sono ato *after that*
yokatta *was good [from **ii/yoi**]*
Tōshōgū *(name of Nikko's most famous shrine)*
Kegon no taki *Kegon waterfall*

shashin *photograph*
torimashita *took [from **toru**, to take]*
san-bon *three (rolls of film)*
totta *took [from **toru**]*
zenbu *all, the whole lot*
dame *no good, useless*
dame ni shimashita *ruined, spoiled*
Dō shita n' desu ka *What happened?*
totte ita toki *when I was taking [from **toru**]*
korobimashita *fell over [from **korobu**, to fall over]*
soshite *and, then*
fuirumu *film (for a camera)*
kawa *river*
otoshimashita *dropped [from **otosu**, to drop, let fall]*
baka-na *stupid, foolish*

✓ Comprehension

1 How was the weather in Nikko?

(*a*) Cold but sunny.
(*b*) Raining.
(*c*) Good, except for a little rain.

2 Did Mr Lloyd take many photographs?
(*a*) Yes, they came out very well.
(*b*) Yes, but he spoilt some of them.
(*c*) Yes, but he ruined all of them.

Notes

1 *Tomodachi no Shimada* (Shimada, a friend)

Note this new use of **no** to give more information about someone.

A Dochira **no** Tanaka san?   *Which Tanaka san?*
B Sensei **no** Tanaka san.   *Tanaka san, the teacher.*

2 *Futari* (Two people)

The counter for people is **-nin**, although the words for *one person* and *two people* are irregular, as you can see below.

hitori	*one person*	roku-**nin**	*six people*
futari	*two people*	shichi-**nin**	*seven people*
san-**nin**	*three people*	hachi-**nin**	*eight people*
yo-**nin**	*four people*	kyū-**nin**	*nine people*
go-**nin**	*five people*	jū-**nin**	*ten people*

A Kinō no mensetsu ni   *How many people altogether came*
   zenbu de **nan-nin**   *to yesterday's interview?*
   kimashita ka.
B Zenbu de **kyū-nin**   *Altogether nine people came. Four*
   kimashita. Otoko no hito   *men and five women.*
   ga **yo-nin**, onna no hito
   ga **go-nin** kimashita.

3 *Itta* (Went)

The plain form of the past tense is entirely regular and straight-forward to form: simply replace the final **-te** of the **-te** form with **-ta**.

dictionary form	-te form	plain past	meaning
iku	itte	itta	*went*
otosu	otoshite	otoshita	*dropped*
toru	totte	totta	*took*
kiku	kiite	kiita	*heard, asked*
tsuku	tsuite	tsuita	*arrived*
nomu	nonde	nonda	*drank*
kau	katte	katta	*bought*
iru	ite	ita	*was in*
suru	shite	shita	*did*
kuru	kite	kita	*came*

It has already been mentioned several times that the plain form of the verb is considered a little too abrupt by itself for everyday polite conversation. However, you will notice from several of the examples given in the rest of this section that the plain form becomes quite acceptable when followed by **n' desu**, even when it is used at the end of a sentence.

Kinō atarashii kamera o **katta n' desu.**	*I bought a new camera yesterday.*
Sono kaisha ni takusan tōshi o **shita n' desu** ga, dame deshita.	*We invested a lot of money in that company, but it didn't work out.*

The plain negative of the past tense is based on the plain negative of the present tense. All that it is necessary is to replace the negative ending **-nai** with **-nakatta**.

iku	ika-nai	ika-**nakatta**	*didn't go*
taberu	tabe-nai	tabe-**nakatta**	*didn't eat*
kuru	ko-nai	ko-**nakatta**	*didn't come*
suru	shi-nai	shi-**nakatta**	*didn't do*
toru	tora-nai	tora-**nakatta**	*didn't take*
au	awa-nai	awa-**nakatta**	*didn't meet*
aru	nai	**nakatta**	*there wasn't*

Jikan ga **nakatta** kara, tomodachi no Shimada san ni **awanakatta** n' desu.	*I didn't meet my friend, Shimada san, because I didn't have the time.*
Densha ga zenzen **konakatta** kara, kekkyoku takushii de ikimashita.	*No trains came at all, so in the end we went by taxi.*

The plain past forms of **desu** are **datta** and **ja nakatta**.

A Kinō no mensetsu wa dō **datta** n' desu ka.

How was the interview yesterday?

B Kinō **ja nakatta** n' desu. Suiyōbi **datta** n' desu.

It wasn't yesterday. It was Wednesday.

The plain past tense of the **-te iru** form of verbs (which shows what is happening at the moment or what was happening at a particular moment in the past) is quite straightforward: **-te iru** becomes **-te ita**, and the negative **-te inai** becomes **-te inakatta**.

Watashi wa sore o tantō shi**te inakatta** kara, yoku wakarimasen.

I wasn't in charge of that, so I don't really know.

Itsu kara itsu made Tōkyō ni sun**de ita** n' desu ka?

When were you living in Tokyo? (Lit. From when to when...)

4 *Tanoshikatta* (Was enjoyable)

As has been mentioned before, **-i** adjectives are very similar to verbs, and in fact they have their own past tense. This is formed by replacing the final **-i** with **-katta**.

present	past	meaning
taka-i	taka-**katta**	was high, expensive
samu-i	samu-**katta**	was cold
atsu-i	atsu-**katta**	was hot
haya-i	haya-**katta**	was early
tsuyo-i	tsuyo-**katta**	was strong
ii, yo-i	yo-**katta**	was good

Nihon e no shutchō wa **mijikakatta** kedo, taihen **tanoshikatta** desu.

My business trip to Japan was only short, but it was extremely enjoyable.

Wāpuro o kau tsumori deshita ga, **takakatta** kara kaimasen deshita.

I was going to buy a word processor, but they were really expensive so I didn't.

Samukatta kara, uchi ni imashita.

It was cold, so I stayed at home (Lit. ... so I was at home).

The negative is formed in the same way as verbs – replace the final **nai** of the negative form with **nakatta**.

present	past	meaning
samuku nai	samuku **nakatta**	*wasn't cold*
atsuku nai	atsuku **nakatta**	*wasn't hot*
yoku nai	yoku **nakatta**	*wasn't good*
ōkiku nai	ōkiku **nakatta**	*wasn't big*
waruku nai	waruku **nakatta**	*wasn't bad*
tsuyoku nai	tsuyoku **nakatta**	*wasn't strong*

Senshū wa **isogashiku nakatta** kara, zangyō ga arimasen deshita.

We weren't busy last week, so there wasn't any overtime.

Kyūryō wa **waruku nakatta** kedo, shigoto wa omoshiroku arimasen deshita.

The salary wasn't bad, but the work wasn't interesting.

-**Na** adjectives do not change their form at all. They are simply followed by the past forms of **desu** rather than the present forms.

Yoku benkyō shita kedo, **dame datta** n' desu.

I studied hard, but it was no good.

Asoko wa **shizuka ja nakatta** kara, betsu no pabu ni ikimashita.

It wasn't quiet there, so we went to another pub.

5 Tenki wa dō deshita ka (How was the weather?)

The weather is as common a topic of small talk and greeting in Japan as it is in Britain, and consequently there are as many set phrases to describe or comment on the weather. Some of the most common are given below.

Kyō wa atsui desu ne!	*It's hot today, isn't it!*
mushiatsui	*humid*
atatakai	*warm*
suzushii	*cool*
samui	*cold*
Ii tenki desu ne.	*Nice weather, isn't it.*
Warui tenki desu ne.	*Bad weather, isn't it.*
Ame ga futte imasu.	*It's raining.*
Yuki ga furimashita.	*It snowed.*
Kaze ga tsuyoi desu ne.	*It's windy, isn't it? (Lit. The wind is strong.)*

6 *Sonna ni samuku nakatta* (Not that cold)

Sonna is from another of the **-ko, -so, -a, -do** group of words.
Konna ni means *this much, to this extent,* **sonna ni** and **anna ni**
mean *that much, to that extent,* and **donna ni** means *to what extent?*

Watashi wa **sonna ni** baka ja arimasen yo.	*I'm not that stupid!*
Konna ni takusan shashin o torimashita yo.	*I took this many photos.*

7 *Nikkō ni tsuita toki* (When we arrived in Nikko)

The word **toki** by itself means *time,* but depending on how it is used,
it can also mean *at the time when.* Thus **gakkō no toki** means *when I
was at school,* **daigaku no toki** means *when I was at university,* and
kodomo no toki means *when I was a child.*

Daigaku no toki, Eigo to Furansugo o naraimashita.	*When I was at university, I learned English and French.*
Kodomo no toki, yoku yama e ikimashita.	*When I was a child, we often went to the mountains.*

If **toki** comes after the plain form of the verb, it indicates the time
when something happened or is happening.

Sochira ni **tsuita toki,** tenki wa dō deshita ka.	*When you got there, how was the weather?*
Rondon de **hataraite ita toki,** doko ni sunde imashita ka.	*When you were working in London, where did you live? (Lit. ...were you living?)*

8 *Dame ni shimashita* (I ruined them)

When **suru** comes after the adverbial form of an adjective (for
example, **ōkiku** or **kirei ni**) it can be thought of as the equivalent of
the English *make something bigger/cleaner/simpler,* etc.

Rajio o **chiisaku shite** kudasai.	*Could you turn down the radio, please? (Lit. make [the sound] smaller)*
Heya o **kirei ni shimashō.**	*Let's clean the room up.*

Kenkyū repōto o mō chotto
kantan ni shite kudasai.

*Could you simplify the research
report a little?*

Expansion activities

1 The crossword below gives practice with the plain past form of
some of the verbs you have come across so far. Notice that some
of the clues are in the positive and some in the negative.

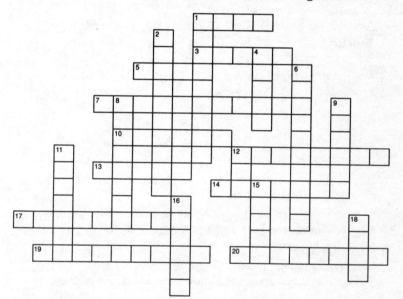

ACROSS		DOWN	
1	*saw*	1	*didn't see*
3	*drank*	2	*didn't do*
5	*came*	4	*was*
7	*didn't take*	6	*didn't go*
10	*finished*	8	*dropped*
12	*wasn't, didn't exist*	9	*went in*
13	*did*	11	*understood*
14	*there wasn't*	12	*was, existed*
17	*worked*	15	*bought*
19	*talked*	16	*went home*
20	*began*	18	*there was*

2 Below is a map showing how the weather was in Japan yesterday. Using the key to the weather symbols, describe the weather in different parts of the country. (Once you know the meaning of the symbols, do this exercise again without referring to the key.)

Example: (Sapporo) Sapporo wa, yuki ga furimashita.

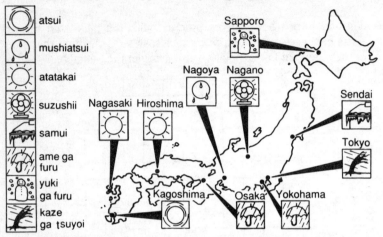

How is the weather where you are today? How was it yesterday? How do you think it will be tomorrow?

3 Look at the situations described below about things which are too long, too small, too loud and so on. How would you ask someone to change the situation?

Example: Someone has a radio turned up very loud.
         Sumimasen ga, mō chotto chiisaku shite kudasai.

(*a*) You have received a report which is much too long, so you would like it made shorter.

(*b*) The meeting room has been left very untidy, so you would like it tidied up.

(*c*) Everyone is making far too much noise.

(*d*) You have been presented with some diagrams which are much too complicated.

(*e*) The illustrations in your company's new catalogue are much too small.

(*f*) The prices for some of your company's products have been set much too low.

4 Dando Sports is looking for a Japanese person to work in its London office, so Mr Lloyd is taking the opportunity while he is in

Japan of interviewing a few prospective candidates. Try to reconstruct some of the facts about one of the candidates from the notes below which Mr Lloyd took during the interview. (Use **toki**.)

Example:

(*child – lived in Scotland*) Kodomo no toki, Sukottorando ni sunde imashita.

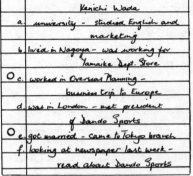

	Kenichi Wada
a	university – studied English and marketing
b	lived in Nagoya – was working for Yamaike Dept. Store
○ c	worked in Overseas Planning – business trip to Europe
d	was in London – met president of Dando Sports
○ e	got married – came to Tokyo branch
f	looking at newspaper last week – read about Dando Sports

5 Noguchi is having a drink with Hotta san, and is telling him about his recent trip abroad during the New Year holiday. See if you can complete their conversation by putting in the correct form of the adjectives shown in brackets.

Hotta Doko ga ichiban (ii) desu ka.

Noguchi Hawaii ga ichiban (ii) desu yo.

Hotta Tenki wa dō deshita ka. (atsui) deshō.

Noguchi Iie, sonna ni (atsui) desu. (suzushii) desu yo.

Hotta Hawaii no doko ga ichiban (ii) desu ka.

Noguchi Mā, Waikiki ga ichiban (tanoshii) desu ne. Amerika no onna no hito ni atta n' desu ga.

Hotta (kawaii) desu ka.

Noguchi (kawaii) n' desu ga, chotto…

Hotta Dō shita n' desu ka.

Noguchi Jitsu wa, kanojo no kamera de, kanojo no shashin o totte ita toki, kamera o otoshita n' desu.

Hotta Kamera wa (daijōbu) deshita ka.

Noguchi Iie, (dame) ni shimashita. (atarashii) kamera o katta n' desu ga, totemo (takai) desu yo.

Hotta Sore wa (taihen) deshita ne.

Noguchi Ē, hontō ni (baka) koto o shimashita ne.

6 Now it's your turn. You are just back from a business trip to Europe, and a Japanese acquaintance is asking you about it.

Him	Yōroppa shutchō wa dō deshita ka.
You	(a) *Well, I was busy, but it was really fascinating.* _____

Him	Tenki wa dō deshita ka. Samukatta deshō.
You	(b) *No, it wasn't that cold. When I arrived in Paris it was raining, but after that the weather was good.* _____

Him	Kankō no jikan wa arimashita ka.
You	(c) *When I was in Rome, I had about three hours.* _____

Him	Sore wa mijikakatta desu ne! Doko ga ichiban yokatta desu ka.
You	(d) *Switzerland (Suisu) was nice. It was a bit expensive, but the mountains were really beautiful.* _____

Him	Shashin o takusan torimashita ka.
You	(e) *I didn't have time, so I didn't take any at all.* _____

Him	Sore wa zannen deshita.

Reading corner

Watanabe san went to Hawaii during the New Year holiday too. Here's one of the postcards she sent to the people back at the office.

じんじ部の みなさん
あけんきですか
POSTCARD
わたしは きのう だいがくの時の ともだちと 三人で ハワイに 来ました。 くうこうに ついた時、 あめが たくさん ふっていたん ですが、 今は とても いい てんきです。 今日 これから ワイキキ に 行くつもりです。 きんよう日 に 日本に かえり ます。 会社は げつよう日から 行きます。
では よろしく おねがいします。
渡辺 けい子

Business briefing

When to visit Japan on business

The development of a good business relationship with a Japanese company depends a great deal on frequent visits to Japan. This is because personal friendships characterise every good partnership be-

tween Japanese and foreign concerns: the ties need constant nurtur-
ing and attention. Not only this, Japan is a fast-changing society with
a market thirsty for innovation and excitement, so it is important to
keep abreast of these changes. No amount of research outside Japan
will give you as much of an insight as a visit there yourself, backed
up by preparatory study and reading.

But when to go? There are a number of national holidays, when
businesses and government offices are closed. The New Year vaca-
tion (December 29th–January 3rd), **O-bon**, the *Festival of the Ancestors*
(approximately August 13th–16th) and Golden Week (April 29th–May
5th) are particularly bad times to visit Japan for business purposes
not only because few offices are operating, but because the whole
country is on the move at these times, travelling back to the family
home or to holiday resorts.

The weather is also a consideration. The end of March and the
months of April and May are pleasant times to visit Japan, particularly
when the cherry trees are in full bloom. It is at this time that you may
be invited to join in a cherry-blossom-viewing party, complete with
snacks (such as **sushi** and **o-senbei** rice crackers), alcohol (beer and
sake), and probably a **karaoke** unit – an invitation not to be turned
down!

June is rainy and not a good time for travelling around unless you are
happy to carry an umbrella with you at all times and don't mind damp
feet. July is humid, with low cloud cover concealing the top of sky-
scrapers, and a heavy atmosphere, although air-conditioning is uni-
versal in large city underground stations, offices and taxis, so it is
still possible to get things done without too much discomfort.

The summer heat peaks in early August and is dispersed eventually
by typhoons in late September. The aftermath of the typhoons leaves
the Japanese islands dry and balmy, so this is an ideal time to visit.
Autumn is also extremely pleasant, with the trees providing beautiful
displays of red, orange and yellow foliage at the end of October and
through into November. The winter, which runs from December to
the beginning of March on the main island of Honshu, is crisp, cold
and sunny, and provides a welcome change for those more accustomed to cold, wet British winters! Snow can be expected on the
Japan Sea side of the country which faces Siberia, but the Pacific side
remains relatively snow-free, with only the occasional snowfall in
Tokyo in mid-February, the coldest time of the year in the Japanese
archipelago.

Japanese National Holidays

January 1st	New Year's Day
January 15th	Adults' Day
February 11th	National Foundation Day
March 21st (or 20th)	Vernal Equinox Day
April 29th	Greenery Day
May 3rd	Constitution Memorial Day
May 5th	Children's Day
September 15th	Respect for the Aged Day
September 23rd (24th)	Autumnal Equinox Day
October 10th	Health Sports Day
November 3rd	Culture Day
November 23rd	Labour Thanksgiving Day
December 23rd	Emperor's Birthday

DAI 13 KA

SONNA NI
ISOGANAIDE
KUDASAI YO

In Lesson 13, you will learn how to:

- ask someone *not* to do something
- use prepositions (*on top of, under, after, in front of*, etc.)
- use the **-te** form of verbs to join sentences together
- explain the reason for something using **no de** (*because*)

The story so far

今日はどよう日ですが、ロイドさんは月よう日にイギリスへ

かえるので、山本部長とミーティングをしています。

きのうのばん、二人はあかさかのバーに行って、たくさんのみ

ました。そのあと、ホテルの上のバーに行って、また、たくさん

のみました。だからロイドさんは、今日はすこしきぶんがわるい

です。

Kyō wa doyōbi desu ga, Roido san wa getsuyōbi ni Igirisu e kaeru no
de, Yamamoto buchō to miitingu o shite imasu. Kinō no ban, futari wa
Akasaka no bā ni itte, takusan nomimashita. Sono ato, hoteru no ue

no bā ni itte, mata, takusan nomimashita. Dakara Roido san wa, kyō wa sukoshi kibun ga warui desu.

Dialogue

山本 きぶんはどうですか。コーヒーでものみますか。

ロイド はい、おねがいします。山本さんはおさけがつよいですね！

山本 えぇ、まぁ、よくのみますから！コーヒーをどうぞ。

ロイド ありがとうございます。

山本 じゃ、これからのスケジュールをかくにんしましょうか。

ロイド はい、そうですね。らいしゅうのすいよう日にきかく部で会議があります。その時、輪島さんのしじょうレポートをせつめいして、はんばいスケジュールをつくるつもりです。

山本 はい。

ロイド そのスケジュールを今月の(looking at his diary)...そうですね... １７日までに輪島さんにおくります。

山本 ちょっとまって！そんなにいそがないで下さいよ。その前に、輪島の中でもミーティングをするので、もうすこし時間がかかります。

ロイド そうですね、すみません！山本さんは今月のおわりにイギリスへ来ますから、その時に、もっとくわしく

しょうひんの話^{はなし}ができますね。

山本^{やまもと}　そうですね。

Yamamoto	Kibun wa dō desu ka. Kōhii demo nomimasu ka.
Lloyd	Hai, onegai shimasu. Yamamoto san wa o-sake ga tsuyoi desu ne!
Yamamoto	Ē, mā, yoku nomimasu kara! Kōhii o dōzo.
Lloyd	Arigatō gozaimasu.
Yamamoto	Ja, kore kara no sukejūru o kakunin shimashō ka.
Lloyd	Hai, sō desu ne. Raishū no suiyōbi ni kikaku-bu de kaigi ga arimasu. Sono toki, Wajima san no shijō repōto o setsumei shite, hanbai sukejūru o tsukuru tsumori desu.
Yamamoto	Hai.
Lloyd	Sono sukejūru o kongetsu no (*looking at his diary*)... sō desu ne...17-nichi made ni Wajima san ni okurimasu.
Yamamoto	Chotto matte! Sonna ni isoganaide kudasai yo. Sono mae ni, Wajima no naka de mo, miitingu o suru no de, mō sukoshi jikan ga kakarimasu.
Lloyd	Sō desu ne, sumimasen! Yamamoto san wa kongetsu no owari ni Igirisu e kimasu kara, sono toki ni, motto kuwashiku shōhin no hanashi ga dekimasu ne.
Yamamoto	Sō desu ne.

no de *since, because*	**kakunin shimashō ka** *Shall we confirm...?* [from **kakunin suru,** *to confirm*]
miitingu *meeting*	
ban *evening, night*	**hanbai** *selling, marketing*
Akasaka *entertainment area of Tokyo*	**tsukuru** *to make, manufacture*
bā *bar*	**kongetsu** *this month*
hoteru no ue *at the top of the hotel*	**made ni** *by, not later than*
ue *top, upper part*	**isoganaide** *don't hurry* [from **isogu**]
mata *again, once more*	**mae** *before, in front of*
dakara *so, therefore, consequently*	**naka** *within, inside*
sukoshi *a little, a small quantity*	**owari** *end, finish*
kibun *feeling, mood*	**shōhin** *goods, merchandise*
o-sake *sake, alcoholic drinks*	**dekimasu** *can do* [from **dekiru** *can, be able to do, or to be done, be completed*]
ē, mā, *yes, well...*	

Comprehension

1 What will Mr Lloyd be doing next Wednesday?
 (*a*) Returning to Britain.
 (*b*) Discussing the sales schedule.
 (*c*) Sending the sales schedule to Wajima.

2 Why does Yamamoto buchō need more time?
 (*a*) Because he's going to have a meeting within Wajima.
 (*b*) Because he doesn't feel well.
 (*c*) Because he has to go to Britain.

Notes

1 No de (So, since)

No de can mean *so*, *since* or *because* and is used to express a reason or cause for something. It comes at the end of the first part of the sentence which shows the reason, and can follow the plain form of a verb, an **-i** adjective, a **-na** adjective (with **datta** instead of **-na** if in the past tense) or a noun with **-na** (or with **datta** if in the past tense).

Mō sukoshi jikan ga kakaru **no de**, mō chotto matte kudasai.	*It will take a little more time, so could you wait a bit longer please?*
Tōkyō no hachi-gatsu wa mushiatsui **no de**, amari suki ja arimasen.	*I don't like August in Tokyo because it's so humid.*
Mokuyōbi wa shutchō na **no de**, miitingu wa suiyōbi ni shimashō.	*I'm away on a business trip on Thursday, so let's have the meeting on Wednesday.*

No de is rather similar in meaning to **kara** (*because, so*), although it is not so strong and somewhat softer in tone. However, it is not used in the case of requests, suggestions, guesses or opinions. In the following sentences, therefore, only **kara** can be used.

Mō osoi **kara**, kaerimashō ka.	*It's late, so shall we go home?* (suggestion)
Roido san wa Nihongo o hanasu **kara**, daijōbu deshō.	*Mr Lloyd speaks Japanese so it should be all right.* (opinion)

2 Akasaka no bā ni itte, takusan nomimashita (They went to a bar in Akasaka, and drank a lot)

One of the main uses of the **-te** form of verbs is to join sentences together. It usually corresponds to the English *and*, although there may be other translations depending on the context. (Note that the word **to** also means *and*, but can only be used to join lists of nouns together e.g. **konpyūtā to wāpuro to kamera**, *computers and word processors and cameras*.)

Hanbai sukejūru o kakunin **shite**, mitsumori o tsukurimashō.	*Let's confirm the sales schedule, and do the estimate.*
Doyōbi no ban, Shinjuku ni **itte**, eiga demo mimashō ka?	*On Saturday evening, shall we go to Shinjuku and see a movie or something?*

The **-te** form can be used more than once in one sentence.

Suitchi o 'on' ni **shite**, furoppii o **irete**, entā kii o oshite kudasai.	*Switch it on, put in the floppy disk and press the 'Enter' key.*

In the case of **desu**, the corresponding **-te** form is **de**.

Shachō no okusan wa daigaku no sensei **de**, Doitsugo o oshiete imasu.	*The president's wife is a university lecturer and she teaches German.*
Ano bā wa shizuka **de**, ii desu.	*That bar is quiet and nice.*

The tone and tense of a sentence is decided by the form of the verb at the end, so the **-te** form can be used in the middle of a sentence regardless of whether it has a past, present or future meaning.

Ano kaisha no shigoto wa taihen **de**, kyūryō mo amari yoku nakatta n' desu.	*At that company the work was tough and the salary wasn't very good.*
Satō buchō ni denwa **shite**, shimekiri o kiite kudasai.	*Please call Satō buchō and ask him about the deadline.*

3 *Hoteru no ue* (At the top of the hotel)

In English, words which show the location of something (prepositions) come before the word they are referring to, for example *on the desk, under the desk, inside the desk*, etc. However, in Japanese they come after the word, joined to it by **no**, so a literal translation is something like *the desk's top, the desk's underneath, the desk's inside*, etc. Some of the most common prepositions are given below.

tsukue no ue	*above, on the desk*
tsukue no shita	*under, below the desk*
tsukue no naka	*in, inside the desk*
tsukue no mae	*in front of the desk*
tsukue no yoko	*by the side of the desk*
tsukue to konpyūtā no aida	*between the desk and the computer*
biru no ushiro	*behind the building*
biru no tonari	*next to the building*
biru no soba	*near the building*

Kinō no ban, yuki **no ue** de korobimashita.
I fell over on the snow yesterday evening.

Eki **no mae** de aimashō.
Let's meet in front of the station.

Hotta san wa, Ikeda san to Noguchi san **no aida** ni suwatte imasu.
Hotta san sits between Ikeda san and Noguchi san.

4 *O-sake ga tsuyoi desu ne* (You can certainly take your drink! [*Lit.* With regard to sake, you're strong])

Being able to drink a lot and still remain in control of one's actions is considered a trait to be admired in Japan, therefore this phrase should be regarded as a compliment. If a Japanese person says this to you, some suitably modest responses are:

Sonna ni tsuyoku arimasen yo. *I'm not really that strong.*
Sō demo nai desu yo. *No, that's not so.*
Ē...mā... *Yes, well...*

5 *Kongetsu* (This month)

The prefixes **sen-** (*last*), **kon-** (*this*) and **rai-** (*next*) are often used with time expressions like the following.

sengetsu	*last month*	**sen**shū	*last week*
kongetsu	*this month*	**kon**shū	*this week*
raigetsu	*next month*	**rai**shū	*next week*

Unfortunately the words referring to years (**nen**) do not all follow this pattern. They are **kyonen** (*last year*), **kotoshi** (*this year*) and **rainen** (*next year*).

> **Raigetsu** kara kinmu jikan o
> mijikaku shimasu.
> *From next month we'll be making the working hours shorter.*
>
> **Raishū** mata denwa shimasu.
> *I'll call again next week.*
>
> **Kotoshi** no owari ni ima no
> gārufurendo to kekkon
> shimasu.
> *I'm marrying my girlfriend at the end of this year.*

6 17-nichi made ni (By the 17th)

Made ni indicates the end of a time limit for a certain action, so it corresponds to the English *by*.

> Kinyōbi **made ni** kikaku-bu no
> atarashii kikaku mitsumori o
> kaite kudasai.
> *Please could you write the Planning Department's new planning estimate by Friday.*
>
> 5-ji han **made ni** kaerimasu.
> *I'll be back by 5:30.*

Remember that if you are talking about a continuous action going on over a period of time, you should use **made** (*until*), and not **made ni**, which only refers to something happening at a particular point in time.

> 5-ji **made** kaigi o shite imasu.
> *I'll be in a meeting until 5:00.*
>
> Kyonen no 10-gatsu **made**,
> Maeda san no okusan mo
> koko de hataraite imashita.
> *Until October of last year, Maeda san's wife worked here too.*
>
> Go-nen mae **made**, Ōsaka ni
> sunde imashita.
> *I lived in Osaka until five years ago.*

7 Isoganaide kudasai (Not so fast)

The **-naide** ending is the negative of the **-te** ending of verbs. Therefore if you want to ask someone *not* to do something, you can use the verb ending **-naide kudasai**.

Sonna ni hayaku hanasa**naide** **kudasai**.   *Please don't talk so quickly.*

Kaigi ni okure**naide kudasai**.   *Don't be late for the meeting, please.*

In very informal situations (when talking to close friends or children, for example) or when you want to make the request sound more like an order, you can leave off the final **kudasai**.

Tsukue no ue ni suwara**naide**.   *Don't sit on the desk.*

In Note 2 above we saw how the -**te** form can be used to join two sentences together. As the -**naide** form is also a kind of -**te** form, this too can be used to join sentences. In this case it means *without -ing*.

Ikeda san wa asa tabe**naide**, kaisha e ikimasu.   *Ikeda san goes to work in the morning without eating anything.*

Depāto e itte, kamera o kau tsumori deshita ga, kekkyoku kawa**naide** kaerimashita.   *I went to the department store intending to buy a camera, but in the end I came home without buying one.*

8 *Itsu made ni dekimasu ka* (When will you be able to do it by?)

The verb **dekimasu** means *to be able to, to be possible, can do*. The thing you are talking about which is possible, or which can be done, is shown by **ga**, and the person who can do it, if mentioned, is indicated by **wa**. With **dekimasu** it is not always necessary to specify the exact verb or action which can be done if this is obvious from context, hence in the following examples it includes the meanings *can do* and *can speak*.

Raishū no kinyōbi made ni, mitsumori ga **dekimasu** ka.   *Will you be able to do the estimate by next Friday?*

Sumimasen ga, Eigo ga **dekimasu** ka.   *Excuse me, can you speak English?*

Roido san wa Nihongo de jiko shōkai ga **dekimashita**.   *Mr Lloyd was able to do his self-introduction in Japanese.*

✔ —— Expansion activities ——

1. Below are some signs that ask you not to do something. What do they mean? Give the meanings in Japanese.

    Example:

    Minaide kudasai.

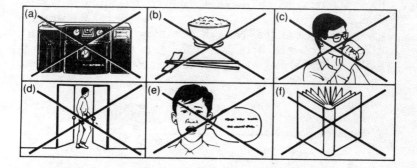

2. Shimada san's wedding went off smoothly and everyone had a good time at the reception, although several of the guests are now a little the worse for wear after consuming rather a lot of beer. They have just gathered outside the wedding hall for some final photographs. Read the description below, and try to identify who is who in the photograph.

Roido san wa kekkon-shiki de takusan nonde, kibun ga totemo
ii no de, kuruma no ue ni suwatte imasu. Kuruma no mae ni
Maekawa san to Maekawa san no okusan ga imasu. Kuruma no
ushiro de Honda san to Toyota san wa mada biiru o nonde imasu.
Kuruma no naka ni Shimada san ga ite, tonari ni okusan ga
suwatte imasu. Kuruma no soba ni wa, Shimada san no mae no
gaarufurendo no Katō san to Satō san ga imasu. Katō san to Satō
san no aida ni, Shimada san no hen-na tomodachi no Itō san ga
imasu. Kuruma no shita ni Shimada san no inu no 'Jūpitā' (*Jupiter*)
ga imasu.

3 Early this morning the cleaners at Wajima decided to give the
   desks a good clean and they cleared everything from Ikeda san's
   desk in order to do so. As the top drawer had been left open, they
   gave that a clean too. Now they're trying to put things back
   exactly where they were before. Look at the picture of Ikeda
   san's desk below and then complete their conversation. (The first
   one has been done for you.)

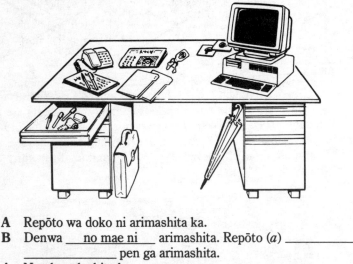

A Repōto wa doko ni arimashita ka.
B Denwa ___no mae ni___ arimashita. Repōto (*a*) _____
   _____ pen ga arimashita.
A Nan-bon deshita ka.
B Ni-hon. Shinbun wa denwa (*b*) _____ atte, shinbun
   (*c*) _____ fairu ga arimashita.
A Ā, sō deshita ne. Wāpuro wa doko ni arimashita ka.
B Wāpuro desu ka. Ēto...wāpuro wa fairu (*d*) _____
   _____ arimashita. Sore kara wāpuro (*e*) _____
   _____, furoppi ga arimashita.

A Kono kagi wa shinbun to furoppi (*f*) _____ arimashita ne.

B Ē, sō desu.

A Tsukue (*g*) _____ nanika arimashita ka.

B Ē, pen ga san-bon to fuirumu ga ni-hon arimashita.

A Kaban wa?

B Kaban wa tsukue (*h*) _____ atte, kaban (*i*) _____ _____ kasa ga ip-pon arimashita.

4 Yamamoto buchō has made a list of the various tasks that need to be done over the next few days, and intends to tell everyone at today's meeting what he wants each of them to do. Look at the list, and decide what he will say to them.

Example:

Ueda san, shijō repōto no shimekiri o shirabete, konpyūtā ni irete kudasai.

```
┌─────────────────────────────────────────────────────────────┐
│ Shōhin hanbai miitingu                                        │
│                                                               │
│ shijō repōto no shimekiri o shiraberu      Ueda               │
│ konpyūtā ni ireru                    Ueda                     │
│ shachō ni denwa o suru, kaigi no hi no tsugō o kiku  Okamoto  │
│ minna no yotei o kiku, tsugō o kakunin suru  Maeda            │
│ miitingu no sukejūru o tsukuru   Maeda                        │
│ shōhin hanbai no dēta o shiraberu   Noguchi                   │
│ mitsumori o tsukuru     Noguchi                               │
│ atarashii shōhin no shorui no kopii o toru   Ikeda            │
│ Nagoya shisha ni fakkusu o okuru   Ikeda                      │
│ kaigi no repōto o kaku, buchō ni miseru   Hotta               │
│ repōto no kopii o totte, fairu ni ireru   Koyama              │
└─────────────────────────────────────────────────────────────┘
```

5 Complete the sentences below (all of which use **no de**) by choosing which of the two endings is most appropriate.

(*a*) Kibun ga warukatta no de,
   (*i*) mō uchi e kaerimashita.
   (*ii*) mō pātii e kaerimashita.

(*b*) Ano heya de kaigi o shite iru no de,
   (*i*) denaide kudasai.
   (*ii*) hairanaide kudasai.

(*c*) Ashita wa isogashii no de,
   (*i*) kinō aimashō.
   (*ii*) asatte aimashō.

(*d*) Eigo ga dekinai no de,
   (*i*) raishū kara narau tsumori desu.
   (*ii*) raishū kara narawanai tsumori desu.

(e) Yoku wakaranai no de,
   (i)   motto kawaiku setsumei shite kudasai.
   (ii) motto kuwashiku setsumei shite kudasai.
(f) Watashi no uchi wa eki no soba na no de,
   (i)   zenzen shizuka ja arimasen.
   (ii) zenzen shinsetsu ja arimasen.
(g) Ashita wa shimekiri na no de,
   (i)   konban zangyō shimasu.
   (ii) kyō wa isogashiku arimasen.
(h) Buchō no okusan wa raishū kara Yōroppa ni ryokō suru no de,
   (i)   ōki-na kaban ni kawarimashita.
   (ii) ōki-na kaban o kaimashita.

6 Now it's your turn. You have just arrived at the office of a regular client and friend, Satō san, in order to discuss a sales schedule, including providing estimates and setting deadlines. However, you're not feeling too good, because you were out drinking until late last night.

Satō Kōhii demo nomimasu ka.
You   (a) *Yes, please.* _____
Satō Dō shimashita ka. Kibun ga warui desu ka.
You   (b) *Yes, a bit. To tell the truth, yesterday evening I drank quite a lot with a friend. That's why I don't feel well today.*

_____

Satō Demo, [your name] san wa o-sake ga tsuyoi deshō.
You   (c) *Not really that much.* _____
Satō Doko de nonda n' desu ka.
You   (d) *We drank a lot at a sushi bar in Shinjuku, and after that we went back to my hotel, and drank some more at the bar at the top of the hotel.* _____

_____

Satō Hontō ni takusan nonda n' desu ne! Daijōbu desu ka. Hanbai sukejūru no hanashi wa dekimasu ka.
You   (e) *Yes, yes, I can. Let me see... We had a meeting at our company last Thursday, and talked about the deadline.* _____

_____

Satō Ē? Mo shimekiri no hanashi o shite iru n' desu ka.
You   (f) *Yes, we'll send you the estimate by the 28th of this month, so could you look at it, and make the sales plan?* _____

Satō	Chotto matte! Sonna ni isoganaide kudasai yo. Sono mae ni, Nagoya shisha de mo sono mitsumori o kakunin shimasu kara, mō sukoshi jikan ga kakarimasu yo.
You	(g) *Oh, yes, sorry. Our president will be coming to Japan at the end of this month, so we could discuss things in more detail then.*
Satō	Sō desu ne. Ja, kōhii o dōzo.

📖 ——— Reading corner ———

Below is a hand-written memo that Okamoto buchō wants Koyama san to type up and distribute for him. Read the memo and see if you can answer the questions that follow.

> 小山さん、 タイプ おねがい
>
> 5月18日 (かようび) に、 なごやししゃ
> の かいがいきかく 部と 本社の かいがい
> きかく部の あいだで 会議が あります。
> 時間は、 3時はん から 6時ごろまでの
> よていです。
> 会議は、本社の じんじ部の となりの
> へやでします。
> さとう 社長も でますから
> おくれないで 下さい。
> くわしいことは きかく部の 岡本まで。

(a) When is the meeting?
(b) Which staff will be attending the meeting?
(c) What time is the meeting?
(d) Where will it be held?
(e) What should the recipients of the memo do if they have any questions about the meeting?

Business briefing

Consensus decision-making and ringisho

New ideas and proposals in a Japanese company are subject to a rigorous and formal system of scrutiny, evaluation, modification and improvement using a document designed to gather group approval known as a **ringisho**. When a proposal needs to be written, the first draft will be shown to the immediate boss, perhaps the **kakarichō**, or assistant manager, if the proposal is being written by an ordinary staff member. If the **kakarichō** decides that the idea has potential, he will invite the person to formulate a concrete proposal, which will be a cleaned-up, revised version to be presented at a section meeting for comment and evaluation from colleagues.

At the section meeting, some people may be quite aggressive about the new idea, and ask questions about whether the proposal is really needed or can be afforded, for example. The proposer has to defend his idea, while at the same time taking note of the comments from the others. The proposal will seldom pass this acid test first time, so it will usually enter a period of correction and rewriting. The next time a section meeting is convened, the new-look proposal is resubmitted and undergoes the same close scrutiny as before. This time people are checking to see whether their comments or suggestions for improvement have been incorporated. Invariably this process is repeated several times until everyone is satisfied that the proposal is in the best form that it can be. Once the section has given its agreement, the proposer and the **kakarichō** can take the document, the **ringishō**, for evaluation and ratification by the **kachō**, or section manager. The **kachō** can veto the idea or ask for changes.

After making the changes, and obtaining the **kachō's** name stamp on the **ringisho** to show his approval, the proposer and **kakarichō** take the document to the **buchō**, or general manager. If the **buchō** likes it, he will approve it by adding his name stamp to the document. The proposal will then become policy.

This process takes quite some time, which is why non-Japanese companies often feel that Japanese companies are slow to reach a decision. It may take time, but most would agree that once made, decisions are swiftly implemented. The quality of decisions is also high because they contain input from everyone who needs to be involved in this decision-making process.

DŌ OMOIMASU KA

In Lesson 14, you will learn how to relate what other people have said, and to explain what you think about something. There will also be more practice with counting and large numbers, and with the use of several adjectives together (including colours) to describe something.

The story so far

<ruby>山本部長<rt>やまもとぶちょう</rt></ruby>と<ruby>岡本課長<rt>おかもとかちょう</rt></ruby>はイギリスへいっしゅうかんしゅっちょうして、おといかえりました。イギリスでは、まいにちダンドー・スポーツの<ruby>本社<rt>ほんしゃ</rt></ruby>に<ruby>行<rt>い</rt></ruby>って、<ruby>会議<rt>かいぎ</rt></ruby>をしました。<ruby>岡本課長<rt>おかもとかちょう</rt></ruby>は、かいがいりょこうは、はじめてだったので、イギリスのしゃしんをたくさんとるつもりでしたが、まいにちまいにち<ruby>会議<rt>かいぎ</rt></ruby>だったので、それはできませんでした。<ruby>岡本課長<rt>おかもとかちょう</rt></ruby>は<ruby>今日<rt>きょう</rt></ruby>、はじめて<ruby>会社<rt>かいしゃ</rt></ruby>へでました。

Yamamoto buchō to Okamoto kachō wa Igirisu e is-shukan shutchō shite, ototoi kaerimashita. Igirisu de wa, mainichi Dandō Supōtsu no honsha ni itte, kaigi o shimashita. Okamoto kachō wa, kaigai ryokō wa, hajimete datta no de, Igirisu no shashin o takusan toru tsumori deshita ga, mainichi mainichi kaigi datta no de, sore wa dekimasen deshita. Okamoto kachō wa kyō, hajimete kaisha e demashita.

Dialogue

前田 おかえりなさい。イギリスはどうでしたか。

岡本 まあまあうまくいきました。ただ、スポーツウェアのサイズといろがもんだいになりました。

前田 どういうことですか。

岡本 ダンドー・スポーツさんは、ぜんぶのサイズを日本にゆしゅつするといいました。

前田 えっ?! Lサイズもですか。Lサイズは日本人には大きいでしょう。

岡本 ええ、だから部長はSとMだけかうといいました。

前田 あぁ、そうですか。それで、もう一つのもんだいはいろだったんですか。

岡本 ええ、ダンドー・スポーツは、パステル・カラーがいいといいましたが、うちは来年のいろは、しろとくろになると思います。だから、それがもんだいです。

前田 それはたいへんですね。かかくはどうなりましたか。

岡本 かかくはだいじょうぶでした。ところで前田さん、(*pointing to his own tie*) このネクタイ、どう思いますか。

前田 みどりときいろとピンク....

岡本 いいいろでしょう。イギリスにはやすくて、いいものがたくさんありますよ。このネクタイも日本では¥25,000ぐらいしますよ。

まえだ
前田 (*thinking to himself*: 日本人はそんないろのネクタイはかわ
にほんじん
ないよ。)

おかもと
岡本 (*giving Maeda a similar necktie*) 前田さんにもイギリスの
まえだ
ネクタイをどうぞ。

Maeda	O-kaeri nasai. Igirisu wa dō deshita ka.
Okamoto	Mā-mā umaku ikimashita. Tada, supōtsu-uea no saizu to iro ga mondai ni narimashita.
Maeda	Dō iu koto desu ka.
Okamoto	Dandō Supōtsu san wa, zenbu no saizu o Nihon ni yushutsu suru to iimashita.
Maeda	Ē?! L saizu mo desu ka. L saizu wa, Nihonjin ni wa ōkii deshō.
Okamoto	Ē, dakara buchō wa S to M dake kau to iimashita.
Maeda	Ā, sō desu ka. Sorede, mō hitotsu no mondai wa iro datta n' desu ka.
Okamoto	Ē, Dandō Supōtsu wa, pasuteru karā ga ii to iimashita ga, uchi wa rainen no iro wa, shiro to kuro ni naru to omoimasu. Dakara, sore ga mondai desu.
Maeda	Sore wa taihen desu ne. Kakaku wa dō narimashita ka.
Okamoto	Kakaku wa daijōbu deshita. Tokorode Maeda san, (*pointing to his own tie*) kono nekutai, dō omoimasu ka.
Maeda	Midori to kiiro to pinku…?
Okamoto	Ii iro deshō? Igirisu ni wa yasukute, ii mono ga takusan arimasu yo. Kono nekutai mo Nihon de wa ¥25,000 gurai shimasu yo.
Maeda	(*thinking to himself*: Nihonjin wa sonna iro no nekutai wa kawanai yo…)
Okamoto	(*giving Maeda a similar necktie*) Maeda san ni mo Igirisu no nekutai o dōzo.

---

is-shūkan *one week*	**L saizu** *large size*
ototoi *the day before yesterday*	**S to M** *small and medium (size)*
mainichi *every day*	**dake** *only, alone*
hajimete *for the first time*	**mō hitotsu** *one more*
kaisha o demashita *went to,*	**pasuteru karā** *pastel colours*
appeared at the office	**uchi** *we, our side*
mainichi mainichi *day after day*	**shiro** *black*
umaku ikimashita *went well, was*	**kuro** *white*
successful	**to omoimasu** *we think that* [from
umai *good, successful*	**omou**, to think]
tada *only, except, it's just that…*	**kakaku** *price, value*

supōtsu-uea *sportswear*	**nekutai** *necktie*
saizu *size*	**midori** *green*
iro *colour*	**kiiro** *yellow*
mondai *problem*	**pinku** *pink*
ni narimashita *became* [from **naru**,	**yasukute, ii** *cheap and good*
to get, become]	**mono** *thing, object*
Dō iu koto desu ka. *What do you*	**Y25,000 gurai shimasu** *cost about*
mean?	*Y25,000*
to iimashita *they said that* [from **iu**,	
to say, to speak]	

✔ ——————— Comprehension ———————

1 What was the problem about the sportswear sizes?

   (*a*)   Dando Sports wanted to export all sizes to Japan.

   (*b*)   The Japanese large size isn't very big.

   (*c*)   Yamamoto buchō didn't want to import small and medium sizes.

2 What was the other problem about?

   (*a*)   Things in Britain are too cheap.

   (*b*)   The two sides disagreed over which colours would sell best in Japan.

   (*c*)   The white started to discolour.

✇ ——————— Notes ———————

1 *Mondai ni narimashita* (It turned into a problem)

The verb **naru** is used to describe a change in condition which occurs naturally, or which isn't controlled by anyone, so it can be translated variously as *get [cold]*, *become [rich]*, *grow [old]*, etc. When **naru** follows a noun or a **-na** adjective, the particle **ni** must be added.

San-nen mae ni sensei **ni** **narimashita**.	*He became a teacher three years ago.*
Hikōki no naka de, byōki **ni** **narimashita**.	*I got sick on the plane.*
Ano kikaku wa dame **ni** **narimashita**.	*That plan didn't work out.* (Lit … *became no good*)

In the case of **-i** adjectives, the **-ku** form is used before **naru**. In other words, drop the final **-i** and add **-ku** (see Lesson 6, Note 8 for formation of the **-ku** form).

Hotta kun wa mainichi Eigo no benkyō o shite imasu ga, zenzen **umaku narimasen**.	*Hotta studies English every day, but he never gets any better.*
Ni-shūkan gurai mae kara, tonari no kōjō wa totemo **urusaku narimashita**.	*Since about two weeks ago, the factory next door has got really noisy.*
Watashi no kuruma wa **furuku natta** no de, atarashii kuruma o kau tsumori desu.	*My car has got old, so I plan to buy a new one.*
Kono shōhin no kakaku wa senshū kara **yasuku narimashita**! Hen desu ne.	*The price of these goods has got cheaper since last week – strange!*

2 Dō iu koto desu ka

This is a set phrase, meaning *What do you mean by that?* and used when you haven't understood the point someone is trying to make.

A Kinō, taihen deshita ne. Demo shizuka de, yokatta desu ne.	*That was terrible yesterday, wasn't it. But it was good that it was so quiet.*
B **Dō iu koto desu ka**.	*What do you mean?*
A Shiranakatta n' desu ka. Kōjō ga sutoraiki de, minna hayaku kaetta n' desu!	*Didn't you know? There was a strike at the factory, and everyone went home early!*

3 To iimashita (They said that...)

Discussing what someone else said is very simple in Japanese. If you want to quote their words, simply add **to iimashita** (*I/he/she, etc. said*).

Hotta san wa 'Kinō hajimete jogingu o shimashita,' **to iimashita**.	*Hotta san said 'I went jogging for the first time yesterday'.*

Indirect speech is equally straightforward to form: all you need do is change anything that was actually said into the plain form before adding **to iimashita**. Hence in the sentence above, Hotta's **shimashita** would become **shita**. Notice that you do not need to change the tense of the verb in the words actually spoken, as you have to in English (where *went jogging* becomes *had gone jogging*).

Hotta san wa, kinō hajimete jogingu o shita **to iimashita**.	*Hotta san said that he had gone jogging for the first time yesterday.*

You can think of the **to** in **to iimashita** either as representing quotation marks in the case of a direct quote, or as the equivalent of *that* in the case of indirect speech (*he said that...*). Here are some more examples of reported speech.

Hanbai sukejūru wa kongetsu no 28-nichi made ni wa dekinai **to iimashita**.	*They said that they couldn't make the sales schedule by the 28th of this month.*
Hotta san wa, kaisha no ryō wa amari atarashiku nai **to iimashita**.	*Hotta san said that the company dormitory wasn't very new.*
Buchō wa nan **to itte imashita** ka.	*What was the buchō saying?*

When relating what someone says in the present tense, the **-te** form is generally used.

Dandō Supōtsu no shōhin no kakaku wa, rainen kara takaku naru **to itte imasu**.	*He says that the price of Dando Sports' goods will go up next year.*

In the past tense too, you will often hear **itte imashita** rather than **iimashita**, even though the English equivalent would be *said* rather than *was saying*.

4 *Nihonjin ni wa* (For Japanese people)

Ni wa used after the topic of a sentence has rather more stress than plain **wa**, and has the meaning of *for...* or *as far as...is concerned*.

Nihonjin **ni wa**, Igirisu no M-saizu wa ōkii deshō.	*The British M-size must be large for Japanese people.*
Hotta san **ni wa**, konpyūta no benkyō wa muzukashikatta desu.	*The study of computers was difficult for Hotta san.*

5 Hitotsu (One)

As we have seen in previous lessons, there are various ways of counting things in Japanese depending on what you are counting (e.g. **biiru ippon**, *one bottle of beer*, **otoko no hito hitori**, *one man*, **mikka**, *the 3rd of the month*), and there is also the series of pure numbers: **ichi, ni, san, shi/yon, go**, etc. However, if you want to count items that have no special counters of their own, then the following series can be used.

	Ikutsu?	*how many?*	
hitotsu	*one (unit)*	muttsu	*six*
futatsu	*two*	nanatsu	*seven*
mittsu	*three*	yattsu	*eight*
yottsu	*four*	kokonotsu	*nine*
itsutsu	*five*	tō	*ten*

After ten, this way of counting reverts back to **jū-ichi, jū-ni, jū-san**, etc. You can always use this series if you don't know, or can't remember, if there is a special way of counting whatever you're counting. Although there is a chance it may not be the correct way, nevertheless it will always be understood.

Supagettii o **mittsu**, hanbāgā o **futatsu**, biiru o ni-hon kudasai.	*Three spaghettis, two hamburgers and two bottles of beer, please.*
Ōki-na mondai ga **hitotsu** dake arimashita.	*There was only one major problem.*

6 *Shiro to kuro* (Black and white [Lit. white and black])

In Japanese, some of the words for colours are nouns, some are adjectives, and some can be both. With those that are **-i** adjectives, the final **-i** can be dropped to make a noun.

kuro(i)	*black*	ao(i)	*blue-green*
shiro(i)	*white*	aka(i)	*red*

Sono **shiroi** sētā o misete kudasai.	*Could you show me that white sweater, please?*
Nihon de wa, **shiro-kuro** no terebi wa mō tsukurimasen.	*Black and white televisions aren't made in Japan any more.*

Other colour words only have a noun form, and so they have to be followed by **no** when used to describe something.

chairo	*brown*	midori	*green*
kiiro	*yellow*	murasaki	*purple*

Tsukue no shita ni, **chairo no** kaban ga arimasen deshita ka.

There wasn't a brown briefcase under the desk, was there?

Watashi no ichiban suki-na iro wa **murasaki** desu.

My favourite colour is purple.

A large number of colour words are derived from English. These are nouns, and so are followed by **no** when used for describing an object.

orenji	*orange*	burū	*blue*
guriin	*green*	gurē	*grey*
pinku	*pink*	buraun	*brown*

Kono **pinku no** mono wa nan desu ka.

What's this pink stuff?

7 *To omoimasu* (We think that)

When you want to talk about your opinions, or ask about someone else's opinions, the pattern is very similar to when you relate what someone said. Just state the thought or opinion, using the plain form, and add **to omoimasu** (*I think*) or **to omoimashita** (*I thought*).

A Atarashii kakaku wa takai **to omoimasu** ka.

Do you think the new pricing is high?

B Mondai nai **to omoimasu** yo.

I don't think it's a problem.

The same pattern is also used when you are talking about something you've heard. In this case you simply use **kiku** (*to hear*) instead of **omou**.

Noguchi kun wa daigaku de, māketingu o benkyō shita to **kikimashita** ga, hontō desu ka.

I heard that Noguchi studied marketing at university, but is it true?

| Ano shorui wa, Tanaka san no jimusho ni okutta **to kikimashita** ga. | *I heard that those documents have been sent to Tanaka san's office.* |

8 *Yasukute, ii mono* (Cheap, good things)

In Lesson 13 you saw how two sentences can be joined together with the **-te** form of the verb, which forms a link usually translated as *and*. This can also be done with **-i** adjectives. When you want to link several adjectives together to describe something, drop the final **-i** and add **-kute**.

| Wajima no ryō wa chotto furu**kute**, kitanai to omoimasen? | *Don't you think that Wajima's dormitory is a bit old and dirty?* |
| Atarashii jimusho wa hiro**kute**, akarui desu. | *The new office is big and bright.* |

9 *¥20,000* (Ni-man en)

When counting large numbers, there is a unit in Japanese which does not exist in English, and that is **man**, or *ten-thousand*. Hence 20,000, for example, is thought of as *two units of ten-thousand*, or **ni-man**. In the same way, 100,000 is *ten units of ten-thousand*, or **jū-man**. Other examples of large numbers are shown below.

10,000	ichi-man
25,000	ni-man go-sen
40,000	yon-man
70,000	nana-man
101,000	jū-man, is-sen
350,000	san-jū-go-man
1,000,000	hyaku-man
4,500,000	yon-hyaku-go-jū-man
20,000,000	ni-sen-man

Expansion activities

1 The sales are on and Ikeda san is out shopping, looking for some bargains. Below are some of the things she's considering buying. Make more sentences like the one in the example about the price cuts on these items.

Example:

Rajio wa ¥35,000 (san-man go-sen en) kara ¥29,000 (ni-man kyū-sen en) ni narimashita.

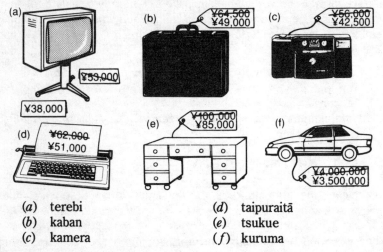

(a) terebi	(d) taipuraitā
(b) kaban	(e) tsukue
(c) kamera	(f) kuruma

2 Imagine that you and a crowd of friends have gone out for something to eat. To avoid confusion, you have taken charge of the ordering, and have made a list of what everyone wants. What would you say to the waiter when he comes to take the order? For example, you would begin: 'Piza o mittsu, kōhii o...'

pizza	× 3
coffee	× 5
orange juice	× 2
1 beer	
cheese sandwich	× 2
ham "	× 3
spaghetti	× 4
1 tuna sandwich	
green salad	× 7

3 Which is the odd man out in each line below? Underline the object which cannot possibly be the colour given at the beginning of the line.

(a)	**aka:**	banana	kuruma	fairu
(b)	**kiiro:**	banana	chiizu	tsuna
(c)	**ao:**	supōtsu-uea	fairu	shinbun
(d)	**midori:**	kasa	inu	o-cha
(e)	**kuro:**	bentō	kaban	nekutai
(f)	**shiro:**	yuki	kōhii	denwa
(g)	**chairo:**	hanbāgā	sake	inu
(h)	**pinku:**	sukāfu	pen	biiru

How would you use these colour words? Imagine you're out shopping with a Japanese friend, and make up mini-dialogues similar to the one below, using the cues that follow.

Example:

A   Kono *kuroi sētā* wa dō omoimasu ka.
B   Watashi wa, *kuro* wa amari suki ja arimasen.

(*i*)   red bag
(*j*)   blue scarf
(*k*)   pink and purple necktie

(*l*)   green car
(*m*)   brown T-shirt

4   Koyama san loves to talk about all the things other people have told her, or that she has overheard in the office, so never tell her a secret. Below are some of the things she overheard today.

In the evening, Koyama san meets Watanabe san from the Personnel Department and tells her all the day's gossip. What does she say?

Example:

(a) <u>Buchō</u> wa, <u>shachō mo fuku-shacho mo kaigi ni deru</u> to itte imashita.

(b) Noguchi san

(c) Hotta san

(d) Ikeda san

(e) Maeda san

(f) Ikeda san

5 Hotta san went home to Sendai at the weekend, and painted a rosy picture of life in Tokyo for his mother, but he told something nearer the truth to his brother, Masao. Later, his mother and Masao discuss what he told them. Complete their dialogue by using the words in brackets. The first one has been done for you. (Note that, as this is a very informal conversation within the family, most of the verbs are in the plain form.) Remember that Hotta's first name is Yūichirō.

O-kāsan   Yūichirō wa, kaisha no ryō wa (atarashii, kirei) ___atarashikute, kirei da___ to itta.

Masao   Sō ja nai, o-kāsan. ([a] kitanai, furui) _____ _____ to itta.

O-kāsan   Ā...sō datta. Demo, Yūichirō no kaisha wa ([b] hiroi, akarui) _____ ne. Shashin o mimashita yo.

Masao   Kaisha wa ([c] hiroi, akarui) _____ kedo, ([d] isogashii, urusai) _____ jimusho da to kiita.

O-kāsan   Ā sō...Demo Yūichirō wa ([e] muzukashii, taihen) _____ shigoto o tantō shite iru to itte ita yo.

Masao   Chigau yo. Totemo ([f] kantan, omoshiroku arimasen) _____ shigoto da to itte ita yo. Tokorode, Yūichirō no gārufurendo wa ([g] shizuka, kirei) _____ hito da to kiita kedo, boku wa hontō ja nai to omou.

O-kāsan   Ē?! Dō iu koto?! Gārufurendo?!

6 Make sentences by joining each phrase in the first group to one in the second group, and finishing them off with **narimashita**, as in the example.

Example:

Watanabe san wa **kachō** ni narimashita.

(a)	Watanabe san	jōzu
(b)	tenki	samui
(c)	Roido san no Nihongo	kachō
(d)	Yamada san no kodomo	raigetsu
(e)	Supōtsu-uea no kakaku	taihen takai
(f)	Kono kikaku	ōkii
(g)	Kono shimekiri	dame
(h)	Watashi no nekutai	kitanai

7 Now it's your turn. You're working for a Japanese company in Tokyo, and you have just been to Sapporo in Hokkaido to sort out some scheduling problems with Tanaka san, your representative there. Now you are reporting back to your buchō on the outcome of your meetings with Tanaka san.

Buchō O-kaeri nasai. Sapporo wa dō deshita ka.

You (a) *It went quite well.* _____

Buchō Ano mondai wa dō narimashita ka.

You (b) *The scheduling problem? That was okay, but Tanaka san said that pricing will become a problem.* _____

Buchō Ja, kakaku no hanashi wa umaku ikanakatta n' desu ne.

You (c) *Yes, that's right, but Tanaka san said he's coming to Tokyo at the end of the month.*

Buchō Ā, sono toki ni motto kuwashiku hanashi ga dekimasu ne. Tokorode, Sapporo wa hajimete itta n' desu ne.

You (d) *Yes, that's right. It's a quiet, beautiful city, isn't it.* __

Buchō Jimusho no tonari ni, chiisa-na kurafuto shoppu* ga arimashita ne.

You (e) *Yes, I went there. They had a lot of interesting things. (taking out a present for the buchō) I thought this was nice. It's for you.* _____

Buchō Dōmo, arigatō gozaimasu. Ā, nekutai desu ne. Kirei-na ao desu ne. Demo, takakatta deshō.

You (f) *No, it wasn't that expensive.* _____

* kurafuto shoppu: craft shop

Reading corner

On page 184 is a fax sent to Ueda Sports Shop by one of its customers, asking for some information. After reading it, see if you can answer the following questions.

1 Who sent the fax?
2 On which day of the week was it sent?
3 What does the customer want to know?
4 When do they want the information by?

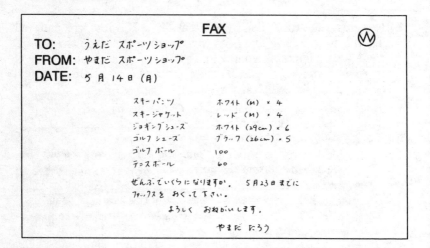

Business briefing

Adapting products for the Japanese market

Many stories have been told about companies which have been unsuccessful in Japan because they failed to take sufficient account of Japanese tastes and preferences when selling their products in this highly sophisticated market. This means that it is not unusual for a distributor or joint-venture partner to insist on changing every aspect of an imported product in the name of 'Japanese taste' alone. In many instances, the packaging of the product will not be transferable to the Japanese market, even though the product may have done well in the United States or Europe.

Personal effects such as cosmetics, shoes and clothes, and household items such as detergents and cleaning materials are all prime targets for 'Japanization'. It can be difficult to accept that a long-striven-for corporate image will not fit the Japanese market, but the best way to cope with this is to be open to suggestions on how to orient the product better to the Japanese consumer. Classic examples of companies which have succeeded in adapting their products to better suit the Japanese market include Unilever in the reworking of the Timotei shampoo brand, Waterford Wedgwood in the design of crystal specifically for the Japanese market, and Rolls Royce in providing left-hand drive cars for a right-hand drive country in order to heighten the 'foreignness' and desirability of its cars.

Daiei Inc., one of Japan's largest retail conglomerates, is constantly searching for high quality, competitively-priced basic products which are carefully adapted for the use of Japanese consumers. When Daiei decided to import canned cream-style sweetcorn from an American company, one of their worries was the colour of the American producer's packaging, which was bright green with blue labels. After discussions, the labels were eventually printed in Japan, in white, and in Japanese.

Not only colour, but size too is an important factor when designing a look for a product destined for the Japanese market. One example of this is a certain brand of English tea, which in Japan is sold in boxes of only 25 teabags, although it is normally sold in boxes of one hundred for the overseas market. The reason for this is that Japanese housewives tend to shop for food every day and do not feel the need to buy consumables like tea in such large quantities. Limited storage space in Japanese kitchens also renders large containers impractical.

Some years ago, a Japanese importer was involved in discussions with an overseas apparel manufacturer. Agreement was reached on the product, but the packaging presented problems. The foreign manufacturer insisted on supplying the product in opaque plastic despite the fact that shirts in Japan are normally offered in smooth, transparent plastic. Needless to say, the import agreement did not go ahead.

MOSHI JIKAN GA AREBA...

In this lesson you will learn one way of making conditional sentences (those that begin with 'If...' in English), and use them to give advice and make suggestions. You will also learn how to:

- use everyday telephone phrases
- talk about things which haven't happened yet or which haven't been finished yet
- say *nothing, no one, nowhere*

The story so far

スポーツウェアのいろとサイズのもんだいについて、もうかいけつしました。輪島で、来月きかく会議がありますから、ロイドさんはまた日本へ来ます。その時、せんでん担当のバーバラ・トーマスさんもいっしょに来ます。そのことについて、ロイドさんは今こくさい電話で山本部長と話をしています。

Supōtsu-uea no iro to saizu no mondai ni tsuite, mō kaiketsu shimashita. Wajima de, raigetsu kikaku kaigi ga arimasu kara, Roido san wa mata Nihon e kimasu. Sono toki, senden tantō no Bābara Tōmasu san mo issho ni kimasu. Sono koto ni tsuite, Roido san wa ima kokusai denwa de Yamamoto buchō to hanashi o shite imasu.

Dialogue

小山　もしもし。輪島しょうしゃでございます。

ロイド　おそれいりますが、山本部長をおねがいします。

小山　しつれいですが、どちらさまでしょうか。

ロイド　ダンドー・スポーツのロイドですが。

小山　はい、しょうしょうおまち下さい。

(Yamamoto buchō comes to the phone.)

山本　山本です。どうも、ロイドさん、おひさしぶりですね。

ロイド　そうですね。おげんきですか。あの....しゅっちょうのことですが。
　　　　来月のきかく会議は13日ですね。

山本　はい、そうです。ただ、ばしょはまだきまっていないんですよ。たぶんなごやになるでしょう。

ロイド　ああ、そうですか。ところで、せんでん担当部のバーバラ・トーマスも会議にでればいいと思いますが、どうでしょうか。

山本　ええ、いっしょにしゅっせきして下さい。

ロイド　それから、もし時間があれば、デパートのけんがくもできますか。

山本　いいですよ。ところで、ひこうきの時間がわかれば、むかえに行きますが。

ロイド　それはどうもありがとうございます。スケジュールはまだくわしくできていませんが、あとでファックスします。

山本 それから、カタログのことですが、あたらしいのがあれ
ば、もって来て下さい。

ロイド はい、もって行きます。では、これで....

山本 じゃ、どうも。しつれいします。(*puts phone down and turns to Koyama san*) バーバラ・トーマスのことについ
て何もしらないけど....「バーバラ」は....じょせいの
名前じゃない?

小山 そうですよ。

山本 えっ?!

Koyama	Moshi moshi. Wajima shōsha de gozaimasu.
Lloyd	Osore-irimasu ga, Yamamato buchō o onegai shimasu.
Koyama	Shitsurei desu ga, dochira sama deshō ka.
Lloyd	Dandō Supōtsu no Roido desu ga.
Koyama	Hai. Shōshō o-machi kudasai. (*Yamamoto buchō comes to the phone.*)
Yamamoto	Yamamoto desu. Dōmo, Roido san, o-hisashiburi desu ne.
Lloyd	Sō desu ne. O-genki desu ka. Anō...shutchō no koto desu ga. Raigetsu no kikaku kaigi wa 13-nichi desu ne.
Yamamoto	Hai, sō desu. Tada, basho wa mada kimatte inai n' desu yo. Tabun Nagoya ni naru deshō.
Lloyd	Ā, sō desu ka. Tokorode, senden tantō-bu no Bābara Tōmasu mo kaigi ni dereba ii to omoimasu ga, dō deshō ka.
Yamamoto	Ē, issho ni shusseki shite kudasai.
Lloyd	Sore kara, moshi jikan ga areba, depāto no kengaku mo dekimasu ka.
Yamamoto	Ii desu yo. Tokorode, hikōki no jikan ga wakareba, mukae ni ikimasu ga.
Lloyd	Sore wa dōmo arigatō gozaimasu. Sukejūru wa mada kuwashiku dekite imasen ga, ato de fakkusu shimasu.
Yamamoto	Sore kara, kataroguma no koto desu ga, atarashii no ga areba, motte kite kudasai.
Lloyd	Hai, motte ikimasu. Dewa, kore de...

Yamamoto Ja, dōmo. Shitsurei shimasu. (*puts phone down and turns to Koyama san*) Bābara Tōmasu no koto ni tsuite nani mo shiranai kedo…'Bābara' wa…josei no namae ja nai?

Koyama Sō desu yo.

Yamamoto Ē?!

---

ni tsuite *regarding, in this connection*

kaiketsu *solution, settlement (of a problem)*

senden *advertising, publicity*

issho ni *together*

…de gozaimasu *This is….*

osore-irimasu ga… *I'm sorry to trouble you, but…*

Dochira sama deshō ka *Who's speaking, please?*

shōshō o-machi kudasai *just a moment, please* [very polite]

dōmo *Hello, there*

o-hisashiburi desu ne *It's been a long time*

basho *place, location*

mada kimatte inai *it hasn't been decided yet* [from **kimaru**, to be decided]

tabun *perhaps, maybe*

dereba *if she attends* [from **deru**, to attend, be present]

shusseki *attendance, presence, appearance*

moshi *if, in case*

areba *if there is* [from **aru**]

kengaku *observation study*

wakareba *if you know* [from **wakaru**]

mada…dekite imasen *it isn't done yet* [from **dekiru**]

ato de *later*

katarogu *catalogue*

atarashii no ga *the new one*

motte kite kudasai *please bring* [from **motte kuru**, to bring]

motte ikimasu *take* [from **motte iku**, to take]

Dewa, kore de… *Well, at this point…*

nani mo shiranai *I don't know anything*

josei *female, woman*

Comprehension

1 Why is Mr Lloyd calling Yamamoto buchō?
   (*a*) Because they haven't spoken for a long time.
   (*b*) Because he wants to know the location of the meeting.
   (*c*) Because he wants to tell Yamamoto buchō about Barbara Thomas.

2 Why doesn't Mr Lloyd tell Yamamoto buchō the arrival time of his plane?
   (*a*) The schedule isn't definite yet.
   (*b*) He's already told Yamamoto buchō by fax.
   (*c*) The flight times will be in the catalogue.

── **Notes** ──

1 Iro to saizu no mondai ni tsuite (Regarding the problems of size and colour)

Ni tsuite means *regarding, in connection with, about*, and comes directly after the topic it is referring to.

Wāpuro B/200 no hanbai jōhō **ni tsuite**, mō wakarimashita ka.	*Have you found out about the sales information on the B/200 wordprocessor yet?*
Pāto no josei no kinmu jikan **ni tsuite** shirabete imasu.	*I'm looking into the working hours of the female part-timers.*

2 Moshi moshi, Wajima shōsha de gozaimasu. (Hello? This is Wajima Trading Company.)

As in English, there are a number of standard phrases in Japanese for use on the telephone, so you might like to consider learning them as set phrases, rather than learning individual words. The first set of phrases below are those needed when making a call.

Moshi moshi, (*company*) **no** (*name*) **desu.**	*Hello, this is (name) from (company).*
(*name*) **san onegai shimasu.**	*Mr/Ms (name), please.*
Naisen 222-ban onegai shimasu.	*Extension 222, please.*
Ato de mata denwa o shimasu.	*I'll call again later.*
Mō sukoshi yukkuri hanashite kudasai.	*Could you speak a bit more slowly, please?*
Mō ichido itte kudasai.	*Could you say that again, please?*

Next are some of the phrases that the other party may say.

Moshi moshi, (*company*) **de gozaimasu.**	*Hello, this is (company).*
Shōshō o-machi kudasai.	*Just a moment, please.*
Shitsurei desu ga, dochira sama deshō ka.	*Excuse me, but could I have your name, please?*
Kochira kara denwa o kakemashō ka.	*Shall I/we call you (as opposed to you calling me/us)?*
Nanika dengon (*or* **messēji**) **ga arimasu ka.**	*Can I take a message?*
Katō san ni o-denwa o kawarimasu.	*I'll pass you over to Kato san.*

O-denwa kawarimashita.	*Hello?* (said by the new person who has come to the phone)
Tadaima seki o hazushite imasu ga.	*He's not at his desk at the moment.*
Tadaima denwa-chū/kaigi-chū desu ga.	*At the moment she's talking on the phone/in a meeting.*
Gaishutsu shite orimasu.	*She's out of the office.*
O-matase shimashita.	*Sorry to have kept you waiting.*

3 Dōmo, Roido san, o-hisashiburi desu ne (It's been some time [since we last spoke])

So far we have only come across **dōmo** when it means *thanks*, but it is also often used as an informal greeting, where it is the equivalent of *Hello, there*. **Hisashiburi desu ne** can be used either on the phone or in face-to-face meetings as a greeting when it has been a long time since you last met, so it means something like *Long time, no see*, or *It's been a long time*. The phrase becomes more courteous when **o-** is added at the beginning.

4 Mada kimatte inai (It hasn't been decided yet)

You have already come across **mada** as meaning *still* when used with a positive verb (Lesson 7, Note 1).

| **Mada** denwa-chū desu. | *He's still on the phone.* |
| Hotta kun wa **mada** katarogu o mite imasu. | *Hotta is still looking at the catalogue.* |

When **mada** is used with a negative verb (usually the **-te inai** form), it indicates that something has not yet happened, or hasn't been completed yet. Note that **mada** can come either at the beginning of the sentence or just before the verb.

Mada Bābara Tōmasu san ni atte imasen.	*I haven't met Barbara Thomas yet.*
Kengaku no hi ni tsuite, **mada** kiite imasen.	*I haven't heard anything about the date for the study trip yet.*
Iro no mondai wa, mō kaiketsu shimashita ga, kakaku no mondai wa **mada** kaiketsu shite imasen.	*The problem about the colour has already been solved, but the price problem hasn't (been solved yet).*
Buchō wa **mada** kite imasen.	*The buchō hasn't come yet.*

5 *Tabun Nagoya ni naru deshō* (It will probably be in Nagoya)

You have already come across **deshō** when it follows a noun or an adjective (Lesson 9, Note 5), but it can also follow the plain form of a verb, with the same range of meanings. For example, when said with a rising intonation, it indicates that the speaker is fairly, but not completely, sure of his facts.

Ano shōhin o terebi de senden shita **deshō**.	*Those goods were advertised on television, right?*
Kare wa, sonna koto wakaru **deshō**!	*Surely he must know that!*

When used as a question with falling intonation, it means *I wonder...*

Hoteru manejimento kōsu wa itsu owaru **deshō** ka.	*I wonder when the hotel management course finishes.*
Miitingu no bashō wa, mō kimatta **deshō** ka ne.	*I wonder if the location for the meeting has been decided yet.*

It can also indicate probability, and this can be emphasised at the beginning of the sentence by using **tabun** (*probably, maybe*).

Tabun shachō mo kaigi ni shusseki suru **deshō**.	*Probably the president will attend the meeting, too.*

6 *Dereba* (If she attends)

There are several ways in Japanese of forming conditional phrases (i.e. those that begin with *if* in English) that will be introduced over the next couple of lessons. The first one we look at is easily recognized by the **-eba** ending of the verbs. For positive verbs, simply drop the final **-u** of the dictionary form and add **-eba**. Notice that even the two irregular verbs **suru** and **kuru** behave regularly here.

dictionary form	-eba form	meaning
ik-u	ik-eba	*if I go*
ar-u	ar-eba	*if there is*
dekir-u	dekir-eba	*if you can*
matomer-u	matomer-eba	*if you collect together*
kaker-u	kaker-eba	*if you call up*
mats-u	mat-eba	*if you wait*

kak-u	kak-eba	*if you write*
mir-u	mir-eba	*if I look*
sur-u	sur-eba	*if you do*
kur-u	kur-eba	*if he comes*

(Note that with verbs which end in **-tsu**, the 's' sound disappears, so **matsu** (*to wait*), for example, becomes **mateba**.)

Mō sukoshi yukkuri **hanaseba**, wakaru to omoimasu.

If you speak a little more slowly, I think I'll understand.

Shain no risuto o **matomereba**, kore de kaigi no junbi ga dekimasu ne?

If we get together a list of the employees, then that'll be the meeting preparations done, right?

If you don't want to wait until the appearance of the verb at the end of the phrase to show that this is an *if* sentence, or if you want to add emphasis, you can begin the sentence with **moshi** (*if*).

Moshi ii kangae ga **areba**, naisen 200-ban made denwa shite kudasai.

If you have any good ideas, call (me on) extension 200.

The negative is equally regular to form: drop the final **-i** from the plain negative form, and add **-kereba**.

plain negative	-nakereba form	meaning
tabena-i	tabena-kereba	if you don't eat
yomana-i	yomana-kereba	if I don't read
wakarana-i	wakarana-kereba	if you don't understand
na-i	na-kereba	if there isn't
ina-i	ina-kereba	if he isn't there
shina-i	shina-kereba	if I don't do (it)
kona-i	kona-kereba	if she doesn't come

Moshi kanojo ga **konakereba**, dō shimashō ka.

If she doesn't come, what shall we do?

Moshi **wakaranakereba**, mō ichido kiite kudasai.

If you don't understand, please ask once again.

The comparable forms of **desu** are **de areba** (positive) and **de nakereba** (negative).

Kachō ga kaigi-chū **de nakereba**, naisen 120-ban made denwa onegai shimasu.

If the kachō isn't in a meeting, could you ask him to call me on extension 120?

The group of -i adjectives also have a conditional form ending with **-eba**. For both the positive and the negative, simply drop the final **-i** and add **-kereba**.

Ima **isogashikereba**, ato de hanashimashō.	*If you're busy at the moment, let's talk later.*
Jōhō wa **atarashiku nakereba**, dame desu.	*If the information isn't new, it's no good.*
Moshi **yokereba**, ima katarogu o misete kudasai.	*If it's all right, please could you show me the catalogue now?*

7 *Dereba ii* (It would be good if she were to attend)

The **-eba** form is often used to ask for or give advice. When linked with **ii desu ka**, it has the literal meaning of *If..., is it good?*

Minna no kangae o **matomereba ii** desu ne.	*It would be good if we got together everybody's ideas.*
Ōsaka e buchō to issho ni **ikeba ii** to omoimasu.	*I think it would be good if you went to Osaka with the buchō.*
Itsu shusseki **sureba ii** desu ka.	*When would it be all right to attend (the meeting)?*
Dō **sureba ii** desu ka.	*What should I do?*

8 *Motte kite kudasai* (Please bring)

The idea of bringing or taking something is conveyed by a combination of two verbs, **iku** or **kuru** with the -te form of **motsu** (*to have, hold, carry*). Hence **motte kuru** means *to bring*, and **motte iku** means *to take*. However, you should remember that **iku** means simply to leave the place where you are now regardless of where you are going (Lesson 7, Note 4), and by extension **motte iku** means to remove something from where it is now, wherever you might be taking it. This means that **motte iku** is sometimes used where in English we would say *bring*, as in the dialogue at the beginning of the lesson and in the example below.

A (*On the telephone*) Jūgyōin no risuto o **motte ikimashō** ka.	*Shall I bring the list of employees?*
B Hai, **motte kite** kudasai.	*Yes, please.*

9 Dewa, kore de.... (Well, at this point...)

This is a useful phrase for when you want to begin making moves to end a conversation, whether you are talking on the phone, finishing a business meeting, or ending a visit to someone's office or home. The sentence is often deliberately left unfinished, but might end in several ways, such as **Dewa, kore de shitsurei shimasu,** (*Well, I will excuse myself now*) or **Dewa, kore de owarimashō,** (*Well, let's finish here*).

10 Nani mo shiranai (I don't know anything)

When the question words **nani, doko** and **dare** are followed by **mo** and a negative verb, they have the meaning of *not any*.

Sono dengon ni tsuite, kanojo wa **nani mo** shirimasen ne.	*She doesn't know anything about that message, does she?*
Dare mo pātii ni kimasen deshita.	*Nobody came to the party.*

The particles **ga, wa** and **o** are usually omitted, but others such as **ni** and **e** are still necessary, coming between the question word and **mo**.

Shūmatsu wa, **doko e mo** ikimasen deshita.	*I didn't go anywhere at the weekend.*
Dare ni mo aimasen deshita.	*We didn't meet anybody.*

☑ —————— **Expansion activities** ——————

1 See how quickly you can complete the crossword below. All the answers are verbs or adjectives which end in **-eba** or **-nakereba.**

ACROSS

2 *if it rains*
4 *if we don't meet*
6 *if it's cold*
7 *if you wait*
12 *if we don't collect them together*
13 *if you don't go*
15 *if I go*
16 *if it's all right*
18 *if we don't buy it*
20 *if I call up*

DOWN

1 *if he comes*
3 *if you write*
5 *if you don't understand*
7 *if I show you*
8 *if she takes it*
9 *if you don't drink it*
10 *if he comes out*
11 *if it's bad*
14 *if he's in*
17 *if you say*

21 *if you do*
22 *if we meet*

18 *if I buy it*
19 *if you have*

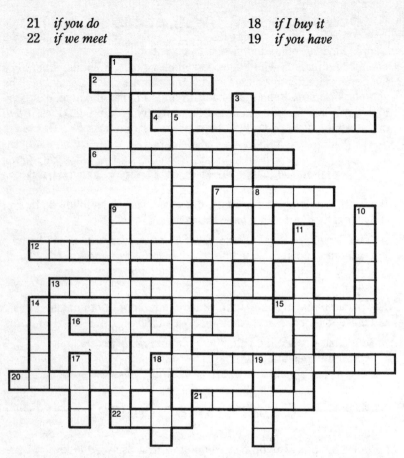

2 Like all managers, Okamoto kachō sometimes has to ask people to do things, and sometimes has to offer advice. To find out some of the things he's said today, fill in the blanks below with the **-eba** form of one of the words from the box. (There are more words than you need, so you will have to choose the most appropriate.)

taberu	suru	dekiru	warui	iru
nomu	matsu	akai	kakeru	aru

Asking people to do things

(*a*) Moshi jikan ga _____, asatte no miitingu ni dete kudasai.

(*b*) _____, kono repōto o mijikaku shite kudasai.

(*c*) Kyonen no katarogu ga _____, motte kite kudasai.

Offering advice

(*d*) Nihonshu o takusan _____, kibun ga waruku narimasu yo.

(*e*) Jinji-bu no Motoyama san ni denwa o _____, wakaru to omoimasu.

(*f*) Mainichi Eigo o benkyō _____, hayaku jōzu ni narimasu yo.

3 Yamamoto buchō has had a busy day since his chat with Mr Lloyd, organising the affairs of everyone in the office. Work out what he's been saying to them by choosing which of the two alternatives is the best way of beginning the sentences.

(*a*) (*i*) Ii kangae ga areba,...
 (*ii*) Watanabe san ni kikeba,...
  ...denwa shite kudasai.

(*b*) (*i*) Dekireba,...
 (*ii*) Kaigi ni shusseki shinakereba,...
  ...hanbai sukejūru ni tsuite wakaranai deshō.

(*c*) (*i*) Kono o-cha o nomeba,...
 (*ii*) Nihon de no senden ni tsuite wakaranakereba,...
  ...ashita kuwashiku setsumei shimasu.

(*d*) (*i*) Igirisu no shinbun o takusan yomeba,...
 (*ii*) Mondai ga areba,...
  ...totemo ii benkyō ni narimasu.

(*e*) (*i*) Ii kangae ga areba,...
 (*ii*) Kono o-cha o nomeba,...
  ...kibun ga yoku naru to omoimasu.

(*f*) (*i*) Kaigi ni shusseki shinakereba,...
 (*ii*) Watanabe san ni kikeba,...
  ...sugu wakaru to omoimasu.

(*g*) (*i*) Igirisu no shinbun o takusan yomeba,...
 (*ii*) Jikan ga areba,...
  ...uchi no kenkyū sentā ni kite kudasai.

(*h*) (*i*) Dekireba,...
 (*ii*) Nihon de no senden ni tsuite wakaranakereba,...
  ...raishū made ni repōto o tsukutte kudasai.

4 Hotta san and the others who joined Wajima at the same time as him have been steadily working through their training programme. Look at the training record below, and make sentences about what tasks Hotta and Morita have and haven't completed. Use **mō** and **mada**, as in the examples below.

Examples:

Hotta san wa, mō wāpuro no renshū o shimashita ga, Morita san wa mada shite imasen.

Hotta san mo, Morita san mo, mō depāto no kengaku o shimashita.

	Torēningu Keikaku	Hotta	Morita	
(a)	Wāpuro no renshū o suru	O	X	
(b)	Depāto no kengaku o suru	O	O	
(c)	Shōhin shijō o shiraberu	X	O	
(d)	Shijō repōto o kaku	X	X	
(e)	Eigo no benkyō o hajimeru	O	O	
(f)	Senden kikaku o tsukuru	X	X	
(g)	Katarogu o miru	X	O	
(h)	Māketingu kōsu ni deru	X	X	

5 Below is a telephone conversation between Mr Priest of ABA Company and someone at Mitsumoto Bank, but the words in each line have been scrambled. See if you can unscramble them to make sense of the conversation.

A gozaimasu Ginkō Mitsumoto de
_____

B Moshi moshi. desu Puriisuto no ga ABA-sha buchō Kitagawa shimasu onegai
_____

A o-machi shōshō kudasai.....tadaima hazushite Kitagawa imasu osorei-irimasu seki ga ga wa o
...
_____

B hanashite mō yukkuri sukoshi sumimasen ga kudasai
_____

A wa ga imasen buchō...arimasu dengon nanika ga wa
...
_____

B denwa iie shimasu ichido ato de mō
_____

A Hai, wakarimashita.

B Shitsurei shimasu.

6 This lunchtime, Hotta has invited Ikeda san out to lunch, and they are talking about Mr Lloyd's unexpected announcement that he will be bringing Barbara Thomas when he next visits Japan. Com-

plete their conversation by filling in the blanks with one of the words or phrases below.

ni tsuite mada dare mo nani mo dare ni mo

Ikeda Nē, mita? Kesa no buchō! Panikku (*panic*) shite imashita ne!

Hotta Ē, mimashita kedo. Demo, dō shite panikku shite ita n' desu ka.

Ikeda Bābara Tōmasu _____, _____ kiite imasen ka.

Hotta 'Bābara' wa josei no namae desu ne. Dare desu ka, sono Bābara Tōmasu wa?

Ikeda Dandō Supōtsu no senden tantō-sha desu yo. _____ _____ kuwashiku kiite inai to omoimasu ga, kanojo wa, raigetsu Roido san to issho ni kuru n' desu.

Hotta Ē?! Roido san to? Demo watashitachi wa sono koto _____ _____ _____ kiite imasen ga.

Ikeda Jitsu wa, buchō mo Bābara Tōmasu _____ _____ shirimasen deshita kara _____ _____ hanashite inai to omoimasu.

Hotta Kanojo wa Roido san no gārufurendo deshō ka ne.

Ikeda Sore wa _____ wakarimasen ga... Demo Igirisu-jin no josei wa hajimete desu ne.

Hotta Omoshiroku narimasu ne.

7 Now it's your turn. You work for a small computer company called Zeron, and you are arranging a meeting with Mr Yamanaka, section manager at Motoyama Kōgyō, to talk about advertising. You also want to bring along Nigel Grey, a colleague who works in your advertising department.

Uketsuke Moshi moshi, Motoyama Kōgyō de gozaimasu.

You (*a*) *I'm sorry to trouble you, but could I speak to Yamanaka kachō please.* _____

_____

Uketsuke Shitsurei desu ga, dochira sama deshō ka.

You (*b*) *It's (your name) from Zeron.* _____

_____

Uketsuke Hai, shōshō o-machi kudasai.

(*You are connected to Yamanaka kachō.*)

Yamanaka Hai, Yamanaka desu. O-hisashiburi desu ne.

You (*c*) *Hello there, how are you? About the advertising meeting – what time is next week's meeting?* _____

Yamanaka	10-ji han kara desu.
You	(d) *I see. The truth is, I think it would be good if Nigel Grey, of our advertising department, was at the meeting too – how would that be?* _____
Yamanaka	Hai, issho ni shusseki shite kudasai.
You	(e) *By the way, is the advertising planning report ready?* _____
Yamanaka	Mada dekite imasen. Ima jōhō o matomete imasu ga...
You	(f) *Right. Well, keep at it.* _____
Yamanaka	Arigatō. Dewa, kore de shitsurei shimasu.
You	(g) *Goodbye.* _____

Reading corner

As you may have noticed, many of the most common Japanese family names are made up of **kanji** which refer to geographical features. Those which have appeared in names so far in this text are:

やま
山 (*mountain*)　　た or だ
田 (*rice field*)　　おか
岡 (*hill*)

しま
島 (*island*)　　かわ
川 (*river*)　　いし
石 (*stone*)

These often occur in combination with the following:

うえ
上 (*upper, above*)　　した
下 (*lower, below*)　　まえ
前 (*in front of*)

なか
中 (*in the middle of*)　　もと
本 (*source, origin*)

Maeda san has been making out the seating plan for the meeting on the 13th. See if you can read the names of the people who will attend, and then answer the questions which follow.

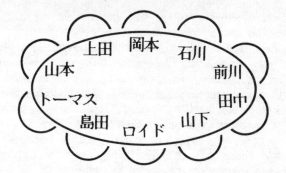

1 山本さんのとなりにだれがすわっていますか。
2 石川さんと上田さんのあいだにだれがすわっていますか。
3 田中さんのとなりにだれがすわっていますか。
4 島田さんと山下さんのあいだにだれがすわっていますか。

Business briefing

Advertising in Japan

Unlike their counterparts in Europe and the United States, Japanese companies tend to keep the advertising agency at arm's length until they have decided their overall marketing strategy. Only then will an advertising agency be called in to take the product from the initial market research stage all the way to the creation of advertisements for magazines and newspapers, and the buying of advertising slots on television. Because they prefer to keep full control of the marketing plan themselves, Japanese companies are in a position to use a variety of advertisers and even pit one against the other if they so wish. The advertisers for their part also have the freedom to work for competing firms in the same industrial or commercial sector.

An increasingly important aspect of the Japanese advertising industry is the promotion of foreign products. In the initial stages of a marketing plan, foreign companies may favour expensive magazine advertisements until they either find a Japanese agent, or set up their own representative office in the country. Once an office is set up, local staff are able to liaise closely with an advertising house on the creation of a more sophisticated advertising campaign.

Most agencies believe that to promote a foreign product in Japan, it is better to hire Japanese copy-writers than to use translated copy. This is probably true, although sometimes the expense of getting Japanese copy-writers to do the job is extremely high, and some companies may feel they have no choice but to use a translated version of the home-produced work. If at all possible, however, it is probably best for the foreign company to leave responsibility for advertising in Japan to the Japanese subsidiary. IBM Japan, for example, portrays IBM products being used by ordinary Japanese people in ordinary Japanese work situations, rather than as American products which Japanese people are expected to buy purely because they are foreign-made. The successful advertising of most foreign products in Japan depends less on the degree of foreign-ness of the product and more on the demonstrable way in which the product has been adapted or groomed for the benefit of the Japanese consumer.

MĀKETINGU NO
—— SHIKATA NI KYŌMI GA ——
ARIMASU

In Lesson 16 you will learn another way of making '*if*' sentences using **to**, how to make strong suggestions using **hō ga ii**, and how to give directions. You will also practise talking about department store facilities and training.

————— **The story so far** —————

バーバラ・トーマスさんはロイドさんといっしょにおととい日本<ruby>日本<rt>にほん</rt></ruby>につきました。かのじょは日本<ruby>日本<rt>にほん</rt></ruby>のマーケティングのしかたやせんでんのしかたなどにきょうみがありますから今日<ruby>今日<rt>きょう</rt></ruby>は東京<ruby>東京<rt>とうきょう</rt></ruby>のゆうめいな高松<ruby>高松<rt>たかまつ</rt></ruby>デパートに来ました。今<ruby>今<rt>いま</rt></ruby>からせんでん部<ruby>部<rt>ぶ</rt></ruby>の小林<ruby>小林<rt>こばやし</rt></ruby>さんとデパートのけんがくをはじめます。

Bābara Tōmasu san wa Roido san to issho ni ototoi Nihon ni tsukimashita. Kanojo wa Nihon no māketingu no shikata ya senden no shikata nado ni kyōmi ga arimasu kara, kyō wa Tōkyō no yūmei-na Takamatsu Depāto ni kimashita. Ima kara senden-bu no Kobayashi san to depāto no kengaku o hajimemasu.

—— **203** ——

Dialogue

小林　1かいのあんないじょからはじめたほうがいいですね。
エレベーターはこちらです。おさきにどうぞ。(*They go down in the lift.*) あんないじょはみぎです。日本では、
あんないじょはデパートの入口にあります。

バーバラ　(*seeing the Information Desk staff*) まあ、とてもスマートなせいふくですね!

小林　デパートのイメージはひじょうにたいせつですから、スマートなせいふくだけでなくいいサービスやてんいんのいいマナーもひつようです。

バーバラ　どんなしゃないきょういくをしていますか。

小林　うちでは、はなしかたやあいさつのしかたなどいろいろなしゃないきょういくをしています。

バーバラ　そうですか。イギリスのデパートでもそんないいしゃないきょういくをしたほうがいいですね。(*looks around and notices the cashpoint*) 入口のひだりがわにキャシュ・コーナーがありますね。

小林　ええ、これもサービスのひとつです。おきゃくさまがおかねをもっていないとしょうばいになりませんから!じゃあ、つぎは、なにをみましょうか。

バーバラ　スポーツウェアのならべかたにきょうみがありますが...

小林　それじゃ、5かいにゴルフ・コーナーがありますから行きましょうか。まっすぐ行ってみぎにまがると、エスカレーターがあります。

Kobayashi　Ik-kai no annai-jo kara hajimeta hō ga ii desu ne.
Erebētā wa kochira desu. O-saki ni, dōzo.
(*They go down in the lift.*) Annai-jo wa migi desu.

	Nihon de wa, annai-jo wa depāto no iriguchi ni arimasu.
Barbara	(*seeing the Information Desk staff*) Mā, totemo sumāto-na seifuku desu ne!
Kobayashi	Depāto no imēji wa hijō ni taisetsu desu kara, sumāto-na seifuku dake de naku, ii sābisu ya ten-in no ii manā mo hitsuyō desu.
Barbara	Donna shanai kyōiku o shite imasu ka.
Kobayashi	Uchi de wa, hanashikata ya aisatsu no shikata nado, iroiro-na shanai kyōiku o shite imasu.
Barbara	Sō desu ka. Igirisu no depāto de mo, sonna ii shanai kyōiku o shita hō ga ii desu ne. (*looks around and notices the cashpoint*) Iriguchi no hidari-gawa ni kyasshu kōnā ga arimasu ne.
Kobayashi	Ē, kore mo sābisu no hitotsu desu. O-kyaku-sama ga o-kane o motte inai to, shōbai ni narimasen kara! Ja, tsugi wa, nani o mimashō ka.
Barbara	Supōtsu-uea no narabekata ni kyōmi ga arimasu ga...
Kobayashi	Sore ja, go-kai ni gorufu kōnā ga arimasu kara ikimashō ka. Massugu itte, migi ni magaru to, esukarētā ga arimasu.

shikata *way of doing, how to do* [from **suru**]	**hitsuyō** *necessary, essential*
ya *and, or*	**shanai** *in-company*
nado *and so on, et cetera*	**kyōiku** *training, education*
...ni kyōmi ga arimasu *is interested in...*	**hanashikata** *way of speaking, how to speak* [from **hanasu**]
ik-kai *first floor* (British ground floor)	**aisatsu** *greetings*
annai-jo *information desk*	**hidari-gawa** *the left-hand side*
-ta hō ga ii *it would be best to, had better*	**hidari** *the left*
erebētā *elevator, lift*	**kyasshu kōnā** *cashpoint*
o-saki ni, dōzo *after you*	**nĕ** *isn't it* [variation of **ne**]
migi *the right*	**o-kyaku-sama** *customer, guest*
iriguchi *entrance*	**o-kane** *money*
sumāto-na *smart*	**motte inai to** *if they don't have*
seifuku *uniform*	**shōbai** *trade, business, commerce*
imēji *image*	**narabekata** *method of display, arrangement* [from **naraberu**, to display, put into position]
hijō ni *extremely, remarkably*	**sore ja** *well then, in that case*
taisetsu *important, valuable*	**go-kai** *fifth floor*
...dake de naku,...mo *not only..., but also...*	**massugu** *straight*
sābisu *service*	**...ni magaru to** *if you turn to the...* [from **magaru**, to turn, bend]
ten-in *sales clerk*	**esukarētā** *escalator*
manā *manners*	

Comprehension

1 Why has Barbara Thomas gone to Takamatsu Department Store today?
   (*a*) Because she's interested in the Japanese way of marketing.
   (*b*) Because it's the most famous department store in Tokyo.
   (*c*) Because she has seen their advertisements.

2 What would Barbara like to see happening in British department stores?
   (*a*) The provision of smarter uniforms for staff.
   (*b*) The provision of more facilities, such as cash machines.
   (*c*) The provision of better staff training.

Notes

1 *Ik-kai* (First floor)

In Japan, unlike Britain, the ground floor of a building is known as the first floor, the next up is the second floor, etc.

	nan-kai? *which floor?*		
ik-kai	*first floor*	**rok-kai**	*sixth floor*
ni-kai	*second floor*	**nana-kai**	*seventh floor*
san-gai	*third floor*	**hachi-kai**	*eighth floor*
yon-kai	*fourth floor*	**kyū-kai**	*ninth floor*
go-kai	*fifth floor*	**jū-kai**	*tenth floor*

Most department stores and office buildings also have several basement floors. The word **chika** means *underground*, so the first basement is known as **chika ik-kai**, the second basement as **chika ni-kai**, etc.

O-tearai wa **ni-kai** to **yon-kai** ni arimasu.
There are toilets on the second floor and the fourth floor.

Chika ik-kai no sushi kōnā wa totemo takai desu.
The sushi corner in the basement is very expensive.

2 ...kara hajimeta hō ga ii (It would be best to start from...)

When the plain past tense of a verb is followed by **hoo ga ii**, it can be translated as *had better, would be best to, should*, so it is often used when giving strong suggestions or advice on what to do or how to behave.

O-bāsan no adobaisu o **kiita hō ga ii** desu yo.	*You should listen to your grandmother's advice.*
Mada 17-sai (jū-nana-sai) dakara, o-sake o **yameta hō ga ii** desu yo.	*You're still only 17 years old, so you'd better stop (drinking) sake.*

If you want to suggest that it is better *not* to take some course of action, then the negative of the plain present tense is used.

Kono shin-shōhin no dezain wa amari yoku nai kara, mae ni **narabenai hō ga ii** desu.	*The design of this new product isn't very good, so it's best not to display it at the front.*
Ashita wa hayai kara, osoku made **nomanai hō ga ii** to omoimasu.	*I have to get up early tomorrow, so I'd better not drink too late.*

3 O-saki ni, dōzo (After you)

You may remember from Lesson 8 that you can use the phrase **O-saki ni, shitsurei shimasu**, to excuse yourself for going on ahead of someone else, or for leaving the office ahead of the others. If you want to invite someone else to go ahead first (when you are showing someone around the office, for example, or holding the door open for someone), the same phrase can be used, but followed by **dōzo**.

4 Seifuku dake de naku, ii sābisu ya, ii ten-in no manā mo... (not only the uniforms, but also good service and good staff manners...)

The phrase...**dake de (wa) naku,...mo** can be translated literally as *not only..., but also...* although in practice this sounds somewhat stilted in English, and there are often other ways of saying it.

Takamatsu Depāto ni wa, Nihon-jin no ten-in **dake de naku**, Amerika-jin no ten-in **mo** imasu.	*At Takamatsu Department Store, there are not only Japanese staff, but American staff too.*
Nihon no depāto wa, doyōbi **dake de naku**, nichiyōbi **mo** aite imasu.	*Department stores in Japan are open on Sundays as well as Saturdays.*
Suchuwādesu wa Nihongo **dake de naku**, Eigo **mo** hanashimasu.	*The stewardesses speak not only Japanese, but English, too.*

5 Ya (And)

The word **ya**, like **to**, means *and*, but the nuance is different. When **ya** is used to link several nouns, it implies that there are perhaps other things to add, and that the items mentioned are only examples of a longer list.

Kinō, zasshi **ya** shinbun no senden ni tsuite hanashimashita.	*Yesterday we talked about advertising in magazines, and newspapers, etc.*

On the other hand, the use of **to** between two nouns indicates that you are talking about those two things only, and that is the end of the matter. Compare the following two sentences.

Depāto de kēki **to** wain o kaimashita.	*I bought cake and wine at the department store.*
Depāto de kēki **ya** wain o kaimashita.	*I bought cake and wine (amongst other things) at the department store.*

To emphasise the fact that the list is unfinished, **nado** (*et cetera*) is sometimes added to the end of the list.

Kaisha no seifuku **ya** shanai kyōiku **nado** ni tsuite, iroiro-na shitsumon ga arimasu.	*I have a number of questions concerning the company uniforms, in-company training, etc.*

6 *Hanashikata* (Way of speaking)

When you come across **-kata** added to the stem of a verb, you can think of it as indicating the manner of doing something, or how to do something. It is formed by dropping **-masu** from the present positive form of the verb, and adding **-kata**. (This makes the word a noun.)

Nihon no shōbai no **shikata** ni tsuite, bideo o mimashita.	*We watched a video about the way of doing business in Japan.*
Kono kanji no **yomikata** ga wakarimasen.	*I don't know how to read this kanji character.*
Fuji Gorufu Kurabu e no **ikikata** o oshiete kudasai.	*Could you tell me how to get to Fuji Golf Club?*

7 *Motte inai to,* (If they don't have)

In the previous lesson we saw how to make *If...* sentences with the verb ending **-eba**. Another way to form such sentences is with the plain form of the verb followed by **to**. The usage is slightly different, however, as sentences with **to** tend to refer to general situations and statements of fact. It can sometimes be translated as *when*.

Shachō ni aisatsu o shinai **to**, shitsurei desu.	*It's impolite if you don't greet the president.*
Chika ik-kai ni iku **to**, kyasshu kōnā ga arimasu.	*If you go to the basement, there's a cash machine there.*
Sukii ni iku **to**, o-kane ga kakarimasu.	*If you go ski-ing, it costs money.*
Mushiatsuku naru **to**, eakon ga hitsuyō ni narimasu.	*When it gets humid, air conditioners become essential.*

8 *...ni kyōmi ga arimasu* (Has an interest in...)

Note that the object of your interest is followed by the particle **ni**.

Nihon no kaisha keiei **ni kyōmi ga arimasu**.	*I'm interested in Japanese company management.*
Māketingu **ni kyōmi ga arimasu** kara, rainen daigaku de māketingu o benkyō suru tsumori desu.	*I'm interested in marketing, so I plan to study it at university next year.*

9 *Massugu itte, migi ni magaru to, esukarētā ga arimasu* (If you go straight ahead, and turn right, you'll see the escalator)

When giving directions in English and pointing out landmarks, we often say *you'll see (a bank)* or *(on your left) you'll see...* but in Japanese it is sufficient simply to use **arimasu** *(there is)*. Some other standard phrases used in Japanese when giving directions are as follows.

hidari/migi ni magaru to	*if you turn left/right*
massugu iku to	*if you go straight ahead*
hidari-gawa ni arimasu	*it's on the left (-hand) side*
migi-gawa ni arimasu	*it's on the right (-hand) side*
tsukiatari ni arimasu	*it's at the end (of the street/aisle)*

Look at the following two examples of usage in relation to the map below.

Takamatsu Depāto wa, massugu itte, hidari ni magaru to, tsukiatari ni arimasu.

It you go straight ahead and turn left, Takamatsu Department Store will be at the end of the street.

Massugu itte, migi ni magaru to, ginkō wa hidari-gawa ni arimasu.

If you go straight ahead and turn right, you'll see the bank on the left-hand side.

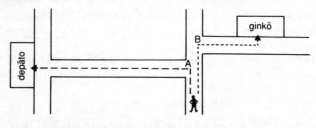

Expansion activities

1 Today Kobayashi san invited Barbara along to a planning meeting with the others in the advertising team. Unfortunately, the most junior member of the team kept interrupting with questions on subjects about which he knew nothing. The others patiently set him right on the appropriate course of action, using answers like the one in the example. See if you can work out what they said in the other cases using the cues below in their answers.

Example: (minna de)

A *Buchō ga* senden kikaku o kimemasu ka.
B Iie, *minna de* senden kikaku o kimeta hō ga ii desu.

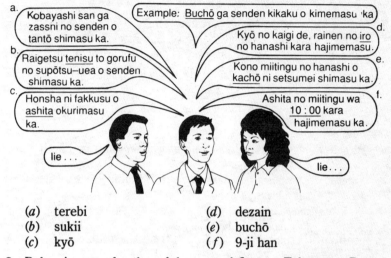

Example: Buchō ga senden kikaku o kimemasu ka.

a. Kobayashi san ga zassni no senden o tantō shimasu ka.

b. Raigetsu tenisu to gorufu no supōtsu–uea o senden shimasu ka.

c. Honsha ni fakkusu o ashita okurimasu ka.

d. Kyō no kaigi de, rainen no iro no hanashi kara hajimemasu.

e. Kono miitingu no hanashi o kachō ni setsumei shimasu ka.

f. Ashita no miitingu wa 10 : 00 kara hajimemasu ka.

Iie...

Iie...

(a) terebi	(d) dezain
(b) sukii	(e) buchō
(c) kyō	(f) 9-ji han

2 Below is part of a plan of the ground floor at Takamatsu Department Store. Several customers have just visited the information desk to ask the way to locations within the department store. Look at their questions below, and see if you can guide them to their destinations using the routes marked on the plan.

Example:

O-kyaku-san Sumimasen ga, denwa kōnā wa doko ni arimasu ka.
Uketsuke Hai. Massugu itte, hidari ni magaru to, denwa kōn; ga arimasu.
O-kyaku-san Dōmo arigatō.

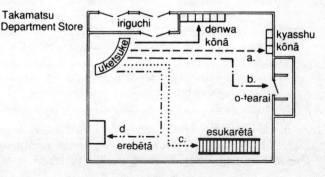

Takamatsu Department Store

iriguchi

denwa kōnā

kyasshu kōnā

a.

b.

o-tearai

Uketsuke

d
erebētā

c.

esukarētā

(a) Osore-irimasu ga, kyasshu kōnā wa doko ni arimasu ka?
(b) Sumimasen. O-tearai wa doko ni arimasu ka.
(c) Sumimasen ga, esukarētā wa doko ni arimasu ka.
(d) Sumimasen. Anō, erebētā wa doko ni arimasu ka.

3 Before her visit to the department store, Barbara prepared some questions to ask people at the store. She marked their answers on her notes too. From these notes, piece together what was said using the first example to help you. All of the replies to her questions follow the pattern:

_____ dake de naku, ii _____ ya ii _____ mo _____.

Example:

Barbara Depāto no keiei ni wa, ii māketingu ga hitsuyō desu ka.

Iwata Ii māketingu dake de naku, ii shōhin ya ii hanbai keikaku mo hitsuyō desu.

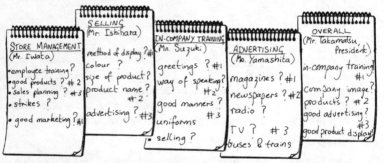

(a) **Barbara** Shin-shōhin no hanbai ni wa, ii narabekata ga taisetsu desu ka.

  Ishihara _____

(b) **Barbara** Shanai kyōiku de, aisatsu no shikata o oshiemasu ka.

  Suzuki _____

(c) **Barbara** Zasshi no senden wa taisetsu desu ka.

  Yamashita _____

(d) **Barbara** Depāto de, taisetsu-na koto wa shanai kyōiku desu ka.

  Shachō _____

4 Later in the day, Kobayashi san shows Barbara a selection of magazines in which the Takamatsu Department Store advertises. In one of the magazines, Barbara pauses to laugh at a column

called **Obāsan no adobaisu,** or *Grandmother's advice*. See if you can work out what Grandmother's words of advice are.

Example:

Q. 18-sai no Saita Etsuko san kara no shitsumon: Suchuwaadesu no shigoto ni kyōmi ga arimasu ga, donna benkyō ga hitsuyō desu ka.

A. (aisatsu no shikata ya Eigo no benkyō o suru) Aisatsu no shikata ya Eigo no benkyō o shita hō ga ii desu ne. Sō suru to, ii suchuwaadesu ni naru to omoimasu.

(a) Q. 23-sai no Ōba Nobuko san kara no shitsumon: Kēki ga daisuki de, mainichi 15 gurai tabemasu. Dō sureba ii deshō ka.

A. (kēki o yamete, guriin sarada o takusan taberu)

Sō suru to, sumāto ni naru to omoimasu.

(b) Q. 26-sai no Tanaka Yasue san kara no shitsumon: Buchō wa kekkon shite imasu ga, watashi wa kare ga dai-suki desu. Dō sureba ii deshō ka.

A. (kaisha o yameru)

Sō shinai to mondai wa ōkiku narimasu yo.

(c) Q. 17-sai no Mary Davis san kara no shitsumon: Kyonen Nihon e kimashita ga, mada kanji no yomikata ga zenzen wakarimasen. Dō sureba ii deshō ka.

A. (Nihongo no kurasu ni hairu)

Sō sureba, kanji no benkyō ga dekimasu.

(d) Q. 19-sai no Kikuchi Tomoko san kara no shitsumon: Uchi no kachō wa muzukashikute, hen-na hito desu kara, kaisha ga kirai ni narimashita. Dō sureba ii desu ka.

A. (Jinji-bu to hanasu)

Sō shinai to, mondai wa ōkiku narimasu.

(e) **Q.** 18-sai no Matsui Yūka san kara no shitsumon: Mainichi mainichi Eigo o benkyō suru n' desu ga, zenzen jōzu ni narimasen. Dō sureba ii deshō ka.

A. (Amerika ni itte, benkyō suru)

Sō sureba, hayaku jōzu ni naru to omoimasu.

5 At the end of the department store tour, Kobayashi san's buchō talks to Barbara about the store's corporate philosophy, and its slogan **Takamatsu Depāto no 5-Y**. Barbara didn't follow the explanation very well, so Kobayashi went over it with her later. Look at the 5-Y slogans below and the cues that follow to see how Kobayashi san clarified things for Barbara.

TAKAMATSU DEPĀTO NO 5-Y

* Yoi shanai kyōiku
* Yoi hanbai keikaku
* Yoi shōhin
* Yoi dezain
* Yoi hanashikata

Example: yoi shanai kyōiku, suru
Yoi shanai kyōiku o **shinai** to, shōbai ni narimasen.

(a) yoi hanbai keikaku, tsukuru
(b) yoi shōhin, tsukuru
(c) yoi dezain, kangaeru (*think about, consider*)
(d) yoi hanashikata, kyōiku suru

6 Now it's your turn. You're showing a Japanese friend around your golf course and clubhouse, trying to create a good impression as you hope he will want to invest in it.

You   (*a*)   *It would be best to start from the reception area, right?* ___

Him   E, sō desu ne. (*At the reception*) Totemo sumāto-na uketsuke desu ne!

You   (*b*)   *Yes, the club's image is extremely important, so it is essential to have not only a smart reception area, but also good service and (the employee's) good manners.* ___

___

Him   Donna kyōiku o shite imasu ka.

You   (*c*)   *We give training in how to speak (well), the way of greeting (customers), etc.* ___

Him   Jūgyōin wa gorufu ni kyōmi ga arimasu ka.

You   (*d*)   *Yes, they are. If they weren't interested, they wouldn't be able to talk about golf to the customers.* ___

Him   Sore wa sō desu ne. Sore ni gorufu wa hijō ni omoshiroi desu kara nē.

You   (*e*)   *Well, shall we go to the restaurant next? If we go straight ahead and then turn left, we'll see the entrance to the restaurant.* ___

___

Him   Wakarimashita.

You   (*f*)   *After you.* ___

━━━━━━━ Reading corner ━━━━━━━

Below is the store guide for Takamatsu Department Store. See if you can work out what is sold on each floor, and then answer the questions which follow.

高松デパートのストア・ガイド

6	<u>スーベニアショップ</u> ゲームコーナー ペットコーナー		レストラン ヘアーサロン	
5	<u>リビング</u> キッチン　　　リビング ベッド　　　　カーテン	エプロン カーペット	タオル	
4	<u>スポーツ＆レジャー</u> テニス　　　ウェア トレーニングウェア	ゴルフウェア スポーツシューズ	トラベルサロン	
3	<u>メンズ　ショップ</u> フォーマル　　　ウェア ジャケット＆スラックス	スーツ	コート キングサイズショップ	
2	<u>レディース　フローア</u> セーター　　　　ドレス ナイトウェア　　　ブラウス	スーツ	ヤングレデース L＆Sサイズショップ	
1	<u>アクセサリー　　　ハンカチ</u> スカーフ　　ハンドバッグ　かさ ネクタイ・ベルト		キャシュコーナー 電話コーナー フラワーショップ	
B1	<u>フード　ギャラリー</u> フルーツ　　　ケーキ ワイン・ビール	コーヒー・ティー すし	レストラン コーナー	

1　ヘアー・サロンは、何かいにありますか。
2　メンズ・ショップは、3がいにありますか。
3　キャシュ・コーナーは、ちか1かいにありますか。

📁 —————— **Business briefing** ——————

The customer is king

One aspect of Japan that never fails to impress the visitor is the very high standard of service to be found in shops, restaurants and hotels, whether big or small. The belief that *The customer is king* is a way of life in the service industries, and no effort is spared in providing the customer with attentive, friendly and polite service.

If you visit a department store when it opens in the morning, you can expect to be greeted at the door by a line of the store staff bowing to you as you enter. Each elevator has a female attendant in a smart uniform who will bow to all customers and assist in helping you find the floor you want. More staff stand at the bottom of each escalator to announce what is on the next floor, thank you for using the store, say good morning, or simply make sure that the moving handrail is clean.

There is no shortage of counter staff in Japanese shops to help you choose your purchases and wrap your goods. All purchases will be beautifully and carefully wrapped, no matter how cheap the item. If it is intended as a present, then extra care will be taken and special gift wrapping and ribbon will be included as a matter of course. Although there is now a growing awareness that over-wrapping of goods may be wasteful of resources, nevertheless beautiful presentation is considered almost as important as the gift itself in Japan, so the Japanese are experts at the art of careful and inventive wrapping. Even at the supermarket your goods will be carefully wrapped for you and bags provided to carry them home in.

In hotels, too, the standards of service are high even in the smallest town. Staff are numerous, attentive and polite. Great attention is paid to small details, and stress is placed on maintaining a clean, pleasant working environment. Lobby staff, for example, are always alert to newspapers which have been left lying around or ashtrays which are less than spotless.

Even at train stations there are platform staff to make sure that the area is kept tidy around the clock, and there are well-stocked kiosks on every platform selling newspapers, snacks, drinks, and anything else you may need for your journey. You will also notice that station guards as well as others in public service such as taxi drivers, station staff, bus drivers and garbage collectors wear neat, white gloves. In fact, if you need any kind of service in Japan, the chances are that you will find yourself dealing with people dressed in smart uniforms who take pride in doing their jobs well, who are courteous and helpful, and who treat the customer as king.

DAI 17 KA

JIKAN GA ATTARA, ATO DE MISEMASHŌ

In Lesson 17 you will find yet another way of making *if* sentences, using the verb ending **-tara**. You will also learn how to:

- ask permission to do something
- grant and refuse permission
- talk about doing two things at the same time
- use vocabulary associated with quality control

The story so far

きのう山本部長がバーバラさんにデパートのけいえいだけでなく、くるまのせいさんについてもべんきょうしたほうがいい、といいました。それで、バーバラさんは、今日はとうざんじどうしゃのこうじょうを見学しています。バーバラさんは工場長の鈴木さんとせいさんラインの見学を今おわりました。

Kinō Yamamoto buchō ga Bābara san ni depāto no keiei dake de naku, kuruma no seisan ni tsuite mo benkyō shita hō ga ii to iimashita. Sorede Bābara san wa, kyō wa Tōzan Jidōsha no kōjō o kengaku shite imasu. Bābara san wa kōjōchō no Suzuki san to seisan rain no kengaku o ima owarimashita.

▶ ——— **Dialogue** ———

バーバラ　せいさんラインのしゃしんをとってもいいですか。

鈴木　はい、どうぞ。たくさんとって下さい。

バーバラ　ところで、くるまのせいさんで何が一番じゅうようですか。

鈴木　そうですね。むずかしいしつもんですね。まあ、くるまのあんぜんせいだと思います。

バーバラ　ふりょうぶひんがでたら、どうしますか。

鈴木　まず、ふりょうぶひんをラインからはずして、ひんしつかんり担当しゃをよびます。そして、ひんしつ担当しゃがオペレーターといっしょにきかいのじょうたいをチェックします。それからふりょうぶひんをひんしつかんりしつへもっていって、もんだいをしらべます。げんいんがわかると、QCサークルで話しあいます。

バーバラ　あぁ、そうですか。それから、ひんしつほしょうもたいせつですか。

鈴木　ええ。ひんしつがよくなかったら、しょうばいになりません！ええと、そこをみぎにまがって下さい。(*They enter a different part of the factory*) そしてひんしつだけでなく、せいさんせいもたいせつです。

バーバラ　そうでしょうね。(*Something catches her eye*) あれは何ですか。ロボットですか。

鈴木　はい、ロボットです。時間があったら、あとで見せま

しょう。

バーバラ　ありがとうございます。(*hearing the signal for the tea break*) あぁ、きゅうけい時間になりましたね....あのう、すみませんが、今から、せいさんラインの人たちにいろいろきいてもよろしいですか。

鈴木　どうぞ、どうぞ。よかったら、みんなでむぎちゃでものみながら、話しましょう。

Barbara　Seisan rain no shashin o totte mo ii desu ka.

Suzuki　Hai, dōzo. Takusan totte kudasai.

Barbara　Tokorode, kuruma no seisan de nani ga ichiban jūyō desu ka.

Suzuki　Sō desu ne. Muzukashii shitsumon desu ne. Mā, kuruma no anzensei da to omoimasu.

Barbara　Furyō buhin ga detara, dō shimasu ka.

Suzuki　Mazu, furyō buhin o rain kara hazushite, hinshitsu kanri tantō-sha o yobimasu. Soshite hinshitsu tantō-sha ga operētā to issho ni kikai no jōtai o chekku shimasu. Sore kara furyō buhin o hinshitsu kanri-shitsu e motte itte, mondai o shirabemasu. Gen-in ga wakaru to, QC sākuru de hanashiaimasu.

Barbara　Ā, sō desu ka. Sore kara, hinshitsu hoshō mo taisetsu desu ka.

Suzuki　Ē. Hinshitsu ga yoku nakattara, shōbai ni narimasen! Ēto, soko o migi ni magatte kudasai. (*They enter a different part of the factory*) Soshite hinshitsu dake de naku, seisansei mo taisetsu desu.

Barbara　Sō deshō ne. (*Something catches her eye*) Are wa nan desu ka. Robotto desu ka.

Suzuki　Hai, robotto desu. Jikan ga attara, ato de misemashō.

Barbara　Arigatō gozaimasu. (*hearing the signal for the tea break*) Ā, kyūkei jikan ni narimashita ne... Anō, sumimasen ga, ima kara seisan rain no hitotachi ni iroiro kiite mo yoroshii desu ka.

Suzuki　Dōzo, dōzo. Yokattara, minna de mugi-cha demo nominagara, hanashimashō.

Tōzan Jidōsha *Tozan Automobiles*	**jōtai** *condition, state*
seisan *production*	**chekku shimasu** *check* [from

kōjōchō *plant manager*	**chekku suru,** *to check*]
seisan rain *production line*	**hinshitsu kanri-shitsu** *quality*
-te mo ii desu ka *Is it all right if I...?*	*control office*
kuruma no seisan de *in the*	**gen-in** *cause*
production of cars,	**kyū shii sākuru** *QC (Quality*
jūyō *important, of importance*	*Control) circle*
anzensei *safety*	**hanashiaimasu** *we discuss* [from
furyō *no good, defective*	**hanashiau,** *to discuss*]
buhin *parts*	**hinshitsu hoshō** *quality assurance*
detara *if they occur* [from **deru,** *to*	**yoku nakattara** *if it isn't good*
come out, appear]	**seisansei** *productivity*
mazu *firstly, first of all*	**robotto** *robot*
hazushite *take off, remove* [from	**attara** *if there is* [from **aru**]
hazusu]	**kyūkei** *rest time, break time*
hinshitsu *quality*	**yoroshii desu ka** *is it all right*
kanri *control, supervision*	**yokattara** *if it's okay (with you)*
yobimasu *call, send for* [from	**mugi-cha** *barley tea*
yobu, *to call*]	**nominagara** *while drinking* [from
operētā *operator*	**nomu**]
kikai *machine*	

Comprehension

1   What are the three things that Suzuki san thinks are most important in automobile production?
  (*a*)   Safety, quality and productivity.
  (*b*)   Safety, productivity and use of robots.
  (*c*)   Safety, QC circles and productivity.

2   Where are defective parts examined?
  (*a*)   By the production line, after removal from the line.
  (*b*)   In the quality control office.
  (*c*)   In the quality control circle.

Notes

1   Bābara san ni (To Barbara)

You will have noticed in the past couple of lessons that the particle **ni** is used to indicate the person who is being spoken to, or asked a question. **Ni** is often used in this way to point out who is on the receiving end of an action, so you will find it used with verbs which mean *ask, speak to, teach, give, write to, show* etc.

| O-kyaku san **ni** Tōzan Jidōsha no katarogu o misemashita ka. | *Did you show the Tozan Automobiles catalogue to the customer?* |
| Noguchi san, Hotta kun **ni** fakkusu no tsukaikata o oshiete kudasai. | *Noguchi san, please show Hotta kun how to use the fax.* |

2 Shashin o totte *mo ii desu ka* (Is it all right if I take some photographs?)

The phrase **mo ii desu ka** after the -te form of a verb is used when you want to ask permission to do something, and corresponds roughly to *Is it all right if I...?* or *Do you mind if I...?* A more polite version is **-te mo yoroshii desu ka**. When someone asks if they can open a window or borrow a pen, etc, appropriate responses are **Hai, dōzo** (*Yes, please go ahead*), or **Mochiron** (Of course), or **Hai, -te mo ii desu yo** (*Yes, it's all right if you...*).

A	Denwa o **karite mo ii desu ka.**	*Can I borrow your phone?*
B	Hai, dōzo, dōzo.	*Yes, please do.*
A	Nihongo ga yoku dekimasen kara, Eigo de **hanashite mo ii desu ka.**	*I can't speak Japanese very well, so is it all right if I talk in English?*
B	Ii desu yo.	*That's fine.*

The negative **-nakute mo ii desu ka** is also possible.

| Ashita wa chotto isogashii desu kara, kaigi ni **denakute mo ii desu ka.** | *I'm rather busy tomorrow, so is it all right if I don't come to the meeting?* |

However, if permission is not going to be granted because something is forbidden, the negative response is **Iie, ikemasen** (*No, you mustn't*), or **Iie, -te wa ikemasen** (*No,... isn't allowed/permitted*). This is a fairly strong refusal.

A	Koko de tabako o sutte mo ii desu ka.	*Is it okay if I smoke here?*
B	**Iie, ikemasen.**	*No, you can't.*
A	Robotto no suitchi o oshite mo ii desu ka.	*Is it all right if I press the buttons on the robot?*
B	**Iie, oshite wa ikemasen.**	*No, you mustn't press them.*

3 Anzensei (Safety)

-sei is a suffix which can be added to some words to turn them into abstract nouns.

anzen-na	*safe*	anzensei	*safety*
jūyō-na	*important*	jūyōsei	*importance*
seisan	*production*	seisansei	*productivity*

Kono kaisha no **seisansei** wa takai desu.
The productivity at this company is high.

Deru Supōtsu to no keiyaku ni **jūyōsei** ga arimasu ka.
Is there any importance attached to having a contract with Dell Sports?

4 Furyō buhin ga detara (If there are any defective parts)

When the plain past tense of a verb or **-i** adjective is followed by **-ra**, it indicates another way of making an *If...* sentence. (In practice this is often called the **-tara** form, as the verb always ends in **-tara**.) Although it can usually be translated as *if*, it is not completely interchangeable with the **to** and **-eba** forms that you learned in the last two lessons, because the **-tara** form can only be used when the action in the main part of the sentence occurs after the action in the *if* part. (Therefore it is NOT correct to use it in sentences like *If I go to the theatre, I prefer to go on a Saturday*, or *If you go, could you let me know beforehand?*) It can sometimes be translated as *when*.

Jishin ga **attara**, shizuka ni ik-kai ni itte kudasai.
If there is an earthquake, please go quietly to the ground floor.

Kyūkei jikan ga **owattara**, issho ni gen-in o shirabemashō.
When the break is over, let's look into the cause (of the problem) together.

Moshi kachō ga **isogashikattara**, watashi ga ikimasu.
If the kachō is busy, I'll go.

When you want to talk about the consequences if something does NOT happen, then **-ra** is added to the negative of the plain past tense of the verb or **-i** adjective.

Repōto no kakikata ga **wakaranakattara**,
If you don't know how to write the report, please call Yamamoto

Yamamoto san made denwa shite kudasai.

san.

Kikai no jōtai ga **warukattara**, tantō-sha o yonde kudasai.

If the machine is in poor condition, call the person in charge.

The corresponding forms for **desu** are **dattara** and **ja (de wa) nakattara**.

Kirai **dattara**, tabenakute mo ii desu.

If you don't like it, it's all right if you don't eat it.

Ni-nen hoshō **ja nakattara**, kaimasen.

If the guarantee isn't for two years, I won't buy it.

5 *Mazu* (Firstly, first of all)

Mazu is often used to begin the description of a process, or the explanation of how to do something. Some other useful words and phrases when explaining a process are **sore kara** (*and then*), **sono tsugi** (*next*), **soshite** (*then*), **sono ato** (*after that*) and **saigo ni** (*finally*).

6 *Hanashiaimasu* (Talk together)

When the verb **au** is added on to the basic stem of **hanasu** (*to talk*), it adds the nuance of both sides talking together or discussing equally. Some other examples of verbs to which **au** can be added are shown below.

miseru	*to show*	miseau	*to show each other*
matsu	*to wait*	machiau	*to wait for each other*
oshieru	*to tell, teach*	oshieau	*to teach each other*

Watashitachi wa keiei no shikata o **oshieaimashita**.

We told each other about our methods of management.

7 *Mugi-cha demo nominagara* (While drinking mugi-cha or something)

-nagara added to the basic stem of a verb means *while ...ing* or *when ...ing* and is used when you want to indicate that the action of that verb is going on at the same time as something else happens.

| Sutereo o **kikinagara** benkyō shite wa ikemasen. | *You mustn't listen to the stereo while studying.* |
| Shokudō de ranchi o **tabenagara** hanashiaimashō. | *Let's talk together over lunch in the dining room.* |

Note that this form can only be used where the subject of both verbs is the same person, so it cannot be used in such cases as *While he was talking, I took notes.*

✓ ———— Expansion activities ————

1 Look at the verbs given at the beginning of each line below, and choose which of the alternatives listed after them is the correct **-tara** form. The first one has been done for you.

(*a*) warui — wattara, <u>warukattara</u>, warattara, wakattara

(*b*) aru — atara, arattara, attara, aratta

(*c*) nai — nakattara, nakatara, nattara, naitara

(*d*) shinai — shinakattara, shittara, shinattara, shinaitara

(*e*) konai — konattara, konokatara, konakattara, konaitara

(*f*) tsukuru — tsukurutara, tsuitara, tsukutara, tsukuttara

(*g*) kariru — karittara, kattara, karitara, kaitara

(*h*) hanashiau — hanashitara, hanattara, hanashiattara, hanashittara

Now choose which of the words you have underlined would be most appropriate in the spaces below.

(*i*) Jishin ga _____, sugu ni kikai no suitchi o OFF ni shite kudasai.

(*j*) Robotto o _____, seisansei ga yoku narimasu.

(*k*) QC sākuru de _____, gen-in ga wakarimasu.

(*l*) Kaisha no kuruma o _____, ato de kagi o uketsuke made motte itte kudasai.

(*m*) Kikai no chekku o mainichi _____, furyō buhin ga demasu.

(*n*) Atarashii buhin ga raigetsu no tōka made ni _____, fakkusu o okutte kudasai.

(*o*) Shitsumon ga _____, kyō no miitingu wa kore de owarimashō.

(*p*) Shin-shōhin no hinshitsu ga _____, dō shimashō ka.

2 During the tea break at the factory, Barbara talks to some of the women who work there about their life in the company dormitory, and what they are and aren't allowed to do. Look at the example below to see the kind of question she asks, and what their reponses are. (Note that in Japan, a circle is used more often than a check mark to indicate *yes*). Barbara's questions all end with **-te mo ii desu ka**, and the responses are either **Hai, (-te mo) ii desu,** or **Iie, (-te wa) ikemasen.**

Example: Heya de o-sake o nonde mo ii desu ka.

Iie, (nonde wa) ikemasen.   Hai, (nonde mo) ii desu.

* bōifurendo: *boyfriend*

3 Inside the factory, Barbara was interested to find the operating standards attached to each operator's machine. The first set of guidelines looked like this:

> **FURYO BUHIN GA DETARA ...**
>
> (1) Furyo buhin o rain kara hazusu
> (2) Hinshitsu kanri tanto-sha o yobu
> (3) Opereta to issho ni kikai no jotai o chekku suru
> (4) Buhin o hinshitsu kanri-shitsu e motte iku
> (5) Mondai o shiraberu

And this was how Suzuki san explained the operating standards:

'Furyō buhin ga de**tara, mazu** furyō buhin o rain kara hazushi**te**, hinshitsu kanri tantō-sha o yobimasu. **Soshite** kare ga operētā to issho ni kikai no jōtai o chekku shimasu. **Sono ato** furyō buhin o hinshitsu kanri-shitsu e motte it**te**, mondai o shirabemasu.'

See if you can work out how he explained the operating standards in the cases below. Use the same pattern as in the example:
_____ -tara, mazu ___(1)___ -te, ___(2)___ . Soshite ___(3)___ .
Sono ato ___(4)___ -te, ___(5)___ .

(a)
> ① KIKAI NO JOTAI GA (warui)
>
> (1)OFF suitchi o osu
> (2)Enjinia o yobu
> (3)Enjinia to issho ni buhin o chekku suru
> (4)Kikai no jotai o shiraberu
> (5)Memo o kaku

(b)
> ① OPERETA GA (tsukareru)...
>
> (1)Betsu no opereta o yobu
> (2)Kyukei o suru
> (3)Zangyo o yameru
> (4)Hayaku uchi e kaeru
> (5)Futsuka gurai yasumu

(c)
> ① JISHIN GA (aru)
>
> (1)Kikai no OFF suitchi o osu
> (2)Shizuka no kojo o deru
> (3)Kojo no mae ni iku
> (4)Kojo ni hairanai
> (5)Kojocho no hanashi o yoku kiku

4 At Tōzan Automobiles, Barbara was given a copy of the company's English-language handbook, produced for use in the various US branches of the company. Some of the company rules are shown below. See if you can work out how they might appear in the Japanese-language handbook.

Example:

(Do not read newspapers or magazines while working.)
Shigoto o shinagara, shinbun ya zasshi o yonde wa ikemasen.

(a) Do not listen to your 'Walkman' while working in the office.
(b) Do not eat while talking on the phone.
(c) Do not drink coffee when using the word processors.
(d) Do not smoke when talking to visitors.
(e) Do not smoke when using the computers.

5 When Hotta san gets back to his dormitory room each evening he gets out his diary and writes about his day, which tends to revolve around life at Wajima. Here is an extract from a recent entry. (Note that all the verbs end in the plain form, as it is a personal piece of writing.) See if you can fill in the gaps with the appropriate particle.

wa   ga   no   ni   de   to

Baabara Toomasu . . . . , senshuu
kinyoobi .... Roido san .... kita
Kanojo ... 34.sai gurai de, ookii hito
da !! Kanojo ... Nihongo ... hontoo
.... joozo da. Ashita, senden-bu
.... miitingu .... aru ga, moshi kanojo
.... shusseki shitara, Eigo .... hanasu!
Kyoo boku-tachi...., kanojo ... issho
.... shokudoo ... ranchi .... tabeta.
Eigo ... hanasu tsumori datta ga,
muzukashikatta kara, yameta. Noguchi
san .... Nyuu Yooku .... Eigo .... ichi-
nen benkyoo shita kara, kirei-na Eigo ....
.... hanashita. Boku mo konban ....
Eigo ... motto benkyoo shita hoo ga ii !!

6 Now it's your turn. You are discussing the purchase of some parts with a supplier in Kawasaki, just outside Tokyo. You're trying to bring up the subject of him reducing his prices.

You (a) *If we import lots of parts, can you make (the price) cheaper?* _____

Him Muzukashii shitsumon desu ne. Demo, shachō ni kikimasu. Ā, mō ranchi no jikan desu ne.

You (b) *We don't have much time, so shall we discuss this while we're eating?* _____

Him Ē, sō desu ne. Kōjō no shokudō de tabete mo ii desu ka.
You (c) *Yes, that's fine.* _____
(d) *Before that, is it all right if I borrow the phone for a moment?* _____

Him Hai, dōzo tsukatte kudasai. Kakekata ga wakarimasu ka.
You (e) *Yes, I do. I used it before. First of all, I press number 9, and call the operator. When the operator comes on the line (**detara**), I tell her my company's phone number, right?* _____
_____
_____

Him Ē, sō desu. Ja, shokudō de matte imasu.
You (f) *Right, I'll come when I've finished the call.* _____

Reading corner

All the people who work at Tōzan Jidōsha are encouraged to make suggestions on how to help the company run more efficiently, and if the suggestion is really useful, there is a cash reward. Below is one of the forms used at Tōzan Jidōsha for submitting suggestions. See if you can work out what it says, and answer the questions that follow.

1 これはだれのアイデアですか。
2 鈴木さんはどこではたらいていますか。
3 きかいについてのもんだいですか。
4 何がよくないですか。
5 部長の名前は何ですか。

Business briefing

Factory life: QC circles and suggestion systems

New recruits to a manufacturing company are often required to undertake factory experience, whether they are destined for a job on the shop floor or a post in a white-collar section. For people who will ultimately work in sales, marketing or human resource management, a spell on the production line brings respect for those who work there every day of their working lives. A month on the welding line in the tremendous heat and humidity of a Japanese summer is a salutary experience.

While on a work placement in the factory, the new recruit has the opportunity to experience at first hand the processes involved in production and, more importantly, the attention to detail and quality control which he will later use in his own white-collar-based job. Quality control circles are one of the methods he will experience. Pioneered by the American William Denning and adopted by the Japanese in the post-war period, QC circles have become well-known in the west as one of the basic techniques of Japanese-style production and factory management. QC circles exist not only to monitor levels of quality and correct errors, but also to encourage workers to think of ways of making their jobs safer and more interesting. For example, in an informal QC circle, the team leader might set up a scene around a particular machine with puddles of oil, bits of scrap metal on the floor, and dirty rags draped over the control consoles. During the tea break everyone gathers around, points out what they think is wrong with the area around the machine, and discusses what might happen should such a situation really occur. Once all the problems have been identified, the workers gather in a ring around the offending area, point at the problem and in unison call out what the error is. This technique serves to emphasise the need for constant vigilance when working on the shop-floor to help people identify potential dangers. It also reminds people doing tedious work to keep safety uppermost in their minds.

More complex problems are handled by groups of QC circles. Problem-solving will be conducted using a variety of standard problem-solving procedures and pro forma documentation, particularly when the rate of defective parts being produced rises suddenly. Teams which hit on the best solution to a problem are often encouraged to take part in company-wide QC circle competitions with prizes for the best team effort.

Suggestion systems, with cash payments for good ideas, are also widely used by Japanese industry. People are not limited to QC circles when it comes to putting forward a new idea; suggestion systems are designed so that whenever an idea for improvement occurs to someone, he or she can note it down, and submit it for immediate consideration. Ideas are the lifeblood of any company anywhere in the world. In Japan, QC circles and suggestion systems are effective in ensuring that the flow of ideas remain constant.

TSUKURITAKU NAI!

At the beginning of this lesson, the Maedas are at home, so you will find practice with informal conversation and plain forms in the opening dialogue. In this lesson you will also find out how to:

● say you want to do something, using the verb ending **-tai**
● talk about your experiences and ask other people about theirs, using **koto ga aru**
● describe one action happening before or after another

The story so far

前田さんはいそがしいサラリーマンです。今日はあさ JETRO で会議にでました。午後はロイドさんたちとはんばいきかくについて話しあいました。8時までざんぎょうをしてから、うちへかえりました。今、前田さんはおくさんとゆうしょくをたべています。

Maeda san wa isogashii sarariiman desu. Kyō wa asa JETRO de kaigi ni demashita. Gogo wa Roido san-tachi to hanbai kikaku ni tsuite hanashiaimashita. Hachi-ji made zangyō o shite kara, uchi e kaerimashita. Ima Maeda san wa okusan to yūshoku o tabete imasu.

Dialogue

前田　このさかなはおいしいね。

おくさん　あぁ、よかったわ。ごはん、おかわりは?

前田　もういいよ。おなかがいっぱいだ。ともこは何時に
じゅくからかえる?

おくさん　もうすぐかえると思います。

前田　あぁ、そうか。(*putting his chopsticks down*) ごちそう
さま。おちゃがのみたいねぇ。

おくさん　はい、すぐ入れます。おふろは後にしますか。

前田　そうだね。おちゃをのんでから入るよ。(*yawning and
stretching*) あぁ、今日は本当にたいへんだった。あさ、
JETRO に行った時、みちがこんでいたから、だいじな
ミーティングにおくれた。そして、JETRO で、フラ
ンスのしじょうについて話したかったけど、ひつよう
なデータを会社にわすれたから、できなかった。

おくさん　まあ、本当。それはたいへんでしたね。はい、おちゃを
どうぞ。(*She pours him a cup of green tea.*)

前田　あぁ、ありがとう。午後、会社にかえってからロイドさ
んたちとはんばいきかくについて8時まで話しあった。

おくさん　それで。ロイドさんたちはいつイギリスにかえりま
すか。

前田　らいしゅうのすいよう日にかえるよていだよ。だから、

かれらがかえる前にいちど、うちによびたいね。

おくさん　ええ？ここに？でもここは、とてもせまいですよ！それ
に、わたしは、イギリスりょうりをつくったことがあ
りませんよ！

前田　ロイドさんたちは、日本りょうりをたべたことがある
から、だいじょぶだよ！すしでもつくったら、どう？

おくさん　いやだ！つくりたくないわ！

Maeda Kono sakana wa oishii ne.

Okusan Ā, yokatta wa. Gohan, o-kawari wa?

Maeda Mō ii yo. O-naka ga ippai da. Tomoko wa nan-ji ni juku kara kaeru?

Okusan Mō sugu kaeru to omoimasu.

Maeda Ā sō ka. (*putting his chopsticks down*) Go-chisō sama. O-cha ga nomitai nē.

Okusan Hai, sugu iremasu. O-furo wa ato ni shimasu ka.

Maeda Sō da ne. O-cha o nonde kara hairu yo. (*yawning and stretching*) Aa, kyō wa hontō ni taihen datta. Asa JETRO ni itta toki, michi ga konde ita kara, daiji-na miitingu ni okureta. Soshite JETRO de, Furansu no shijō ni tsuite hanashitakatta kedo, hitsuyō-na dēta o kaisha ni wasureta kara, dekinakatta.

Okusan Mā, hontō. Sore wa taihen deshita ne. Hai, o-cha o dōzo. (*She pours him a cup of green tea.*)

Maeda Ā, arigatō. Gogo, kaisha ni kaette kara, Roido san-tachi to hanbai kikaku ni tsuite hachi-ji made hanashiatta.

Okusan Sorede, Roido san-tachi wa itsu Igirisu ni kaerimasu ka.

Maeda Raishū no suiyōbi ni kaeru yotei da yo. Dakara, karera ga kaeru mae ni ichido, uchi ni yobitai ne.

Okusan Ē? Koko ni? Demo koko wa totemo, semai desu yo! Sore ni, watashi wa, Igirisu ryōri o tsukutta koto ga arimasen yo!

Maeda Roido san-tachi wa, Nihon ryōri o tabeta koto ga aru kara, daijōbu da yo! Sushi demo tsukuttara, dō?

Okusan Iya da! Tsukuritaku nai wa!

gogo *afternoon*
JETRO *Japan External Trade Organisation*
Roido san-tachi *Mr Lloyd and the other(s) with him*
zangyō shite kara *after doing overtime*
yūshoku *evening meal*
sakana *fish*
oishii *tasty, good*
(yokatta) wa [*sentence ending used by women*]
gohan *rice*
o-kawari *another helping*
mō ii *I've had enough*
o-naka ga ippai *I'm full*
ippai *full*
Tomoko *girl's first name, Maeda san's daughter*
juku *private school for extra tuition*
nomitai *want to drink* [*from* **nomu**]
iremasu *make (some tea)* [*from* **ireru**]
o-furo *bath*
nonde kara *after drinking* [*from* **nomu**]
itta toki *when I went* [*from* **iku**]

michi *road, way*
konde ita *was crowded* [*from* **komu**, *to be crowded*]
daiji-na *important, serious*
hanashitakatta *wanted to talk* [*from* **hanasu**]
dēta *data*
wasureta *forgot* [*from* **wasureru**, *to forget, leave behind*]
kaette kara *after returning* [*from* **kaeru**]
kaeru yotei *plan to return*
kaeru mae *before returning*
yobitai *want to invite* [*from* **yobu**, *to call, invite*]
semai *small (in area)*
sore ni *moreover, on top of that*
ryōri *cooking, cuisine*
tsukutta koto ga arimasen *have never made* [*from* **tsukuru**]
tabeta koto ga aru *have eaten* [*from* **taberu**]
iya da! *no way, I'm not going to do that*
iya-na *unpleasant, nasty*
tsukuritaku nai *don't want to make* [*from* **tsukuru**]

Comprehension

1   Why was Maeda san late for the meeting at JETRO?
   (*a*)   He left some important data at the office.
   (*b*)   The roads were crowded.
   (*c*)   He forgot where the meeting was being held.

2   How does Maeda san's wife feel about Mr Lloyd and Barbara coming to visit their home?
   (*a*)   She's a little concerned because she's never met any foreigners before.
   (*b*)   She thinks it's a wonderful idea because she can cook British food.
   (*c*)   She thinks it's a terrible idea.

Notes

1 8-ji made zangyō o shite kara,... (After working overtime until 8:00,...)

The construction **-te kara** corresponds to the English *after -ing*, and so is used when you want to talk about two consecutive actions. The **-te** form is used here regardless of whether the actions are in the future or the past.

Kono dēta o konpyūtā ni **irete kara**, ranchi ni itte mo ii desu ka.	*After I've input the data into the computer, is it all right if I go to lunch?*
Kikai no jōtai o **shirabete kara**, repōto o kaite kudasai.	*After you've checked out the condition of the machine, please write a report on it.*

Take care not to confuse **-te kara** with **-ta kara**, which shows reason or cause for something (see Lesson 10, Note 4).

2 Okusan (His wife)

Like all the Japanese vocabulary for family members, there are different ways of saying *wife*, depending on whether you are talking about your own family or someone else's. The word **okusan** is a courtesy title, and so is used only to refer to someone else's wife. When talking about one's own wife, the words **kanai**, or **tsuma** are used. In the same way, there are several words for *husband*. When referring to someone else's husband, the polite form is **go-shujin**; when talking about one's own husband, the words are **shujin**, or **otto**.

A	Suzuki san, ashita, **okusan** mo issho ni ikimasu ka.	*Suzuki san, is your wife going along tomorrow, too?*
B	Iie, **kanai** wa ashita chotto isogashii desu kara...	*No, my wife is rather busy tomorrow, so...*

3 Yokatta wa (Good, I'm glad)

In informal situations such as within the family, it is very common to use the plain form of verbs and adjectives at the end of sentences, as Maeda san and his wife are doing in this dialogue. Men tend to use the plain form more than women, although women also commonly use it with their close friends or family members. However, when women end a sentence with the plain form, they often follow it with the sentence ending **wa**, which has no meaning in itself, but which softens the tone of the whole sentence, and makes it very feminine sounding. Note that in the next sentence in the dialogue (**Gohan, o-kawari wa?**), the **wa** at the end of the phrase is not the feminine sentence-ending, but the particle **wa**, as the complete sentence would be **Gohan, o-kawari wa ikaga desu ka**.

4 *Mō ii yo* (I've had enough)

The phrase **Mō ii desu**, or **Iie, mō ii desu** can be used when you want to refuse an offer of more food or drink, and corresponds to the English *No, I'm fine* or *I've had enough*. A more polite alternative is **Iie, mō kekkō desu**.

A	Biiru mō sukoshi ikaga desu ka.	*How about a little more beer?*
B	Iie, **mō kekkō desu**, arigatō.	*No. I'm fine, thank you.*

5 *Tomoko wa nan-ji ni juku kara kaeru* (What time will Tomoko be back from the *juku*?)

After the school day has finished in Japan, it is very common for even small children to go on to a private school for further tuition in subjects such as kanji, mathematics, and English. The schools, called **juku**, are intended to help the students get through the all-important school exams, so they are sometimes referred to as 'cram schools'. Note that Maeda san refers to his daughter simply as 'Tomoko' as it is quite acceptable within the family not to use the respect title **san** with children. However it is quite common to use the affectionate diminutive **chan**, especially with young children.

6 *O-cha ga nomitai* (I'd like some green tea)

When **-tai** is added to the basic stem of a verb, it expresses a desire or wish to do something. Hence **tabetai** means *I want to eat* and **ikitai** means *I want to go*. To make this form of the verb, drop **-masu** from the plain present form and add **-tai**. Except in very informal situations, it is best to finish the sentence by adding **desu** or **n' desu**.

| Honkon e **ikitai** ne. | *I'd love to go to Hong Kong.* |
| Suisu ni itte, utsukushii yama no naka o **arukitai desu**. | *I'd like to go to Switzerland and walk in the beautiful mountains.* |

Verbs ending in **-tai** act like **-i** adjectives, so they have a negative form ending in **-ku arimasen**, and past tenses ending in **-katta** and **-ku nakatta** (or **-ku arimasen deshita**).

| Sono romanchikku-na eiga o **mitakatta** kedo, totemo konde ita kara, mimasen deshita. | *We wanted to see that romantic movie, but it was really crowded, so we didn't.* |
| Samukute, kurakatta kara, soto e **detaku nakatta** n' desu. | *It was cold and dark, so I didn't want to go out.* |

A word of warning though. This form is only used when talking about yourself. It is not used to refer to someone else's desire to do something, because it is generally considered that you cannot see into another person's mind. When you want to talk about what someone else wants to do you need to be indirect by adding **to omoimasu**, **deshō** or **to iimashita** to the end of the sentence.

| Buchō wa sono keiyaku ni mada sain **shitaku nai deshō**. | *It seems as if the buchō doesn't want to sign the contract yet.* |
| Ne, kikimashita ka. Kachō no okusan ga Rondon daigaku de seiji o benkyō **shitai to itte imashita**. | *Hey, have you heard? The kachō's wife said she wants to study politics at London University!* |

Note that *like* in the English question *What would you like to drink?* or *What would you like to do next?* has a different meaning, and so should not be translated into Japanese using the **-tai** form. Instead, ask **Nani o nomimasu ka**, or **Tsugi wa nani o shimasu ka**.

7 *Raishū no suiyōbi ni kaeru yotei* (They plan to return next Wednesday)

In this sentence, the whole phrase **raishū no suiyōbi ni kaeru** is used to describe **yotei**, so it can be treated almost like a very long adjective (*next-Wednesday-return-home plan*), in the same way as **atarashii yotei** (*a new plan*) or **iroiro-na yotei** (*various plans*). Any phrase which is used like this to describe something, or someone, always has verbs in the plain form.

Rainen sekai ryokō o **suru** **yotei** desu.	*Next year I plan to go on a trip around the world* (Lit: *Next year there is a do-a-world-trip plan*).
Ashita no gogo, Watanabe san ni **au yotei** desu.	*Tomorrow afternoon, I plan to meet Watanabe-san* (Lit: *There is a meet-Watanabe-san plan*).

Other words which can be used in the same way as **yotei** are **chansu** (*chance, opportunity*) and **toki** (*time, the time when*).

Pari ni iku **chansu** ga attara, subarashii Furansu ryōri o tabetai desu.	*If I get the chance to go to Paris, I want to try the wonderful French cooking.*
Densha o orita **toki**, daiji-na shorui o otoshimashita.	*When I got off the train, I dropped some important papers.*

8 *Karera ga kaeru mae ni* (Before they return)

When you want to talk about one action happening before another, simply add **mae ni** after the plain form of the verb. Remember that the verb here is always in the present tense even in cases where the past would be used in English. Hence **iku mae ni** can mean *before going, before I went, or before I go*.

Hikōki ni **noru mae ni**, denwa shite kudasai.	*Before you get on the plane, please give me a call.*
Minna ni **hanasu mae ni**, mō ichido kakunin shita hō ga ii desu.	*Before you tell everyone, you'd better confirm it once more.*

9 *Koko wa totemo semai desu yo* (This place is really small)

Japanese homes are often quite small, especially in the larger cities where land prices are prohibitively high. In addition, they are considered to be very private places just for the family, so there tends to be very little socialising done at home. Instead, people meet friends or entertain clients at restaurants, bars or coffee shops. Maeda san's wife is not accustomed to relative strangers coming to the house, so she is understandably nervous.

10 Tsukutta koto ga arimasen (I've never made it)

When the word **koto** (*thing, fact*) comes after a verb or verb phrase, it does the job of turning the whole phrase into one long noun. If the verb used is in the past tense, then it comes to mean an experience of doing something. So **Nihon ni itta koto** means *the experience of having been to Japan*, and **sono hon o yonda koto** means *the experience of having read that book*. The phrase **-ta koto ga arimasu ka** is therefore the equivalent of asking someone *Have you ever...?*

Nihon no o-furo ni **haitta koto ga arimasu ka.** — *Have you ever taken a Japanese-style bath?*

Konna ni utsukushii umi o **mita koto ga arimasen.** — *I've never seen such a beautiful sea.*

Sono atarashii konpyūtā o **tsukatta koto ga arimasu ka.** — *Have you ever used that new computer?*

The response to a question with **-ta koto ga arimasu ka** is usually **Hai, arimasu** (*Yes, I have*) or **Iie, arimasen** (*No, I haven't*).

☑ ———— Expansion activities ————

1   Watanabe san of the Personnel Department has short-listed three people from Wajima Trading to go for an internship at Dando Sports' head office. Look at the rough notes she has made below about each candidate.

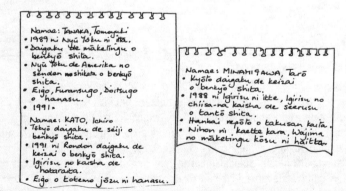

In a meeting with Watanabe san, Mr Lloyd asks about the various candidates. Using the information in the notes above, make questions and answers like the following.

Example: Minamigawa, Igirisu ni iku

Lloyd   Minamigawa san wa Igirisu ni itta koto ga arimasu ka.

Watanabe   Hai, arimasu.

Example: Tanaka, māketingu o tantō suru

Lloyd   Tanaka san wa māketingu o tantō shita koto ga arimasu ka.

Watanabe   Iie, arimasen.

(a) Minamigawa, hanbai repōto, kaku
(b) Tanaka, senden no shikata, benkyō suru
(c) Katō, Igirisu no kaisha de hataraku
(d) Tanaka, Igirisu no kaisha de hataraku
(e) Katō, sērusu o tantō suru
(f) Minamigawa, Igirisu de māketingu o benkyō suru

2 Watanabe san and Koyama san are talking over lunch about how lucky Mr Lloyd and Barbara Thomas are to be able to travel the world, and wishing that they could do the same. Complete their dialogue by changing the verbs in brackets to the **-tai** form.

Watanabe   Watashi wa Pari o (miru) wa.

Koyama   Watashi mo. Pari ni itte, dezain o benkyō (suru) to omou wa.

Watanabe   Sore kara, Amerika ni mo kyōmi ga aru kara, Nyū Yōku ni mo (iku) wa.

Koyama   O-kane ga takusan attara, sekai ryokō o (suru) ne.

Watanabe   Sō ne. Bōifurendo to issho ni (iku)?

Koyama   Ē. Honkon de oishii chūka ryōri* o (taberu) wa ne. Sore kara, Indo no Taji Mahāru** o (miru) to omou wa.

Watanabe   Ii wa ne! Watashi wa bōifurendo to Suisu e itte, yama o (aruku) wa.

Koyama   Romanchikku ne!

* Chūka ryōri   Chinese cuisine
** Indo no Taji Mahāru   the Taj Mahal, in India

3 This evening Mr Lloyd and Barbara Thomas are at the Maedas' house having dinner, and talking about some of the things they

weren't able to do during this trip. Make sentences using the same pattern as in the example.

Example: Kyōto o ryokō suru, jikan ga nai
Kyōto o ryokō shitakatta kedo, jikan ga nakatta kara, dekimasen deshita.

(a) **Barbara**   Tōzan Jidōsha no robotto o miru, jikan ga nai
(b) **Mr Lloyd** Okamoto kachō to gorufu o suru, tenki ga warui
(c) **Mr Lloyd** Watashi mo Takamatsu Depāto o kengaku suru, miitingu ga aru
(d) **Barbara**   Takamatsu Depāto de shōhin no narabekata o motto kiku, tantō-sha ga isogashii
(e) **Barbara**   Ginza de kaimono o suru, depāto ga konde iru

4   Yesterday Okamoto kachō prepared a list of action items to be taken care of before the contract with Dando Sports is signed, and he's just given it to Ikeda san for typing. This is the list.

- shōhin no iro ya saizu o kimeru
- kakaku o kakunin suru
- hanbai sukejūru o chekku suru
- senden kikaku o kakunin suru
- keiyaku no shorui o matomeru
- minna de keiyaku ni tsuite hanashiau
- keiyaku o kaku
- Dandō Supōtsu ni keiyaku no kopii o okuru
- keiyaku o chekku suru
- Nihon de keiyaku ni sain suru

Ikeda san gets confused with the layout of the list, so she asks Okamoto kachō to clarify things. Work out what her questions and Okamoto kachō's answers are, using the example below and the cues that follow. (All of the questions and answers use -te kara or mae.)

Example: Confirm price, then decide colour/size of product?

Ikeda   Kakaku o kakunin shite kara, shōhin no iro ya saizu o kimemasu ka.

Okamoto   Iie, chigaimasu. Kakaku o kakunin suru mae ni, shōhin no iro ya saizu o kimemasu.

(a) Confirm advertising plan, then check sales schedule?

(b) Discuss the contract together, then collect together contract documents?

(c) Sign the contract in Japan, then send a copy to Dando Sports?

5 Maeda san had a bad day yesterday. Today was even worse. What happened? Use the pictures and cues to make sentences describing his day, like the one in the example. This exercise gives further practice in the use of **toki**, and in making complex sentences.

Example:

Tōkyō eki de takushii o oriru, kaban o wasureru, miitingu ni okureru

Tōkyō eki de takushii o orita toki, kaban o wasureta kara, miitingu ni okuremashita.

(a) Nagoya shisha ni iku, densha ga konde iru, tsukareru

(b) Miitingu o shite iru, jishin ga aru, soto ni deru

(c) Kaisha de zangyō o shite iru, kibun ga waruku naru, uchi e kaeru

(d) Uchi e kaeru, kurai, korobu

(e) O-furo ni haite iru, buchō kara denwa ga aru, o-furo kara deru

6 Now it's your turn. You are at Narita Airport waiting for your flight home. You've bought quite a few souvenirs at the duty-free shop and you're trying to get them all into your flight bag. The Japanese businessman sitting next to you starts a conversation.

Him Takusan kaimono o shimashita ne.
You (a) *Yes, I have. I wanted to buy a kimono but they were extremely expensive, so I didn't.* _____

Him Kankō ryokō deshita ka?
You (b) *No, I was on business. I wanted to go to Kyōto, but there wasn't time, and so I didn't go.* _____

Him Sore wa zannen deshita ne. Ēto, shitsurei desu ga, Amerika no kata* desu ka.
You (c) *No, I'm British. Have you ever been to Britain?* _____

Him Iie, mada itta koto ga arimasen. Kyonen iku tsumori deshita ga, o-kane ga nakute, ikimasen deshita.
You (d) *We've still got some time, so shall we have a beer or something? I always have a beer before boarding a plane.* ___

Him Sore wa ii desu ne. Sō shimashō.
You (e) *There's a bar over there, so shall we go?* _____

Him Jitsu wa, watashi wa hikōki ni notta koto ga arimasen.
You (f) *Oh, really? It'll be all right! But in that case, maybe it would be better not to drink too much.* _____

* **Amerika no kata:** polite form of **Amerika-jin**

Reading corner

Ikeda san and Koyama san have been looking at holiday brochures and trying to decide where to go for a late summer holiday. Now they're thinking about Okinawa, one of the most southern of the Japanese islands. See if you can read this brochure on the hotel they're considering now.

沖縄のおいしいおりょうりをたべたことがありますか。

沖縄のすばらしいうみを見たことがありますか。

沖縄のきれいなさかなを見たことがありますか。

松島ビーチ・ホテルは沖縄で一番うつくしいところです。

沖縄でたのしいホリデーを！

おきなわに
行きたいわ！

Business briefing

The Japanese home

Japanese homes range from the large traditional farmhouse in the country with three or four generations living under one roof, to the modern houses and apartments in the large cities that by western standards would be considered very small and cramped. Nevertheless, there are certain elements that are common to almost all houses, whether large or small, opulent or modest.

The floors of Japanese homes were traditionally made of **tatami** mats, and even modern, westernised houses still have at least one room with **tatami** flooring. **Tatami** mats are made of layers of thick rush matting edged with fabric, and come in standard sizes, so rooms are generally measured by the number of mats they have. A **tatami** floor has some bounce to it, which makes it a comfortable base on which to lay **futon** bedding at night. Each **tatami** mat is about the size of one person's **futon**, so a six-**tatami** room could traditionally sleep six people.

Another feature of the Japanese home is the **genkan**, or entrance hall, which is set at the same level as the ground outside, with a step up into the rest of the house. The **genkan** is the dividing line between **uchi**, or *inside* and **soto**, or *outside*. Outdoor shoes are left in the **genkan** and exchanged for slippers, a complicated procedure which involves stepping out of the shoes one by one and, without touching the floor of the **genkan** in stockinged feet, putting on the slippers which are laid out ready on the step up into the house proper. In other words, shoes never come inside the house, and bare feet or slippers never touch the floor of the **genkan**, which although physically inside the house, is still considered **soto**. Never bringing shoes into the house means the floors are kept clean, the **tatami** mats are not damaged, and the symbolic separation of **soto** and **uchi** is maintained.

Another aspect of cleanliness in the Japanese home is the use of the **o-furo**, or bath. The Japanese bath tub is for soaking in, not for washing in. Washing is done outside the bath, either using water taken in a bowl from the already-filled bath, or nowadays under a shower. Japanese bathrooms have a drain set in to the floor, so water can be freely sloshed around the waterproofed room. Because such care is taken to wash thoroughly before getting into the bath, the actual bath water remains clean and the whole family can use it to relax in after washing. The Japanese like to have a long soak in extremely hot water, so it is kept hot with a water heater on the side of the bath, and there is usually a cover which fits over the bath to keep the water warm between bathers. Traditionally, the husband or any guests would be invited to take a bath first, followed by sons, daughters and finally the wife, who would have had the task of preparing the bath in the first place. Taking a Japanese bath is a wonderfully relaxing, soothing experience, and one not to be missed if you have the opportunity of staying in a Japanese home or a **ryokan**.

DAI 19 KA

DORU-DATE YORI
EN-DATE NO HŌ
GA II

In Lesson 19, you will learn how to make comparisons and talk about your preferences. You will also find out how to say *must, have to* using the verb ending **-nakereba narimasen**, and how to talk about things you can or can't do, using **suru koto ga dekimasu**.

——— The story so far ———

<ruby>岡本<rt>おかもと</rt></ruby><ruby>課長<rt>かちょう</rt></ruby>と<ruby>前田<rt>まえだ</rt></ruby>さんは<ruby>今<rt>いま</rt></ruby>ダンドー・スポーツとのけいやくスケジュ
ールや<ruby>社員旅行<rt>しゃいんりょこう</rt></ruby>について<ruby>話<rt>はな</rt></ruby>しあっています。でも、<ruby>課長<rt>かちょう</rt></ruby>はけいや
くの<ruby>話<rt>はなし</rt></ruby>より、<ruby>社員旅行<rt>しゃいんりょこう</rt></ruby>の<ruby>話<rt>はなし</rt></ruby>のほうがしたいです。かれは、まいねん
<ruby>社員旅行<rt>しゃいんりょこう</rt></ruby>をたのしみにしていますから。

Okamoto kachō to Maeda san wa ima Dandō Supōtsu to no keiyaku sukejūru ya shain ryokō ni tsuite hanashiatte imasu. Demo, kachō wa keiyaku no hanashi yori, shain ryokō no hanashi no hō ga shitai desu. Kare wa, mainen shain ryokō o tanoshimi ni shite imasu kara.

Dialogue

岡本 えぇと、いつまでにダンドー・スポーツにけいやくしょるいをおくらなけばなりませんか。

前田 来月の15日までにおくらなければなりません。

岡本 けいやくのじょうけんをぜんぶめいかくにしましたか。

前田 はい、ほうりつ担当の森さんとよく話しあいましたから、もんだいてんはぜんぶかいけつしました。

岡本 それで、しはらいは円だてにしますね。

前田 えぇ、ドルだてより円だてのほうがいいと思いますから。

岡本 わかりました。ごくろうさまでした。(*He looks at the agenda for the meeting.*) つぎは社員旅行のけんですね。

前田 はい、そうです。みんなで、いろいろ話しあいましたが、けっきょく日本アルプスの青山こうげんというところにしました。

岡本 あぁ、わたしもうみより山のほうがすきです。おんせんに入って、ゆっくりすることができますからね。

前田 ええ、わたしもそう思います。それに、青山こうげんでは、おいしいさんさいりょうりをたべることができます。

岡本 あぁ、いいですね。それで、イベントの担当者をきめなければなりませんね。

前田 イベントというのは...?

岡本 えんかいですよ。えんかいがなければ、いい社員旅行になりません。じゃ...前田さんにまかせますよ。

まえだ
前田　あぁ、はい...

Okamoto	Ēto, itsu made ni Dandō Supōtsu ni keiyaku shorui o okuranakereba narimasen ka.
Maeda	Raigetsu no 15-nichi made ni okuranakereba narimasen.
Okamoto	Keiyaku no jōken o zenbu meikaku ni shimashita ka.
Maeda	Hai, hōritsu tantō no Mori san to yoku hanashiaimashita kara, mondai ten wa zenbu kaiketsu shimashita.
Okamoto	Sorede, shi-harai wa en-date ni shimasu ne.
Maeda	Ē, doru-date yori en-date no hō ga ii to omoimasu kara.
Okamoto	Wakarimashita. Go-kurō sama deshita. (*He looks at the agenda for the meeting*.) Tsugi wa shain ryokō no ken desu ne.
Maeda	Hai, sō desu. Minna de, iroiro hanashiaimashita ga, kekkyoku Nihon Arupusu no Aoyama Kōgen to iu tokoro ni shimashita.
Okamoto	Ā, watashi mo umi yori yama no hō ga suki desu. Onsen ni haitte, yukkuri suru koto ga dekimasu kara ne.
Maeda	Ē, watashi mo sō omoimasu. Sore ni, Aoyama Kōgen de wa, oishii sansai ryōri o taberu koto ga dekimasu.
Okamoto	Ā, ii desu ne. Sorede, ibento no tantō-sha o kimena-kereba narimasen ne.
Maeda	Ibento to iu no wa...?
Okamoto	Enkai desu yo. Enkai ga nakereba, ii shain ryokō ni narimasen. Jā... Maeda san ni makasemasu yo.
Maeda	Ā, hai...

shain ryokō *company trip*	**Go-kurō sama deshita** *Thank you for doing a good job*
yori *rather than*	
mainen *every year*	**ken** *matter, item*
tanoshimi ni shite imasu *is looking forward to*	**...to iu tokoro** *a place called...*
okuranakereba narimasen *have to send* [from **okuru**]	**tokoro** *place*
	onsen *hot springs*
jōken *terms, conditions*	**yukkuri suru koto ga dekimasu** *can take it easy*
meikaku *clear, distinct*	**sansai ryōri** *mountain-style cooking*
hōritsu *law*	**taberu koto ga dekimasu** *can eat*
mondai ten *problem points*	**ibento** *event*
shi-harai *payment*	**enkai** *party, banquet*
en-date *in yen, a yen base*	**Maeda san ni makasemasu yo** *I'll leave it up to you, Maeda san* [from **makaseru**, to entrust, leave (to someone's care)]
doru-date *in dollars, a dollar base*	
doru-date yori *rather than paying in dollars...*	

✓ ──────────── **Comprehension** ────────────

1 How will the payment be made?
   (a) In dollars.
   (b) In yen.
   (c) It can be either in yen or in dollars.

2 Why is Okamoto buchō pleased to hear the company trip is to the
   Japan Alps?
   (a) He enjoys the local events.
   (b) He enjoys relaxing in the hot springs.
   (c) He enjoys climbing mountains.

🔊 ──────────────── **Notes** ────────────────

1 *Keiyaku no hanashi yori shain ryokō no hanashi no hō ga shitai desu* (He wants to talk about the company trip rather than the contract)

There are no comparative forms of adjectives or adverbs in Japanese.
Instead, when you want to make comparisons or talk about your
preferences, the pattern to use is **A yori, B no hō ga (ii desu)**. Literally, this means *Rather than A, B is (better)*, or more colloquially *B
is (better) than A*.

Sutēki **yori**, sakana **no hō ga**   *I like fish better than steak.*
   suki desu.
Hoteru **yori**, ryokan **no hō ga**   *You can relax more in a ryokan*
   yukkuri dekimasu.   *(Japanese inn) than in a hotel.*

When the topic you are talking about is already understood, you can
omit the part with **yori**.

Higashi biru **no hō ga** saki ni   *The east building was finished*
   dekimashita.   *first.*

When you want to ask a question about which of two things is taller,
or more expensive, or better, use the pattern **A to B to, dochira no
hō ga (ii) desu ka**, or *Of A and B, which is (better)*?

A Dandō Supōtsu **to** Miki   *Which exports more, Dando Sports*
   Supōtsu **to**, **dochira no**   *or Miki Sports?*
   hō ga yushutsu ga ōi
   desu ka.

B Mochiron Dandō Supōtsu *Dando Sports, of course.*
no hō desu.

It is also possible to leave out **no hō** in this kind of question.

A Mae no shōhin to atarashii *Which do you think is better, this*
shōhin to, dochira ga ii *new product or the previous*
to omoimasu ka. *one?*

B Sō desu ne. Atarashii
shōhin no hō ga ii to *Mmm, I think the new one is*
omoimasu. *better.*

2 *Okuranakereba narimasen* (Have to send)

Japanese uses the double negative **-nakereba narimasen** to express
the idea of obligation. It actually means something like *If you don't (do
it), it won't do* but it is more likely to be translated as *must* or *have to.*

Hikōki no shuppatsu wa asa *The plane departs at 7:30 a.m., so*
7-ji han desu kara, mae no *I'll have to stay in Tokyo the*
ban wa Tōkyō ni *night before.*
**tomaranakereba
narimasen.**

Ato de unten **shinakereba** *I have to drive later, so it's better if*
naranai no de, o-sake o *I don't have any sake.*
nomanai hō ga ii desu.

Keiyaku shorui wa mada *The contract papers aren't ready*
dekite imasen kara, *yet, so we'll have to extend the*
shimekiri o *deadline.*
**nobasanakereba
narimasen.**

The negative *do not have to* cannot be expressed with this pattern. Instead, you need to use **-nakute mo ii desu.** (See Lesson 17, Note 2.)

A En-date de *Do we have to pay in yen?*
harawanakereba
narimasen ka.

B Iie, en-date de *No, it's all right if you don't pay in*
harawanakute mo ii *yen.*
desu.

3 *Go-kurō sama deshita* (Thank you for doing a good job)

This phrase is a way of saying thank you to someone for having worked hard, and shows your appreciation of their labour. It is therefore used only when they have performed some duty well, rather than when they have done something as a favour. Hence you might say it to the man delivering your new washing machine, but if you say it to a colleague who holds a door open for you, it sounds as if you consider this to be his role in life. It is not generally said to superiors.

4 *Aoyama Kōgen to iu tokoro* (A place called Aoyama Kōgen)

The phrase **to iu** is used to point out a name or word that the speaker thinks the listener might be unfamiliar with, and which therefore needs identification or explanation. In this way it is similar to the English *called* as shown in the examples below.

'Miki Supōtsu' **to iu** kaisha o kiita koto ga arimasu ka.
Have you ever heard of a company called 'Miki Sports'?

Buchō, Watanabe **to iu** hito ga uketsuke ni imasu ga...
Buchō, there's a man called Watanabe in reception...

Kyonen Igirisu ni itta toki, nan **to iu** ryokō-gaisha o tsukaimashita ka.
When you went to Britain last year, what travel agent did you use? (Lit. ...what-called travel agent?)

5 *Onsen* (Hot springs)

Being a volcanic country, Japan has a wealth of natural hot springs, and it is a common leisure pursuit to go to the mountains for the weekend and soak in the hot water. In easily accessible locations, whole resort towns have grown up around the springs, while in the more remote areas it may be necessary to leave the car and hike through the hills to get to a **ryokan**, or Japanese inn, built next to the hot spring waters.

6 *Yukkuri suru koto ga dekimasu* (You can take it easy)

When you want to talk about ability to do something (*can, be able to*) in Japanese, the easiest way is simply to add **koto ga dekiru** to the plain present form of the verb. This phrase can be used to talk both about skills (*Can you play the piano?*) and about possibilities (*Can I get* *there in half an hour?*).

Hashi o tsukau **koto ga dekimasu** ka.

Can you use chopsticks?

Sono kaisha ni hairu to, mainen Yōroppa ni **iku koto ga dekimasu**.

If you join that company, you'll be able to go to Europe every year.

Kono shūmatsu no ibento o tantō **suru koto ga dekimasu** ka.

Can you be in charge of the events this weekend?

Expansion activities

1 Which of the things shown below can you do? How would you ask someone else if they can do them? Using the illustrations and the cues, make questions and answers like the ones in the example.

Example: **Q** Nihongo o hanasu koto ga dekimasu ka.

A Hai, dekimasu. (*or* Iie, dekimasen.)

Nihongo, hanasu.

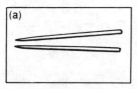

hashi, tsukau

kanji, kaku

kuruma, unten suru

tabako, yameru

Nihon no shinbun, yomu

2 At the morning meeting, Okamoto kachō has just introduced the topic of this summer's company trip. The Wajima summer trip is always an enjoyable affair, so everyone wants to know all the details as soon as possible. Work out what their questions and the kachō's answers are, using the same pattern as in the example.

Example: tokoro – iku? Aoyama kōgen

  Q Nan to iu tokoro ni ikimasu ka.
  A Aoyama Kōgen to iu tokoro ni ikimasu.

(*a*)	hoteru – tomaru?	Arupusu Puraza
(*b*)	ryokō-gaisha – tsukau?	Tanaka Toraberu
(*c*)	onsen – iku?	Yamanaka Onsen
(*d*)	eki – oriru?	Nishi Aoyama
(*e*)	gaido san (*guide*) – desu?	Itō Kumiko san

3 Noguchi san is in charge of organising party games for the company trip, and at the moment he's making up questions for a general knowledge quiz. See how many of the questions you can answer – in Japanese of course.
  (*a*) Nihon to Igirisu to, dochira no hō ga ōkii desu ka.
  (*b*) Shinkansen to hikōki to, dochira no hō ga hayai desu ka.
  (*c*) Piramiddo to Koroshiamu (*Coliseum*) to, dochira no hō ga saki ni dekimashita ka.
  (*d*) Noruē to Suēden to, dochira no hō ga kita ni arimasu ka.
  (*e*) Rondon to Tōkyō to, dochira no hō ga ame ga ōi desu ka.
  (*f*) Fuji san to Mattahōn to, dochira no hō ga takai desu ka.

4 Look at the pairs of pictures below, and make comparisons by asking and answering questions like the ones in the example.

Example

Nihon no sutēki   (takai)   Amerika no sutēki

  Q Nihon no sutēki to Amerika no sutēki to, dochira no hō ga takai desu ka.
  A Nihon no sutēki no hō ga takai desu.

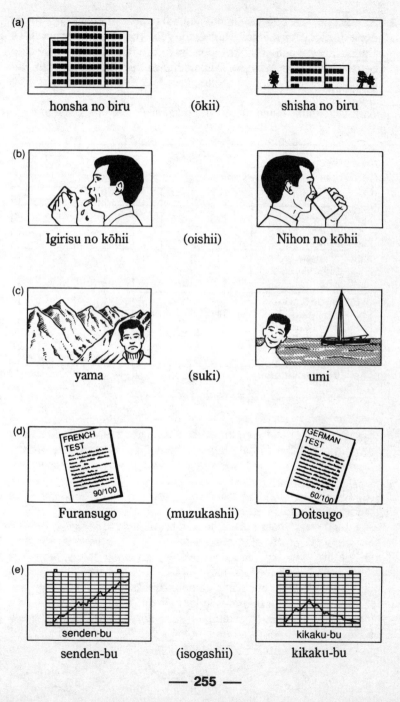

(a) honsha no biru   (ōkii)   shisha no biru

(b) Igirisu no kōhii   (oishii)   Nihon no kōhii

(c) yama   (suki)   umi

(d) Furansugo   (muzukashii)   Doitsugo

(e) senden-bu   (isogashii)   kikaku-bu

5 At today's meeting, Okamoto kachō explained what has to be done in preparation for the signing of the next contract with Dando Sports and what the deadlines are. Look at the schedule below to work out what he said, using **-nakereba narimasen.**

Example

Ku-gatsu itsuka made ni keiyaku o kakanakereba narimasen.

		Ku-gatsu					Jū-gatsu		
	1–5	8–12	15–19	22–26	29–3	6–10	13–17	20–24	27–31
keiyaku o kaku	*								
(a) hōritsu tantō no Mori san to hanashiau		*							
(b) mondai ten o zenbu kaiketsu suru			*						
(c) Dandō Supōtsu ni keiyaku shorui o okuru				*					
(d) jōken o kimeru								*	
(e) keiyaku ni sain suru									*

6 Some people at the meeting were concerned that these deadlines were too tight and that they might not be able to meet them. Look at what they said below, and choose which of the responses Okamoto kachō is likely to have given.

(*a*) Ku-gatsu itsuka made ni keiyaku o kaku koto ga dekinakereba dō shimasu ka.

    (*i*) Ja, jū-gatsu made nobashite mo ii desu.

    (*ii*) Ja, asatte okutte mo ii desu.

(*b*) Mori san ga mondai ten o kaiketsu suru koto ga dekinakereba, dō shimasu ka.

    (*i*) Sō desu ne, buchō ga nobashimashō.

    (*ii*) Chotto wakarimasen kara, buchō ni kikimasho.

(*c*) Jōken o zenbu meikaku ni suru koto ga dekinakereba, dō shimasu ka.

(i) Ja, keiyaku ni sain shinai hō ga ii desu.
(ii) Ja, kikaku ni sain shinai hō ga ii desu.
(d) En-date ni suru koto ga dekinakereba, dō shimasu ka.
(i) Ja, doru-date ni shite mō ii desu.
(ii) Ja, doru o karite kudasai.
(e) Joken ga yoku nakereba, dō shimasu ka.
(i) Ja, mō ichido keiyaku shimashō.
(ii) Ja, mō ichido kangaemashō.

7 Now it's your turn. You and a couple of friends are thinking of taking a weekend trip to an **onsen**. At work you ask your colleague Itō san whether she would like to come along too.

You (a) *This weekend I'm going on a trip with some friends – would you like to come too?* _____

Itō Ii desu ne. Doko ni ikimasu ka.
You (b) *It isn't decided yet, but I like the mountains better than the sea, so I'm considering an onsen called Shirakawa.* _____

Itō Onsen ni tomaru n' desu ka. Ii desu ne.
You (c) *Yes, because you can take it easy at an onsen, can't you.* _

Itō Shirakawa no sansai ryōri wa oishii desu yo.
You (d) *Well, shall we decide on Shirakawa then?* _____

Itō Ē, sō shimashō. Nan-ji ni demashō ka.
You (e) *We'll have to take an 8:00 train, so can you come to the station by 7:30?* _____

Itō Hai, ja 7-ji han desu ne. Tanoshimi ni shite imasu.

—————— Reading corner ——————

Ikeda san has just finished typing up the schedule for the company trip next week. After reading it, see if you can answer the questions overleaf.

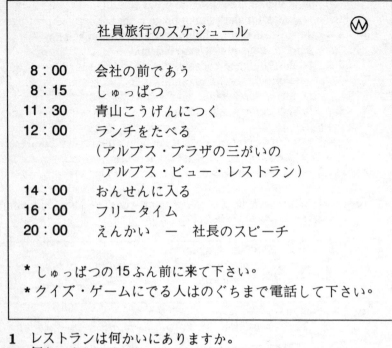

社員旅行のスケジュール

8：00	会社の前であう
8：15	しゅっぱつ
11：30	青山こうげんにつく
12：00	ランチをたべる
	（アルプス・プラザの三がいの
	アルプス・ビュー・レストラン）
14：00	おんせんに入る
16：00	フリータイム
20：00	えんかい　ー　社長のスピーチ

＊しゅっぱつの15ふん前に来て下さい。

＊クイズ・ゲームにでる人はのぐちまで電話して下さい。

1　レストランは何かいにありますか。
2　何というレストランですか。
3　えんかいは何時からですか。

Business briefing

Company trips

The Japanese like group outings, and it is a common sight around the tourist spots to see organised groups of schoolchildren, business people or tourists trailing along behind the guide with her inevitable flag. The company trip, however, is a decidedly more relaxed affair. Most companies organise at least one trip a year, and more often than not it is exclusively for the employees of the company, so wives, husbands and children tend to get left behind. An **onsen**, or hot-spring resort, not too many hours distant from the company is a popular destination, and many once-picturesque **onsen** sites have been spoiled by enormous concrete hotels specifically designed for large, low-paying tour groups.

If the group is staying at a **ryokan**, or Japanese-style inn, then they will be sharing **tatami**-mat rooms together, with perhaps as many as eight or ten people in one room. The **futon** bedding will be laid out at night side by side, and then put away again during the daytime. At meal times the group will all sit down to eat together in a large **tatami**-mat room which has several rows of individual low black tables set out on floor. Each small table will be laid out with a variety of small and colourful dishes, usually including local specialities such as particular kinds of fish, vegetables or pickles. In the evening, the meal is likely to be washed down with copious amounts of beer and sake, and as the evening progresses, so the group will get more raucous, and the games and singing begin. Singing, whether unaccompanied or with a background **karaoke** tape, is a great way of breaking down reserve, and when everyone joins in it also helps to foster the group spirit.

One of the main purposes of the company trip is to strengthen the feeling of group solidarity, and so most of the time will be spent in group activities such as sports, games, visits to tourist spots and parties. Not to join in these activities is likely to be frowned upon, and in fact such trips are a very good way of getting to know your colleagues better, and of discovering their hidden talents as singers, comedians, quizmasters or baseball players. Although some younger employees these days may try to find ways of avoiding the company trip, nevertheless it is a tradition which is likely to continue flourishing for a very long time.

DAI 20 KA

MINNA TANOSHI-
SŌ DESU NE

In Lesson 20 you will find information on respect language, or **keigo**, and there is also practice with saying how something looks or appears, reporting on hearsay, and using relative clauses (such as *The company which I visited yesterday was in Shinjuku.*) At the end of the lesson is a quiz to test your general knowledge about Japan.

The story so far

<ruby>輪島<rt>わじま</rt></ruby>はせんしゅうダンドー・スポーツとのけいやくにサインをしましたから、<ruby>山本部長<rt>やまもとぶちょう</rt></ruby>はホッとしています。<ruby>今日<rt>きょう</rt></ruby>は<ruby>社員旅行<rt>しゃいんりょこう</rt></ruby>の<ruby>日<rt>ひ</rt></ruby>だから、みんなでバスにのって、<ruby>青山<rt>あおやま</rt></ruby>こうげんに<ruby>来<rt>き</rt></ruby>ました。8<ruby>時<rt>じ</rt></ruby>からえんかいがはじまって、みんな<ruby>楽<rt>たの</rt></ruby>しそうに<ruby>歌<rt>うた</rt></ruby>を<ruby>歌<rt>うた</rt></ruby>っています。<ruby>山本部長<rt>やまもとぶちょう</rt></ruby>もうれしそうにおさけをのみながら、<ruby>野口<rt>のぐち</rt></ruby>さんと<ruby>話<rt>はなし</rt></ruby>をしています。

Wajima wa senshū Dandō Supōtsu to no keiyaku ni sain o shimashita kara, Yamamoto buchō wa hotto shite imasu. Kyō wa shain ryokō no hi dakara, minna de basu ni notte, Aoyama Kōgen ni kimashita. 8-ji kara enkai ga hajimatte, minna tanoshi-sō ni uta o utatte imasu.

Yamamoto buchō mo ureshi-sō ni o-sake o nominagara, Noguchi san
to hanashi o shite imasu.

Dialogue

野口 よかったですね、ダンドー・スポーツとのけいやくがうま
くいって…

山本 野口くんもいそがしそうでしたね。会社のために、いっしょ
うけんめいはたらいたから…

野口 いいえ、とんでもない。

山本 (looking around) みんな楽しそうですね。あそこで今歌を歌
っている人はだれですか。

野口 あの人はなごや支社から来た田中という人です。かれはひ
じょうにさけにつよいという話ですよ。

山本 あぁ、そう、そう… 岡本課長のうしろでおどっている人
は…？

野口 部長！ わからないんですか。あれは堀田くんですよ。 部長
もよっぱらっていますね。

(The obāsan from the hotel opens the door to the room, and bows.)

おばあさん おそれいりますが、山本さんというかた、いらっしゃ
いますか。

山本 はい、わたしですが、何か…？

おばあさん お電話でございますが。

山本 あぁ、どうも。だれだろう？ ちょっと、しつれいしま
す。(He goes out to the phone.)

もしもし、山本ですが...

中川 もしもし、山本部長ですか。輪島の中川ともうします が、えんかい中にお電話して、もうしわけありませ ん。じつは、さっきイギリスのロイドさんからお電 話がありました。

山本 えぇ？ロイドさんから？それで、何でしたか。

中川 さあ、よくわかりませんが、できるだけはやくお電 話下さいとおっしゃっていました。

山本 ええ？何だろう！

Noguchi Yokatta desu ne, Dandō Supōtsu to no keiyaku ga umaku itte...

Yamamoto Noguchi kun mo isogashi-sō deshita ne. Kaisha no tame ni, isshōkenmei hataraita kara...

Noguchi Iie, tonde mo nai.

Yamamoto (*looking around*) Minna tanoshi-sō desu ne. Asoko de ima uta o utatte iru hito wa dare desu ka.

Noguchi Ano hito wa Nagoya shisha kara kita Tanaka to iu hito desu. Kare wa hijō ni sake ni tsuyoi to iu hanashi desu yo.

Yamamoto Ā, sō, sō... Okamoto kachō no ushiro de odotte iru hito wa...?

Noguchi Buchō! Wakaranai n' desu ka. Are wa Hotta kun desu yo. Buchō mo yopparatte imasu ne. (*The* obāsan *from the hotel opens the door to the room, and bows.*)

Obāsan Osore-irimasu ga, Yamamoto san to iu kata, irasshaimasu ka.

Yamamoto Hai, watashi desu ga, nanika...?

Obāsan O-denwa de gozaimasu ga.

Yamamoto Ā, dōmo. Dare darō? Chotto, shitsurei shimasu. (*He goes out to the phone.*) Moshi moshi, Yamamoto desu ga...

Nakagawa Moshi moshi, Yamamoto buchō desu ka. Wajima no

	Nakagawa to mōshimasu ga, enkai-chū ni o-denwa shite, mōshiwake arimasen. Jitsu wa, sakki Igirisu no Roido san kara o-denwa ga arimashita.
Yamamoto	Ē, Roido san kara? Sorede, nan deshita ka.
Nakagawa	Sā, yoku wakarimasen ga, dekiru dake hayaku o-denwa kudasai to osshatte imashita.
Yamamoto	Ē? Nan darō!

hotto shite imasu *is feeling relieved*	**yopparatte imasu** *is drunk* [from
hajimatte began [from **hajimaru**, *it*	**yopparau**, *to get drunk*]
begins]	**....irasshaimasu ka** *Is....here?*
tanoshi-sō ni *enjoyably, having fun*	[from **irassharu**, *honorific form of*
uta *song*	**iru**]
utatte imasu *are singing* [from	**O-denwa de gozaimasu** *There's a*
utau, *to sing*]	*call for you* [from **gozaru**, *honorific*
ureshi-sō *looking happy, happily*	*form of* **desu**]
isogashi-sō deshita *looked busy,*	**darō** [plain form of **deshō**]
was busy	**Saitō to mōshimasu** *My name is*
no tame ni *for, for the sake of*	*Saitō* [from **mosu**, *humble form of*
isshōkenmei *as hard as you could,*	**iu**]
with great effort	**enkai-chū** *in the middle of the party*
tonde mo nai *Not at all, please*	**mōshiwake arimasen** *I apologise, I*
don't mention it	*owe you an apology*
uta o utatte iru hito *the person*	**mōshiwake** *apology, excuse*
who's singing a song	**sakki** *just now, a little while ago*
to iu hanashi desu *it is said that,*	**dekiru dake hayaku** *as soon as*
they say that	*possible*
odotte iru hito wa..? *and the*	**o-denwa kudasai** *please telephone*
person who's dancing? [from	**to osshatte imashita** *he said* [from
odoru, *to dance*]	**ossharu**, *honorific form of* **iu**]

✔ ——— Comprehension ———

1 Why is Yamamoto buchō able to relax now?
(a) Because the party is going well.
(b) Because the contract with Dando Sports finally got signed.
(c) Because Noguchi san worked hard to get the contract signed.

2 What is Tanaka san doing at the moment?
(a) He's singing a song.
(b) He's drinking sake.
(c) He's dancing.

Notes

1 8-ji ni enkai ga hajimatte... (the party began at 8:00, and...)

There are a number of verbs in Japanese that have both transitive and intransitive forms, or in other words, those that need an object, and those that don't. For example, the verb **hajimeru** is transitive, so it needs an object, and means *to begin (something)*.

1981-nen ni kokusai tōshi o **hajimemashita**.
In 1981 we began (making) international investments.

The verb **hajimaru**, on the other hand, is intransitive, so it does not need an object, and means *something begins*.

Seminā ga mō sugu **hajimarimasu** yo.
The seminar is about to begin.

Two more verbs which act in the same way are **shimeru** (*to close something*) and **shimaru** (*to be closed*).

Kuruma no doa o **shimete** kudasai.
Please close the car door.

Kono ginkō wa nan-ji ni **shimarimasu** ka.
What time does this bank close?

We have already come across the intransitive verb **kimaru** (*to be decided*), and this too has a corresponding transitive version in **kimeru** (*to decide something*).

Kyō torēningu no basho o **kimenakereba** narimasen.
Shimekiri no hi wa mō **kimarimashita**.
Today we have to decide the location for the training (session).
The day for the deadline has been decided.

Other examples of similar pairs of verbs are:

tomeru	(*to stop, halt something*)	tomaru	(*to come to a halt*)
akeru	(*to open something*)	aku	(*to open, be open*)
ireru	(*to insert something*)	hairu	(*to go in, enter*)
kaeru	(*to change something*)	kawaru	(*to change, be changed*)

2 Tanoshi-sō (Looks happy)

The -sō ending added on to adjectives is used when you want to comment on how someone or something appears, so it can be variously translated as *looks, looks like, seems, appears*. With -i adjectives, the final -i needs to be dropped before adding -sō, but it can be added directly to -na adjectives (without the -na).

Kono keizai no hon wa nagakute, **muzukashi-sō** desu ne.	*This economics book looks long and difficult, doesn't it.*
Tsugi no supiikā wa **omoshiro-sō** desu.	*The next speaker looks interesting.*

When the adjective to be used is **ii/yoi** (*good*), the formation is irregular, becoming **yosa-sō**.

Kono kōsu no naiyō wa **yosa-sō** desu ne.	*The contents of this course look good, don't they.*

When the negative form of the adjective is used, ending in **nai**, the corresponding form is **nasa-sō** (*doesn't look ...*).

Kyō wa, kachō wa kibun ga yoku **nasa-sō** desu.	*The kachō looks as if he doesn't feel well today.*

When new compound words are formed by adding the suffix -sō, these words themselves then become -na adjectives.

Noguchi san wa **taka-sō-na** sūtsu o kite imasu ne.	*Noguchi san is wearing an expensive-looking suit, isn't he.*
Atarashii hisho wa atama ga **yosa-sō-na** hito desu.	*The new secretary seems an intelligent person.*

Words ending in -sō can also be used as adverbs, to describe how someone appears as they do something.

Ano hito wa itsumo **isogashi-sō ni** hataraite imasu ga, hontō wa sonna ni isogashiku nai n' desu yo.	*He always looks as if he's working busily, but really he's not that busy.*

3 Kaisha no tame ni (For the company)

In this sentence, **tame ni** means *for the benefit of, for the sake of*, but it can also have the wider meaning of *for the purpose of, in order to*.

Igirisu to Nihon no kankei o yoku suru **tame ni**, watashitachi wa Nihongo o benkyō shite imasu.	*We're learning Japanese so that we can improve relations between Britain and Japan.*

Ii shōhin o uru **tame ni**, ii   *In order to sell good products, a*
dezain ga hitsuyō desu.   *good design is necessary.*

4 *Iie, tonde mo nai* (Please don't mention it)

This expression is used as a gracious response when someone heaps
praise or compliments on you. In various situations it can mean *No,
no, not at all* or *It's nothing* or *Please don't mention it.*

A   Obata san wa Tōkyō   *You went to Tokyo University,*
     Daigaku o deta n' desu   *Obata san? You must be clever!*
     ka. Atama ga ii desu ne!

B   **Iie, tonde mo nai** desu   *No, it's nothing.*
     yo.

5 *Uta o utatte iru hito wa* (The person who's singing a song)

In Lesson 18, we saw how whole sentences including the verb can be
used like extended adjectives before words like **yotei** (*plan*), **chansu**
(*chance*) and **toki** (*the time when*). Such verb phrases can in fact be
used to describe any noun, and correspond to clauses in English
which are introduced with *who, which, that,* etc. In English, these
clauses come after the word they describe; in Japanese, they come
before it, like any adjective, and this can be seen in the examples below, where corresponding sections in English and Japanese have
been printed in bold type.

Maitsuki QC sākuru de   *The reports **which they write in***
kaku repōto wa yoku yaku   ***the QC circle** are very useful,*
ni tachimasu ne.   *aren't they.*

Kono haru* haitta shain wa   *The employees **who joined (the***
minna isshōkenmei   ***company) this spring** all*
hatarakimasu.   *work very hard.*

Kono robotto o tsukutte iru   *The company **which is making***
kaisha wa, kokusai-teki ni   ***these robots** is internationally*
yūmei desu.   *famous.*

Remember that the verbs which come within the clauses can all be in
the plain form, as it is only the politeness level of the verb at the end
of the sentence which affects the tone of the sentence.

* For your information, the other seasons are **aki**, autumn, **fuyu**, winter and **natsu**, summer.

6 *...to iu hanashi desu* (It is said that)

When the phrase **to iu hanashi** is used at the end of a sentence, it means *it is said that* or *the story is that*, and so is used to report on hearsay.

Kinō buchō wa taihen yopparatta **to iu hanashi desu** yo!	*They say that the buchō was really drunk last night!*
Raishū Roido san ga kuru **to iu hanashi** o sakki kikimashita.	*I heard the news just now that Mr Lloyd is coming next week.*

7 *...irasshaimasu ka* (Is...here?)

As you have seen throughout this text, there are many different ways of saying the same thing in Japanese, depending on who you are speaking to, and the degree of formality and respect required by the situation. For example, the following three sentences all mean *Koyama san is in the meeting room*.

Koyama san wa kaigi-shitsu ni iru.
Koyama san wa kaigi-shitsu ni iru n' desu.
Koyama san wa kaigi-shitsu ni imasu.

It is also possible to show respect to someone of higher status or greater age not just by using different verb endings, but by using completely different verbs altogether. The verb **irassharu**, for example, means *to be, to exist* as does the verb **iru** in the three sentences above, but it is used to emphasise the fact that the person being referred to is of much higher status than the speaker. For example, a reception desk clerk may use this so-called 'honorific' language when greeting guests to the company, staff in a department store may use it towards customers, and junior office workers will probably use it if they find themselves talking to the company president and his wife. Some other verbs which are used in this way are on the next page.

Dictionary form	Ordinary polite form	Honorific form	Meaning
kuru	kimasu	irasshaimasu	*to come*
iku	ikimasu	irasshaimasu	*to go*
taberu	tabemasu	meshiagarimasu	*to eat*
iu	iimasu	osshaimasu	*to say*
suru	shimasu	nasaimasu	*to do*
miru	mimasu	goran ni narimasu	*to see*
da	desu	de gozaimasu	*to be, is*

Following are some examples of how these verbs might typically be used.

Mazu shachō no okusama ga supiichi o **nasaimasu** kara, sono ato de kanpai o shimashō.

First the president's wife will give a speech, so let's have a toast after that.

Shachō, kono keiyaku shorui o mō **goran ni narimashita ka.**

Mr President, have you already seen the contract papers?

As mentioned above, such honorific language is only used when the subject is someone other that yourself. (It is somewhat similar to the use of words like **san**, which you only use when referring to other people, not to yourself.) However, another way to emphasise or show recognition of differences in status is by using so-called 'humble' language when talking about yourself, and so elevating the other person by implication. Some examples of verbs which are used in this way are shown below.

Dictionary form	Ordinary humble form	Humble form	Meaning
kuru	kimasu	mairimasu	*to come*
iku	ikimasu	mairimasu	*to go*
taberu	tabemasu	itadakimasu	*to eat*
nomu	nomimasu	itadakimasu	*to drink*
suru	shimasu	itashimasu	*to do*
iu	iimasu	mōshimasu	*to say, speak*
iru	imasu	orimasu	*to be,*

Some typical sentences using these humble forms are as follows.

O-saki ni shitsurei **itashimasu.**

Excuse me, I'm leaving now (before you).

| Mō takusan **itadakimashita** kara, kekkō desu. | *I've eaten such a lot, it's been quite enough, thank you.* |

There are other ways of forming verbs and other set phrases for use in respect language, or **keigo**, but this section is intended simply as an introduction to the subject. Although it is important to be aware of these honorific and humble forms, and to recognise them when you hear them being used, you should not worry too much about trying to memorise them or use them all just yet. For the time being, the ordinary polite **-masu** form of verbs will probably be sufficient.

8 *O-denwa de gozaimasu* (There's a telephone call for you)

As the Wajima group are guests, the *obāsan*, or elderly lady, who is in charge of the hotel naturally uses respect language with them. **De gozaimasu** is a more formal equivalent of **desu**, although it is not used when talking about people outside one's own group. Instead, the honorific equivalent **de irasshaimasu** is used.

| Moshi moshi, Watanabe san **de irasshaimasu** ka. | *Hello? Is that Watanabe san?* |

Gozaimasu by itself is the formal equivalent of **arimasu**.

| Mōshiwake **gozaimasen**. | *I apologise* (Lit. *I have no excuse*.) |

9 *...to mōshimasu ga* (The name's...)

As in English, people tend to use more formal Japanese on the telephone, except in cases where they know each other very well. The start of a typical call to a company might go as follows:

Caller	Osore-irimasu ga, Okamoto buchō wa irasshaimasu deshō ka. *I'm very sorry to bother you, but I wonder if Okamoto buchō is there at the moment?*
Secretary	Mōshiwake gozaimasen. Tadaima seki o hazushite orimasu ga, dochira sama deshō ka. *I'm sorry, but he's not at his desk right now. Could I ask who's calling, please?*
Caller	Yamada to mōshimasu ga. *The name's Yamada.*

10 *Dekiru dake hayaku* (As soon as possible)

The phrase **dekiru dake** is used before adjectives, adverbs, verbs or nouns to mean *as...as possible*.

Jikan ga amari arimasen kara, supiichi wa **dekiru dake** mijikaku onegai shimasu.

We don't have much time, so please could you make the speech as short as possible.

Kachō wa Eigo ga wakaranai no de, **dekiru dake** Nihongo de hanashimashō.

The kachō doesn't understand English, so let's speak in Japanese as much as possible.

☑ ——————— **Expansion activities** ———————

1 Find out what the missing words are from the sentences below in order to complete the crossword.

ACROSS
3 Kono furoppii o doko ni _____ n' desu ka.
5 Nagoya wa Tōkyō to Ōsaka no _____ ni arimasu.
7 Mō _____ ni sain o shimashita ka.
9 Igirisu e _____ koto ga arimasu ka.
11 Kanji o kirei ni _____ koto ga dekimasu ka.
13 Kinō no tanjōbi de nan- _____ ni narimashita ka.
14 5-ji made ni kono fakkusu o okuranakereba _____.
16 Kono _____ wa oishii desu ne.
19 Kono kikai o tsukatta _____ ga arimasu ka.
20 Ano hito wa Tanaka san _____ okusan desu.
21 Kono mondai o mō _____ shimashita ka.
24 Nihon no kōhii wa, Igirisu no kōhii yori _____ desu ne.
25 Mainen 4- _____ ni atarashii shain ga hairimasu.
26 _____ de haratta hō ga ii desu.
28 Chotto nonda kara, _____ shinai hō ga ii desu yo.

DOWN
1 Atarashii shōhin no _____ wa ¥2,500 ni kimarimashita.
2 _____ da! Ryōri o shitaku nai!
3 Kengaku ni _____ jikan ga arimasen.
4 Shachō-shitsu wa ichiban _____ ni arimasu.

5 Kinō Nagoya shisha kara kita fakkusu wa doko ni _____ ka.
6 Terebi o _____ benkyō shite wa ikemasen.
8 Tōkyō kara Ōsaka made, Shinkansen de nan-_____ kakarimasu ka.
10 Keiyaku no jōken o zenbu _____ ni shimashita ka.
12 Pari ni ittara, oishii Furansu ryōri o _____ ne.
15 Jitsu _____, Suzuki san wa kyō konai to itte imashita.
16 Asoko ni suwatte iru hito o _____ imasu ka.
17 Roido san wa itsu Igirisu e _____ yotei desu ka.
18 Itaria _____ Supein ni tōshi shita hō ga ii desu.
21 Kono heya no _____ o futatsu tsukurimashita.
22 Biiru o _____ -bon kudasai.
23 Kinō osoku made benkyō _____ kedo, mada yoku wakarimasen.
26 _____ to doru to, dochira ga tsuyoi desu ka.
27 Kanojo wa doko _____ hataraite imasu ka.

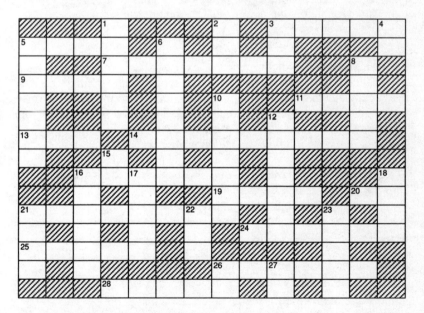

2 Everyone is having a good time at the party in Aoyama Kōgen. However, there are a lot of people from the branch offices, and Yamamoto buchō is not always sure who everyone is, so he asks Noguchi san. Look at the picture, and make sentences like the one in the example below.

Yamamoto Uta o utatte iru hito o shitte imasu ka.
Noguchi Are wa Tanaka to iu hito desu.

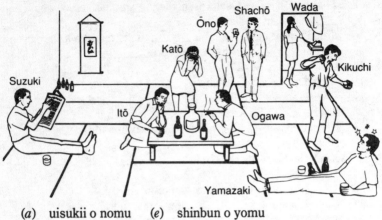

(a) uisukii o nomu   (e) shinbun o yomu
(b) shashin o toru   (f) shachō to hanasu
(c) tabako o sū   (g) yopparau
(d) denwa o kakeru   (h) odoru

3 Recently some of the middle level staff at Wajima have been attending a series of seminars connected with training and personnel matters, and after each seminar they are asked to give feedback on what they thought of it. The chart below shows the results of the feedback for April and May.

	4-gatsu	5-gatsu	6-gatsu
bideo*	omoshiroi	omoshiroku nai	
(a) ryōri	oishii	amari oishiku nai	
(b) supiichi	nagai	mijikai	
(c) heya	hiroi	chiisai	
(d) hoteru	yoi	warui	
(f) naiyō	yaku ni tatsu	yaku ni tatanai	

* bideo: *video*

Based on the information above and the verbs supplied below, make sentences about the April and May seminars, using the same pattern as in the example.

Example: (bideo, miru) 4-gatsu ni **mita bideo** wa omoshirokatta kedo, 5-gatsu ni **mita bideo** wa omoshiroku nakatta desu.

(a) taberu   (d) tomaru
(b) kiku   (e) benkyō suru
(c) tsukau

4 Hotta san is somewhat naive, and tends to take things at face value, so more worldly Noguchi san often has to set him straight as to the real facts. Using the cues provided, create more exchanges between Hotta and Noguchi like the one below.

Example: shigoto, taihen
Hotta   Ano *shigoto* wa *taihen-sō* desu ne.
Noguchi *Taihen-sō-na shigoto* desu kedo, hontō wa sonna ni *taihen ja nai* n' desu yo.

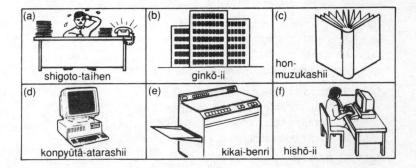

5 At the party, Umeda san, one of the new reception clerks, has been telling Hotta about her induction training which included instruction in the use of **keigo**, or respect language. For fun, Umeda san tested Hotta san to see how much **keigo** he knew. Below are the sentences she gave him, and three possible **keigo** equivalents for each sentence, only one of which is correct. Hotta san got all the answers right – see if you can do as well.

Example: 'Tanaka san desu ka.'
  ✓(i)   Tanaka san de irasshaimasu ka.
  ___(ii) Tanaka san orimasu ka.
  ___(iii) Tanaka sama osshaimasu ka.

(*a*) 'Nani ni shimasu ka.'
___(*i*) Nani gozaimasu ka.
___(*ii*) Nani ni nasaimasu ka.
___(*iii*) Nani o shimasu ka.

(*b*) 'Ohayō gozaimasu, Wajima desu ga.'
___(*i*) Ohayō gozaimasu, Wajima de gozaimasu ga.
___(*ii*) Ohayō gozaimasu, Wajima de irasshaimasu ga.
___(*iii*) Ohayō gozaimasu, Wajima de mōshimasu ga.

(*c*) 'Shachō wa nan to iimashita ka.'
___(*i*) Shachō wa nan to osshaimashita ka.
___(*ii*) Shachō wa nan to mairimashita ka.
___(*iii*) Shachō wa nan to oshiemashita ka.

(*d*) 'Shachō-shitsu wa koko desu.'
___(*i*) Shachō-shitsu wa kochira imasu.
___(*ii*) Shachō-shitsu wa koko de irasshaimasu.
___(*iii*) Shachō-shitsu wa kochira de gozaimasu.

(*e*) 'Chotto matte kudasai.'
___(*i*) Chotto o-machimasu.
___(*ii*) Shōshō o-machi kudasai.
___(*iii*) Shōshō o-machi irraishaimasu.

(*f*) 'Uchi no katarogu o mimashita ka.'
___(*i*) Uchi no katarogu o nasaimashita ka.
___(*ii*) Uchi no katarogu o goran ni narimashita ka.
___(*iii*) Uchi no katarogu o goran nasaimashita ka.

(*g*) 'Uchi no Watanabe wa sugu kimasu.'
___(*i*) Uchi no Watanabe wa sugu mairimasu.
___(*ii*) Uchi no Watanabe wa sugu irasshaimasu.
___(*iii*) Uchi no Watanabe wa sugu orimasu.

6 The **enkai** is drawing to a close, and Yamamoto buchō decides to ask all the new staff members to stand up and announce their mid-year resolutions to the rest of the group. Use the words and phrases in the box below to complete their responses. (You will need to use some of them more than once.)

dekiru dake	no tame ni
isshōkenmei	ni tsuite
to iu hanashi	

Buchō   Kono natsu haitta shain no hitotachi, shigoto
(*a*) _____ omotta koto o hanashite kudasai. Ja, Hotta
san kara onegai shimasu.

Hotta   Kaigai ryokō ga ōi (*b*) _____ desu ga, watashi mo
ikitai desu.

Umeda   (*c*) _____ hayaku wāpuro o narau tsumori desu.

Saitō   Kaisha (*d*) _____ (*e*) _____ hataraku tsumori
desu.

Itō   Kore kara wa (*f*) _____ Eigo no kurasu ni shusseki
shimasu.

Ogawa   Senden (*g*) _____ motto (*h*) _____ benkyō shitai
to omoimasu.

7 Now it's your turn. You've been attending a series of seminars
being held at a client company, and today's is the third in the
series. While drinking coffee in the reception area before it
begins, you see an acquaintance of yours, Shirai san, and go over
to say hello.

You   (*a*) *Good morning, Shirai san. It's crowded, isn't it!*

Shirai   Hontō ni konde imasu ne. Kyō wa yūmei-na supiikā ga
takusan kite imasu kara ne.

You   (*b*) *Is this the first time you've been to this seminar?*

Shirai   Iie, maitsuki kimasu. Ni-gatsu ni kita seminā wa taihen
yaku ni tachimashita.

You   (*c*) *By the way, who's the person over there drinking
coffee? He's wearing an expensive-looking suit, isn't he!*

Shirai   Shiranai n' desu ka. Are wa uchi no shachō desu yo.

You   (*d*) *Oh, really. Who's the attractive woman talking to
him?*

Shirai   Kanojo wa atarashii shachō-hisho desu yo.

You   (*e*) *She looks clever, doesn't she.*

Shirai   Kanojo wa Okkusufōdo de keizai o benkyō shita to iu
hanashi desu yo.

Uketsuke   Osore-irimasu ga, [*your name*] san, irrasshaimasu
deshō ka.

You	(f) *Yes, that's me. Was there something…?* _____
	_____
Uketsuke	O-denwa de gozaimasu.
You	(g) *Thank you. I wonder who it is?* _____
	_____

📖 ──────── **Reading corner** ────────

Below is a page from Hotta san's diary. See if you can read it, and then answer the questions which follow.

この しゅうまつ 中野にある けんきゅうじょで
トレーニングが あった。 その トレーニングに しゅっせき
した人たちは 本社の人 だけでなく なごや支社
の人も たくさん いた。 となりに すわった人は
なごや支社から 来た 山口さんと いう人だった。
かのじょは とても きれいで しんせつな人だった。
今月のトレーニングは ひじょうに やくにたった。
トレーニングの あとで みんなで カラオケバーに 行った。
そこで 歌った えいごの歌は とても ロマンチックだった。
その歌を 歌いながら ぼくは 山口さんのことを
かんがえた。 来月に ある トレーニングにも
かのじょは 来る だろうか …

1 トレーニングにしゅっせきした人たちは、どこから来ましたか。
2 山口さんはどんな人ですか。
3 今月のトレーニングはどうしたか。
4 堀田さんは、山口さんのことをどう思いましたか。
5 来月もトレーニングがありますか。

Business Briefing

True or False? – Japan Quiz

How much do you know about Japan? Mark which of the statements below you think are false, and which true, then check your answers at the end of the book.

		True	False
1	Japan is larger in area than the UK.	____	____
2	Tipping is common in Japan.	____	____
3	Most offices are open-plan in design.	____	____
4	Slippers, but not outdoor shoes, may be worn on tatami mats.	____	____
5	Japan is in the same time zone as Hong Kong.	____	____
6	Name stamps are often used instead of signatures.	____	____
7	The second largest city after Tokyo is Yokohama.	____	____
8	The handshake is now more common between Japanese people than the bow.	____	____
9	Cars are driven on the left.	____	____
10	Life expectancy for Japanese women is the highest in the world.	____	____
11	Japan Standard Time is nine hours ahead of GMT.	____	____
12	Industrial strikes are common.	____	____
13	It is quite usual to feel mild earthquakes.	____	____
14	Christmas Day is not a national holiday.	____	____
15	Tokyo is on approximately the same latitude as Paris.	____	____
16	The Japanese parliament is known as the Diet.	____	____
17	The symbol of the imperial family is the cherry blossom.	____	____
18	The placename **Tōkyō** means *New Capital*.	____	____
19	When it is summer in Japan, it is winter in Britain.	____	____
20	In restaurants, Japanese food is eaten with chopsticks and western-style food is eaten with a knife and fork.	____	____

TRANSLATIONS AND ANSWERS

Lesson 1

8   taxi, passport, computer, necktie, data
9   fruit, fried chicken, pilaf, beef steak,
knife   10   London, escalator, printer,
America, elegant, golf   11   Mitsubishi
(company name), tuna, suit, two-piece
(suit or dress), tweed   12   Nissan
(company name), Nippon (Japanese
word for *Japan*), pocket, cassette,
panic, soccer, rush (hour), match
15   uētoresu, sarada, bideo, erebētā,
pabu   16   blues, strike, bus, taxi,
schedule, salesman, report, sales,
message, printer, computer, data, report,
memo, typist, type up, copy, lunch, ham
sandwich, coffee, coffee shop, table,
carpet, coffee, suit, necktie, panic,
elevator, manager, sales, cancel, sales,
engineer, manager, girlfriend, restaurant,
date, pizza, beer, stereo.

Lesson 2

Dialogue   Reception   Good morning.
Maeda   Good morning.   **Reception**
Are you checking out?   **Maeda**   Yes,
please.   **Reception**   Your name?
Maeda   It's Maeda.   **Reception**   And
your room number?   **Maeda**   3812.
Reception   3812?   **Maeda**   Yes,
that's right.   **Reception**   *(handing over
the bill)*   Here you are.   **Maeda**   Thank
you. Ah! The key!   **Reception**   Thank
you.

Comprehension   1 (*a*)   2 (*c*)
Expansion activities   1 (*a*) ohayō
gozaimasu   (*b*) konnichiwa
(*c*) konnichiwa   (*d*) konbanwa
2 (*a*) Yon-san-go desu.   (*b*) Ni-ichi-ichi
desu.   (*c*) San-ichi-ni desu.
(*d*) Go-roku-kyū desu.   (*e*) Hachi-san-
kyū desu.   3 (*a*) zero-go-roku-go no
ni-roku-yon no ni-roku-yon   (*b*) zero-san
no yon-roku-roku-go no san-ichi-zero-
nana   (*c*) zero-san no san-kyū-ni-zero no

ichi-nana-nana-roku   (*d*) zero-yon-ni-
nana no kyū-nana no ni-roku-roku-ichi
(*e*) zero-nana-hachi no hachi-roku-ichi no
san-san-yon-san   4 (*a*) Okamoto san wa
kachō desu ka. OR Kachō wa Okamoto san
desu ka.   (*b*) O-heya bangō wa ni-san-go
desu ka.   .(*c*) Denwa bangō wa nan desu
ka.   (*d*) Wajima wa shōsha desu.
(*e*) Denwa bangō wa 03-4836-0862 desu.
5 Food and drink: hamburger, whisky,
salad, beer; At the office: file, typewriter,
computer, database; Jobs: waitress,
engineer, consultant, announcer
6 (*a*) Hai, onegai shimasu.   (*b*) (your
name) desu.   (*c*) Ni-zero-yon desu.
(*d*) Dōmo/ Dōmo arigatō.
Reading corner   Watanabe   Maeda
san wa kakarichō desu ka (*Is Maeda san
an assistant manager?*)   **Koyama**   Hai,
sō desu (*Yes, that's right*)   **Watanabe**
Okamoto san wa? (*How about Okamoto
san?*)   **Koyama**   Okamoto san wa
kaachō desu (*He's a manager*)

Lesson 3

Dialogue   Hotta   Excuse me.   **Kiosk
clerk**   Yes?   **Hotta**   How much are
the lunchboxes?   **Kiosk clerk**   They're
¥800.   **Hotta**   How about the
sandwiches?   **Kiosk clerk**   The cheese
sandwiches are ¥700. The tuna
sandwiches are ¥750.   **Hotta**   The tuna
sandwich, please. I love tuna!   **Kiosk
clerk**   Here you are.   **Hotta**   Oh, and
a Nikkei newspaper too, please.   **Kiosk
clerk**   Thank you.
Comprehension   1 (*b*)   2 (*b*)
Expansion activities   1 (*a*) shinbun,
hyaku nana-jū en   (*b*) kasa, ni-sen
go-hyaku en   (*c*) kōhii, yon-hyaku go-jū
en   (*d*) orenji jūsu, san-byaku go-jū en
(*e*) biiru, rop-pyaku en   (*f*) pen,
kyū-hyaku en   2   kaban o kudasai,
fairu o kudasai, pen o kudasai,
Yomiuri shinbun o kudasai,
kasa o kudasai   3   (follow

example given in exercise) **4** (free answers) **5** (*a*) (*i*) (*b*) (*ii*) (*c*) (*ii*) (*d*) (*i*) (*e*) (*i*) **6** (*a*) Sumimasen (*b*) Nyūs Juiik (OR *Newsweek*) wa ikura desu ka. (*c*) Taimu (OR *Time*) wa? (*d*) Taimu o kudasai. (*e*) Ā, pen mo kudasai.
Reading corner shopping list: kasa, bentō, kaban, Asahi shinbun, nihonshu, kagi

Lesson 4

Dialogue Hotta Hello? **Tanaka** Hello? **Hotta** Is that Tanaka san? **Tanaka** Yes, this is Tanaka. **Hotta** Er, this is Hotta... **Tanaka** (*unable to hear because of background noise*) Eh? Ōta san? **Hotta** No, it's Hotta. Hotta from Sendai. **Tanaka** Ah, Hotta san! Hello! How's your father? **Hotta** He's fine. **Tanaka** Where are you now? **Hotta** I'm at Shinjuku station. **Tanaka** Sightseeing? That's nice, isn't it. **Hotta** No, (I'm in Tokyo) for a job interview.
Comprehension **1** (*c*) **2** (*b*)
Expansion activities **1** (*a*) shachō (*b*) konpyūtā (*c*) ano (*d*) mā-mā (*e*) kankō (*f*) Tōkyō **2** (It is best to say non-Japanese names with Japanese pronunciation if possible, e.g. Rarufu Jēmuzu, but for the sake of ease of reading, the spellings have been given here in their original form.) (*a*) Hajimemashite, Autodoor no Ralph James desu. (*b*) Hajimemashite, Meito no Masato Iwata desu. (*c*) Hajimemashite, Kictec no Susan Ellis desu. (*d*) Hajimemashite, ENA no Richard Moor desu. (*e*) Autodoor no shisha wa doko desu ka. Fukuoka desu. (*f*) Meito no honsha wa doko desu ka. Nagoya desu. (*g*) Kictec no honsha wa doko desu ka. Nagoya desu. (*h*) ENA no shisha wa doko desu ka. Ena-shi desu. **3** (*a*) Hai, sō desu. (*b*) Iie (chigaimasu), buchō desu. (*c*) Hai, sō desu. (*d*) Iie (chigaimasu), fuku-shachō desu. (*e*) Hai, sō desu. **4** (*a*) (*iv*) (*b*) (*vii*) (*c*) (*i*) (*d*) (*v*) (*e*) (*ii*) (*f*) (*iii*) **5** (*e*) (*a*) (*f*) (*i*) (*b*) (*g*) (*c*) (*h*) (*j*) (*d*) **6** (*a*) (your name) desu. (*b*) (your company's name) desu. (*c*) Hai, sō desu./Iie, (country name) no kaisha desu. (*d*) (location of head office) desu. (*e*) Hai, suki desu.

(*f*) Shumi wa (your interests) desu. (*g*) Dō itashimashite.
Reading corner **O-kāsan** Moshi moshi, Hotta desu ga... Hai, ... hai... Yūichirō, denwa! (*Hello, this is Hotta speaking. Yes... Yes... Yūichirō, telephone!*) **Hotta** Dare? (*Who is it?*) **O-kāsan** Wajima no jinji-bu no Ishii san. (*Ishii san, from the personnel department at Wajima.*) **Hotta** Ē! Wajima no Ishii san?! (*What? Ishii san from Wajima?!*)

Lesson 5

Dialogue Noguchi (*to Okamoto*) Kachō, this is Mr Hotta. Today is his first day in our department. **Hotta** I'm Hotta. Pleased to meet you. **Okamoto** Ah, Hotta! Well, work hard! **Hotta** Yes, I certainly will. Excuse me. (*Noguchi takes Hotta over to Yamamoto san's desk, but the buchō is not there.*) **Noguchi** (to Ikeda) Where's the buchō? **Ikeda** He's not here today. He's at the Nagoya office. He'll be back tomorrow. **Noguchi** Oh right, thank you. **Hotta** (*aside to Noguchi*) Who's that? **Noguchi** That's Ikeda san. **Hotta** I see. She's pretty, isn't she! **Noguchi** (introducing Hotta to Ikeda) Ikeda san, this is Hotta san. **Hotta** I'm Hotta. Pleased to meet you. **Ikeda** Pleased to meet you too. Oh, Noguchi san, there's a message from the Nagoya office. Ishihara san can't come to the meeting next week. **Noguchi** What? Why not? Has he got something else on? **Ikeda** I don't know. Shall I call the Nagoya office and see? **Noguchi** Yes, please.
Comprehension **1** (*a*) **2** (*b*)
Expansion activities **1** (*a*) go (*b*) speak (*c*) return (*d*) begin (*e*) teach (*f*) drink (*g*) write (*h*) come (*i*) eat (*j*) see (*k*) understand GANBARIMASU **2** (*a*) Repōto o yomimasu. (*b*) Repōto o kakimasu. (*c*) Shachō ni hanashimasen. (*d*) Wāpuro no renshū o shimasu. (*e*) Denwa o shimasu. (*f*) Nagoya shisha ni ikimasen. (*g*) Sendai ni kaerimasen. (*h*) Terebi o mimasu. (*i*) Kōhii o nomimasu. **3** imasu: (*a*) (*c*) (*f*) (*g*) arimasu: (*b*) (*d*) (*e*) (*h*) **4** ikimasu, kaerimasu, ikimasu, wakarimasen,

kikimasu, hairimasu   5 Takeshita san wa
Ōsaka kara (Tōkyō ni) kaerimasu. Maeda
san wa kaisha ni imasu. Tani san wa (OR
mo) kaisha ni imasu. Noguchi san wa
Nagoya shisha ni ikimasu. Hotta san wa
kenkyū sentā ni ikimasu. Koyama san to
Ikeda san wa wāpuro no kurasu ni
hairimasu.   6 (*a*) wa, no, o   (*b*) no, wa
(*c*) no, wa, ni   (*d*) wa, ni, o   (*e*) wa, ga
(*f*) wa, no, o   (*g*) no, ni/wa, ga   (*h*) o
7 (*a*) Miura san desu ka.   (*b*) [your
name] desu.   (*c*) Hai, genki desu. Ēto,
raishū no kaigi ni kimasu ka.   (*d*) Takagi
san wa?   (*e*) Dō shite? Tsugō ga warui
desu ka.   (*f*) Shigoto desu ka.

Reading corner   Watanabe san, Ikeda
san kara denwa. Ashita wa Hotta san no
pātii desu. Kaigai kikaku-bu no minna
ikimasu. Watanabe san mo ikimasu ka.
Ikeda san ni denwa onegai shimasu.
Michiko. (*Watanabe san, Ikeda san called.*
Tomorrow is Hotta san's party. Everyone
from the Overseas Planning Department is
going. Are you going? Please call Ikeda
san. Michiko.)

Ikeda san, denwa arigatō. Watashi mo
ikimasu. Konban denwa shimasu ne.
Keiko. (*Ikeda san, thanks for the call. Yes,*
I'll come. I'll call you tonight. Keiko.)

Lesson 6

Dialogue   **Kachō**   Morning everyone.
All   Good morning   **Kachō**   Where's
Hotta?   **Maeda**   He'll be here soon.
Shall we wait?   **Kachō**   It's already
10:00.   **Maeda**   Right, let's begin.
Tomorrow Mr Boyd, from the British
company Dando Sports, will be coming.
Noguchi   (*whispering*)   Maeda san,
excuse me. It's not Mr Boyd. It's Mr
Lloyd.   **Maeda**   Ah, yes, Mr Lloyd.
Sorry. Uh, the person in charge is
Noguchi kun, right? What time will Mr
Lloyd be arriving, Noguchi kun?
Noguchi   He'll be arriving at 8:00 in the
morning at Narita airport. I'll be going to
meet him.   **Kachō**   That's early! How
are you going? By limousine bus?
Noguchi   I don't know yet. I'll check
the times of the trains and limousine
buses later.   **Kachō**   You're going too,
aren't you, Maeda san.   **Maeda**   Well...

Kachō   Is there a problem? Are you
busy?   **Maeda**   No, I'm not busy. It's
fine.   **Kachō**   Good.   **Noguchi**
Thank you, Maeda san.
Comprehension   1 (*b*)   2 (*c*)
Expansion activities   1 (*a*)   shichi-ji
ni-jū-go-fun   (*b*)   san-ji   (*c*)   roku-ji
san-jū-ni-fun   (*d*)   jū-ji yon-jū-hap-pun
(*e*)   ni-ji han   (*f*)   hachi-ji yon-jū-go-
fun   2 London – 4:30; Delhi – 9:05;
Singapore – 11:40; Tokyo – 12:45;
Sydney – 12:50; Vancouver – 19:55; New
York – 23:00   3 (*a*)   densha/Shinkansen
(*b*)   denwa/Eigo   (*c*)   terebi
(*d*)   fakkusu   (*e*)   denwa/Eigo
(*f*)   densha   4 (free answers)
5 (*a*)   Roido san wa māketingu no
manējā desu./Māketingu no manējā wa
Roido san desu.   (*b*)   Ashita no asa
Narita kūkō ni tsukimasu.   (*c*)   Roido
san no shumi wa gorufu desu.
(*d*)   Rondon wa suki ja arimasen.
(*e*)   Kare no kaisha wa Igirisu no kaisha
desu.   (*f*)   Roido san wa totemo
isogashii hito desu.   (*g*)   Raishū
Wajima no kenkyū sentā ni ikimasu.
6 (*a*)   Shigoto desu. Shinkansen de Kōbe
ni ikimasu.   (*b*)   8-ji desu. 11-ji 20-pun
goro ni Kōbe ni tsukimasu.
(*c*)   Sō desu ne.   (*d*)   Chotto
muzukashii desu.   (*e*)   Hai, totemo
omoshiroi desu. Nihongo no benkyō wa
tanoshii desu.   (*f*)   Arigatō. Ikura desu
ka.   (*g*)   Y2,500? Takai desu ne!
(*h*)   Hai, ganbarimasu.
Reading corner   8:15   Eigo no
class (*English class*)   9:30   atarashii
part-time no mensetsu (*interview for*
new part-time staff)   11:00   Kaigai
kikaku-bu no kaigi (*overseas planning*
department meeting)   12:00   **Lloyd** san
to **lunch** (*lunch with Mr Lloyd*)
2:00   **Singapore** ni kokusai denwa
(*internatonal phone call to Singapore*)
4:00   Tōkyō eki ni shachō o mukae ni
ikimasu (*go to meet the president at Tokyo*
station)   6:00   **Marathon** no renshū
(*training for the marathon*)

Memo   ● Nagoya shisha no Ishihara
san ni denwa (*call Ishihara san in*
Nagoya)   ● **Dando Sports** no shorui o
Yokohama ni **Fax** (*fax the Dando Sports*
documents to Yokohama)   ● Ashita no
golf wa nan-ji kara? (*What time is*
tomorrow's golf?)

Lesson 7

Dialogue **Koyama** Where are you?
Maeda Still at the airport. Is Okamoto kachō there? **Koyama** Um... (*looking around*) he's making a phone call at the moment. **Maeda** Okay, could you get Ikeda san please? **Koyama** Ikeda san is just sending a fax – just a moment. (*calling to Ikeda*) Ikeda san, it's Maeda san. **Ikeda** Just coming. (*comes over and takes the receiver*) Hello, this is Ikeda. **Maeda** Morning, it's Maeda. Well, how are the preparations for tomorrow's meeting? **Ikeda** I'm seeing to it now. I'll soon be finished. **Maeda** Right. How about Hotta kun? What's he doing? **Ikeda** Hotta san? He's been doing all sorts of things since morning. At the moment he's practising on the word processor, but he's not very good yet. **Maeda** (*laughing*) Slow? **Ikeda** Yes, extremely slow! But he's trying very hard. So, what time will you be taking the bus back? **Maeda** I don't know yet. Noguchi kun is just checking the times of the buses now. **Ikeda** Right, I see.

Comprehension 1 (*a*) 2 (*b*)

Expansion activities 1 (*a*) A: Kono heya wa kirei desu ne. B: Ē, hontō-ni kirei-na heya desu ne. (*b*) A: Kono shigoto wa taihen desu ne. B: Ē, honto-ni taihen-na shigoto desu ne. (*c*) A: Ano kōjō wa ōkii desu ne. B: Ē, honto-ni ōki-na kōjō desu ne. (*d*) A: Ano sensei wa shinsetsu desu ne. B: Ē, hontō-ni shinsetsu-na sensei desu ne. (*e*) A: Ano kaisha wa yūmei desu ne. B: Ē, hontō-ni yūmei-na kaisha desu ne. (*f*) A: Kono messēji wa hen desu ne. B: Ē, hontō-ni hen-na messēji desu ne. 2 (*a*) F (*b*) F (*c*) T (*d*) T (*e*) F (*f*) F (*g*) F (*h*) T 3 (*a*) Yamamoto buchō wa ima kōhii o nonde imasu. (*b*) Noguchi san wa ima repōto o yonde imasu. (*c*) Ueno san wa Ikeda san no hanashi o kiite imasu. (*d*) Maeda san wa shorui o kaite imasu. (*e*) Okamoto kachō wa denwa de hanashite imasu. (*f*) Koyama san wa wāpuro no renshū o shite imasu. (*g*) Ikeda san wa Ueno san ni hanashite imasu. 4 **Part A** (*a*) iv (*b*) iii (*c*) i (*d*) v (*e*) vi (*f*) ii **Part B** **Ikeda**: Ja, 'ON' suitchi o oshite kudasai. **Clerk**: Hai. **Ikeda**: 10–byō matte kudasai. **Clerk**: Hai. **Ikeda**: Ēto, furoppii o irete kudasai, ne. **Clerk**: Hai, iremasu. **Ikeda**: Tsugi wa jikan o entā shite kudasai. **Clerk**: Jikan desu ka. Ima 5-ji desu ne. **Ikeda**: Sō desu ne. Sore kara 'RETURN' kii o oshite kudasai. **Clerk**: Ā, menyū desu! **Ikeda**: Ii desu ne. **Clerk**: Hai. Arigatō gozaimasu. 5 okutte kudasai, hajimete kudasai, shite imasu, shite kudasai, irete kudasai 6 (*a*) Hai, muzukashii desu ga, omoshiroi desu. (*b*) Hai, takai desu ga, yoku arimasen. (*c*) Hai, chiisai desu ga, yūmei desu. (*d*) Hai, omoshiroi desu ga, taihen desu. (*e*) Hai, suki desu ga, jōzu ja arimasen. (*f*) Hai, takusan arimasu ga, sugu owarimasu. 7 (*a*) Repōto desu ka. Anō, ima kaite imasu ga... (*b*) Ēto ne, mada iroiro-na koto o shirabete imasu ga... (*c*) Chotto matte kudasai. Tantō-sha ni kikimasu. Sumimasen ga, tantō-sha wa imasen. (*d*) Ima kaigi o shite imasu ga... (*e*) Hai, ashita denwa shimasu.

Reading corner Ima no jikan o kaite kudasai. (*Please write the current time.*) Bu, ka no namae o kaite kudasai. (*Please write your department and section.*)
1 Asa, nani o tabemasu ka. (*What do you eat in the mornings?*) 2 Asa, nani o nomimasu ka. (*What do you drink in the mornings?*) 3 Asa, terebi o mimasu ka. (*Do you watch television in the mornings?*) 4 Shinbun wa nani o yomimasu ka. (*What newspaper do you read?*) 5 Nan-ji ni, kaisha ni ikimasu ka. (*What time do you go to work?*) 6 Densha de kaisha ni ikimasu ka. (*Do you go to work by train?*) 7 Nan-ji ni kaisha ni tsukimasu ka. (*What time do you arrive at the office?*) 8 Shigoto wa nan desu ka. (*What is your job?*) 9 Nan-ji ni kaerimasu ka. (*What time do you go home?*)

Lesson 8

Dialogue **Maeda** I'm back!
Koyama That was really late! **Maeda** Boy, I'm exhausted. **Koyama** What time did Mr Lloyd's plane arrive in the end? **Maeda** It arrived at 11:30. **Koyama** That was really late! **Maeda** The return journey was even worse. It took three and a half hours from the airport to the hotel. **Koyama** You must be really tired. Would you like some green tea or something? **Maeda**

Please. Uh, where's Ikeda san?
Koyama She's already gone home.
Maeda What? What about the
preparations for the meeting? **Koyama**
It's all done. The papers are just there –
shall I show them to you? **Maeda**
Yes, but I'll have that tea first, please.
Comprehension 1 (*c*) 2 (*b*)
Expansion activities 1 (*a*) Tadaima.
(*b*) O-kaeri nasai. (*c*) Wakarimashita.
(*d*) Hajimemashite. (*e*) Moshi moshi.
(*f*) Ganbatte kudasai. (*g*) Shitsurei
shimasu (or shimashita). (*h*) Tsukareta.
(*i*) O-tsukare sama deshita (*j*) O-saki ni
shitsurei shimasu. (*k*) Dō itashimashite.
2 (*a*) Shinkansen de, Tōkyo kara Ōsaka
made, nan-jikan kakarimasu ka. San-
jikan gurai kakarimasu. (*b*) Kuruma
de, Ōsaka kara Kōbe made, nan-jikan
kakarimasu ka. Ichi-jikan gurai
kakarimasu. (*c*) Kuruma de, Tōkyō
kara Nagoya made nan-jikan kakarimasu
ka. San-jikan han gurai kakarimasu.
(*d*) Hikōki de, Ōsaka kara Tōkyō made
nan-jikan kakarimasu ka. Ichi-jikan
gurai kakarimasu. (*e*) Shinkansen
de, Kyōto kara Nagoya made, nan-
jikan kakarimasu ka. Go-jippun
gurai kakarimasu. 3 Kaigi-shitsu
o katazukemashita ka. Hai,
katazukemashita. Mensetsu no
junbi o shimashita ka. Hai, shimashita.
Shinkansen no jikan o shirabemashita ka.
Iie, shirabemasen deshita. Kikaku-bu
no repōto o kopii shimashita ka. Hai,
kopii shimashita. Dandō Supōtsu no
dēta o konpyūtā ni iremashita ka. Iie,
iremasen deshita. 4 Kaigi-shitsu o
katazukemashō ka. Mō katazukemashita.
Mensetsu no junbi o shimashō ka. Mō
shimashita. Shinkansen no jikan o
shirabemashō ka. Hai, shirabete kudasai.
Kikaku-bu no repōto o kopii shimashō ka.
Mō kopii shimashita. Dandō Supōtsu no
dēta o konpyūtā ni iremashō ka. Hai,
irete kudasai. 5 ikimashō, owarimashō,
shimashō, nomimashō, ikimashō,
machimashō, ikimashō, aimashō
6 (*a*) Ohayō gozaimasu. (*b*) Hai,
ikimashita ga, kaeri wa taihen deshita.
(*c*) Yokohama eki ni ōkii jiko ga
arimashita. (*d*) Ē, ichi-jikan mo
machimashita ga, densha wa kimasen
deshita. (*e*) Takushii noriba e ikimashita
ga, hito ga takusan matte imashita. Soko
de yon-jippun mo machimashita.

Kekkyoku jū-ji ni uchi ni kaerimashita.
(*f*) Ē, hontō ni takai desu ne. Demo sore
kara ga motto taihen deshita. (*g*) Uchi
no kagi ga arimasen deshita.
Reading corner Ichi: Kaigai kikaku-bu
no kaigi wa ni-ji kara yo-ji made desu.
(*1 The Overseas Planning Department
meeting is from 2:00 to 4:00.*) Ni: Kachō
no denwa bangō wa zero-go-ni no
san-hachi-ni no san-go-yon-kyū desu.
(*2 The kachō's telephone number is 052–
382–3549.*) San: Kaeri no takushii wa
san-zen go-hyaku roku-jū en deshita.
Takai desu ne. (*3 The taxi back was
¥3,560. Expensive, eh?*) Yon: Ano
roku-sen en no sukāfu o kudasai. (*4 I'll
have the scarf which is ¥6,000, please.*)
Go: Jū-ji no Shinkansen de Nagoya ni
ikimasu. (*5 I'm going to Nagoya on the
10:00 Shinkansen.*)

Lesson 9

Dialogue Shimada Are you still in
the Overseas Planning Department?
Lloyd Yes, I am, but I work in a
different section now. I've been in charge
of marketing since February. **Shimada**
That's hard work. You must be busy.
Lloyd Yes, there's a lot of overtime
too. **Shimada** You're off on Saturdays
and Sundays, right? **Lloyd** Yes, but I
sometimes go to the office on Saturdays.
There are business trips too. **Shimada**
By the way, you're here on this trip until
May 3rd, aren't you. **Lloyd** Yes, that's
right. **Shimada** Are you free on the
first? **Lloyd** The first is a Saturday,
isn't it. Yes, I'm free. Is there
something...? **Shimada** Actually,
there's a wedding on that day. **Lloyd**
Whose wedding? **Shimada** Mine!
Lloyd Well, congratulations!
Comprehension 1 (*c*) 2 (*b*)
Expansion activities 1 (*a*) Doko de
eiga o mimasu ka. Shinjuku de mimasu.
(*b*) Doko de biiru o nomimasu ka. Kanda
de nomimasu. (*c*) Doko de Eigo no
benkyō o shimasu ka. Shibuya de
shimasu. (*d*) Doko de tenisu o shimasu
ka. Ueno de shimasu. (*e*) Doko de
gorufu no renshū o shimasu ka. Kawasaki
de shimasu. (*f*) Doko de karate no
renshū o shimasu ka. Nakano de
shimasu. 2 (*a*) Shimada san no o-kāsan

no tanjōbi wa roku-gatsu jū-ni-nichi desu.
(*b*) Shimada san no kekkon-shiki wa
go-gatsu tsuitachi desu. (*c*) Roido san
no tanjōbi wa jū-ni-gatsu muika desu.
(*d*) Buchō no tanjōbi wa jū-ichi-gatsu
ni-jū-roku-nichi desu. (*e*) Honda san no
kekkon-shiki wa ku-gatsu jū-ku-nichi
desu. (*f*) Nagoya shutchō wa go-gatsu
jū-yokka desu. (*g*) Atarashii shain no
mensetsu wa roku-gatsu futsuka desu.
(*h*) Tanaka san no tanjōbi wa ichi-gatsu
hatsuka desu. **3** 19th: meeting at
Wajima from 1:00 21st: appointment at
2:30 22rd: go to Nagoya on the 10:15
Shinkansen 23rd: go to Kyoto 27th:
return to Tokyo **4** (*a*) (*iii*) (*b*) (*iv*)
(*c*) (*ii*) (*d*) (*v*) (*e*) (*vi*) (*f*) (*i*) **5** 1 (*f*)
2 (*c*) 3 (*d*) 4 (*b*) 5 (*g*) 6 (*a*) 7 (*e*)
6 (*a*) Isogashii deshō! (*b*) Ima mo
jinji-bu de hataraite imasu ka. (*c*) Iie,
ima betsu no kaisha ni tsutomete imasu.
(*d*) Iie, Nihon no kaisha desu. (*e*) Mada
chiisai desu. (*f*) Hontō ni takusan
arimasu yo. Tokidoki doyōbi mo kaisha ni
ikimasu.
Reading corner Okamoto san:
shi-gatsu tōka, Noguchi san: roku-gatsu
jū-roku-nichi, Maeda san: shichi-gatsu
itsuka, Ikeda san: ku-gatsu ni-jū-ichi-
nichi, Koyama san: jū-gatsu tsuitachi,
Yamada san: jū-ichi-gatsu yokka, Takeshita
san: jū-ni-gatsu ni-jū-roku-nichi.

Lesson 10

Dialogue Okamoto I believe there
are a lot of strikes in Britain. **Lloyd**
Well, there are strikes sometimes, but
we never have any at Dando Sports.
Okamoto Why's that? **Lloyd** The
workers don't strike because they get
treated well! The salaries are good too.
(*everyone laughs*) **Okamoto** Dando
Sports exports to Europe, right? **Lloyd**
Yes, we do. Germany is our biggest
market. **Okamoto** How about
Eastern Europe? **Lloyd** Not much.
But we hope to invest more there in the
future. **Okamoto** Is that so. Dando
Sports is a really energetic company,
isn't it! **Lloyd** Thank you.
Comprehension 1 (*b*) **2** (*a*)
Expansion activities 1 (*a*) Fuji-san
desu. (*b*) 3-gatsu desu. (*c*) Tōkyō
desu. (*d*) Batikan Shitii (Vatican City)

desu. (*e*) Shinkansen desu. (*f*) Narita
desu. **2** (*a*) (*iii*) (*b*) (*vi*) (*c*) (*ii*)
(*d*) (*v*) (*e*) (*i*) (*f*) (*vii*) (*g*) (*iv*)
3 (You may find some other ways of
expressing these ideas than the ones
below.) Yōka ni kaigai kikaku-bu no kaigi
o shimashita. Kokonoka ni kenkyū
sentā ni ikimashita. Jū-san-nichi ni kōjō
no jūgyōin no mensetsu o shimashita.
Jū-yokka ni kaigai kikaku-bu no kaigi o
shimashita. Jū-go-nichi ni Nagoya ni
shutchō shimashita. Jū-roku-nichi ni
Roido san ni aimashita. Jū-shichi-nichi
ni Satō san no kekkon-shiki ni demashita.
Jū-hachi-nichi ni gorufu o shimashita.
(*a*) Iie, mokuyōbi wa kaigai kikaku-bu
no kaigi o shimashita kara, kinyōbi ni
(kenkyū sentā ni) ikimashita. (*b*) Iie,
kayōbi ni kōjō no jūgyōin no mensetsu
o shimashita kara, suiyōbi ni (kaigai
kikaku-bu no kaigi o) shimashita. (*c*) Iie,
kinyōbi ni Roido san ni aimashita kara,
mokuyōbi ni (Nagoya ni) shutchō
shimashita. (*d*) Iie, doyōbi ni Satō san
no kekkon-shiki ni demashita kara,
nichiyōbi ni (gorufu o) shimashita.
4 Dandō Supōtsu no dairiten wa Nyū
Yōku to Sōru ni arimasu ga, Deru no
dairiten wa Hyūston to Manira ni
arimasu. Dandō Supōtsu no kōjō wa
Gurazugō to Buristoru ni arimasu ga,
Deru no kōjō wa Dābii to Kādifu ni
arimasu. Dandō Supōtsu no kinmu jikan
wa 9-ji kara 6-ji made desu ga, Deru no
kinmu jikan wa 9-ji kara 5-ji made desu.
Dandō Supōtsu no ichiban ōkii shijō wa
Doitsu desu ga, Deru no ichiban ōkii shijō
wa Furansu desu. Dandō Supōtsu wa
Amerika ni yushutsu shimasu ga, Deru
wa Amerika ni yushutsu shimasen.
5 (Free answers) **6** (*a*) (*ii*) (*b*) (*ii*)
(*c*) (*i*) (*d*) (*ii*) (*e*) (*i*) **7** (*a*) Ima wa
Furansu desu. (*b*) Ima wa zenzen shite
imasen ga, kore kara tōshi o shimasu.
Nihon wa totemo enerugisshu-na kuni
desu kara. (*c*) Iie, chigaimasu. Dairiten
wa Rondon desu ga, honsha wa Ribapūru
ni arimasu. (*d*) E? Ribapūru o shitte
imasu ka. (*e*) Sō desu ka. Igirisu-jin wa
ima amari kikimasen.
Reading corner
Dandō Supōtsu san • Igirisu no
ichiban ōki-na supōtsu-uea no kaisha wa?
(*What's the biggest sportswear company in
Britain?*) • Ichiban ōki-na shijō wa?
(*Where's the biggest market?*)

● Kōjō wa doko? (*Where are its factories?*) ● Sutoraiki wa? (*How about strikes?*) ● Roido san wa suiyōbi no kaigi ni deru? (*Is Mr Lloyd going to attend the Wednesday meeting?*) ● Roido san wa itsu kenkyū sentā ni iku? Ni-jū-shichi-nichi? Ni-jū-hachi-nichi? (*When is Mr Lloyd going to the research centre? 27th? 28th?*)

Lesson 11

Dialogue Ishikawa Mr Lloyd, please come this way. **Lloyd** Right, thank you. **Ishikawa** Shall we have some beer? (*to waiter*) Five bottles of beer, please. (*The waiter brings the beer.*) Mr Lloyd, how about some beer? **Lloyd** (*holding his glass to be filled*) Thank you. **Ishikawa** Well, everybody, many thanks for all your hard work today. Cheers! **Everyone** Cheers! **Ishikawa** Mr Lloyd, welcome to Japan. How about a few words? **Lloyd** You mean introduce myself? But, my Japanese really isn't very good yet... **Ishikawa** It's okay, just keep it simple. **Lloyd** My name's Richard Lloyd and I'm in charge of overseas marketing at Dando Sports. We look forward to your support in the future. Many thanks for your help. **Ishikawa** Thank you very much. How long are you in Japan for, Mr Lloyd? **Lloyd** Until May 3rd. It's a bit short, but still. **Ishikawa** Do you have any time for sightseeing? **Lloyd** Not really, but I intend to go to Nikko. **Ishikawa** That's good.
Comprehension 1 (*c*) 2 (*b*)
Expansion activities 1 Across
4 tsukareru 5 tsutomeru 7 wakaranai 11 owaranai 12 inai 14 nomanai 15 konai 16 matanai 17 nai 18 shinai 19 oshieru **Down** 1 kaeru 2 okuru 3 tabenai 4 tsukanai 6 kikanai 8 awanai 9 yomanai 10 narawanai 13 ikanai 2 (*a*) Nikkō e iku, ikanai, ikanai, jikan ga nai (*b*) Tanaka san wa kuru, konai, konai, yotei ga aru (*c*) buchō wa ashita no kaigi ni deru, denai, denai, shutchō ga aru (*d*) kyō wa hayaku kaeru, kaeranai, kaeranai, zangyō ga takusan aru 3 (Note: Although non-Japanese names have been given here with their original spelling, it would

be helpful to Japanese listeners if, during your self-introduction, you gave a Japanese pronunciation to such names. For example, (*a*) might be said **Pāfekuto Konpyūtā Shisutemu no...** etc.) (*a*) Perfect Computer Systems no konsarutanto no Tyrone Jones desu. (*b*) Ross Engineering no Engineering Design-bu no Jane Rockwell desu. (*c*) Hotel Shangri-la no Sales-bu no Tony Marshall desu. (*d*) Dell Sporting Goods no kokusai kikaku-bu no Anna Taylor desu. 4 (*a*) Jōzu ni Nihongo o hanashimashita. (*b*) Hayaku kaisha ni tsukimashita. (*c*) Osoku uchi ni kaerimashita. (*d*) Kantan ni jiko shōkai o shimashita. (*e*) Kuwashiku repōto o kakimashita. (*f*) Kirei ni kaigi-shitsu o katazukemashita. **5 Dialogue 1**
A Kochira e dōzo. B Ā, dōmo.
A Biiru wa dō desu ka. B Hai, itadakimasu. A Ja, kanpai shimashō.
B Kanpai! **Dialogue 2** A Menyū o kudasai. B Hai, dōzo. A Biiru o kudasai. B Nan-bon desu ka.
A Ip-pon onegai shimasu. Sore kara, supagetti o kudasai. B Hai, wakarimashita. 6 (*a*) Tanaka san, kochira e dōzo. (*b*) Biiru ni shimashō ka. (*c*) Biiru o rop-pon kudasai. (*d*) Itsu made Igirisu ni imasu ka. (*e*) Kankō no jikan wa aru n' desu ka. (*f*) Sore wa ii desu ne. Biiru wa dō desu ka. (*g*) Ja, mina san, Igirisu e yōkoso! Kanpai! (*h*) Ēto, nani ni shimashō ka. **Reading practice** Coffee Shop 'Rin'; Soft Drinks: Blended coffee, cafe au lait, lemon tea, milk tea, milk, cocoa; Juices: orange juice, grapefruit juice, tomato juice, cola, cream soda

Lesson 12

The story so far Yesterday, Mr Lloyd went to Nikko with his friend Mr Shimada. Today he has come to Wajima because he has a meeting with Yamamoto buchō. The buchō is now asking him about his trip to Nikko.
Dialogue Yamamoto Did you go to Nikko in the end? **Lloyd** Yes, I went with a friend of mine, Shimada san. I really enjoyed it. **Yamamoto** How was the weather? I imagine it was a bit cold. **Lloyd** No, it wasn't that cold. When we arrived in Nikko, it was raining,

but after that the weather was good.
Yamamoto Where did you like best?
Lloyd Toshogu was really good. And
Kegon Waterfall was very beautiful.
Yamamoto Did you take many photos?
Lloyd Yes, I took three rolls, but I
ruined all of them. **Yamamoto** What
happened? **Lloyd** When I was taking a
photo of Kegon Waterfall, I fell over. And
I dropped the films into the river...
Yamamoto (*laughing*) That's terrible!
Lloyd It was really stupid of me, wasn't
it.
Comprehension 1 (*c*) 2 (*c*)
Expansion Activities 1 **Across**
1 mita 3 nonda 5 kita 7 toranakatta
10 owatta 12 inakatta 13 shita
14 nakatta 17 hataraita 19 hanashita
20 hajimeta **Down** 1 minakatta
2 shinakatta 4 datta 6 ikanakatta
8 otoshita 9 haitta 11 wakatta 12 ita
15 katta 16 kaetta 18 atta 2 Sapporo
wa yuki ga furimashita. Sendai wa
samukatta desu. Nagano wa
suzushikatta desu. Tōkyō wa kaze ga
tsuyokatta desu. Yokohama wa ame ga
furimashita. Nagoya wa mushiatsukatta
desu. Ōsaka wa ame ga furimashita.
Hiroshima wa atatakakatta desu.
Nagasaki wa (or mo) atatakakatta desu.
Kagoshima wa atsukatta desu.
3 (*a*) Sumimasen ga, mō chotto mijikaku
shite kudasai. (*b*) Sumimasen ga,
mō chotto kirei ni shite kudasai.
(*c*) Sumimasen ga, mō chotto, shizuka
ni shite kudasai. (*d*) Sumimasen ga,
mō chotto kantan ni shite kudasai.
(*e*) Sumimasen ga, mō chotto ōkiku shite
kudasai. (*f*) Sumimasen ga, mō chotto
takaku shite kudasai. 4 (*a*) Daigaku no
toki, Eigo to māketingu o benkyō
shimashita. (*b*) Nagoya ni sunde ita toki,
Yamaike Depāto de hataraite imashita.
(*c*) Kaigai kikaku-bu de hataraite ita toki,
Yōroppa e shutchō shimashita.
(*d*) Rondon ni ita toki, Dandō Supōtsu no
shachō ni aimashita. (*e*) Kekkon shita
toki, Tōkyō shisha ni kimashita.
(*f*) Senshū shinbun o mite ita toki,
Dandō Supōtsu no koto o yomimashita.
5 yokatta, yokatta, atsukatta, atsuku
nakatta, suzushikatta, yokatta,
tanoshikatta, kawaikatta, kawaikatta,
daijōbu, dame, atarashii, takakatta, taihen.
baka-na 6 (*a*) Mā, isogashikatta kedo,
taihen omoshirokatta desu. (*b*) Iie,

sonna ni samuku nakatta desu. Parii ni
tsuita toki, ame ga futte ita kedo, sono
ato ii tenki deshita. (*c*) Roma ni ita toki,
san-jikan gurai arimashita. (*d*) Suisu ga
yokatta desu ne. Chotto takakatta kedo,
yama ga totemo kirei deshita. (*e*) Jikan
ga nakatta kara, zenzen torimasen
deshita.
Reading corner Jinji-bu no mina san
o-genki desu ka. Watashi wa kinō daigaku
no toki no tomodachi to san-nin de
Hawaii ni kimashita. Kūkō ni tsuita toki,
ame ga takusan futte ita n' desu ga, ima
wa totemo ii tenki desu. Kyō kore kara
Waikiki ni iku tsumori desu. Kinyōbi ni
Nihon ni kaerimasu. Kaisha wa getsuyōbi
kara ikimasu. Dewa, yoroshiku onegai
shimasu. Watanabe Keiko (*To everyone in
the Personnel Department: How are you?
Yesterday three of us – two friends from
university days and I – came to Hawaii.
When we arrived at the airport, it was
raining hard, but today the weather is
great. We plan to go to Waikiki after this.
I'll be back in Japan on Friday. I'll be at
work from Monday. Well, regards to you
all. Keiko Watanabe*)

Lesson 13

The story so far Mr Lloyd is returning
to Britain on Monday, so, although today
is Saturday, he's having a meeting with
Yamamoto buchō. Yesterday evening, the
two of them went to a bar in Akasaka,
and drank a lot. After that, they went to a
bar at the top of Mr Lloyd's hotel, and
drank a lot more. That's why Mr Lloyd is
feeling a little unwell today.
Dialogue Yamamoto How are you
feeling? Would you like some coffee or
something? **Lloyd** Yes, please. You
can certainly drink, Yamamoto san!
Yamamoto Yes, well, that's because I
do it often! Here's your coffee. **Lloyd**
Thank you. **Yamamoto** Right, shall
we confirm the next part of the schedule?
Lloyd Yes. Next Wednesday we're
having a meeting in the planning
department. At that time I plan to explain
Wajima's market report, and make the
sales schedule. **Yamamoto** Right.
Lloyd I'll send the schedule to you
by... (*looking at his diary*) let me see...
by the 17th. **Yamamoto** Just a
minute! Not so fast! Before that, we'll be

having a meeting within Wajima, so it'll take a little more time. **Lloyd** Of course, sorry! You're coming to Britain at the end of this month, so we can talk about the products in more detail then. **Yamamoto** Right.
Comprehension 1 (*b*) 2 (*a*)
Expansion activities 1 (*a*) Shashin o toranaide kudasai. (*Please don't take pictures.*) (*b*) Tabenaide kudasai. (*Please don't eat this.*) (*c*) Nomanaide kudasai. (*Please don't drink this.*) (*d*) Hairanaide kudasai. (*Please don't enter.*) (*e*) Hanasanaide kudasai. (*Please don't talk.*) (*f*) Yomanaide kudasai. (*Please don't read this.*) 2 (*a*) Maekawa san no okusan (*b*) Maekawa san (*c*) Shimada san (*d*) Shimada san no okusan (*e*) Roido san (*f*)/(*g*) Honda san, Toyota san (*h*) 'Jūpitā' (*i*)/(*k*) Katō san to Satō san (*j*) Itō san 3 (*a*) no ue ni (*b*) no yoko ni (*c*) no mae ni (*d*) no yoko ni (*e*) no ushiro ni (*f*) no aida ni (*g*) no naka ni (*h*) no shita ni (*i*) no soba ni 4 Okamoto san, shachō ni denwa o shite, kaigi no hi no tsugō o kiite kudasai. Maeda san, minna no yotei o kiite, tsugō o kakunin shite, miitingu no sukējuru o tsukutte kudasai. Noguchi kun, shōhin hanbai no dēta o shirabete, mitsumori o tsukutte kudasai. Ikeda san, atarashii shōhin no shorui no kopii o totte, Nagoya shisha ni fakkusu o okutte kudasai. Hotta san, kaigi no repōto o kaite, buchō ni misete kudasai. Koyama san, repōto no kopii o totte, fairu ni irete kudasai.
5 (*a*) (*i*), (*b*) (*ii*), (*c*) (*ii*), (*d*) (*i*), (*e*) (*ii*), (*f*) (*i*), (*g*) (*i*), (*h*) (*ii*)
6 (*a*) Hai, onegai shimasu. (*b*) Ē, chotto. Jitsu wa, kinō no ban, tomodachi to takusan nonda n' desu. Dakara kyō wa kibun ga warui desu. (*c*) Sonna ni tsuyoku arimasen yo. (*d*) Shinjuku no sushi-ya de takusan nonde, sono ato watashi no hoteru e kaette, hoteru no ue no bā de mata nomimashita. (*e*) Hai, hai, dekimasu. Ēto… senshū no mokuyōbi ni uchi no kaisha de miitingu ga atte, shimekiri no hanashi o shimashita. (*f*) Ē, kongetsu no 28-nichi made ni Sato san ni mitsumori o okuru no de, sore o mite, hanbai kikaku o tsukutte kudasai. (*g*) Sō desu ne, sumimasen. Uchi no shachō ga kongetsu no owari ni Nihon ni kimasu kara, sono toki ni motto kuwashiku hanashi ga dekimasu ne.

Reading corner

Go-gatsu jū-hachi-nichi (kayōbi) ni, Nagoya shisha no kaigai kikaku-bu to honsha no kaigai kikaku-bu no aida de kaigi ga arimasu. Jikan wa, san-ji han kara roku-ji goro made no yotei desu. Kaigi wa, honsha no jinji-bu no tonari no heya de shimasu. Satō shachō mo demasu kara okurenaide kudasai. Kuwashii koto wa kikaku-bu no Okamoto made. (*Koyama san, please type this up. On May 18th [Tuesday], there will be a meeting of the Nagoya branch Overseas Planning Department and the head office Overseas Planning Department. It is scheduled to run from 3:30 to approximately 6:00. The meeting will be held in the room next to the Personnel Department at the head office. The president, Satō san, will also attend, so please don't be late. For more details, contact Okamoto in the Planning Department.*)

Lesson 14

The story so far Yamamoto buchō and Okamoto kachō went to Britain for a week on business, and came back the day before yesterday. While they were in Britain, they went to the Dando Sports head office and had meetings every day. For Okamoto kachō, it was his first time abroad, so he had planned to take lots of photographs of Britain, but the meetings went on day after day, so he wasn't able to. Today he has come back to the (Wajima) office for the first time.
Dialogue Maeda Welcome back. How was Britain? **Okamoto** It went pretty well. Only there were problems with the colours and the sizes of the sportswear. **Maeda** What do you mean? **Okamoto** Dando Sports said they were going to export all sizes to Japan. **Maeda** What? Large sizes too? But isn't the Large too big for the Japanese? **Okamoto** Yes, so the buchō said we would only buy Small and Medium. **Maeda** Really. And another problem was the colours? **Okamoto** Yes, Dando Sports said pastel colours would be best, but we think that black

and white will be next year's colours in Japan. So that's a problem. **Maeda** That's serious. What happened about prices? **Okamoto** The prices were OK. By the way, Maeda san, what do you think of this tie? **Maeda** Green and yellow and pink...? **Okamoto** Nice colours, eh? In Britain there are a lot of cheap, good-quality goods. This tie is about Y25,000 in Japan, you know. **Maeda** (*Thinking to himself: But Japanese wouldn't buy a tie in those colours...*) **Okamoto** Here's a British tie for you too.

Comprehension 1 (*a*) 2 (*b*)

Expansion activities 1 (*a*) Terebi wa ¥53,000 (go-man san-zen en) kara ¥38,000 (san-man has-sen en) ni narimashita. (*b*) Kaban wa ¥64,500 (roku-man yon-sen go-hyaku en) kara ¥49,000 (yon-man kyū-sen en) ni narimashita. (*c*) Kamera wa ¥56,000 (go-man roku-sen en) kara ¥42,500 (yon-man ni-sen go-hyaku en) ni narimashita. (*d*) Taipuraitā wa ¥62,000 (roku-man ni-sen en) kara ¥51,000 (go-man is-sen en) ni narimashita. (*e*) Tsukue wa ¥100,000 (jū-man en) kara ¥85,000 (hachi-man go-sen en) ni narimashita. (*f*) Kuruma wa ¥4,000,000 (yon-hyaku-man en) kara ¥3,500,000 (san-byaku-go-jū-man en) ni narimashita.
2 Piza o mittsu, kōhii o itsutsu, orenji jūsu o futatsu, biiru o ippon, chiizu sando-(itchi) o futatsu, hamu sando(itchi) o mittsu, supagetii o yottsu, tsuna sando-(itchi) o hitotsu to guriin sarada o nanatsu kudasai. 3 (*a*) banana (*b*) tsuna (*c*) shinbun (*d*) inu (*e*) bentō (*f*) kōhii (*g*) sake (*h*) biiru (*i*) akai kaban, aka (*j*) burū no/aoi sukāfu sukāfu, burū/ao (*k*) pinku to murasaki no nekutai, pinku to murasaki (*l*) midori/guriin no kuruma, midori/ guriin (*m*) chairo/buraun no T-shatsu, chairo/buraun 4 (*b*) Noguchi san wa, shūmatsu ni gārufurendo to yama ni iku to itte imashita. (*c*) Hotta san wa, L-saizu ni natta kara, mainichi jogingu o suru to itte imashita. (*d*) Ikeda san wa, shachō no okusan wa sengetsu daigaku no sensei ni natta to itte imashita.
(*e*) Maeda san wa, kinō jikan ga nakatta kara mitsumori o tsukuranakatta to itte imashita. (*f*) Ikeda san wa, kachō wa Eigo ga zenzen dekinai to itte

imashita. 5 (*a*) kitanakute, furui (*b*) hirokute, akarui (*c*) hirokute, akarui (*d*) isogashikute, urusai (*e*) muzukashikute, taihen-na (*f*) kantan de, omoshiroku nai (*g*) shizuka de, kirei na 6 (*b*) Tenki wa samuku narimashita. (*c*) Roido san no Nihongo wa jōzu ni narimashita. (*d*) Yamada san no kodomo wa ōkiku narimashita. (*e*) Supōtsu-uea no kakaku wa taihen takaku narimashita. (*f*) Kono kikaku wa dame ni narimashita. (*g*) Kono shimekiri wa raigetsu ni narimashita. (*h*) Watashi no nekutai wa kitanaku narimashita. 7 (*a*) Mā mā umaku ikimashita. (*b*) Sukejūru no mondai desu ka. Sore wa daijōbu deshita ga, Tanaka san wa kore kara kakaku ga mondai ni naru to iimashita. (*c*) Ē, sō desu ga, Tanaka san wa kongetsu no owari ni Tōkyō e kuru to iimashita. (*d*) Hai, sō desu. Shizuka de, kirei na machi desu ne. (*e*) Ē, ikimashita. Omoshiroi mono ga takusan arimashita. Kore wa ii to omoimashita. Dōzo. (*f*) Iie, sonna ni takaku nakatta n' desu.

Reading corner To: Ueda Supōtsu Shoppu, From: Yamada Supōtsu Kurabu, Date: Go-gatsu jū-yokka (getsu), Sukii pantsu – howaito (M) × 4; sukii jaketto – reddo (M) × 4; jogingu shūzu – howaito (29 cm) × 6; gorufu shūzu – burakku (26 cm) × 5; gorufu bōru – 100; tenisu bōru – 60. Zenbu de ikura ni narimasu ka. Go-gatsu ni-jū-san-nichi made ni fakkusu o okutte kudasai. Yoroshiku onegai shimasu. Yamada Tarō (*To: Ueda Sports Shop, From: Yamada Sports Club, Date: May 14 (Monday), ski pants – white; ski jacket – red; jogging shoes – white; golf shoes – black; golf balls; tennis balls; How much will that be altogether? Please let me know by fax by May 23. Many thanks. Tarō Yamada.*)

Lesson 15

The story so far The problems about the sizes and colour of the sportswear have been solved. Next month there will be a planning meeting at Wajima, so Mr Lloyd will be coming to Japan again. At that time, Barbara Thomas, who is in charge of advertising, will come with him. Mr Lloyd is now talking to Yamamoto

buchō about this matter on the phone.
Dialogue Koyama Hello, Wajima
Trading. **Lloyd** Sorry to bother you,
but could I speak to Yamamoto buchō
please? **Koyama** Excuse me, but
could I have your name, please? **Lloyd**
It's Lloyd, from Dando Sports. **Koyama**
Right, just a moment please. (*Yamamoto
buchō comes to the phone.*) **Yamamoto**
Yamamoto speaking. Hello there, Mr
Lloyd, it's been a long time! **Lloyd** It
certainly has. How are you? It's about my
business trip. The planning meeting next
month is on the 13th, right?
Yamamoto Yes, that's right. The only
thing is, the location hasn't been decided
yet. It'll probably be in Nagoya. **Lloyd**
Right. By the way, I thought it would be a
good idea if Barbara Thomas of our
advertising department came to the
meeting. How would that be?
Yamamoto Yes, please, both of you
attend. **Lloyd** Also, if there's time,
could we visit some department stores?
Yamamoto Of course. By the way, if
you know the time of the plane, I'll come
to meet you. **Lloyd** That's very kind.
The details of the schedule aren't
finalised yet, but I'll send you a fax later.
Yamamoto Also, about the catalogue,
if you have the new one, could you bring
it? **Lloyd** Yes, I will. Well, that's
about it ..... **Yamamoto** Thanks,
then. Goodbye. (*puts phone down and
turns to Koyama san*) I don't know
anything about Barbara Thomas ...
'Barbara' ... isn't that a woman's name?
Koyama That's right. **Yamamoto**
Eh?!
Comprehension 1 (*c*) **2** (*a*)
Expansion activities 1 Across
2 fureba 4 awanakereba 6 samukereba
7 mateba 12 matomenakereba
13 ikanakereba 15 ikeba 16 yokereba
18 kawanakereba 20 kakereba
21 sureba 22 aeba **Down** 1 kureba
3 kakeba 5 wakaranakereba
7 misereba 8 toreba 9 nomanakereba
10 dereba 11 warukereba 14 ireba
17 ieba 18 kaeba 19 areba
2 (*a*) areba (*b*) dekireba (*c*) areba
(*d*) nomeba (*e*) kakereba/sureba
(*f*) sureba **3** (*a*) (*i*) (*b*) (*ii*) (*c*) (*ii*)
(*d*) (*i*) (*e*) (*ii*) (*f*) (*ii*) (*g*) (*ii*) (*h*) (*i*)
4 (*c*) Hotta san wa, mada shōhin shijō o
shirabete imasen ga, Morita san wa mō

shirabemashita. (*d*) Hotta san mo,
Morita san mo, mada shijō repōto o kaite
imasen. (*e*) Hotta san mo, Morita san
mo, mō Eigo no benkyō o hajimemashita.
(*f*) Hotta san mo, Morita san mo, mada
senden kikaku o tsukutte imasen.
(*g*) Hotta san wa mada katarogu o mite
imasen ga, Morita san wa mō mimashita.
(*h*) Hotta san mo Morita san mo, mada
māketingu kōsu ni dete imasen.
5 A: Mitsumoto Ginkō de gozaimasu.
B: Moshi moshi. ABA-sha no Puriisuto
desu ga, Kitagawa buchō onegai shimasu.
A: Shōshō o-machi kudasai...
Osorei-irimasu ga, tadaima Kitagawa
wa seki o hazushite imasu ga.
B: Sumimasen ga, mō sukoshi yukkuri
hanashite kudasai. A: Buchō wa imasen
ga...nanika dengon ga arimasu ka.
B: Iie, ato de mō ichido denwa shimasu.
6 ni tsuite, mada, mada, dare mo, ni
tsuite, mada, nani mo, ni tsuite, nani mo,
mada, dare ni mo, mada **7** (*a*)
Osore-irimasu ga, Yamanaka kachō
onegai shimasu. (*b*) Zeron no (*your
name*) desu ga. (*c*) Dōmo, o-genki desu
ka. Senden no kaigi no koto desu ga,
raishū no kaigi wa nan-ji desu ka.
(*d*) Wakarimashita. Jitsu wa, uchi no
senden-bu no Naijeru Gurē mo kaigi ni
dereba ii to omoimasu ga, dō deshō ka.
(*e*) Tokorode, senden kikaku no repōto
wa mō dekimashita ka. (*f*) Sō desu ka.
Ja, ganbatte kudasai ne. (*g*) Shitsurei
shimasu.
Reading corner (clockwise from top
centre) Okamoto, Ishikawa, Maekawa,
Tanaka, Yamashita, Lloyd, Shimada,
Thomas, Yamamoto, Ueda **1** Yamamoto
san no tonari ni dare ga suwatte imasu
ka. (*Who's sitting next to Yamamoto san?*)
2 Ishikawa san to Ueda san no aida ni
dare ga suwatte imasu ka. (*Who's sitting
between Ishikawa san and Ueda san?*)
3 Tanaka san no tonari ni dare ga suwatte
imasu ka. (*Who's sitting next to Tanaka
san?*) **4** Shimada san to Yamashita san
no aida ni dare ga suwatte imasu ka.
(*Who's sitting between Shimada san and
Yamashita san?*)

Lesson 16

The story so far Barbara Thomas
arrived in Japan with Mr Lloyd the day

before yesterday. She's interested in the Japanese way of marketing and advertising, so today she has come to Tokyo's famous Takamatsu Department Store. She is just going to begin a tour of the store with Kobayashi san, of the advertising department.

Dialogue Kobayashi I think we should begin from the information desk on the first floor. The elevator is this way. After you. (*They go down in the lift.*) The information desk is on the right. In Japan, information desks are at the entrance of the store. **Barbara** (*seeing the information desk staff*) Well, those are really smart uniforms, aren't they! **Kobayashi** The image of the store is extremely important, so it's essential not just to have smart uniforms, but also to have good service and good staff manners too. **Barbara** What kind of in-company training do you do? **Kobayashi** We do all kinds of training, such as how to speak (well), greetings, and that kind of thing. **Barbara** Really. It would be good to have that kind of training in Britain too. (*looks around and notices the cashpoint*) I see that there's a cashpoint on the left side of the entrance. **Kobayashi** Yes, this is also part of the service. If customers don't have money, there's no business for us! Well, what shall we see next? **Barbara** I'm interested in how the sportswear is displayed... **Kobayashi** Well, on the fifth floor there's a golf corner, so let's go there.

Comprehension 1 (*a*) 2 (*c*)
Expansion activities 1 (*a*) Iie, terebi no senden o tantō shita hō ga ii desu. (*b*) Iie, sukii to gorufu no supōtsu-uea o senden shita hō ga ii desu. (*c*) Iie, kyō okutta hō ga ii desu. (*d*) Iie, dezain no hanashi kara hajimeta hō ga ii desu. (*e*) Iie, buchō ni setsumei shita hō ga ii desu. (*f*) Iie, 9-ji han kara hajimeta hō ga ii desu. 2 (*a*) Hai, massugu iku to, tsukiatari ni arimasu. (*b*) Hai, massugu itte, migi ni magaru to, hidari (-gawa) ni arimasu. (*c*) Hai, migi ni magatte, massugu iku to, hidari (-gawa) ni arimasu. (*d*) Hai, migi ni magatte, massugu iku to, migi (-gawa) ni arimasu. 3 (*a*) Ii narabekata dake de naku, ii namae ya ii senden mo taisetsu desu. (*b*) Aisatsu no shikata dake de naku, ii

hanashikata ya ii manā mo oshiemasu. (*c*) Zasshi no senden dake de naku, ii shinbun no senden ya ii terebi no senden mo taisetsu desu. (*d*) Shanai kyōiku dake de naku, ii shōhin ya ii senden mo taisetsu desu. 4 (*a*) Kēki o yamete, guriin sarada o takusan tabeta hō ga ii desu ne. (*b*) Kaisha o yameta hō ga ii desu ne. (*c*) Nihongo no kurasu ni haitta hō ga ii desu ne. (*d*) Jinji-bu to hanashita hō ga ii desu ne. (*e*) Amerika ni itte, benkyō shita hō ga ii desu ne. 5 (*a*) Yoi hanbai keikaku o tsukuranai to, shōbai ni narimasen. (*b*) Yoi shōhin o tsukaranai to, shōbai ni narimasen. (*c*) Yoi dezain o kangaenai to, shōbai ni narimasen. (*d*) Yoi hanashikata o kyōiku shinai to, shōbai ni narimasen. 6 (*a*) Uketsuke kara hajimeta hō ga ii desu ne. (*b*) Ē, kurabu no imēji wa hijō ni taisetsu desu kara, sumāto-na uketsuke dake de naku, ii sābisu ya ii jūgyōin no manā mo hitsuyō desu. (*c*) Uchi de wa, hanashikata ya aisatsu no shikata nado no kyōiku o shite imasu. (*d*) Ē, arimasu. Kyōmi ga nai to okyaku-sama to gorufu ni tsuite no hanashi ga dekimasen. (*e*) Jā, tsugi wa resutoran e ikimashō ka. Massugu itte, hidari ni magaru to, resutoran no iriguchi ga arimasu. (*f*) O-saki ni dōzo.

Reading corner Floor B1: Fūdo gyarari (*food gallery*), furūtsu (*fruit*), kēki (*cake*), kōhii.tii (*coffee and tea*), resutoran (*restaurant*), wain.biiru (*wine and beer*), sushi kōnā (*sushi corner*) **Floor 1:** akusesarii (*accessories*), hankachi (*handkerchiefs*), kyasshu kōnā (*cashpoint*), sukāfu (*scarves*), handobaggu (*handbags*), kasa (*umbrellas*), denwa kōnā (*telephone corner*), nekutai.beruto (*ties and belts*), furawā shoppu (*flower shop*) **Floor 2: Rediizu furōa** (*ladies' floor*), sētā (*sweaters*), doresu (*dresses*), sūtsu (*suits*), yangu rediizu (*young ladies'*), naito uea (*nightwear*), burausu (*blouses*), L&S saizu shoppu (*L&S size shop*) **Floor 3: Menzu shoppu** (*men's shop*), fōmaru uea (*formal wear*), sūtsu (*suits*), kōto (*coats*), jaketto & surakkusu (*jackets and slacks*), kingu saizu shoppu (*king-size shop*) **Floor 4: Supōtsu & rejā** (*Sports and leisure*), tenisu uea (*tennis wear*), gorufu uea (*golf wear*), toraberu saron (*travel salon*), torēningu uea (*training wear*), supōtsu shūzu (*sports shoes*) **Floor 5: Ribingu**

(*living*), kitchin ribingu (*kitchen living=kitchen goods*), epuron (*aprons*), taoru (*towels*), beddo (*beds*), kāten (*curtains*), kāpetto (*carpets*) **Floor 6:** Sūbenia shoppu (*souvenir shop*), gēmu kōna (*game corner*), resutoran (*restaurants*), petto kōnā (*pet corner*), heā saron (*hair salon*) **1** Heā saron wa, nan-kai ni arimasu ka. (*Which floor is the hair salon on?*) **2** Menzu shoppu wa, san-gai ni arimasu ka. (*Is the men's shop on the third floor?*) **3** Kyasshu kōnā wa, chika ik-kai ni arimasu ka. (*Is the cashpoint in the basement?*)

Lesson 17

The story so far Yesterday, Yamamoto buchō mentioned to Barbara that it would be best not only to study about department store management, but about car production too. So today she has come to look around the Tozan Automobile factory. She has just finished an inspection of the production line with Suzuki san, the plant manager. **Dialogue Barbara** Is it all right if I take some photographs of the production line? **Suzuki** Yes, of course. Take lots. **Barbara** By the way, in the production of automobiles, what (do you consider) as most important? **Suzuki** Mm, that's a difficult question. Well, I think it's the car's safety. **Barbara** What do you do if you get defective parts? **Suzuki** First, we remove the defective part from the production line, and call the person in charge of quality control. Then he and the operator check the condition of the machine together. After that the defective part is taken to the quality control office, and the problem is investigated. When they find the cause, we discuss it together in the QC circle. **Barbara** I see. And, is quality assurance important too? **Suzuki** Yes, if the quality isn't good, there's no business! Uh, turn right there. (*They enter a different part of the factory.*) And not only is quality important, but productivity too. **Barbara** Yes, you're right. (*Something catches her eye.*) What are those? Are they robots? **Suzuki** Yes, they are. If there's time, I'll show you them later. **Barbara** Thank you. (*hearing the signal for the tea break*) Ah,

it's the tea break, isn't it. Um, excuse me but would it be all right to ask some questions of the people on the production line? **Suzuki** Of course, please go ahead. If it's all right with you, let's talk to them while we have some mugi-cha or something.
Comprehension 1 (*a*) **2** (*b*)
Expansion activities 1 (*b*) attara (*c*) nakattara (*d*) shinakattara (*e*) konakattara (*f*) tsukuttara (*g*) karitara (*h*) hanashiattara (*i*) attara (*j*) tsukattara (*k*) hanashiattara (*l*) karitara/tsukattara (*m*) shinakattara (*n*) konakattara (*o*) nakattara (*p*) warukattara **2** (*a*) Heya de sutereo o kiite mo ii desu ka. Ē, (kiite mo) ii desu. (*b*) Heya de pātii o shite mo ii desu ka. Iie, (pātii o shite wa) ikemasen. (*c*) Yoru osoku kaette mo ii desu ka. Iie, (osoku kaette wa) ikemasen. (*d*) Heya de terebi o mite mo ii desu ka. Ē, (mite mo) ii desu. (*e*) Ryō e bōifurendo o yonde mo ii desu ka. Iie, (bōifurendo o yonde wa) ikemasen. (*f*) Heya de tabete mo ii desu ka. Ē, (tabete mo) ii desu. **3** (*a*) Kikai no jōtai ga warukattara, mazu OFF suitchi o oshite, enjinia o yobimasu. Soshite enjinia to issho ni buhin o chekku shimasu. Sono ato kikai no jōtai o shirabete, memo o kakimasu. (*b*) Operētā ga tsukaretara, betsu no operētā o yonde, kyūkei o shimasu. Soshite zangyō o yamemasu. Sono ato hayaku uchi e kaette, futsuka gurai yasumimasu. (*c*) Jishin ga attara, kikai no OFF suitchi o oshite, shizuka ni kōjō e demasu. Soshite kōjō no mae ni ikimasu. Sono ato kōjō ni hairanaide, kōjōchō no hanashi o yoku kikimasu.
4 (*a*) Jimusho de hatarakinagara, 'Walkman' o kiite wa ikemasen. (*b*) Denwa de hanashinagara, tabete wa ikemasen. (*c*) Wāpuro o tsukainagara, kōhii o nonde wa ikemasen. (*d*) O-kyaku-san to hanashinagara, tabako o sutte wa ikemasen. (*e*) Konpyūtā o tsukainagara, tabako o sutte wa ikemasen. **5** ga/wa, no, ni, to. wa. wa, ga, ni. no/de, ga, ga, de/o. wa, to, ni, de, o. de/o. wa, de, o, o/de. o.
6 (*a*) Takusan buhin o yunyū shitara yasuku dekimasu ka. (*b*) Amari jikan ga arimasen kara, ranchi o tabenagara hanashimashō ka. (*c*) Hai, ii desu yo. (*d*) Sono mae ni, chotto denwa o karite

mo ii desu ka. (e) Hai, wakarimasu. Mae ni tsukaimashita. Mazu kyū-ban o oshite, operētā o yobimasu. Operētā ga detara, uchi no kaisha no denwa bangō o iimasu ne. (f) Hai, denwa ga owattara ikimasu.

Reading corner Kongetsu no aidea (This month's idea) Namae: Suzuki Masato (*Name: Suzuki Masato*) Kōjō: Tōkyō (*Factory: Tokyo*) Bu: Hinshitsu kanri-bu (*Department: Quality control department*) Gappi: hachi-gatsu ni-jū-ichi-nichi (*Date: August 21st*) Mondai: TPI no furyō buhin ga ima takusan dete iru. (*Problem: there are currently a lot of defective parts coming from the TPI.*) Gen-in: Operētā no tsukaikata ga warui. (*Cause: The operator's method of using [the machine] is poor.*) Aidea: Operētā ga honsha no kenkyūjo e itte, TPI no tsukaikata o motto benkyō shita hō ga yoi. (*Idea: The operator should go to the head office's research centre and study more about how to operate the TPI.*) Kōjōchō (*plant manager*), buchō (*general manager*), kachō (*section manager*), kakarichō (*assistant manager*) **1** Kore wa dare no aidea desu ka. **2** Suzuki san wa doko de hataraite imasu ka. **3** Kikai ni tsuite no mondai desu ka. **4** Nani ga yoku nai desu ka.

Lesson 18

The story so far Maeda san is a busy man. Today, he attended a meeting in the morning at JETRO. In the afternoon he talked with Mr Lloyd and the others about the sales plan. After working overtime until 8:00, he went home. At the moment Maeda san is having dinner with his wife.

Dialogue **Maeda** This fish is good. **Okusan** Good, I'm glad. Do you want some more rice? **Maeda** This is enough, I'm full. What time is Tomoko coming back from the **juku**? **Okusan** I think she should be back soon now. **Maeda** Oh. (*putting his chopsticks down.*) Thanks for the meal. I'd love some green tea. **Okusan** I'll make some now. Will you take your bath later? **Maeda** Yes, I'll have it after I've drunk my green tea. (*yawning and stretching*) Aa, today was really awful. When I went to JETRO this morning, the roads were really crowded and so I was late for the

meeting. Then at JETRO I wanted to talk about the French market, but I'd left the necessary data at the office, so I couldn't. **Okusan** Really, that's terrible. Here's your tea. (*She pours him a cup of green tea.*) **Maeda** Thanks. And in the afternoon, after I'd got back to the office, I talked with Mr Lloyd and the others about the sales plan until 8:00. **Okusan** So when are Mr Lloyd and Barbara going back to Britain? **Maeda** They plan to return next Wednesday. So before they go I'd like to ask them over here. **Okusan** What? Here? But this place is so small! And on top of that, I've never cooked British food! **Maeda** Mr Lloyd and Barbara have eaten Japanese food before, so it's all right! How about doing sushi or something? **Okusan** No way! I don't want to!

Comprehension **1** (b) **2** (c)
Expansion activities
1 (a) Minamigawa san wa hanbai repōto o kaita koto ga arimasu ka. Hai, arimasu. (b) Tanaka san wa senden no shikata o benkyō shita koto ga arimasu ka. Hai, arimasu. (c) Katō san wa Igirisu no kaisha de hataraita koto ga arimasu ka. Hai, arimasu. (d) Tanaka san wa Igirisu no kaisha de hataraita koto ga arimasu ka. Iie, arimasen. (e) Katō san wa sērusu o tantō shita koto ga arimasu ka. Iie, arimasen. (f) Minamigawa san wa Igirisu de māketingu o benkyō shita koto ga arimasu ka. Iie, arimasen. **2** mitai, shitai, ikitai, shitai, ikitai, tabetai, mitai, arukitai **3** (a) Tōzan Jidōsha no robotto o mitakatta kedo, jikan ga nakatta kara, dekimasen deshita. (b) Okamoto kachō to gorufu o shitakatta kedo, tenki ga warukatta kara, dekimasen deshita. (c) Watashi mo Takamatsu Depāto o kengaku shitakatta kedo, miitingu ga atta kara, dekimasen deshita. (d) Takamatsu Depāto de shōhin no narabekata o motto kikitakatta kedo, tantō-sha ga isogashikatta kara, dekimasen deshita. (e) Ginza de kaimono o shitakatta kedo, depāto ga konde ita kara, dekimasen deshita. **4** (a) Senden kikaku o kakunin shite kara, hanbai sukejūru o chekku shimasu ka. Iie, senden kikaku o kakunin suru mae ni, hanbai sukejūru o chekku shimasu. (b) Minna de keiyaku ni tsuite hanashiatte kara, keiyaku no shorui o matomemasu ka. Iie, minna de keiyaku

ni tsuite hanashiau mae ni, keiyaku no shorui o matomemasu. (*c*) Nihon de keiyaku ni sain shite kara, Dandō Supōtsu ni kopii o okurimasu ka. Iie, Nihon de keiyaku ni sain suru mae ni, Dandō Supōtsu ni kopii o okurimasu.
5 (*a*) Nagoya shisha ni itta toki, densha ga konde ita kara, tsukaremashita. (*b*) Miitingu o shite ita toki, jishin ga atta kara, soto ni demashita. (*c*) Kaisha de zangyō o shite ita toki, kibun ga waruku natta kara, uchi e kaerimashita. (*d*) Uchi e kaetta toki, kurakatta kara, korobimashita. (*e*) O-furo ni haite ita toki, buchō kara denwa ga arimashita kara, o-furo kara demashita. 6 (*a*) Ē, shimashita. Kimono o kaitakatta n' desu ga, taihen takakatta kara, yamemashita. (*b*) Iie, shigoto deshita. Kyōto ni ikitakatta ga, jikan ga nakute, ikimasen deshita. (*c*) Iie, Igirisu-jin desu. Igirisu ni itta koto ga arimasu ka. (*d*) Mada jikan ga arimasu kara, biiru demo nomimashō ka. Watashi wa itsumo hikōki ni noru mae ni biiru o nomimasu. (*e*) Asoko ni bā ga arimasu kara, ikimashō ka. (*f*) Ā, sō desu ka. Daijōbu desu yo! Demo, sore ja, amari takusan nomanai hō ga ii desu ne.
Reading corner Okinawa no oishii o-ryōri o tabeta koto ga arimasu ka. (*Have you ever tasted the delicious cuisine of Okinawa?*) Okinawa no subarashii umi o mita koto ga arimasu ka. (*Have you ever seen Okinawa's wonderful ocean?*) Okinawa no kirei-na sakana o mita koto ga arimasu ka. (*Have you ever seen Okinawa's beautiful fish?*) Matsushima biichi hoteru wa Okinawa de ichiban utsukushii tokoro desu. (*Matsushima Beach Hotel is the most beautiful place in Okinawa.*) Okinawa de tanoshii horidē o! (*Have a wonderful holiday in Okinawa!*) Okinawa ni ikitai wa! (*I want to go to Okinawa!*)

Lesson 19

The story so far Okamoto kachō and Maeda san are talking together about the contract schedule, the company trip, and other things. However, the kachō wants to talk about the company trip more than the contracts, because every year he really looks forward it.

Dialogue **Okamoto** Let's see, when do we have to send the contract papers to Dando Sports by? **Maeda** We have to send them by the 15th of next month. **Okamoto** Have all the terms been clarified? **Maeda** Yes, we had lots of talks with Mori san, who's in charge of legal matters, and all the problem points have been cleared up. **Okamoto** And, payment will be in yen, right? **Maeda** Yes, we thought that payment in yen would be better than in dollars. **Okamoto** Fine. Thank you for all the hard work. (*He looks at the agenda for their meeting.*) The next item is the company trip, isn't it. **Maeda** Yes, that's right. Everyone has talked together, and we finally decided on a place called Aoyama Kōgen in the Japan Alps. **Okamoto** Ah, I prefer the mountains to the sea, too. You can go in the **onsen** and relax, can't you. **Maeda** Yes, I agree. And also, at Aoyama Kōgen you can eat really delicious mountain-style cooking. **Okamoto** That's good. So, we have to decide on a person to be in charge of the events. **Maeda** 'Events'...? **Okamoto** The party. If we don't have a party, it won't be a good company outing. Well, I'll leave that up to you, Maeda san. **Maeda** Uuh, yes...
Comprehension 1 (*b*) 2 (*b*)
Expansion activities 1 (*a*) Hashi o tsukau koto ga dekimasu ka. (*b*) Kanji o kaku koto ga dekimasu ka. (*c*) Kuruma o unten suru koto ga dekimasu ka. (*d*) Tabako o yameru koto ga dekimasu ka. (*e*) Nihon no shinbun o yomu koto ga dekimasu ka. 2 (*a*) Nan to iu hoteru ni tomarimasu ka. Arupusu Puraza to iu hoteru ni tomarimasu. (*b*) Nan to iu ryokō-gaisha o tsukaimasu ka. Tanaka Toraberu to iu ryokō-gaisha o tsukaimasu. (*c*) Nan to iu onsen ni ikimasu ka. Yamanaka Onsen to iu onsen ni ikimasu. (*d*) Nan to iu eki de orimasu ka. Nishi Aoyama to iu eki de orimasu. (*e*) Nan to iu gaido san desu ka. Itō Kumiko san to iu gaido san desu.
3 (*a*) Nihon no hō ga ōkii desu. (*b*) Hikōki no hō ga hayai desu. (*c*) Piramiddo no hō ga saki ni dekimashita. (*d*) Noruē no hō ga kita ni arimasu. (*e*) Tōkyō no hō ga ame ga ōi

desu. (*f*) Mattahōn no hō ga takai desu.
4 (*a*) Honsha no biru to shisha no biru to,
dochira (no hō) ga takai desu ka. Honsha
no biru no hō ga takai desu.
(*b*) Igirisu no kōhii to Nihon no kōhii to,
dochira (no hō) ga oishii desu ka. Nihon
no kōhii no hō ga oishii desu. (*c*) Yama
to umi to, dochira (no hō) ga suki
desu ka. Umi no hō ga suki desu.
(*d*) Furansugo to Doitsugo to, dochira (no
hō) ga muzukashii desu ka. Doitsugo no
hō ga muzukashii desu. (*e*) Senden-bu
to kikaku-bu to, dochira (no hō) ga
isogashii desu ka. Senden-bu no hō ga
isogashii desu. 5 (*a*) Ku-gatsu
jū-ni-nichi made ni hōritsu tantō
no Mori san to hanashiawanakereba
narimasen. (*b*) Ku-gatsu ni-jū-roku-
nichi made ni mondai ten o zenbu
kaiketsu shinakereba narimasen.
(*c*) Jū-gatsu mikka made ni, Dandō
Supōtsu ni keiyaku shorui o
okuranakereba narimasen. (*d*) Jū-gatsu
jū-shichi-nichi made ni jōken o
kimenakereba narimasen. (*e*) Jū-gatsu
san-jū-ichi-nichi made ni keiyaku ni sain
shinakereba narimasen. 6 (*a*) (*i*)
(*b*) (*ii*)　(*c*) (*i*)　(*d*) (*i*)　(*e*) (*ii*)
7 (*a*) Kono shūmatsu ni tomodachi to
ryokō shimasu ga, Itō san mo issho ni
ikimasen ka. (*b*) Mada kimatte inai n'
desu ga, umi yori yama no hō ga suki
desu kara, Shirakawa to iu onsen o
kangaete imasu. (*c*) Ē, onsen de wa
yukkuri suru koto ga dekimasu kara
ne. (*d*) Ja, Shirakawa ni kimemashō
ka. (*e*) 8-ji no densha ni noranakereba
narimasen kara, 7-ji han made ni eki ni
kuru koto ga dekimasu ka.
Reading corner Shain ryokō no
sukejūru (*Schedule for the company trip*)
8:00 Kaisha no mae de au (*meet in front
of the company*) 8:15 Shuppatsu
(*departure*) 11:30 Aoyama Kōgen ni
tsuku (*arrive at Aoyama Kōgen*) 12:00
Ranchi o taberu (*eat lunch*) Arupusu
Puraza no san-gai no Arupusu Byū
Resutoran (*Alps View Restaurant on the
third floor of the Alps Plaza*) 14:00
Onsen ni hairu (*go into the hot springs*)
16:00 Furii taimu (*free time*) 20:00
Enkai – shachō no supiichi (*party – speech
by the president*) * Shuppatsu no 15-fun
mae ni kite kudasai. (*Please arrive 15
minutes before departure.*) * Kuizu

gēmu ni deru hito wa Noguchi made
denwa shite kudasai. (*anyone who wants
to join in the quiz game, please call
Noguchi.*) 1 Resutoran wa nan-kai ni
arimasu ka. 2 Nan to iu resutoran desu
ka. 3 Enkai wa nan-ji kara desu ka.

Lesson 20

The story so far Last week Wajima
signed the contract with Dando Sports,
so Yamamoto buchō is feeling relieved.
Today is the day of the company trip,
and everyone took the bus together to
Aoyama Kōgen. The party began at 8:00,
and now everyone is enjoying themselves
singing songs. Yamamoto buchō is
happily drinking sake while talking to
Noguchi san.
Dialogue **Noguchi** It's good isn't it,
the contract with Dando Sports going so
well... **Yamamoto** You were busy
too, weren't you. You really worked hard
for the company... **Noguchi** No, it
was nothing. **Yamamoto** (*looking
around*) Everyone looks as if they're
having a good time, eh? Who's that
singing a song over there? **Noguchi**
He's called Tanaka, and he's from the
Nagoya branch. They say he can really
hold his drink. **Yamamoto** Ah yes,
that's right... And how about the person
dancing behind Okamoto kachō?
Noguchi Buchō! Don't you know?
That's Hotta kun! You're tipsy too, aren't
you! (*The obāsan from the hotel opens the
door to the room and bows.*) **Obāsan**
I'm sorry to disturb you, but is there
someone here called Yamamoto san?
Yamamoto Yes, that's me. Was there
something...? **Obāsan** There's a
telephone call for you. **Yamamoto**
Thank you. I wonder who it is? Excuse
me a moment. (*He goes out to the phone.*)
Hello? This is Yamamoto. **Nakagawa**
Hello? Yamamoto buchō? My name is
Nakagawa, from Wajima. I'm very sorry
to disturb you in the middle of the party,
but the fact is, there was a call from
Britain from Mr Lloyd just now.
Yamamoto What? From Mr Lloyd? So,
what was it about? **Nakagawa** Well, I
don't really know, but he asked if you
would call him as soon as possible.
Yamamoto Eh? I wonder what it is!

Comprehension 1 (*b*) 2 (*a*)
Expansion activities **1 Across:**
3 ireru 5 aida 7 keiyaku 9 itta
11 kaku 13 sai 14 narimasen
16 sakana 19 koto 20 no 21 kaiketsu
24 oishii 25 gatsu 26 endate
28 unten **Down:** 1 kakaku 2 iya
3 iku 4 ue 5 arimasu 6 minagara
8 jikan 10 meikaku 12 tabetai 15 wa
16 shitte 17 kaeru 18 yori 21 kagi
22 san 23 shita 26 en 27 de
2 (*a*) Uisukii o nonde iru hito o shitte
imasu ka. Are wa Itō to iu hito desu.
(*b*) Shashin o totte iru hito o shitte
imasu ka. Are wa Katō to iu hito desu.
(*c*) Tabako o sutte iru hito o shitte imasu
ka. Are wa Ogawa to iu hito desu.
(*d*) Denwa o kakete iru hito o shitte
imasu ka. Are wa Wada to iu hito desu.
(*e*) Shinbun o yonde iru hito o shitte
imasu ka. Are wa Suzuki to iu hito desu.
(*f*) Shachō to hanashite iru hito o shitte
imasu ka. Are wa Ōno to iu hito desu.
(*g*) Yopparatte iru hito o shitte imasu
ka. Are wa Yamazaki to iu hito desu.
(*g*) Odotte iru hito o shitte imasu ka. Are
wa Kikuchi to iu hito desu. **3** (*a*) 4-gatsu
ni tabeta ryōri wa oishikatta kedo,
5-gatsu ni tabeta ryōri wa amari oishiku
nakatta desu. (*b*) 4-gatsu ni kiita
supiichi wa nagakatta kedo, 5-gatsu ni
kiita supiichi wa mijikakatta desu.
(*c*) 4-gatsu ni tsukatta heya wa hirokatta
kedo, 5-gatsu ni tsukatta heya wa
chiisakatta desu. (*d*) 4-gatsu ni tomatta
hoteru wa yokatta kedo, 5-gatsu ni
tomatta hoteru wa warukatta desu.
(*e*) 4-gatsu ni benkyō shita naiyō wa yaku
ni tatta kedo, 5-gatsu ni benkyō shita
naiyō wa yaku ni tatanakatta desu.
4 (*a*) shigoto, taihen-sō, taihen-sō-na
shigoto, taihen ja nai. (*b*) ginkō, yosa-sō,
yosa-sō-na ginkō, yoku nai (*c*) hon,
muzukashi-sō, muzukashi-sō-na hon,
muzukashiku nai (*d*) konpyūta,
atarashi-sō, atarashi-sō-na konpyūta,
atarashiku nai (*e*) kikai, benri-sō,
benri-sō-na kikai, benri ja nai (*f*) hisho,
yosa-sō, yosa-sō-na hisho, yoku nai
5 (*a*) (*ii*) (*b*) (*i*) (*c*) (*i*) (*d*) (*iii*)
(*e*) (*ii*) (*f*) (*ii*) (*g*) (*i*) **6** (*a*) ni tsuite
(*b*) to iu hanashi (*c*) dekiru dake (*d*) no
tame ni (*e*) isshōkenmei (*f*) dekiru
dake (*g*) ni tsuite (*h*) isshōkenmei
7 (*a*) Ohayō gozaimasu, Shirai san. Konde
imasu, ne. (*b*) Kono seminā wa hajimete

desu ka. (*c*) Tokorode, asoko de kōhii o
nonde iru hito wa dare desu ka. Taka-sō-
na sūtsu o kite imasu, ne! (*d*) Ā, sō
desu ka. Kare to hanashite iru kirei-na
onna no hito wa dare desu ka. (*e*) Atama
ga yosa-sō desu ne. (*f*) Hai, watashi
desu ga. Nanika... (*g*) Arigatō
gozaimasu. Dare deshō ka.
Reading corner Kono shūmatsu,
Nakano ni aru kenkyūjō de torēningu ga
atta. Sono torēningu ni shusseki shita
hitotachi wa honsha no hito dake de naku,
Nagoya shisha no hito mo takusan ita.
Tonari ni suwatta hito wa Nagoya shisha
kara kita Yamaguchi san to iu hito datta.
Kanojo wa totemo kirei de, shinsetsu-na
hito datta. Kongetsu no torēningu wa hijō
ni yaku ni tatta.
Torēningu no ato de, minna de karaoke
baa ni itta. Soko de utatta Eigo no uta wa
totemo romanchikku datta. Sono uta o
utainagara, boku wa Yamaguchi san no
koto o kangaeta. Raigetsu aru
torēningu ni mo kanojo wa kuru darō
ka... (*This weekend, there was a
training session at the research centre
(which is) in Nakano. The people who
attended the training were not only from
head office, there were a lot from the
Nagoya branch too. The person who sat
next to me was from the Nagoya branch,
and she was called Yamaguchi san.
She was very pretty and sweet. This
month's training was extremely
useful.*
*After the training we all went together to a
karaoke bar. The English song that we
sang there was very romantic. While we
were singing that song, I thought about
Yamaguchi san. I wonder if she'll be
coming to next month's training...*)
1 Torēningu ni shusseki shita hitotachi
wa, doko kara kimashita ka. (*Where did
the people who attended the training come
from?*) **2** Yamaguchi san wa donna
hito desu ka. (*What kind of person is
Yamaguchi san?*) **3** Kongetsu no
torēningu wa dō deshita ka. (*How was
this month's training session?*) **4** Hotta
san wa, Yamaguchi san no koto o dō
omoimashita ka. (*What did Hotta san
think of Yamaguchi san?*) **5** Raigetsu
mo torēningu ga arimasu ka. (*Is there a
training session next month?*)
Business briefing 1-T 2-F 3-T
4-F 5-F 6-T 7-T 8-F 9-T 10-T

11-T 12-F 13-T 14-T 15-F 16-T
17-F 18-F 19-F 20-T

Aural comprehension answers

Lesson 2 First dialogue: 1 Morning.
2 Her key. Second dialogue: 1 He's
the kachō (section manager).
2 314–718.

Lesson 3 First dialogue:
1 Newspapers. 2 ¥320. Second
dialogue: 1 Yes. 2 Golf.

Lesson 4 First dialogue: 1 The
kachō's mother. 2 She's a teacher.
Second dialogue: 1 No. 2 London.

Lesson 5 First dialogue:
1 Tomorrow. 2 The buchō (general
manager). Second dialogue: 1 Check his
schedule for tomorrow. 2 Yes.

Lesson 6 First dialogue: 1 Ōsaka.
2 2:30. Second dialogue: 1 Yes. 2 No.

Lesson 7 First dialogue: 1 Yes.
2 Write his name and his company's
name. Second dialogue: 1 France.
2 No.

Lesson 8 First dialogue: 1 Yes.
2 He went home. Second dialogue:
1 No. 2 Now.

Lesson 9 First dialogue: 1 Tuesday.
2 By car. Second dialogue:
1 Attending English class.
2 At the company.

Lesson 10 First dialogue: 1 Yes.
2 Two days. Second dialogue: 1 Yes.
2 Yes.

Lesson 11 First dialogue: 1 The end
of the working day. 2 No. Second
dialogue: 1 20 bottles 2 No.

Lesson 12 First dialogue: 1 No.
2 The pubs. Second dialogue:
1 During university. 2 No.

Lesson 13 First dialogue:
1 Explained about the sales/marketing.
2 At 5:00. Second dialogue: 1 In the
desk. 2 Yes, the kachō has.

Lesson 14 First dialogue: 1 At the
department store in front of the station.
2 ¥11,000. Second dialogue: 1 The
president of the company. 2 In the
sales/marketing department.

Lesson 15 First dialogue: 1 He's in a
meeting. 2 No, he's going to call again
later. Second dialogue: 1 No. 2 No.

Lesson 16 First dialogue: 1 The
president's office. 2 Straight ahead, and
then turn left. Second dialogue: 1 To a
French restaurant. 2 The service at the
restaurant.

Lesson 17 First dialogue: 1 No.
2 Automobile safety. Second dialogue:
1 Use the word processor. 2 Smoke.

Lesson 18 First dialogue: 1 Yes.
2 His wife. Second dialogue: 1 Yes.
2 No.

Lesson 19 First dialogue:
1 Sightseeing in Kyoto or going to a hot
spring. 2 The buchō. Second
dialogue: 1 The contract (for the car).
2 By fax.

Lesson 20 First dialogue: 1 A
computer training course. 2 One week.
Second dialogue: 1 Their company's.
2 Sing the song.

APPENDICES

Appendix 1: verbs

The following list shows all the verbs which appear in this text, except those which are made up of a noun plus **suru**, such as **benkyō suru, ryokō suru, kopii suru**, etc. The abbreviation [iv] shows an intransitive verb, and [tv] shows a transitive verb.

dictionary form	-masu form	-te form	meaning	lesson
akeru	akemasu	akete	*open* [tv]	20
aku	akimasu	aite	*be open, free* [iv]	9
aru	arimasu	atte	*have, exist*	5
aruku	arukimasu	aruite	*walk*	18
asobu	asobimasu	asonde	*play*	7
au	aimasu	atte	*meet*	8
chigau	chigaimasu	chigatte	*be different*	4
dekiru	dekimasu	dekite	*can, be done*	13
deru	demasu	dete	*come out, appear*	7
furu	furimasu	futte	*fall, come down*	12
ganbaru	ganbarimasu	ganbatte	*try hard, persist*	5
hairu	hairimasu	haitte	*join, enter*	5
hajimaru	hajimarimasu	hajimatte	*start, begin* [iv]	20
hajimeru	hajimemasu	hajimete	*start, begin* [tv]	5
hanashiau	hanashiaimasu	hanashiatte	*talk together*	17
hanasu	hanashimasu	hanashite	*speak, talk*	5
harau	haraimasu	haratte	*pay*	19
hataraku	hatarakimasu	hataraite	*work*	9
hazusu	hazushimasu	hazushite	*leave (one's seat)*	15
iku	ikimasu	itte	*go*	5
irassharu	irasshaimasu	irasshite	*be* [honorific]	20
ireru	iremasu	irete	*put in*	7
iru	imasu	ite	*be, exist*	5
isogu	isogimasu	isoide	*hurry*	7
itadaku	itadakimasu	itadaite	*eat, drink* [humble]	20
itasu	itashimasu	itashite	*do* [humble]	20
iu	iimasu	itte	*speak, say*	14
kaeru	kaerimasu	kaette	*return, go home*	5
kaeru	kaemasu	kaete	*change* [tv]	20
kakaru	kakarimasu	kakatte	*take, need, require*	8
kakeru	kakemasu	kakete	*call, ring up*	15
kaku	kakimasu	kaite	*write*	5
kangaeru	kangaemasu	kangaete	*think about, consider*	16

kariru	karimasu	karite	*borrow*	17
katazukeru	katazukemasu	katazukete	*put in order*	8
kau	kaimasu	katte	*buy*	12
kawaru	kawarimasu	kawatte	*replace* [iv]	7
kiku	kikimasu	kiite	*ask, hear*	5
kimaru	kimarimasu	kimatte	*be decided* [iv]	15
kimeru	kimemasu	kimete	*decide* [tv]	20
kiru	kimasu	kite	*wear, put on*	20
komu	komimasu	konde	*be crowded*	18
korobu	korobimasu	koronde	*fall over*	12
kuru	kimasu	kite	*come*	5
machiau	machiaimasu	machiatte	*wait for each other*	17
magaru	magarimasu	magatte	*turn, bend*	16
mairu	mairimasu	maitte	*come, go* [humble]	20
makaseru	makasemasu	makasete	*entrust, leave*	19
matomeru	matomemasu	matomete	*collect together*	15
matsu	machimasu	matte	*wait*	6
meshiagaru	meshiagarimasu	meshiagatte	*eat* [honorific]	20
miru	mimasu	mite	*see, look at*	5
miseau	miseaimasu	miseatte	*show each other*	17
miseru	misemasu	misete	*show*	8
mōsu	mōshimasu	mōshite	*say, tell* [humble]	20
motsu	mochimasu	motte	*have, hold*	15
motte iku	motte ikimasu	motte ite	*take*	15
motte kuru	motte kimasu	motte kuru	*bring*	15
naraberu	narabemasu	narabete	*display*	16
narau	naraimasu	naratte	*learn*	7
naru	narimasu	natte	*become, get*	14
nasaru	nasaimasu	nasatte	*do* [honorific]	20
nobasu	nobashimasu	nobashite	*extend, lengthen*	19
nomu	nomimasu	nonde	*drink*	5
noru	norimasu	notte	*get on, in*	18
odoru	odorimasu	odotte	*dance*	20
okureru	okuremasu	okurete	*be late*	8
okuru	okurimasu	okutte	*send*	5
omou	omoimasu	omotte	*think*	14
oriru	orimasu	orite	*get off, out of*	18
oru	orimasu	otte	*be* [humble]	20
oshieau	oshieaimasu	oshieatte	*teach each other*	17
oshieru	oshiemasu	oshiete	*teach, tell*	5
ossharu	osshaimasu	osshatte	*say, tell* [honorific]	20
osu	oshimasu	oshite	*push, press*	7
otosu	otoshimasu	otoshite	*drop, let fall*	12
owaru	owarimasu	owatte	*finish, end*	7
shimaru	shimarimasu	shimatte	*close* [iv]	20
shimeru	shimemasu	shimete	*close* [tv]	20
shinu	shinimasu	shinde	*die*	7
shiraberu	shirabemasu	shirabete	*investigate*	6
shiru	shirimasu	shitte	*know, be acquainted*	9
suku	sukimasu	suite	*become empty*	9

sumu	sumimasu	sunde	*live, reside*	12
suru	shimasu	shite	*do*	5
sū	suimasu	sutte	*inhale, smoke*	17
suwaru	suwarimasu	suwatte	*sit*	13
taberu	tabemasu	tabete	*eat*	5
tomaru	tomarimasu	tomatte	*stop, halt* [iv]	20
tomeru	tomemasu	tomete	*stop, halt* [tv]	20
toru	torimasu	totte	*take*	12
tsukareru	tsukaremasu	tsukarete	*get tired*	8
tsukau	tsukaimasu	tsukatte	*use*	17
tsuku	tsukimasu	tsuite	*arrive*	6
tsukuru	tsukurimasu	tsukutte	*make*	13
tsutomeru	tsutomemasu	tsutomete	*be employed*	9
uru	urimasu	utte	*sell*	20
utau	utaimasu	utatte	*sing*	20
wakaru	wakarimasu	wakatte	*understand*	5
wasureru	wasuremasu	wasurete	*forget*	18
yaku ni tatsu	yaku ni tachimasu	yaku ni tatte	*be of use*	20
yameru	yamemasu	yamete	*stop, discontinue*	16
yobu	yobimasu	yonde	*call, send for*	17
yomu	yomimasu	yonde	*read*	5
yopparau	yopparaimasu	yopparatte	*get drunk*	20
da	desu	de	*be, is*	2

Appendix 2: adjectives

The following list shows all **-i** and **-na** adjectives which appear in this text.

adjective	meaning	lesson
akai	*red*	14
akarui	*light, bright*	14
anzen-na	*safe*	17
aoi	*blue-green*	14
atarashii	*new*	6
atatakai	*warm*	12
atsui	*hot*	12
baka-na	*stupid, foolish*	12
byōki-na	*ill*	14
chiisai, chiisa-na	*small*	7
daiji-na	*important, serious*	18
daijōbu-na	*all right, okay*	6
dai-kirai-na	*hateful*	3
dai-suki-na	*like very much*	3
dame-na	*no good, useless*	12

enerugisshu-na	*energetic*	10
furui	*old*	14
genki-na	*fine, healthy*	4
hayai	*early, fast*	6
hen-na	*strange, odd*	7
hiroi	*big, spacious*	6
hitsuyō-na	*necessary*	16
ii	*nice, good*	4
iroiro-na	*various, all kinds of*	7
isogashii	*busy*	6
iya-na	*unpleasant, nasty*	18
jōzu-na	*skilful, good at*	7
jūyō-na	*important*	17
kantan-na	*simple, brief*	11
kawaii	*cute, pretty*	5
kirai-na	*dislike, horrible*	3
kirei-na	*pretty, clean*	7
kitanai	*dirty*	14
kurai	*dark, gloomy*	18
kuroi	*black*	14
kuwashii	*detailed*	11
meikaku-na	*clear, distinct*	19
mijikai	*short*	11
mushiatsui	*humid*	12
muzukashii	*difficult*	6
nagai	*long*	20
oishii	*tasty, good*	18
ōi	*lots of, many*	10
ōkii, ōki-na	*big, large*	7
omoshiroi	*interesting*	6
osoi	*late, slow*	6
romanchikku-na	*romantic*	10
samui	*cold*	12
sekushii-na	*sexy*	10
semai	*small (in area)*	18
shinsetsu-na	*kind*	7
shiroi	*white*	14
shizuka-na	*quiet, peaceful*	11
subarashii	*wonderful, marvellous*	18
suki-na	*like*	3
sumāto-na	*smart*	16
suzushii	*cool*	12
taihen-na	*tough, terrible*	7
taisetsu-na	*important, valuable*	16
takai	*expensive, high*	6
tanoshii	*enjoyable, fun*	6
tsuyoi	*strong*	12
umai	*good, successful*	14
ureshii	*happy*	20
urusai	*noisy*	14

utsukushii	beautiful	18
warui	bad, wrong	5
yasui	cheap	10
yoroshii	all right, fine	17
yūmei-na	famous	7
zannen-na	regrettable, disappointing	11

Appendix 3: particles

The relationship of nouns to the rest of the sentence is generally shown by the small words called particles which follow them.

wa Indicates the topic of the sentence, which is often, but not always, the grammatical subject.

| Ano kaisha **wa** ōkii desu. | *That company is large.* |
| Tanaka san **wa** mō kaerimashita. | *Tanaka san has already gone home.* |

ga Points out the subject of the verb, especially when the information is being introduced for the first time, or with WH-question words when they are the subject.

| Dare **ga** kore o kakimashita ka? | *Who wrote this?* |
| Kinō Roido san kara tegami **ga** kimashita yo. | *Yesterday a letter came from Mr Lloyd.* |

o Shows the object of the verb.

| Kare wa o-sake **o** nomimashita. | *He drank sake.* |
| Fakkusu **o** okurimashita. | *I sent the fax.* |

ka Comes at the end of the sentence to indicate that it is a question.

| Kore ga atarashii kikai desu **ka**. | *Is this a new machine?* |
| Eiga o mimashō **ka**. | *Shall we watch a film?* |

ni (*to*) Shows the indirect object of the verb, usually the person on the receiving end of an action.

| Tomodachi **ni** tegami o kakimashita. | *I wrote a letter to a friend.* |
| Kono repōto o Nagoya shisha **ni** okutte kudasai. | *Please could you fax this report to the Nagoya branch office.* |

ni (*in, at*) Indicates the place where a person or thing exists.

| Kaisha wa Tōkyō **ni** arimasu. | *The company is in Tokyo.* |

| Kanojō wa kaigi-shitsu **ni** imasu. | *She's in the meeting room.* |

ni (*at, on*) Indicates a point in time.

| Kaigi wa 2-ji **ni** arimasu. | *The meeting is at 2:00.* |
| Doyōbi **ni** aimashō. | *Let's meet on Saturday.* |

ni (*to, toward*) Shows movement towards a place, so it is often used with verbs meaning *go, come, return, travel*, etc.

| Sono konsāto **ni** ikimashita ka. | *Did you go to that concert?* |
| Ano resutoran **ni** hairimashō. | *Let's go into that restaurant.* |

e (*to, toward*) Like **ni** above, **e** also shows movement towards a place.

| Itsu Nihon **e** kimashita ka. | *When did you come to Japan?* |
| Kare wa 30-pun mae ni uchi **e** kaerimashita. | *He went home half an hour ago.* |

de (*at, in*) Shows the place where an action is performed or where something happens.

| Igirisu **de** Eigo o benkyō shita hō ga ii desu. | *It's best to study English in Britain.* |
| Doko **de** aimashō ka. | *Where shall we meet?* |

de (*with, by*) Shows the instrument or means used to perform some action.

| Takushii **de** ikimashō. | *Let's go by taxi.* |
| Eigo **de** hanashite kudasai. | *Please speak in English.* |

mo (*also, too*)

| Ashita **mo** kimasu ka. | *Are you coming tomorrow too?* |
| Tanaka san **mo** sono daigaku de benkyō shimashita. | *Tanaka san studied at that university, too.* |

mō (*already, yet*)

| **Mō** ranchi o tabemashita. | *I've already had lunch.* |
| Shigoto wa **mō** owarimashita ka. | *Have you finished your work yet?* |

no (*of, 's*) Shows possession or belonging to.

| Kore wa Koyama san **no** kaban desu ka. | *Is this Koyama san's briefcase?* |
| Igirisu **no** tenki wa ima dō desu ka. | *How's the weather in Britain at the moment?* |

no Used in apposition to give more information about someone or something.

Enjinia **no** Itō san ga uketsuke ni imasu.	*Mr Ito, the engineer, is in reception.*
Kochira ga hōritsu tantō **no** Mori san desu.	*This is the person in charge of legal matters, Mori san.*

—— Appendix 4: days of the month ——

tsuitachi	1st	jū-roku-nichi	16th
futsuka	2nd	jū-shichi-nichi	17th
mikka	3rd	jū-hachi-nichi	18th
yokka	4th	jū-ku-nichi	19th
itsuka	5th	hatsuka	20th
muika	6th	ni-jū-ichi-nichi	21st
nanoka	7th	ni-jū-ni-nichi	22nd
yōka	8th	ni-jū-san-nichi	23rd
kokonoka	9th	ni-jū-yokka	24th
tōka	10th	ni-jū-go-nichi	25th
jū-ichi-nichi	11th	ni-jū-roku-nichi	26th
jū-ni-nichi	12th	ni-jū-shichi-nichi	27th
jū-san-nichi	13th	ni-jū-hachi-nichi	28th
jū-yokka	14th	ni-jū-ku-nichi	29th
jū-go-nichi	15th	san-jū-nichi	30th
		san-jū-ichi-nichi	31st

—— Appendix 5: counters ——

The counters which have been covered in this book are given below.

(a) Counting cylindrical objects such as umbrellas, pencils, cigarettes, bottles, etc.:

1 ip-pon   2 ni-hon   3 san-bon   4 yon-hon   5 go-hon
6 rop-pon   7 nana-hon   8 hap-pon   9 kyū-hon   10 jip-pon

(b) Counting people:

1 hitori   2 futari   3 san-nin   4 yo-nin   5 go-nin   6 roku-nin
7 shichi-nin   8 hachi-nin   9 kyū-nin   10 jū-nin

(c) Counting floors in a building:

1 ik-kai   2 ni-kai   3 san-gai   4 yon-kai   5 go-kai   6 rok-kai
7 nana-kai   8 hachi-kai   9 kyū-kai   10 jū-kai

(*d*)   Counting objects which have no other special counter:
1 hitotsu   2 futatsu   3 mittsu   4 yottsu   5 itsutsu   6 muttsu
7 nanatsu   8 yattsu   9 kokonotsu   10 tō

(*e*)   Counting minutes:
1   ip-pun   2   ni-fun   3   san-pun   4   yon-pun.   5   go-fun
6   rop-pun   7   nana-fun   8   hap-pun/hachi-fun   9   kyū-fun
10 jip-pun

Appendix 6: occupations

Among the following list of occupations are some which have not appeared in the lessons.

bengoshi	*lawyer*	kenchikuka	*architect*
dezainā	*designer*	kokku/shefu	*chef*
enjinia	*engineer*	kōmuin	*public service*
gakusei	*student*		*employee*
haisha	*dentist*	kyōju	*professor*
hisho	*secretary*	operētā	*operator*
honyakuka	*translator*	seijika	*politician*
isha	*doctor*	sensei	*teacher*
jānarisuto	*journalist*	taipisuto	*typist*
jimuin	*clerk*	ten-in	*shop assistant*
kangofu	*nurse*	tsūyaku-sha	*interpreter*
keikan/o-mawari-san	*policeman*	uētā	*waiter*
		uētoresu	*waitress*
		uketsuke	*receptionist*
		untenshu	*driver*

Appendix 7: kanji

Following is a list of the kanji characters which are introduced in this text. The same character may be shown more than once if it appears with a different way of reading in different lessons.

Dai	Kanji	Way of reading	Meaning
5	ぶちょう 部長	bu-chō	*general manager*
5	かちょう 課長	ka-chō	*section manager*

5	でんわ 電話	den-wa	*telephone*
6	き 来ます	ki-masu	*to come*
6	い 行きます	i-kimasu	*to go*
6	なん 何	nan, nani	*what?*
7	いま 今	ima	*now*
7	はな 話す	hana-su	*to talk, speak*
7	くだ 下さい	kuda-sai	*please*
8	なんじ 何時	nan-ji	*what time, hour*
8	かいぎ 会議	kai-gi	*meeting*
8	いち に さん 一, 二, 三	ichi, ni, san	*one, two, three*
8	よん/しご 四、五	you shi, go	*four, five*
8	ろく しち/なな 六、七	roku, shichi/nana	*six, seven*
8	はち きゅう じゅう 八、九、十	hachi, kyū, jū	*eight, nine, ten*
8	ひゃく 百	hyaku	*hundred*
8	せん 千	sen	*thousand*
9	しまだ 島田	Shima-da	*(family name)*
9	にがつ 二月	ni-gatsu	*February*
9	び どよう日	doyō-bi	*Saturday*
9	ごがつ 五月	go-gatsu	*May*
9	みっか 三日	mik-ka	*the third (of the month)*
9	ついたち 一日	tsuitachi	*the first (of the month)*
9	ひ その日	sono hi	*that day*
9	なまえ 名前	na-mae	*name*
9	がっぴ 月日	gap-pi	*month and day*
9	ほった 堀田	Hot-ta	*(family name)*
9	おかもと 岡本	Oka-moto	*(family name)*
9	のぐち 野口	No-guchi	*(family name)*
9	まえだ 前田	Mae-da	*(family name)*

9	いけだ 池田	Ike-da	(family name)
9	こやま 小山	Ko-yama	(family name)
9	やまだ 山田	Yama-da	(family name)
9	たけした 竹下	Take-shita	(family name)
10	おお 多い	ō-i	lots of, many
10	ときどき 時々	toki-doki	sometimes
10	おお 大きい	ō-kii	big
10	かいしゃ 会社	kai-sha	company
11	いしかわ 石川	Ishi-kawa	(family name)
11	ごほん 五本	go-hon	five (bottles)
11	きょう 今日	kyō	today
11	ほんとう 本当	hon-tō	really
11	にほん 日本	Ni-hon	Japan
11	ひと 一こと	hito-koto	one word
11	じかん 時間	ji-kan	hour, time
12	ふたり 二人	futari	two people
12	わじま 輪島	Wa-jima	(company name)
13	げつ　び 月よう日	getsu-yō-bi	Monday
13	うえ 上	ue	above, on top
13	こんげつ 今月	kon-getsu	this month
13	なか 中	naka	middle, centre
13	はなし 話	hanashi	talk, conversation
14	にほんじん 日本人	Ni-hon-jin	Japanese person
14	らいねん 来年	rai-nen	next year
14	おも 思います	omo-imasu	to think
15	たんとう 担当する	tan-tō suru	to be in charge
16	とうきょう 東京	Tō-kyō	(city name)
16	たかまつ 高松	Taka-matsu	(place or family name)

16	こばやし 小林	Ko-bayashi	*(family name)*
16	いりぐち 入口	iri-guchi	*entrance*
17	けんがく 見学	ken-gaku	*observation study*
17	すずき 鈴木	Suzu-ki	*(family name)*
17	いちばん 一番	ichi-ban	*best, most*
17	み 見せる	mi-seru	*to show*
17	ひと 人	hito	*person*
17	こうじょう 工場	kō-jō	*factory*
18	ご ご 午後	go-go	*afternoon*
18	い 入れる	i-reru	*to insert, put in*
18	あと 後	ato	*after, latter*
18	はい 入る	hai-ru	*to enter, go in*
19	しゃいん 社員	sha-in	*company employee*
19	りょこう 旅行	ryo-kō	*trip , travel*
19	もり 森	mori	*(family name)*
19	えん 円	en	*yen*
19	あおやま 青山	Ao-yama	*(place or family name)*
19	たんとうしゃ 担当者	tan tō-sha	*(person in charge)*
20	うた 歌	uta	*song*
20	うた 歌う	uta-u	*to sing*
20	たの 楽しい	tano-shii	*enjoyable, fun*
20	ししゃ 支社	shi-sha	*branch office*

ENGLISH-JAPANESE GLOSSARY

The number in brackets following each entry indicates the lesson in which the word or phrase first appears. [v] indicates a verb, [n] a noun, [adj] an adjective, [iv] an intransitive verb, and [tv] a transitive verb.

about, around — goro (6)

about, approximately — gurai (kurai) (8)

accident — jiko (8)

advertising, publicity — senden (15)

advice — adobaisu (16)

Africa — Afurika (11)

after — ato (12)

after a long interval — hisashiburi (15)

afternoon — gogo (18)

again, once more — mata (13)

airport — kūkō (6)

all, the whole lot — zenbu (12)

all of you — minna (4)

all right, okay — daijōbu (-na) (6), yoroshii [polite version of ii] (17)

already — mō (6)

also, too — mo (3)

altogether — zenbu de (12)

always — itsumo (10)

America — Amerika (11)

another helping — o-kawari (18)

and — to (5), ya (16)

and, then — soshite (12)

and, so, thereupon — sorede (14)

announcer — anaunsā (2)

another, separate — betsu no (9)

anyone — dareka (9)

anything — nanika (9)

anytime — itsuka (9)

anywhere — dokoka (9)

apartment, flat — apāto (3)

apology, excuse — mōshiwake (20)

April — shi-gatsu (9)

arrive [v] — tsuku (6)

as...as possible — dekiru dake (20)

ask, hear [v] — kiku (5)

as much as — mo (8)

assistant manager — kakarichō (2)

at, in — de (9)

attend, be present [v] — deru (15)

attendance, presence — shusseki (15)

August — hachi-gatsu (9)

automobile — jidōsha (17)

bad, wrong — warui (5)

bank — ginkō (16)

bar — bā (13)

barley tea — mugi-cha (17)

bath — furo, o-furo (18)

be [v] — desu (2), de gozaimasu [formal] (20)

be, exist [v] — [animate things] iru (5), irassharu [honorific] (20), oru [humble] (20)

be, exist [v] — [inanimate objects] aru (5), gozaimasu [formal] (20)

be crowded [v] — komu (18)

be decided [v] — kimaru (15)

be done, be completed [v] — dekiru (13)

be employed [v] — tsutomeru (9)

be in charge [v] — tantō suru (9)

be late [v] — okureru (8)

be of use [v] — yaku ni tatsu (20)

be open, be free [v] — aku (9)

be out, not at home [v] — gaishutsu suru (15)

be relieved [v] — hotto suru (20)

beautiful — utsukushii (18)

because, since — kara (10)

become, get [v] — naru (14)

become empty [v] — suku (9)

beer — biiru (2)

before, in front of — mae (13)

begin [iv] — hajimaru (20)

behind — ushiro (13)

between — aida (13)

big (large) — ōkii (6), ōki-na (7)

big (spacious) — hiroi (6)

birthday	tanjōbi (9)	*come [v]*	kuru (5), mairu [humble] (20)
black	kuro(i) (14)		
blue	burū (14)	*come out, appear [v]*	deru (7)
blue-green	ao(i) (14)	*company*	kaisha (4)
bon appétit/yes, please	itadakimasu (11)	*computer*	konpyūtā (2)
		condition, state	jōtai
borrow [v]	kariru (17)	*confirm [v]*	kakunin suru (13)
boyfriend	bōifurendo (17)	*congratulations*	omedetō gozaimasu (9)
briefcase, bag	kaban (3)		
bring [v]	motte kuru (15)	*consultant*	konsarutanto (2)
brown	chairo, buraun (14)	*contents*	naiyō (20)
building	biru (13)	*contract*	keiyaku (17)
bus	basu (6)	*control, supervision*	kanri (17)
business trip	shutchō (8)	*convenience, circumstances*	tsugō (5)
busy	isogashii (6)		
but	demo, ga (7)	*conversation, talk*	hanashi (6)
buy [v]	kau (12)	*cooking, cuisine*	ryōri (18)
by [instrument]	de (6)	*cool*	suzushii (12)
by, not later than	made ni (13)	*country*	kuni (10)
by the side	yoko (13)	*course (of study)*	kōsu (15)
		cram school	juku (18)
call (on the phone), ring up [v]	kakeru (15)	*customer, guest*	o-kyaku san/sama
		cute, pretty	kawaii (5)
cake	kēki (16)		
call, invite [v]	yobu (18)	*dance [v]*	odoru (20)
camera	kamera (12)	*dark, gloomy*	kurai (18)
cashpoint	kyasshu kōnā (16)	*data*	dēta (18)
can, be able to do [v]	dekiru (13)	*day*	hi (9)
car	kuruma (8)	*day after tomorrow*	asatte (5)
caretaker	kanrinin (6)	*day before yesterday*	ototoi (14)
catalogue	katarogu (15)	*deadline*	shimekiri (13)
cause	gen-in (17)	*December*	jū-ni-gatsu (9)
chance, opportunity	chansu (18)	*decide [tv]*	kimeru (20)
change [tv]	kaeru (20)	*defective*	furyō (no) (17)
change, replace, take the place of [iv]	kawaru (7)	*department (of a company)*	-bu (4)
cheap	yasui (10)	*department store*	depāto (3)
check [v]	chekku suru (17)	*departure*	shuppatsu (19)
check out (of a hotel)	chekku-auto (2)	*desk*	tsukue (4)
		detailed	kuwashii (11)
cheers	kanpai (11)	*design*	dezain (16)
cheese	chiizu (3)	*die [v]*	shinu (7)
child	kodomo (12)	*difficult*	muzukashii (6)
Chinese characters	kanji (5)	*dining room, cafeteria*	shokudō (17)
chopsticks	hashi (19)		
Chinese cooking	chūka ryōri (18)	*dirty*	kitanai (14)
cigarette	tabako (17)	*dislike, detestable*	kirai (-na) (3)
class	kurasu (5)	*display, put into position [v]*	naraberu (16)
clear, distinct	meikaku-na (19)		
close [iv]	shimaru (20)	*division (of a company)*	jigyō-hon-bu (4)
close [tv]	shimeru (20)		
club	kurabu (16)	*do [v]*	suru (5), itasu [humble] (20), nasaru [honorific] (20)
coffee	kōhii (2)		
cold	samui (12)		
collect together, put in order [v]	matomeru (15)		
		document	shorui (6)
colour	iro (14)	*dog*	inu (5)

door	doa (20)	extension	naisen (15)
dormitory	ryō (14)	(telephone)	
dollars, in dollars	doru, doru-date	extremely	zuibun (8), hijō ni
	(19)		(16)
drink [v]	nomu (5)	factory	kōjō (4)
drive [v]	unten suru (19)	fall, come down [v]	furu (12)
drop, let fall [v]	otosu (12)	fall over [v]	korobu (12)
during, in the	-chū (15)	famous	yūmei (-na) (7)
course of		father	chichi [familiar],
early	hayai (6)		o-tōsan [polite]
earthquake	jishin (17)		(4)
east	higashi (10)	fax	fakkusu (5)
eat [v]	taberu (5); itadaku	February	ni-gatsu (9)
	[humble] (20);	feeling, mood	kibun (13)
	meshiagaru	female, woman	josei (15)
	[honorific] (20)	file	fairu (2)
economics	keizai (18)	film, movie	eiga (9)
education, training	kyōiku (16)	film (for a camera)	fuirumu (12)
employees, workers	jūgyōin (10)	finally, in the end	kekkyoku (8),
elevator	erebētā (16)		saigo ni (17)
end, finish	owari (13)	fine, healthy	genki (-na) (4)
end (of the street,	tsukiatari (16)	finish, end [v]	owaru (7)
aisle, etc.)		first floor (UK	ik-kai (16)
energetic	enerugisshu-na	ground floor)	
	(10)	first of all, ahead	saki ni (8)
engineer	enjinia (2)	first time	hajimete (14)
England, Britain	Igirisu (4)	firstly, first of all	mazu (17)
English language	Eigo (5)	__floor	-kai (16)
enjoyable, fun	tanoshii (6)	fish	sakana (18)
enough, that'll do	kekkō desu (18)	floppy disk	furoppii (7)
enter (information	entā suru (7)	for, for the purpose	no tame ni (20)
into a computer)		of	
[v]		forget, leave behind	wasureru (18)
enter, put in [v]	ireru (7)	Friday	kinyōbi (9)
entrance, exit	-guchi (10),	friend	tomodachi (12)
	iriguchi (16)	from	kara (5)
entrust, leave (to	makaseru (19)	France	Furansu (4)
someone's care)		full	ippai (18)
escalator	esukarētā (16)	general manager	buchō (4)
estimate, quotation	mitsumori (13)	Germany	Doitsu (10)
et cetera, and so on	nado (16)	get drunk [v]	yopparau (20)
Europe	Yōroppa (10)	get in, on (a vehicle,	noru (18)
evening, night	ban (13)	lift, etc.)	
evening meal	yūshoku (18)	get off, out of (a	oriru (18)
event	ibento (19)	vehicle, lift, etc.)	
every day	mainichi (14)	get tired [v]	tsukareru (8)
every month	maitsuki (20)	girlfriend	gārufurendo (13)
every year	mainen (19)	go [v]	iku (5), mairu
excuse me	sumimasen (3),		[humble] (20)
	shitsurei	go to meet [v]	mukae ni iku (6)
	shimasu (5)	golf	gorufu (3)
expensive, high	takai (6)	good, successful	umai (14)
explain [v]	setsumei suru	good, tasty	oishii (18)
	(11)	good evening	konbanwa (2)
export [v]	yushutsu suru (10)	good morning	ohayō gozaimasu (2)
extend, lengthen [v]	nobasu (19)	goods, merchandise	shōhin (13)

grandmother, old woman	o-bāsan (16)	*inhale, smoke [v]*	sū (17)
		inside, within	naka (13)
green	guriin, midori (14)	*intend to [v]*	tsumori desu (11)
green tea	o-cha (8)	*interest*	kyōmi (16)
greetings	aisatsu (16)	*interesting*	omoshiroi (6)
grey	gurē (14)	*international*	kokusai (4)
guarantee	hoshō (17)	*internationally*	kokusai-teki (20)
guide	gaido san (19)	*interview*	mensetsu (4)
half	han (6)	*investigate, check up [v]*	shiraberu (6)
happy	ureshii (20)		
hate, hateful	dai-kirai (-na) (3)	*investment*	tōshi (10)
have, exist [for inanimate objects] [v]	aru (5)	*isn't*	ja arimasen [negative of desu] (6)
have, hold, carry [v]	motsu (15)	*Italy*	Itaria (18)
he, him	kare (4)		
head	atama (20)	*January*	ichi-gatsu (9)
head office	honsha (4)	*Japan*	Nihon (3)
hello	konnichiwa (2)	*Japanese language*	Nihongo (5)
hello (on the phone)	moshi moshi (4)	*Japanese-style inn*	ryokan (19)
here	koko (8)	*jogging*	jogingu (14)
hobby, pastime	shumi (4)	*join, enter [v]*	hairu (5)
holiday, day off	yasumi (9)	*juice*	jūsu (2)
Hong Kong	Honkon (18)	*July*	shichi-gatsu (9)
hot	atsui (12)	*June*	roku-gatsu (9)
hot spring	onsen (19)	*just now*	sakki (20)
hotel	hoteru (6)		
house, home	uchi (8)	*key*	kagi (2)
how? by what means?	nani de (6)	*key (on a keyboard)*	kii (7)
		kind	shinsetsu (-na) (7)
how?	dō (7)	*know, understand [v]*	wakaru (5)
how do you do?	hajimemashite (4)		
how much (money)?	ikura (3)	*know, be acquainted [v]*	shiru (9)
however, but, although	kedo, keredo, keredomo (10)		
humid	mushiatsui (12)	*late, slow*	osoi (6)
hundred	hyaku (3)	*later*	ato de (15)
hurry [v]	isogu (7)	*last month*	sengetsu (13)
husband, your/her	go-shujin (18)	*last week*	senshū (9)
husband, my	otto, shujin (18)	*last year*	kyonen (13)
I, me	watashi (4), boku [male, informal] (9)	*law*	hōritsu (19)
		learn [v]	narau (7)
		leave (one's seat) [v]	hazusu (15)
		left	hidari (16)
I'm home	tadaima (8)	*light, bright*	akarui (14)
if, in case	moshi (15)	*like, liking*	suki (-na), dai-suki (-na) (2)
if, when	to (16)		
ill	byōki (-na) (14)	*list*	risuto (15)
image	imēji (16)	*little, slightly*	chotto (6), shōshō (15)
import [v]	yunyū suru (10)		
importance	jūyōsei (17)	*little, a small quantity*	sukoshi (13)
important, principal	jūyō-na (17)		
important, valuable	taisetsu-na (16)	*live, reside [v]*	sumu (12)
in-company	shanai (16)	*look forward to, hope for [v]*	tanoshimi ni suru (19)
India	Indo (18)		
information	jōhō (15)	*long*	nagai (20)
information desk	annai-jo (16)	*lots, many*	takusan (7)
		lunch	ranchi (17)

machine	kikai (17)	no one	dare mo (15)
make, manufacture [v]	tsukuru (13)	nothing	nani mo (15)
		north	kita (10)
magazine	zasshi (16)	not at all	zenzen (10)
man	otoko no hito (10)	not much, not usually	amari (10)
management	manejimento (15) keiei (16)	November	jū-ichi-gatsu (9)
manager	kachō (2), manējā (6)	now, at the moment	ima (4)
		nowhere	doko e/ni mo (15)
manners	manā (16)	number	bangō (2)
many, lots of	ōi (10)	number ___	-ban (2)
March	san-gatsu (9)		
market	shijō (10)	o'clock	-ji (6)
marketing	māketingu (6)	observation study	kengaku (15)
marry [v]	kekkon suru (13)	October	jū-gatsu (9)
matter, item	ken (19)	of course	mochiron (17)
May	go-gatsu (9)	office, place of business	jimusho (14)
meet [v]	au (8)		
meeting	kaigi (5), miitingu (13)	office worker	sarariiman (4)
		often, usually	yoku (10)
menu	menyū (7)	old	furui (14)
message	messēji (5), dengon (15)	once, one time	ichido (15)
		one (item)	hitotsu (14)
minute	fun (6)	one person	hitori (12)
Monday	getsuyōbi (9)	one week	is-shūkan (14)
money	o-kane (16)	only, alone	dake (14)
more	motto (8)	only, except, it's just that	tada (14)
moreover	sore ni (18)		
morning	asa (5)	open [tv]	akeru (20)
most, -est	ichiban (10)	operator	operētā (17)
mother	haha [familiar], o-kāsan [polite] (4)	orange	orenji (2)
		our	uchi no (5)
		outside	soto (18)
Mount –	-san (10)	overseas	kaigai (4)
mountain	yama (10)	over there	asoko (8)
Mr, Mrs, Ms, Miss	san (2)	overtime work	zangyō (9)
Mr [informal]	kun (5)	part(s)	buhin (17)
mustn't, forbidden, no good	ikemasen (17)	part-time worker	pāto (15)
		party	pātii (5)
name	namae (2)	party, banquet	enkai (19)
near	soba (13)	pastel colours	pasuteru karā (14)
necktie	nekutai (14)	pay [v]	harau (19)
necessary, essential	hitsuyō (16)	payment	shi-harai (19)
new product	shin-shōhin (16)	pen	pen (3)
newspaper	shinbun (3)	people	hitotachi (4)
next	tsugi no (6)	perhaps, maybe	tabun (15)
next month	raigetsu (13)	person	hito (4), kata [polite] (18)
next to	tonari (13)		
next week	raishū (5)	person in charge	tantō-sha (6)
next year	rainen (13)	person (of a country)	-jin (5)
new	atarashii (6)		
nice, good	ii (4)	personnel	jinji (4)
no	iie (4)	photocopy	kopii (7)
no good, useless	dame (-na) (12) furyō (17)	photograph	shashin (12)
		pink	pinku (14)
noisy	urusai (14)	place, location	basho (15), tokoro (19)

plan, schedule	yotei (5)	robot	robotto (17)
plane	hikōki (8)	romantic	romanchikku (-na) (10)
planning, a plan	kikaku (4)		
plant manager	kōjō-chō (17)	room	heya (2)
play [v]	asobu (7)	-room	-shitsu (5)
please (do that)	onegai shimasu (2)	safe	anzen-na (17)
please (give me)	kudasai (3)	safety	anzensei (17)
please (take it); here you are	dōzo (2)	sake	nihonshu (3), sake (13)
pleased to meet you	dōzo yoroshiku (5)	salary	kyūryō (10)
point, spot, mark	ten (19)	sales	sērusu (6)
politics	seiji (18)	sandwich	sando(itchi) (3)
practice	renshū (5)	sales clerk	ten-in (16)
preparations	junbi (7)	Saturday	doyōbi (9)
president	shachō (4)	schedule	sukejūru (10)
pretty, clean	kirei (-na) (7)	school	gakkō (4)
price, value	kakaku (14)	sea	umi (18)
problem	mondai (14)	seat, place	seki (15)
production	seisan (17)	secretary	hisho (20)
production line	seisan rain (17)	section (of a company)	-ka (4)
productivity	seisanseī (17)		
pub	pabu (8)	see, look at [v]	miru (5), goran ni naru [honorific] (20)
purple	murasaki (14)		
push, press [v]	osu (7)		
put in, insert [v]	ireru (7)	self-introduction	jiko shōkai (11)
quality	hinshitsu (17)	sell [v]	uru (20)
quality control circle	QC sākuru (17)	selling, marketing	hanbai (13)
question	shitsumon (16)	seminar	seminā (20)
quiet, peaceful	shizuka (-na) (11)	send, despatch [v]	okuru (5)
radio	rajio (12)	September	ku-gatsu (9)
rain	ame (12)	serious, grave	daiji (-na) (18)
rather than	yori (19)	service	sābisu (16)
read [v]	yomu (5)	sexy	sekushii (-na) (10)
really, very	totemo (6)	she, her	kanojo (4)
really, truly	hontō ni (7)	shopping	kaimono (9)
reception	uketsuke (6)	short	mijikai (11)
reception clerk (at a hotel)	furonto no hito (2)	show [v]	miseru (8)
		show each other [v]	miseau (17)
red	aka(i) (14)	-side	-gawa (16)
regarding, in this connection	ni tsuite (15)	sightseeing	kankō (4)
		sign [v]	sain suru (18)
regrettable, disappointing	zannen (-na) (11)	simple, brief	kantan (-na) (11)
		since, because	no de, na no de (13)
relations, relationship	kankei (20)	sing [v]	utau (20)
		sit [v]	suwaru (13)
report	repōto (5)	size (of clothing)	saizu (14)
representative office	dairiten (10)	skiing	sukii (16)
research, study	kenkyū (5)	skilful, good at	jōzu (-na) (7)
respect language	keigo (20)	slowly	yukkuri (15)
rest time, break	kyūkei (17)	small (in size)	chiisai, chiisa (-na) (7)
return, go home [v]	kaeru (5)		
return trip	kaeri (8)	small (in area)	semai (18)
rice (cooked)	gohan (18)	smart	sumāto-na (16)
right	migi (16)	snow	yuki (12)
river	kawa (12)	so, like that	sō (2)
road	michi (18)		

so, therefore, consequently — dakara (13)
solution — kaiketsu (15)
someone — dareka (9)
something — nanika (9)
sometime — itsuka (9)
sometimes — tokidoki (9)
somewhere — dokoka (9)
song — uta (20)
soon — sugu (6)
so-so — mā-mā (3)
sorry to trouble you — osore-irimasu (15)
south — minami (10)
spaghetti — supagettii (11)
speak, talk, say [v] — hanasu (5), iu (14), mosu [humble] (20), ossharu [honorific] (20)
speaker — supiikā (20)
sport — supōtsu (7)
sportswear — supōtsu-uea (14)
station — eki (4)
staff members — shain (9), [without titles] hira shain (4)
start, begin [v] — hajimeru (5)
stay overnight [v] — tomaru (19)
steak — sutēki (19)
stereo — sutereo (17)
stewardess — suchuwādesu (16)
still — mada (7)
stomach — o-naka (9)
stop, cease [v] — yameru (16)
stop, come to a halt [iv] — tomaru (20)
stop, bring to a halt [tv] — tomeru (20)
straight, direct — massugu (16)
strange, odd — hen (-na) (7)
strike — sutoraiki (10)
strong — tsuyoi (12)
study — benkyō (5)
suit — sūtsu (20)
Sunday — nichiyōbi (9)
sushi bar — sushi-ya (9)
sweater — sētā (14)
switch — suitchi (7)
Switzerland — Suisu (18)
take, need, require [v] — kakaru (8)
take, hold [v] — toru (12)
take, take away [v] — motte iku (15)
talk together, discuss [v] — hanashiau (17)
taxi — takushii (8)
taxi stand — takushii noriba (8)

teach, tell [v] — oshieru (5)
teach each other [v] — oshieau (17)
teacher — sensei (4)
telephone — denwa (2)
television — terebi (3)
ten thousand — man (14)
tennis — tenisu (3)
terms, conditions — jōken (19)
thanks — dōmo (2)
thank you — arigatō gozaimasu (2)
thank you [when receiving something] — itadakimasu (11)
thank you for the meal — go-chisō sama deshita (11)
that — sono [adj], sore [n] (4)
that much — anna ni, sonna ni (12)
that over there — ano [adj], are [n] (4)
that way — sochira (11)
that way over there — achira (11)
there — soko (8)
they, them — karera (4)
thing, object — mono (14)
things, matters — koto (7)
think [v] — omou (14)
think about, consider [v] — kangaeru (16)
this — kono [adj], kore [n] (4)
this month — kongetsu (13)
this much — konna ni (12)
this way — kochira (11)
this week — konshū (13)
this year — kotoshi (13)
thought, idea — kangae (15)
thousand — sen (3)
Thursday — mokuyōbi (9)
tidy up, put in order [v] — katazukeru (8)
time, hour — jikan (6)
time, the time when — toki (12)
to — ni (5)
to, towards — e (8)
to, until, as far as — made (8)
today — kyō (5)
together — issho ni (15)
toilet — o-tearai (4)
tomorrow — ashita (5)
top, upper part — ue (13)
tough, terrible — taihen (-na) (7)
town, city — machi (10)
trade, business, — shōbai (16)

commerce	
trading company	shōsha (2)
train	densha (6)
training	torēningu (20)
travel, trip	ryokō (9)
truth, to tell the truth	jitsu wa (9)
try hard, persist [v]	ganbaru (5)
Tuesday	kayōbi (9)
turn, bend [v]	magaru (16)
two people	futari (12)
typewriter	taipuraitā (2)
typist	taipisuto (2)
umbrella	kasa (3)
under, below	shita (13)
underground/ basement	chika (16)
uniform	seifuku (16)
university	daigaku (12)
unpleasant, nasty	iya-na (18)
use [v]	tsukau (17)
various, all kinds of	iroiro (-na) (7)
vice-president	fuku-shachō (4)
video	bideo (20)
wait [v]	matsu (6)
wait for each other [v]	machiau (17)
waitress	uētoresu (2)
walk [v]	aruku (18)
warm	atatakai (12)
waterfall	take (12)
way of -ing	-kata (16)
we, our side	uchi (14)
wear, put on [v]	kiru (20)
weather	tenki (6)
wedding ceremony	kekkon-shiki (9)
Wednesday	suiyōbi (9)
week	shūkan (14)
weekend	shūmatsu (8)
welcome back	o-kaeri nasai (8)
welcome	yōkoso (11)
well then, in that case	dewa (6), sore ja (16)
well...	sā... (7), maa (10)
well, often	yoku (11)

well, by the way	tokorode (7)
west	nishi (10)
what?	nan (2), nani (5)
what extent?	donna ni (12)
what time?	nan-ji? (6)
when?	itsu (5)
where?	doko (4)
which?	dono [adj], dore [n] (3)
which way?	dochira (11)
which one?	dochira (19)
whisky	uisukii (2)
white	shiro(i) (14)
who?	dare (4)
why?	dō shite (5)
wife, your/his	okusan (13), okusama [formal] (20)
wife, my	kanai, tsuma (18)
wind	kaze (12)
with, together with	to (12)
with great effort	isshōkenmei (20)
woman	onna no hito (10)
wonderful, marvellous	subarashii (18)
word or two, a single word	hitokoto (11)
word processor	wāpuro (3)
work [v]	hataraku (9)
work, job	shigoto (3)
work, duty	kinmu (10)
world	sekai (18)
write [v]	kaku (5)
year	nen (13)
- years old	-sai (16)
yellow	kiiro (14)
yen, in yen	en (3), en-date (19)
yes	hai (2)
yet	mada (6)
you	anata [singular], anatatachi [plural] (4)
you're welcome	dō itashimashite (2)
zero, nought	zero (2)

JAPANESE-ENGLISH
GLOSSARY

The number in brackets following each entry indicates the lesson in which the word or phrase first appears. [v] indicates a verb, [n] a noun, [adj] an adjective, [tv] a transitive verb and [iv] an intransitive verb.

achira (11)	*that way over there*	atsui (12)	*hot*
adobaisu (16)	*advice*	au (8)	*to meet*
Afurika (11)	*Africa*	bā (13)	*bar*
aida (13)	*between*	baka (-na) (12)	*stupid, foolish*
aisatsu (16)	*greetings*	ban (13)	*evening, night*
aka(i) (14)	*red*	-ban (2)	*number ____*
akarui (14)	*light, bright*	bangō (2)	*number*
akeru (20)	*to open [tv]*	basho (15)	*place, location*
aki (20)	*autumn*	basu (6)	*bus*
aku (9)	*to be open, be free [iv]*	benkyō (5)	*study*
		bentō (3)	*packed lunch*
amari (10)	*not much, not usually*	betsu no (9)	*another, separate*
		bideo (20)	*video*
ame (12)	*rain*	biiru (2)	*beer*
Amerika (11)	*America*	biru (13)	*building*
anaunsā (2)	*announcer*	-bu (4)	*department (of a company)*
anata (4)	*you [singular]*		
anatatachi (4)	*you [plural]*	bōifurendo (17)	*boyfriend*
annai-jo (16)	*information desk*	buchō (4)	*general manager*
anna ni (12)	*that much*	buhin (17)	*parts*
ano (4)	*that over there [adj]*	buraun (14)	*brown*
anō (4)	*er...*	burū (14)	*blue*
anzen-na (17)	*safe*	byōki (-na) (14)	*ill*
anzen-sei (17)	*safety*	chairo (14)	*brown*
ao(i) (4)	*blue-green*	chansu (18)	*chance, opportunity*
apāto (3)	*apartment, flat*	chika (16)	*underground, basement*
are (4)	*that over there [n]*		
arigatō gozaimasu (2)	*thank you*	chekku-auto (2)	*check out (of a hotel)*
aru (5)	*to have, exist [for inanimate objects]*	chekku suru (17)	*to check*
		chichi (4)	*(my) father [familiar]*
aruku (18)	*to walk*	chigaimasu (4)	*that's not correct*
asa (5)	*morning*	chigau (4)	*to be different from*
asatte (5)	*the day after tomorrow*	chiisai, chiisa-na (7)	*small*
ashita (5)	*tomorrow*	chiizu (3)	*cheese*
asobu (7)	*to play*	chotto (6)	*a little*
asoko (8)	*over there*	-chū (15)	*during, in the course of*
atama (20)	*head*		
atarashii (6)	*new*	chūka ryōri (18)	*Chinese cooking*
atatakai (12)	*warm*	da (6)	*is [plain form of desu]*
ato (12)	*after*		
ato de (15)	*later*		

dai (number) ka (1) — *lesson (number)*
daigaku (12) — *university*
daiji-na (18) — *important, serious*
daijōbu (-na) (6) — *all right, okay*
dai-kirai (-na) (3) — *hate, hateful*
dairiten (10) — *representative office*
dai-suki (-na) (3) — *like very much*
dakara (13) — *so, therefore, consequently*
dake (14) — *alone, only*
dame (-na) (12) — *no good, useless*
dare (4) — *who?*
dareka (9) — *someone, anyone*
dare mo (15) — *no one [with negative verb]*
darō (20) — *[plain form of* **deshō***]*
de (6) — *by [instrument or means]*
de (9) — *at, in*
de gozaimasu (20) — *is [formal equivalent of* **desu***]*
dēta (18) — *data*
dētabēsu (2) — *database*
dekiru (13) — *1) to be done, be completed 2) can, to be able to do*
dekiru dake (20) — *as....as possible*
demo (7) — *but*
demo (8) — *or something*
dengon (15) — *message*
densha (6) — *train*
denwa (2) — *telephone*
depāto (3) — *department store*
deru (7) — *to come out, appear*
deru (15) — *to attend, be present*
desu (2) — *am, is, are*
dewa (6) — *well then, in that case*
dezain (16) — *design*
doa (20) — *door*
dochira (11) — *which way?*
dochira (19) — *which one?*
donna ni (12) — *to what extent?*
dō (7) — *how?*
dō itashimashite (2) — *you're welcome*
Doitsu (10) — *Germany*
doko (4) — *where?*
dokoka (9) — *somewhere, anywhere*
doko e/ni mo — *not anywhere (with negative verb)*
dōmo (2) — *thanks*

dōmo (15) — *Hello, there.*
dono (4) — *which? [adj]*
dore (4) — *which one?*
doru (19) — *dollars*
doru-date (19) — *in dollars*
dō shite (5) — *why?*
doyōbi (9) — *Saturday*
dōzo (2) — *please (take it); here you are*
dōzo yoroshiku (5) — *pleased to meet you*

e (8) — *to, towards*
eakon (3) — *air conditioner*
eiga (9) — *film, movie*
Eigo (5) — *English language*
eki (4) — *train station*
en (3) — *yen*
en-date (19) — *in yen*
enerugisshu (-na) (10) — *energetic*
enjinia (2) — *engineer*
enkai (19) — *party, banquet*
entā suru (7) — *to enter (information into a computer)*
erebētā (16) — *elevator*
esukarētā (16) — *escalator*
fairu (2) — *file*
fakkusu (5) — *fax*
fuirumu (12) — *film (for a camera)*
fuku-shachō (4) — *company vice-president*
fun (6) — *minute*
Furansu (4) — *France*
furonto no hito (2) — *reception clerk (at a hotel)*
furoppii (7) — *floppy disk*
furu (12) — *to fall, come down*
furui (14) — *old*
furyō (no) (17) — *no good, defective*
futari (12) — *two people*
futsuka (9) — *2nd of the month*
fuyu (20) — *winter*
ga (4) — *[sentence ending to soften the tone of the sentence]*
ga (5) — *[particle indicating subject of verb]*
ga (7) — *but*
gārufurendo (13) — *girlfriend*
gaido san (19) — *guide*
gairaigo (10) — *words of non-Japanese origin*
gaishutsu suru (15) — *to be out, not at home*

gakkō (4) — school
ganbaru (5) — to try hard, persist
-gawa (16) — the ___ side
gen-in (17) — cause
genki (-na) (4) — fine, healthy
getsuyōbi (9) — Monday
ginkō (16) — bank
go (2) — five
-go (5) — language (of a country)
go-chisō sama deshita (11) — thank you for the meal
go-gatsu (9) — May
gogo (18) — afternoon
gohan (18) — cooked rice
goran ni naru (20) — to see, look [honorific]
goro (6) — about, around [with time, month, etc.]
gorufu (3) — golf
go-shujin (18) — (your, her) husband
gozaimasu (20) — have, exist [formal equivalent of **arimasu**]
-guchi (10) — -entrance, -exit
gurai (kurai) (8) — about, approximately
gurē (14) — grey
guriin (14) — green
hachi (2) — eight
hachi-gatsu (9) — August
haha (4) — (my) mother [familiar]
hai (2) — yes
hairu (5) — to join, enter
hajimaru (20) — to begin [iv]
hajimemashite (4) — how do you do?
hajimeru (5) — to start, begin [tv]
hajimete (14) — for the first time
han (6) — a half
hanashi (6) — conversation, talk
hanashiau (17) — to talk together, discuss
hanasu (5) — to speak, talk
hanbāgā (2) — hamburger
hanbai (13) — selling, marketing
harau (19) — to pay
haru (20) — spring
hashi (19) — chopsticks
hataraku (9) — to work
hayai (6) — early, fast
hazusu (15) — to leave (one's seat)
hen (-na) (7) — strange, odd
heya (2) — room
hi (9) — day

hidari (16) — the left
higashi (10) — east
hijō ni (16) — extremely, remarkably
hikōki (8) — plane
hinshitsu (17) — quality
hira shain (4) — staff members (without titles)
hiroi (6) — big (spacious)
hisashiburi (15) — after a long interval
hisho (20) — secretary
hito (4) — person
hitokoto (11) — a word (or two), a single word
hitori (12) — one person
hitotachi (4) — people
hitotsu (14) — one (item)
hitsuyō (-na) (16) — necessary, essential
-hon (11) — [counter for long, cylindrical objects]
Honkon (18) — Hong Kong
honsha (4) — head office
hontō ni (7) — really, truly
hōritsu (19) — law
hoshō (17) — guarantee
hoteru (6) — hotel
hotto suru (20) — to be relieved
hyaku (3) — hundred
ibento (19) — event
ichi (2) — one
ichiban (10) — most, -est
ichido (15) — once, one time
ichi-gatsu (9) — January
Igirisu (4) — England, Britain
ii (4) — nice, good
iie (4) — no
ikemasen (17) — mustn't, forbidden, no good
ik-kai (16) — first floor
iku (5) — to go
ikura (3) — how much (money)?
ima (4) — now, at the moment
imēji (16) — image
Indo (18) — India
inu (5) — dog
ippai (18) — full
irassharu (20) — to be [honorific]
ireru (7) — to put in
iriguchi (16) — entrance
iro (14) — colour
iroiro (-na) (7) — various, all kinds of
iru (5) — to be, exist [for animate things]
isogashii (6) — busy
isogu (7) — to hurry

issho ni (15) — *together*
isshōkenmei (20) — *with great effort*
is-shūkan (14) — *one week*
itadakimasu (11) — *thank you [when receiving something]*
itadaku (20) — *to eat, drink [humble]*
Itaria (18) — *Italy*
itasu (20) — *to do [humble]*
itsu (5) — *when?*
itsuka (9) — *5th of the month*
itsuka (9) — *sometime, anytime*
itsumo (10) — *always*
iu (14) — *to speak, say*
iya-na (18) — *unpleasant, nasty*
ja (3) — *well, in that case*
ja arimasen (6) — *isn't [negative of **desu**]*
-ji (6) — *___ o'clock*
jidōsha (17) — *automobile*
jigyō-hon-bu (4) — *division (of a company)*
jikan (6) — *time, hour*
jiko (8) — *accident*
jiko shōkai (11) — *self-introduction*
jimusho (14) — *office, place of business*
-jin (5) — *person (of a country)*
jinji (4) — *personnel*
jishin (17) — *earthquake*
jitsu wa (9) — *in fact, to tell the truth*
jōhō (15) — *information*
jōken (19) — *terms, conditions*
jōtai (17) — *condition, state*
josei (15) — *female, woman*
jōzu (-na) (7) — *skilful, good at*
jogingu (14) — *jogging*
juku (18) — *cram school*
jū (2) — *ten*
jū-gatsu (9) — *October*
jūgyōin (10) — *employees, workers*
jū-ichi-gatsu (9) — *November*
jūyō (-na) (17) — *important*
jūyōsei (17) — *importance*
junbi (7) — *preparations*
jū-ni-gatsu (9) — *December*
jūsu (2) — *juice*
ka (2) — *[sentence ending to indicate a question]*
-ka (4) — *section (of a company)*
kaban (3) — *bag, briefcase*

kachō (2) — *manager*
kaeri (8) — *return (trip)*
kaeru (20) — *to change [tv]*
kaeru (5) — *to return, go home*
kagi (2) — *key*
kaigai (4) — *overseas*
kaigi (5) — *meeting*
kaiketsu (15) — *solution, settlement (of a problem)*
kaimono (9) — *shopping*
kaisha (4) — *company*
kakaku (14) — *price, value*
kakarichō (2) — *assistant manager*
kakaru (8) — *to take, need, require*
kakeru (15) — *call (on the phone), ring up*
kaku (5) — *to write*
kakunin suru (13) — *to confirm*
kamera (12) — *camera*
kanai (18) — *my wife*
kangae (15) — *thought, idea*
kangaeru (16) — *to think about, consider*
kanji (5) — *Chinese characters*
kankei (20) — *relations, relationship*
kankō (4) — *sightseeing*
kanojo (4) — *she, her*
kanpai (11) — *cheers*
kanri (17) — *control, supervision*
kanrinin (6) — *caretaker*
kantan (-na) (11) — *simple, brief*
kara (5) — *from*
kara (10) — *since, because*
kare (4) — *he, him*
karera (4) — *they, them*
kariru (17) — *to borrow*
kasa (3) — *umbrella*
-kata (16) — *way of ---ing*
kata (18) — *person (polite form of **jin** or **hito**)*
-kai (16) — *___floor*
katarogu (15) — *catalogue*
katazukeru (8) — *to tidy up, put in order*
kau (12) — *to buy*
kawa (12) — *river*
kawaii (5) — *cute, pretty*
kawaru (7) — *to replace, take the place of*
kayōbi (9) — *Tuesday*
kaze (12) — *wind*
kedo, keredo, keredomo (10) — *however, but, although*
keiei (16) — *management,*

	administration
keigo (20)	*respect language*
kēki (16)	*cake*
keiyaku (17)	*contract*
keizai (18)	*economics*
kekkon-shiki (9)	*wedding ceremony*
kekkon suru (13)	*to marry, get married*
kekkō desu (18)	*I've had enough, that'll do*
kekkyoku (8)	*finally, in the end*
ken (19)	*matter, item*
kengaku (15)	*observation study*
kenkyū (5)	*research, study*
kibun (13)	*feeling, mood*
kii (7)	*key (on a keyboard)*
kiiro (14)	*yellow*
kikai (17)	*machine*
kikaku (4)	*planning, a plan*
kiku (5)	*to ask, to hear*
kimaru (15)	*to be decided [iv]*
kimeru (20)	*to decide [tv]*
kinmu (10)	*work, duty*
kinō (8)	*yesterday*
kinyōbi (9)	*Friday*
kiosuku (3)	*kiosk*
kirai (-na) (3)	*dislike, detestable*
kirei (-na) (7)	*pretty, clean*
kiru (20)	*to wear, put on*
kita (10)	*north*
kitanai (14)	*dirty*
kochira (11)	*this way*
kodomo (12)	*child*
koko (8)	*here*
kokonoka (9)	*9th of the month*
kokusai (4)	*international*
kokusai-teki (20)	*internationally*
komu (18)	*to be crowded*
konban (5)	*this evening*
konbanwa (2)	*good evening*
kongetsu (13)	*this month*
konna ni (12)	*this much*
konnichiwa (2)	*hello*
kono (4)	*this [adj]*
konpyūtā (2)	*computer*
konsarutanto (2)	*consultant*
konshū (13)	*this week*
kōhii (2)	*coffee*
kōjō (4)	*factory*
kōjōchō (17)	*plant manager*
kopii (7)	*photocopy*
kore (4)	*this [n]*
korobu (12)	*to fall over*
kōsu (15)	*course (of study)*
koto (7)	*things, matters*
kotoshi (13)	*this year*

kudasai (3)	*please (give me)*
ku-gatsu (9)	*November*
kun (5)	*Mr [informal]*
kuni (10)	*country*
kurabu (16)	*club*
kurai (18)	*dark, gloomy*
kurasu (5)	*class*
kuro(i) (14)	*black*
kuru (5)	*to come*
kuruma (8)	*car*
kūkō (6)	*airport*
kuwashii (11)	*detailed*
kyasshu kōnā (16)	*cashpoint*
kyonen (13)	*last year*
kyō (5)	*today*
kyōiku (16)	*training, education*
kyōmi (16)	*interest*
kyū (2)	*nine*
kyūkei (17)	*rest time, break*
kyūryō (10)	*salary*
mā (10)	*well, I think, let me see*
māketingu (6)	*marketing*
mā-mā (3)	*so-so*
machi (10)	*town, city*
machiau (17)	*to wait for each other*
mada (6)	*(not) yet [with negative verb]*
mada (7)	*still [with positive verb]*
made (8)	*to, until, as far as*
made ni (13)	*by, not later than*
mae (13)	*before, in front of*
magaru (16)	*to turn, bend*
mainen (19)	*every year*
mainichi (14)	*every day*
mairu (20)	*to come, go [humble]*
maitsuki (20)	*every month*
makaseru (19)	*to entrust, leave, (to someone's care)*
man (14)	*ten thousand*
manā (16)	*manners*
manējā (6)	*manager*
manejimento (15)	*management*
marason (5)	*marathon*
massugu (16)	*straight, direct*
mata (13)	*again, once more*
matomeru (15)	*to collect together, put in order*
matsu (6)	*to wait*
mazu (17)	*firstly, first of all*
meikaku (-na) (19)	*clear, distinct*
mensetsu (4)	*interview*
menyū (7)	*menu*

meshiagaru (20)   *to eat [honorific]*
messēji (5)   *message*
michi (18)   *road*
midori (14)   *green*
migi (16)   *the right*
miitingu (13)   *meeting*
mijikai (11)   *short*
mikka (9)   *3rd of the month*
minami (10)   *south*
minna, mina (4)   *all of you*
miru (5)   *to see, to look at*
miseau (17)   *to show each other*
miseru (8)   *to show*
mitsumori (13)   *estimate, quotation*
mo (3)   *also, too*
mo (8)   *as much as*
mō (6)   *already*
mochiron (17)   *of course*
mokuyōbi (9)   *Thursday*
mondai (14)   *problem*
mono (14)   *thing, object*
moshi (15)   *if, in case*
moshi moshi (4)   *hello? [on the phone]*
mōshiwake (20)   *apology, excuse*
mōsu (20)   *to say, tell [humble]*
motsu (15)   *to have, hold, carry*
motte iku (15)   *to take*
motte kuru (15)   *to bring*
motto (8)   *more*
mugi-cha (17)   *barley tea*
muika (9)   *6th of the month*
mukae ni iku (6)   *to go to meet*
murasaki (14)   *purple*
mushiatsui (12)   *humid*
muzukashii (6)   *difficult*
nado (16)   *and so on, et cetera*
nagai (20)   *long*
naisen (15)   *(telephone) extension*
naiyō (20)   *contents*
naka (13)   *within, inside*
namae (2)   *name*
nan (2), nani (5)   *what?*
nan-ban (2)   *what number?*
nani de (6)   *how?, by what means?*
nanika (9)   *something, anything*
nani mo (15)   *nothing [with negative verb]*
nan-ji (6)   *what time?*
nanoka (9)   *7th of the month*
naraberu (16)   *to display, put into position*
narau (7)   *to learn*
naru (14)   *to become, get*

nasaru (20)   *to do [honorific]*
natsu (20)   *summer*
ne (4)   *isn't it*
nekutai (14)   *necktie*
nen (13)   *year*
ni (2)   *two*
ni (5)   *[particle indicating: 1) place toward which something moves; 2) location where something or someone exists; 3) indirect object of verb]*
nichiyōbi (9)   *Sunday*
ni-gatsu (9)   *February*
Nihon (2)   *Japan*
Nihongo (5)   *Japanese language*
nihonshu (3)   *sake*
nishi (10)   *west*
ni tsuite (15)   *regarding, in this connection*
no (4)   *[particle indicating possession]*
no de, na no de (13)   *since, because*
nobasu (19)   *to extend, lengthen*
nomu (5)   *to drink*
noru (18)   *to get on, in (a vehicle, escalator, etc.)*
o (3)   *[particle indicating object of verb]*
o- (2)   *[prefix to indicate politeness]*
o-bāsan (16)   *grandmother, old woman [polite]*
o-cha (8)   *green tea*
odoru (20)   *to dance*
o-furo (18)   *bath*
ohayō gozaimasu (2)   *good morning*
ōi (10)   *lots of, many*
oishii (18)   *tasty, good*
o-kāsan (4)   *mother [polite]*
o-kaeri nasai (8)   *welcome back*
o-kane (16)   *money*
o-kawari (18)   *another helping*
okusan (13)   *(your) wife*
okusama (20)   *(your, his) wife [formal]*
onsen (19)   *hot spring*
ōkii (6), ōki-na (7)   *big, large*
okureru (8)   *to be late*
okuru (5)   *to send, dispatch*

o-kyaku san/sama (16)	customer, guest	romanchikku (-na) (10)	romantic
omedetō gozaimasu (9)	congratulations	ryokan (19)	Japanese-style inn
omoshiroi (6)	interesting	ryō (14)	dormitory
omou (14)	to think	ryokō (9)	travel, trip
o-naka (9)	stomach	ryōri (18)	cooking, cuisine
onegai shimasu (2)	please (do that)	sā... (7)	well...
onna no hito (10)	woman	sābisu (16)	service
onsen (19)	hot spring	-sai (16)	_years old
operētā (17)	operator	saigo ni (17)	in the end, finally
orenji (2)	orange	sain suru (18)	to sign
oriru (18)	to get off, out of (a vehicle, escalator, etc.)	saizu (14)	size (of clothing)
		sakana (18)	fish
		sake (13)	sake, alcoholic drinks
oru (20)	to be [humble]	saki ni (8)	first of all, ahead
o-sewa ni naru (11)	to receive assistance	sakki (20)	just now, a little while ago
oshieau (17)	to teach each other		
oshieru (5)	to teach, tell	samui (12)	cold
osoi (6)	late, slow	san (2)	three
osore-irimasu ga (15)	sorry to trouble you, but	san (2)	Mr, Mrs, Miss, Ms
		-san (10)	Mount –
ossharu (20)	to say, tell [honorific]	sando(itchi) (3)	sandwich
		san-gatsu (9)	March
osu (7)	to push, press	sansai ryōri (19)	mountain-style cooking
o-tearai (4)	toilet		
otoko no hito (10)	man	sarada (2)	salad
o-tōsan (4)	father [polite]	sarariiman (4)	office worker
otosu (12)	to drop, let fall	seifuku (16)	uniform
ototoi (14)	the day before yesterday	seisan (17)	production
		seisan rain (17)	production line
otto (18)	my husband	seisansei (17)	productivity
owari (13)	finish, end	sekai (18)	the world
owaru (7)	to finish, end	seki (15)	seat, place
pabu (8)	pub	sekushii (-na) (10)	sexy
pasuteru karā (14)	pastel colour	sērusu (6)	sales
pātii (5)	party	sētā (14)	sweater
pāto (15)	part-time worker	seiji (18)	politics
pen (3)	pen	semai (18)	small (in area)
pinku (14)	pink	seminā (20)	seminar
QC sākuru (17)	QC (quality control) circle	sen (3)	thousand
		senden (15)	advertising, publicity
raigetsu (13)	next month	sengetsu (13)	last month
rainen (13)	next year	sensei (4)	teacher
raishū (5)	next week	senshū (9)	last week
rajio (12)	radio	sentā (5)	a centre
ranchi (17)	lunch	setsumei suru (11)	to explain
renshū (5)	practice	shachō (4)	company president
repōto (5)	a report	shain (4)	staff member
rimujin basu (6)	airport limousine bus	shanai (16)	in-company
		shashin (12)	photograph
risuto (15)	list	shi/yon (2)	four
robotto (17)	robot	shichi/nana (2)	seven
roku (2)	six	shichi-gatsu (9)	July
roku-gatsu (9)	June	shi-gatsu (9)	April

shigoto (3)	*work, job*	Suisu (18)	*Switzerland*
shi-harai (19)	*payment*	suitchi (7)	*switch*
shijō (10)	*market*	suiyōbi (9)	*Wednesday*
shimaru (20)	*to close [iv]*	sukāfu (4)	*scarf*
shimekiri (13)	*deadline*	sukejūru (10)	*schedule*
shimeru (20)	*to close [tv]*	suki (-na) (3)	*like*
shinbun (3)	*newspaper*	sukii (16)	*skiing*
shin-shōhin (16)	*new products*	sukoshi (13)	*a little, a small*
shinsetsu (-na) (7)	*kind*		*quantity*
shinu (7)	*to die*	suku (9)	*to become empty*
shiraberu (6)	*to investigate, check*	sumāto (-na) (16)	*smart*
	up	sumimasen (3)	*excuse me*
shiro(i) (14)	*white*	sumu (12)	*to live, reside*
shiru (9)	*to know, be*	supagettii (11)	*spaghetti*
	acquainted	supiikā (20)	*speaker*
shisha (4)	*branch office*	supōtsu (7)	*sport*
shita (13)	*under, below*	supōtsu-uea (14)	*sportswear*
-shitsu (5)	*-room*	suru (5)	*to do*
shitsumon (16)	*question*	sushi (8)	*sushi (raw fish on*
shitsurei shimasu	*excuse me*		*rice)*
(5)		sushi-ya	*sushi bar*
shizuka (-na) (11)	*quiet, peaceful*	sutereo (17)	*stereo*
shujin (18)	*my husband*	sutoraiki (10)	*strike*
shokudō (17)	*dining room,*	sū (17)	*to inhale, smoke*
	cafeteria	sūpā (3)	*supermarket*
shūmatsu (19)	*weekend*	sūtsu (20)	*suit*
shuppatsu (19)	*departure*	suwaru (13)	*to sit*
sutēki (19)	*steak*	suzushii (12)	*cool*
sutereo (17)	*stereo*		
shōbai (16)	*trade, business,*	tabako (17)	*cigarette*
	commerce	taberu (5)	*to eat*
shōhin (13)	*goods, merchandise*	tabun (15)	*perhaps, maybe*
shōsha (2)	*trading company*	-tachi (7)	*[plural ending for*
shōshō (15)	*a few, little*		*people]*
shorui (6)	*document*	tada (14)	*only, except, it's just*
shūkan (14)	*week*		*that*
shumi (4)	*hobby, pastime*	tadaima (8)	*I'm back*
shusseki (15)	*attendance, presence*	taihen (-na) (7)	*tough, terrible*
shutchō (8)	*business trip*	taipisuto (2)	*typist*
soba (13)	*near*	taipuraitā (2)	*typewriter*
sochira (11)	*that way*	taisetsu (-na) (16)	*important, valuable*
soko (8)	*there*	takai (6)	*expensive, high*
sonna ni (12)	*that much*	taki (12)	*waterfall*
sono (4)	*that [adj]*	takusan (7)	*a lot, many*
sō (2)	*so*	takushii (8)	*taxi*
sore (4)	*that [n]*	takushii noriba (8)	*taxi stand*
sorede (14)	*and, so, thereupon*	tame ni (20)	*for the purpose of,*
sore ja (16)	*well, in that case*		*for the sake of*
sore ni (18)	*moreover, on top of*	tanjōbi (9)	*birthday*
	that	tanoshii (6)	*enjoyable, fun*
soshite (12)	*and, then*	tanoshimi ni suru	*to look forward to,*
soto (18)	*outside*	(19)	*hope for*
subarashii (18)	*wonderful,*	tantō-sha (6)	*person in charge*
	marvellous	tantō suru (9)	*to be in charge*
sugu (6)	*soon*	ten (19)	*point, spot, mark*
suchuwādesu (16)	*stewardess*	ten-in (16)	*sales clerk*
		tenisu (3)	*tennis*

tenki (6) — *weather*
terebi (3) — *television*
to (5) — *and*
to (12) — *with, together with*
to (16) — *if, when*
toki (12) — *time, the time when*
tokidoki (9) — *sometimes*
tokoro (19) — *place, location*
tokorode (7) — *well, by the way*
tomaru (19) — *to stay overnight*
tomaru (20) — *to stop, halt [iv]*
tomeru (20) — *to stop, halt [tv]*
tomodachi (12) — *friend*
tonari (13) — *next to*
tonde mo nai (20) — *it's nothing*
tōka (9) — *10th of the month*
torēningu (20) — *training*
toru (12) — *to take*
tōshi (10) — *investment*
totemo (6) — *really*
tsugi no (6) — *next*
tsugō (5) — *convenience, circumstances*
tsuitachi (9) — *lst of the month*
tsukareru (8) — *to get tired*
tsukau (17) — *to use*
tsukiatari (16) — *at the end (of the street)*
tsuku (6) — *to arrive*
tsukue (4) — *desk*
tsukuru (13) — *to make, manufacture*
tsuma (18) — *my wife*
tsumori desu (11) — *to intend to*
tsuna (3) — *tuna (canned)*
tsutomeru (9) — *to be employed*
tsuyoi (12) — *strong*
uchi (8) — *house, home*
uchi (14) — *we, our side*
uchi no (5) — *our*
ue (13) — *top, upper part*
uētoresu (2) — *waitress*
uisukii (2) — *whisky*
uketsuke (6) — *reception*
umai (14) — *good, successful*
umi (18) — *sea*
unten suru (19) — *to drive*
ureshii (20) — *happy*
uru (20) — *to sell*
urusai (14) — *noisy*
ushiro (13) — *behind*
uta (20) — *song*

utau (20) — *to sing*
utsukushii (18) — *beautiful*
wa (2) — *[particle indicating topic of sentence]*
wāpuro (3) — *word processor*
wakaru (5) — *to know, understand*
warui (5) — *bad, wrong*
wasureru (18) — *to forget, leave behind*
watashi (4) — *I, me*
ya (16) — *and, or*
yaku ni tatsu (20) — *to be of use*
yama (10) — *mountain*
yameru (16) — *to stop, cease, discontinue*
yasui (10) — *cheap*
yasumi (9) — *holiday, day off*
yo (6) — *[sentence ending to show emphasis]*
yobu (17) — *to call, send for, invite*
yoko (13) — *by the side*
yōka (9) — *8th of the month*
yokka (9) — *4th of the month*
yoku (10) — *usually, often*
yoku (11) — *well*
yomu (5) — *to read*
yōkoso (11) — *welcome*
yopparau (20) — *to get drunk*
Yōroppa (10) — *Europe*
yori (19) — *rather than*
yoroshii (17) — *all right, fine [polite version of ii]*
yotei (5) — *plan, schedule*
yuki (12) — *snow*
yukkuri (15) — *slowly*
yūmei (-na) (7) — *famous*
yunyū suru (10) — *to import*
yūshoku (18) — *evening meal*
yushutsu suru (10) — *to export*
zangyō (9) — *overtime work*
zannen (-na) (11) — *regrettable, disappointing*
zasshi (16) — *magazine*
zenbu (12) — *all, the whole lot*
zenbu de (12) — *altogether*
zenzen (10) — *not at all*
zero (2) — *zero, nought*
zuibun (8) — *extremely*

─── PHRASES ───

This list shows the phrases which have been introduced in this text. The number after each entry indicates the lesson in which it first appears.

Dō itashimashite. (2)	*You're welcome, not at all.*
Arigatō gozaimasu. (2)	*Thank you very much.*
Dōmo arigatō. (2)	*Thank you.*
Konbanwa. (2)	*Good evening.*
Ohayō gozaimasu. (2)	*Good morning.*
Onegai shimasu. (2)	*Please (do that for me).*
Hajimemashite. (4)	*How do you do?*
Moshi moshi. (4)	*Hello? (on the phone).*
Dōzo yoroshiku. (5)	*Pleased to meet you.*
Ganbatte kudasai. (5)	*Do your best, try hard.*
Shitsurei shimasu. (5)	*Excuse me, sorry to disturb you.*
Tadaima. (8)	*I'm back, I'm home.*
O-kaeri nasai. (8)	*Welcome back.*
Omedetō gozaimasu. (9)	*Congratulations.*
O-tsukare sama deshita. (8)	*You must be really tired.*
O-saki ni (shitsurei shimasu). (8)	*I'm off (Lit: Excuse me for leaving before you).*
(iroiro) O-sewa ni narimasu. (11)	*We look forward to your support in the future.*
(iroiro) O-sewa ni narimashita. (11)	*Many thanks for all your help.*
Kanpai. (11)	*Cheers!*
Itadakimasu. (11)	*Bon appétit; yes, please (when offered food or drink).*
Go-chisō sama deshita. (11)	*Thank you for the meal.*
Nihon e yōkoso. (11)	*Welcome to Japan.*
Dō shita n' desu ka. (12)	*What happened?*
Zannen desu. (11)	*What a pity.*
Dō iu koto desu ka. (14)	*What do you mean by that?*
Osore-irimasu ga... (15)	*I'm sorry to trouble you but...*
O-hisashiburi desu ne. (15)	*Long time, no see.*
Naisen __ onegai shimasu. (15)	*Extension __, please.*
Mō sukoshi yukkuri hanashite kudasai. (15)	*Could you speak a little more slowly, please?*
Mō ichido itte kudasai. (15)	*Could you say that again, please?*

Shōshō o-machi kudasai. (15)	*Just a moment, please.*
O-matase shimashita. (15)	*Sorry to have kept you waiting.*
__ dake de naku, __ mo (16)	*Not only __, but also __*
O-saki ni dōzo. (16)	*After you.*
Kekkō desu. (18)	*I've had enough, thank you.*
Go-kurō sama deshita. (19)	*Thank you for your hard work.*
Tonde mo nai. (20)	*It's nothing. Please don't mention it.*
Atama ga ii desu ne. (20)	*He's very clever, isn't he.*
...to iu hanashi desu. (20)	*They say that....*
Mōshiwake arimasen. (20)	*I apologise, I'm extremely sorry.*

JAPANESE
H. Ballhatchet and S. Kaiser

A clearly structured course designed to help you achieve basic fluency in modern colloquial Japanese.

This book is designed to take the student with no previous experience of the language to the point where he or she is able to hold a conversation in everyday Japanese with confidence. Principal points of grammar and vocabulary are introduced using realistic dialogues, example sentences and exercises. These are written in the Roman alphabet, according to modern practice. The dialogues are also available on a specially prepared optional cassette. A section of Japanese social customs is included.

TEACH YOURSELF BOOKS